From the Pages of *Hollywood on Lake Michigan*

"The fact that Chicago is not a film industry town makes people here want to really work extra hard, really be craftsmen at what they do."
—Steven A. Jones, producer

"There are a lot of good synergies between different groups and people in Chicago. There's a certain amount of support for each other. Chicago is a very good climate to remain independent but not have to compete so hard for your survival."
—Gordon Quinn, producer/filmmaker, Kartemquin Films

"We have been fortunate to make six films in Chicago. From finding the quintessential house in Oak Park for *Soul Food*, to shooting *Barbershop* on 79th and Exchange in the heart of the South Side, to capturing Humboldt Park in *Nothing Like the Holidays*, Chicago has always been a character in our films. Much like a leading actor, it is unique, original, and always holds your attention. And it will always hold a special place in my heart."
—Bob Teitel, producer of *Soul Food*, from the foreword

Hollywood on Lake Michigan

100+ Years of Chicago and the Movies

Second Edition

Michael Corcoran and Arnie Bernstein

CHICAGO
REVIEW
PRESS

For the companion website to *Hollywood on Lake Michigan*, visit www.chicagocinema.net. It features information about events related to the book, bonus interviews and content, reviews of recent Chicago films, and various entries on Chicago film, art, music, culture, and history.

Visit Michael Corcoran's website, www.brainsnack.net, for more information about Chicago tours, lectures, and performances.

To learn more about Arnie Bernstein and his award-winning books, visit www.arniebernstein.com.

Copyright © 2013 by Michael Corcoran and Arnie Bernstein
Foreword copyright © 2013 by Bob Teitel
All rights reserved
Second edition
Published by Chicago Review Press Incorporated
814 North Franklin Street
Chicago, Illinois 60610
ISBN 978-1-61374-575-5

First edition published in 1998 by Lake Claremont Press

Library of Congress Cataloging-in-Publication Data
Is available from the Library of Congress.

Cover and interior design: Visible Logic Inc.
Cover photograph: iStockphoto.com/kedan

Printed in the United States of America
5 4 3 2 1

To John and Merrilie Corcoran, who taught me to read, to love learning, and to be strong.   —Michael Corcoran

To Cassandra Garber, Matthew J. Frawley, and Lisa Pevtzow, great movie lovers and great friends.   —Arnie Bernstein

Contents

Foreword

Bob Teitel

The first time I ever saw a movie being filmed was in 1979 when I was 11 years old. My family and I were driving down the 294, and lo and behold in the middle of the freeway pass was this police car wedged into the bed of a semi truck. My little brother and I just lit up with excitement as my dad mentioned that he'd read that they were shooting this movie all around Chicago called *The Blues Brothers*. That image has stayed with me forever.

Then in 1984 I rode my bike to watch the filming of John Hughes's *The Breakfast Club* for six days straight. It had to be a 10-mile round trip, but I didn't care. I had to be there to see an actual movie being made with my own eyes. Movies became a huge part of my teenage years. Every Friday night with my friends and Saturdays with my dad, I was at the movie theater.

When my directing partner George Tillman Jr. and I were attending Columbia College in the heart of the city, we walked down Wabash and watched Robert DeNiro shooting *Midnight Run*. I remember saying to George, "Wouldn't it be amazing to make a movie with DeNiro someday?" Little did we know that we'd get that opportunity in late 1999 when we made *Men of Honor* with him.

I mention these moments because they have all had such a profound impact on me. I knew from watching these films being made that I had found what I always wanted to do. And more important, to do it in my hometown of Chicago.

We have been fortunate to make six films in Chicago. From finding the quintessential house in Oak Park for *Soul Food* to shooting *Barbershop* on 79th and Exchange in the heart of the South Side, to capturing Humboldt Park in *Nothing Like the Holidays*, Chicago has always been a character in our films. Much like a leading actor, it is unique, original, and always holds your attention. And it will always hold a special place in my heart.

Preface

Arnie Bernstein

A little over 15 years ago, I was just another Chicago movie nut, a denizen of many darkened rooms illuminated by flickering images projected onto a screen. The Music Box was a personal mecca. When I wasn't in a movie theater, I was riveted to the television screen, watching hour upon hour of movies on VHS tapes (remember those?). Movies made in Chicago particularly intrigued me. Forget mise-en-scène, auteur theories, and other highfalutin verbal baubles of my fellow cinephiles. It was *fun* to see Chicago in the movies. I was intrigued by the lost world of 1940s Chicago in *Call Northside 777*. *The Blues Brothers* was as much an icon of the city as Al Capone or Michael Jordan. The darker realms of Chicago seethed to the surface in a masterpiece of psychological filmmaking, *Henry: Portrait of a Serial Killer*. The "I will" spirit of Chicago informed every moment of *Hoop Dreams*, both on-screen and behind the camera. And then there were those guilty pleasures found only in the gut-spatterin' glee of Herschell Gordon Lewis's *The Wizard of Gore*, *The Gore Gore Girls*, and my personal favorite of his grindhouse oeuvre, *Blood Feast*.

I wanted to translate this love for my hometown and its movies into a guidebook showcasing the city via the many locations used by Hollywood productions and independent filmmakers, insights from practitioners, and a seemingly forgotten local movie history that dates back to the birth of the revolutionary cinema medium. Thanks to Sharon Woodhouse of Lake Claremont Press, my passions were channeled into the first edition of *Hollywood on Lake Michigan: 100 Years of Chicago and the Movies*. I had a good time with it, and the wonderful feedback I've received from readers over the years has been flattering, thoughtful, and often quite entertaining.

Like any parental author, I'm taking great pride and pleasure in seeing my baby all grown up and now a completely different book, reinvigorated by one of the few people I know whose love for Chicago movies (and movie Chicago) equals and often exceeds my own strange obsessions. I've brushed up the silent section—silent films being a great cinematic romance of mine that I just *couldn't* part with—but don't think of this volume as some sort of sequel, innocuously dubbed *Return to Hollywood on Lake Michigan* or *Hollywood on Lake Michigan II: Temple of Oprah*. It's a fresh look at a favored topic, filled with terrific stuff I never dreamed of. Just like any good movie or book should be.

Michael Corcoran

When I began as a Chicago tour guide in 2003, my most popular offering was my Chicago Cinema Tour, which explored locations where Chicago movies were shot and provided tales about those films. In my research for this tour, I came upon Arnie's excellent volume *Hollywood on Lake Michigan: 100 Years of Chicago and the Movies*, and it formed the basis of the tour. Groups howled at my retellings of Arnie's stories of Colonel Selig and the couple who tried to pick up the poor baby outside of Marshall Field's during the filming of a scene in *Baby's Day Out* (written and directed by the recently departed Chicago film legend John Hughes), and the exhaustive list of locations allowed me to route a tour with relative ease.

My only problem was that the book had been written five years previously, and it was difficult, even as a movie fan, to keep track of all the various locations of all the films that were now being produced here with such regularity. If only this Arnie Bernstein fellow would update his damn book!

Strolling one day in Lincoln Square, I passed the storefront office of Lake Claremont Press (they've since moved downtown). I paused, looking at the titles in the window. To my amazement, here was not only Arnie's book but also many of the great Chicago guidebooks and histories whose information formed the backbone of my best tours! Finally putting two and two together, I went in to bother the woman working at a desk inside.

Fortunately, she didn't mind my interruption, and we had a lovely chat about Chicago and her publishing house. I mentioned that I was a tour guide and belonged to a guild of Chicago tour guides (the Chicago Tour-Guide Professionals Association), and we made plans for an event where members would come and check out their array of Chicago-centric works. That was how I met Sharon Woodhouse, founder of Lake Claremont Press. A year or so later, I got to meet that Arnie Bernstein fellow. I told him how much I loved his book and thanked him profusely for the success of my Chicago Cinema Tour. I was also able to beg him personally, instead of via Sharon, to create an updated version. Having made my plea to the source, I then forgot about it, as other tours, mainly my Columbian Exposition Tour, began to generate more heat.

Little did I know that my campaign had borne fruit. Sharon and Arnie had serious talks about a sequel, but Arnie was busy with other projects and didn't have the time to dedicate to a second edition. They discussed finding someone to do the update, and my name came up. I'd like to think I'd impressed Sharon with my keen intellect and scholarly nature, but I suspect it was the rousing rendition of Lynyrd Skynyrd's "Gimme Three Steps" that I had belted out at a karaoke session following a Lake Claremont party.

Whatever her reason, she offered me the task of updating Arnie's work. I was hesitant at first. Although I loved Chicago movies, did I really have the time and wherewithal to go down that rabbit hole, to seek out the dozens of films made here in the intervening years? What's more, did I have the time to conduct what would amount to a large fieldwork project on the Chicago film scene? Only a full immersion could do justice to the original; was I prepared for that? I thought long and hard, and as I heard someone say once, "Sometimes you've just got to say yes."

I watched more than 100 films over a seven-month period and spent countless hours tracking down various figures of the Chicago film community, both here and in other locales, for interviews and consultation. As much time as I spent and as many films as I watched, I know I barely scratched the surface of Chicago's fertile film scene, and I apologize for all the people, places, and films I was unable to either include or to discover. I also apologize to fans of the first volume for all the items that I had to cut for the second edition. There were many difficult choices to make; please forgive me if they weren't the ones you would have made.

So much has changed in this city in the last 15 years, and not just in the film community. The world has changed as well. With the Internet now ubiquitous, I tried to create content that couldn't just be discovered by a few minutes of Web surfing. I also wanted to include more about the people behind the camera whose talent, artistry, and hard work are integral to the creation of a film.

A subject as large as this could never be done justice in a series of volumes, much less a single book, but I hope that readers will enjoy the fruits of my efforts. I thank Arnie and Sharon for this opportunity, as well as everyone who has ever been a part of film in Chicago.

Introduction

Legend has it that early in his reign as mayor, Richard J. Daley saw a television show that had a scene in which a Chicago cop accepted a bribe. He was so enraged by this insult to his beloved city that he forbade all movie and television productions from shooting in Chicago.

Whether or not that's the actual reason, only a scant few film crews were allowed to shoot here during his administration. It was not until after Daley's death in 1976 that the Hollywood studios were finally allowed back to the city that gave birth to them, and what could be characterized as the contemporary era of Chicago feature film production began in earnest.

Many would mourn the lost decades in which Chicago's visual riches were left unseen by the filmgoing world, but it allowed the city to evolve without the intrusive gaze of the camera's eye. Chicagoans, already an unself-conscious lot, were able to construct their own reality, fashioning a narrative far deeper than can be written on a studio back lot.

From its birth as a sleepy fur trading outpost, Chicago has been a haven for the displaced, the oppressed, the persecuted, the radical, the eccentric, the mad dreamer, and the insane schemer. Its patterns of population growth mirror the troubles of mankind in the last two centuries: Irish fleeing a famine, Polish Jews fleeing a pogrom, and everyone fleeing poverty and war.

Chicago has always been a place where anyone can come and try to live their dreams. Where you can start from scratch and reinvent yourself, again and again if you wish. Where you can live the life you want, not the life you're born into. Where you can write your own story. Where you can do whatever the hell you want as long as you don't bother anyone else.

Without the pressures of conformity found elsewhere, artists, writers, actors, architects, musicians, philosophers, scientists, and chefs developed new methods and styles. Fusing disparate elements together, building upon traditions while simultaneously ignoring them. The Chicago school of architecture shares this bond with the Chicago school of sociology, as the Chicago blues does with the Chicago style of acting, house music with improvisation, and the gyro with Chicago-style pizza.

What is Chicago other than an immense film set? Built on stilts of concrete, hovering above a swamp. A patchwork constructed of dreams from across the globe. A set for the greatest movie ever made, the story of Chicago.

And Chicago was ready for its close-up.

1

The Silent Era

The neighborhood at Western Avenue and Irving Park Road, bordered by Byron Street and Claremont Avenue, is as typical as any stretch of Chicago. A gas station on the corner of Western and Irving Park. Houses, apartment buildings, and condo blocks. It's a quiet, residential area, with only the sounds of people and traffic in the air.

There is one oddity to the neighborhood: a building at the northeast corner of Byron and Claremont with a mysterious letter *S* emblazoned in concrete above the doorway of a condominium building called St. Ben's Lofts. Imprinted in a diamond shape, that *S* is the only hint that this neighborhood was once a thriving hub for moviemaking.

The building is the last remnant of one of Chicago's major silent film factories. At its peak, this lot was teeming with movie people, equipment, and a menagerie of exotic animals. The cacophony of those lions, monkeys, wolves, and actors has long been replaced by the more innocuous sound of traffic. The distinguishing *S* was the trademark emblem of the Selig Polyscope Company, where "Colonel" William Selig presided over his personal moviemaking workshop.

Though now condos, the former Selig Polyscope Co. building at Claremont and Byron still bears the trademark *S*. *(Photo by Kate Corcoran)*

1

A few miles north and east of Colonel Selig's former film studio is St. Augustine College, a bilingual facility for Chicago's Hispanic community. Located at 1333–1345 W. Argyle Street, St. Augustine is another link to Chicago's great silent movie past. The entrance at 1345 W. Argyle features an Indian-head logo set in colored terra cotta. This doorway marks the former entrance to the Essanay Film Manufacturing Company, Chicago's most important silent film studio. Today, students walk through the same buildings once used by Charlie Chaplin, Gloria Swanson, Wallace Beery, Ben Turpin, and Essanay's leading heartthrob, Francis X. Bushman. One of popular cinema's first matinee idols, Bushman spent his off-hours tooling around Chicago in a lavender sedan. Fans were known to follow him in packs whenever he went shopping in the Loop. Eventually one store's proprietors were forced to ask Bushman to no longer frequent their place of business—they couldn't keep up with the herd that always followed the handsome actor!

In the first two decades of the 20th century, the impact of motion pictures was felt at every level of society. "The time is not far in the distant future when the moving picture apparatus will be in the equipment of every schoolhouse," wrote one *Chicago Daily News* columnist in 1911. "The attempt to teach without it will be absurd." Replace the words "moving picture apparatus" with "computer technology" and you have a better understanding of how revolutionary motion pictures were to everyday culture. In a much-criticized move, social reformer Jane Addams exhibited films at her Hull-House location at 800 S. Halsted Street. Charging five cents admission, the same as local theaters, Addams's in-house motion picture venue became a neighborhood staple. An audience was an audience in Addams's mind. She realized the power of motion pictures as an important tool for both entertainment and enlightenment.

Today, Chicago is a well-known world-class center for film production; major Hollywood productions like *The Dark Knight* (2008) showcase the city in ways the men behind Selig and Essanay studios could only dream of. Yet while the technologies have undergone radical change, the basic techniques of telling a story on-screen remain virtually unchanged. Another factor is unequivocal: Chicagoans have a creative spirit coupled with a dynamic city that puts a unique stamp on moviemaking. We have been an important factor in the film world, from the dawn of cinema and its rudimentary technology to today's computer-enhanced blockbusters.

The Movies Come to Chicago

Chicagoans were first introduced to moving pictures at the Columbian Exposition of 1893 with a special pavilion devoted to Kinetoscopes, a viewing machine created by Thomas Edison's labs in West Orange, New Jersey. Developed under Edison's supervision by Edison assistant William Kennedy Laurie Dickson, the Kinetoscope was the forerunner to the modern motion picture. Basically, the Kinetoscope was a large box that contained several spools and a 50-foot loop of exposed moving picture film. By looking into the eyepiece at the top, viewers could watch such entertainments as Edison worker Fred Ott sneezing, dancers performing, and other simple motion attractions.

However, due to production delays, the Kinetoscopes never arrived in time, and the fair closed before the machines could be installed. Though many Chicagoans claim to have viewed Kinetoscope films at the Columbian Exposition, these early moving picture devices would have to wait a bit longer before arriving in Chicago.

Despite this inauspicious beginning, the movies eventually took their hold on Chicago in a big way. By the first decade of the new century, Chicago was a thriving center for moving picture production, while nickelodeon theaters opened throughout the city. As advancing technology brought moving pictures out of the Kinetoscope and projected them onto screens, nickelodeons became the new standard for film exhibitors. Charging five cents for admission (hence the name "nickelodeon"), these theaters operated out of storefronts and other handy locations. Musical accompaniment was usually provided by a piano player improvising popular tunes to fit the on-screen action.

With the proliferation of movies and exhibition spaces came the need for many moving picture–related jobs. Chicagoans eager to get in on

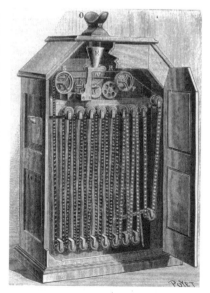

Schematic drawing of W. K. L. Dickson's Kinetoscope, mid-1890s. *(Wikimedia Commons)*

the many aspects of the film industry began advertising in the *Chicago Daily News*, *Chicago Tribune*, and other newspapers, offering a wide variety of film-related services. "Moving picture music especially arranged is taught by Chas. Quinn, 59 E. Van Buren, Room 206" and "Experienced lady pianist desires position in first class picture theater. Drexel 6051" were typical classified ads, focusing on the unique musical needs of nickelodeons.

Other advertisements attracted would-be movie stars with such enticing copy as "Motion picture instruction. Gilbert Shorter has new department under direction of competent director who has been connected with several feature productions. Exceptional opportunity for competent students. Day and evening classes. 50 Auditorium Building." Another ad read, "The College Film Company, Peoples Gas building, Suite 928. Lessons: will teach limited number of students and place them in big feature films which will be exhibited all over the world. Visitors welcome. Classes for children. Terms reasonable." A classified for screenwriters read, "Write moving picture plays. $25 weekly, sparetime: literary ability unnecessary. Free particulars. Atlas Publication Company, Cincinnati, Ohio."

While fans flocked to the nickelodeons, studios and entrepreneurs worked throughout the city to provide moving picture entertainments. The movies became an important aspect of Chicago's artistic and business world. At their height in the late 1910s, one out of every five movies in the world was produced in Chicago.

Selig Polyscope Company (1896–1919)

43 Peck Court (now E. 8th Street)

3945 N. Western Avenue (southeast corner of Western Avenue and Irving Park Road)

45 E. Randolph Street

William Nicholas Selig, a product of the Chicago streets, brought a good sense for show business, along with his personal style of savvy and bluster, to the fledgling movie industry. Selig was born in Chicago on March 14, 1864. As a young man ill health forced him to relocate to a more hospitable climate. He first moved to Colorado and then to California, where his well-being improved. Selig became manager of a West Coast health spa ironically named "Chicago Park."

Eventually Selig found his calling in the world of vaudeville and sideshows. He took up magic and achieved some success as a parlor performer. Eager to expand in the world of show business, Selig adopted the sobriquet "Colonel" and put together a traveling minstrel show. One member of the troupe was a young performer named Bert Williams, who would later achieve great success as a comedian in the Ziegfeld Follies.

While traveling through Texas in 1895, Selig saw his first Kinetoscope parlor. With his show business sensibilities, the Colonel perceived the enormous financial potential of further developing moving picture technology. Selig returned to his hometown and rented office space at 43 Peck Court (now E. 8th Street), in the heart of what was then Chicago's brothel-filled "Levee" district. Selig had no interest in opening his own string of Kinetoscope parlors. Understanding that the real money was to be in filling theaters, Selig turned his attention to developing technology that would project filmstrips onto a wall or screen.

To keep his cash flow going, Selig operated a photography studio out of his Peck Court office. His major source of income was providing carbon prints for Chicago portrait studios and working on landscape photography for the railway industry. Simultaneously, Selig looked at attempts of other early film projection pioneers. He was particularly interested in the efforts of Major Woodville Latham, a retired Confederate soldier, and Louis Lumière of France. In 1895, after seeing an exhibit of Latham and Lumière's machines at Chicago's Schiller Theater at 103 E. Randolph Street, Selig knew what he was up against.

Major Latham had developed a successful motion picture projection system while working on expanding the Edison Kinetoscope. Latham's so-called "Latham Loop," a basic setup for threading motion picture film through a projector, has essentially remained the same since its invention in 1895. Lumière, who had seen an exhibition of the Kinetoscope in Paris, coupled moving picture technology with his own ideas. His invention, dubbed the "Cinématographe," was capable of both recording movement on film and projecting the exposed film onto a screen.

Through his talent as a conniver, Selig got his hands on Latham's and Lumière's devices and began experimenting with projection machines in his Peck Court office. His trial runs were successful ventures. Often Selig's offices would be teeming with friends interested in seeing the Colonel's moving picture exhibitions. Yet Selig still was frustrated by his inability to create his own technology.

In desperation, he turned to the Union Model Works, a local Chicago machine shop located at 193 N. Clark Street. Hoping to find a mechanic that could help develop his ideas, Selig met Andrew Schustek, the leading machinist and model-maker for the shop.

Serendipity ensued.

It seemed that Schustek had been deeply involved in creating machine parts for a mysterious foreign-born customer. This gentleman had been coming to the shop week by week, asking Schustek to reproduce specific items for some sort of mechanical device. Though the enigmatic stranger never revealed what he was developing, Schustek had taken an interest in the project and carefully sketched out plans for each piece.

Finally, Schustek learned his customer was French and had been involved with the Lumière demonstration at the Schiller Theater. Essentially, the tight-lipped client was having Schustek reproduce a Lumière Cinématographe piece by piece. Who this customer was and why he had Schustek create the device is a great unknown. The Frenchman paid Schustek $210 cash for his work (350 hours of labor at the sum of 60 cents an hour) and never left a name. What he did leave was a perfect set of plans, created by Schustek, for building a motion picture recording and projection machine.

When Selig met Schustek to explain his own interest in motion pictures, the Colonel looked on Schustek's workspace and was surprised to see a blueprint for the Lumière Cinématographe. The two men quickly hatched a deal. Schustek left Union Model Works for employment with Selig.

Needing a larger workspace, Selig opened a second office at 3945 N. Western Avenue, located in the far reaches of Chicago. Settling into the southeast corner of the intersection of Western Avenue and Irving Park Road, Selig and Schustek devised a plan to recreate the Lumière Cinématographe, make slight changes, and give the contraption a new name to avoid any claims of patent infringement. Essentially, they created a front by which Schustek would build cameras and projectors for a sole customer—who was of course Selig. The Lumière Cinématographe, as reproduced by the two men, became the Selig Standard Camera for recording film and the Selig Polyscope, which was the projection system.

Christening his business Mutoscope & Film Company, then W. N. Selig Company, and finally the Selig Polyscope Company, Selig opened up one of the world's first film studios at his Western and Irving Park office. Using this North Side setting as a headquarters, Selig made his first narrative, *The Tramp and the Dog*, in 1896. Shot in a wooded area in what is today the Rogers Park neighborhood, this simple film involves a

Selig Polyscope projector and logo, from the collection of Michael and Kate Corcoran. *(Photo by Kate Corcoran)*

hobo going door to door, looking for a meal. At one house he is met by an ill-tempered bulldog that chases him over a fence. Since such movie conventions as stuntmen and trained animals were years away, Selig's comedy took an unexpected turn when the dog sank his teeth into the actor's pants while the camera continued rolling. It was said that the look on the hobo's face was genuine fear—here was the original method actor. Audiences, slowly warming up to this new medium, enjoyed *The Tramp and the Dog* as filler in between acts at Chicago vaudeville houses.

Selig's ventures into the fledgling film industry continued with smaller (and safer) productions, essentially 50-foot reels documenting the city on film. Selig Polyscope produced such turn-of-the-century titles as *Chicago Police Parade, Gans-McGovern Fight, Chicago Fire Run, View of State Street,* and *Chicago Fireboats on Parade*. Realizing that audiences wanted to see other locales besides their own neighborhoods, Selig sent camera crews out to Colorado and the southwestern states. This footage was incorporated into the popular Hale's Tours films.

Meanwhile, on the East Coast, Thomas Edison was attempting to broaden the base of motion picture audiences by creating "story films." His first success was the 1903 film *The Great Train Robbery*, directed by Edwin S. Porter. *The Great Train Robbery* was a landmark picture on many fronts. It was one of the first American films to effectively tell a story by editing together different shots from various locations. As an adventure of the Old West, it introduced many motifs—such as bandits, train robberies, and wild shoot-outs—that became stock elements of westerns well into the sound era. *The Great Train Robbery* featured a young actor by the name of William G. Anderson (formerly Max Aronson, the son of Jewish immigrants and a native of Pine Bluff, Arkansas). Anderson, a fledgling stage actor and magazine model, was trying to work his way into the growing motion picture business. He took on the screen name "Bronco Billy" for his alleged horse-riding skills, though Anderson's saddle experience was largely the product of his imagination. Early in the filming of *The Great Train Robbery*, Anderson was thrown from his horse and ended up missing a good deal of production time. Consequently, most of his scenes were completed sans bronco.

Nevertheless, Anderson was hooked on the movie business. Brushing up on his horsemanship, Anderson moved west to Chicago. To compete with the success of *The Great Train Robbery*, the Colonel hired Anderson to produce, direct, and star in Selig Polyscope westerns. Circus horse riders were hired to play cowboys, and Native Americans were brought in from Michigan as Selig's Indians. Teepees were erected on the studio lot that doubled as both housing for the Native American actors and sets for the Selig westerns.

These films proved to be a financial success, though not without certain production problems inherent to shooting movies near a major metropolis. Scenes occasionally had to be scrapped when the exposed footage revealed western landscapes with laundry flapping in the breeze. Other problems included curious neighborhood children who could be seen hiding in the shrubbery to watch cowboy shoot-outs.

Selig western movie poster originally published by Goes Litho Co., circa 1914. *(Library of Congress, Prints and Photographs Division)*

Selig, realizing that authentic western locations would attract even more viewers, ordered Anderson and a cameraman to California. In autumn, Anderson became the first filmmaker to set up shop in the Golden State, working on the outskirts of Los Angeles. He filmed numerous location westerns for Selig, beginning with *The Girl from Montana* (filmed in both California and Montana), *His First Ride*, and *The Bandit King*. The result was more-realistic-looking pictures that raked in money for the Colonel.

By 1907, the Western Avenue studio grew to include both indoor and outdoor facilities. Now bounded by Western Avenue, Irving Park Road, Claremont Avenue, and Byron Street, the Selig Polyscope studio billed itself as "the biggest motion picture plant in the country . . . [with] the largest skylight of any west of the Hudson River." By the end of the year, Anderson left Selig to form his own company with Spoor (see page 14), though the defection barely made a dent in the Selig operation. Expanding the market beyond westerns, Selig Polyscope also produced romances, comedies, jungle stories, pirate adventures, and historical pictures.

In the fall of 1908, Selig had some high-level meetings with President Theodore Roosevelt, who was planning a hunting trip to Africa for when his term ended in the spring. Selig pitched the idea of documenting Roosevelt's exploits with a camera crew and even proposed taking Roosevelt's son Kermit to Chicago and teaching him how to use a Polyscope camera. Roosevelt loved the idea, and Selig made trips back and forth from Chicago to Washington to finalize plans. But in the spring of 1909, Roosevelt reneged on his deal. Via arrangements made for his trip through the Smithsonian Institution, the former president left for Africa in May, taking along an English camera crew hired by the museum.

Not to be outdone, Selig developed an alternative plan. He revamped one section of his studio to resemble an African location. A local actor, well known for his Roosevelt impersonations, was hired to play the former president. Selig next went up to Milwaukee, Wisconsin, where for $400 he purchased an aging yet still feisty lion from a failing zoo and brought him back to the Selig lot. Several African Americans—many of whom worked during the week as Pullman porters—were hired as members of Roosevelt's hunting party and outfitted in "native" costumes. With all the players set up, Selig's African hunting party was ready for production.

According to accounts, Selig's Roosevelt was a lousy shot, so a marksman was hired to shoot the lion from offscreen while the on-screen actor fired blanks. "Roosevelt," his hunting party, and the lion were contained in a cage on the set. Unfortunately, the hired gunman missed the beast on his first shot. Instead, the lion became angry from being socked with a blank cartridge from "Roosevelt's" prop gun. The hunting party escaped through an emergency door while the faux Roosevelt scrambled to the top of the cage. Hanging onto the top with a very real and very angry lion roaring beneath him, the actor sweated it out while Selig's director, Tom

Persons, reset the scene for a close-up. With "Roosevelt" quaking above, the marksman finally killed the lion. One costume change and camera setup later, "Roosevelt" posed as the Great White Hunter, standing triumphantly above the lion's corpse.

After completing production, Selig bided his time. Finally, word came that the real Roosevelt had felled his first lion. As newspapers headlines throughout the nation trumpeted this news, Selig rushed his film, dubbed *Hunting Big Game in Africa* (1909), to the theaters. Though Roosevelt was never mentioned by name in either the film or the advertisements, audiences assumed the movie was authentic. *Hunting Big Game in Africa* was extremely popular, making Selig Polyscope loads of money in the process. When the by-then-former president learned of the situation, he was outraged, but there was nothing Roosevelt could do.

With the success of *Hunting Big Game in Africa*, Selig developed a livestock company of animal performers. He specialized in exotic creatures that could be used for jungle films, as well as adventures set in the frozen north. In 1911, one writer visiting the Selig lot cataloged the menagerie as "12 lions, 9 lion cubs, 1 elephant, 10 leopards, 7 leopard cubs, 5 pumas, 1 monkey, 3 bears, 2 deer, 10 Eskimo dogs, 8 grey wolves, not to mention mules, geese, dogs, horses, etc."

The Colonel also built up a stock troupe of human actors, drawing on the large pool of talent living in the area. Centrally located, Chicago was a logical home for many vaudeville performers of the day. Well-known writers in the Chicago area were also brought into the fold, including L. Frank Baum, creator of the Oz stories. Baum got started in Chicago as a reporter for the *Chicago Evening Post*, and then switched to penning children's stories. He hit the jackpot with his 1900 book *The Wonderful Wizard of Oz*. In 1908, Baum turned to theatrical entertainment, creating a combination stage and film show called *Fairylogue and Radio-Plays*. Eventually Baum ended up at Selig, who released the film portion of *Fairylogue* in 1910. Selig also made the first film version of Baum's *Wizard of Oz* that same year. But by the end of the year, Baum had moved to California; he later opened his own film studio devoted to producing Oz films, the Oz Film Manufacturing Company.

As the Western Avenue studio thrived, Selig opened up a suite of offices downtown at 45 E. Randolph Street. Selig even maintained a special room there specifically for local censors to screen films. The Chicago Film Board was formed in 1907 to regulate the content of the growing movie industry. Fearing the possible moral corruption of audiences who flocked to the movies, the city council gave the board power to ban any seemingly objectionable film. Rather than fight this governing body, Selig played the game by their rules and consequently experienced no trouble.

Conforming to stereotypes of the day, Selig used ethnic actors, such as Native Americans or African Americans, to give his films a sense of supposed realism. For example, a 1909 exploit in the "Arctic" used Japanese acrobats as authentic-looking "Eskimos." Sent to a wintry location in Michigan that doubled for the North Pole, the troupe tracked down and shot a domesticated polar bear for Selig's cameras.

Selig also made imaginative use of Chicago and the surrounding area. In one Selig adventure, the Indiana Dunes served as the Sahara Desert. The Des Plaines River near the Chicago Canal doubled as a Boer War location. And in one of his most ambitious and internationally successful films, Selig turned the yacht basin at Jackson Park into the landing site of Christopher Columbus.

The Colonel had come into possession of three ships, replicas of the *Niña*, the *Pinta*, and the *Santa Maria*, left over from the Columbian Exposition of 1893. Originally brought to Chicago by the Spanish government, the vessels were now in pretty sorry shape. Nevertheless, Selig made the ships seaworthy (or Lake Michigan–worthy, as the case was) and hired crews to sail them into the Jackson Park Yacht Basin. Shooting was delayed by bad weather. Complicating matters, Columbus (played by Selig actor Charles Clary) and his crewmates, unused to choppy water, got seasick. Once they recovered, the production ran into further problems when the *Santa Maria* became stranded on a sandbar. Finally, as the re-creation of this historic landing was about to unfold for the cameras, the filmmakers encountered a problem never imagined by the real Columbus: scores of curiosity-seekers circled the three ships in small boats of their own, eager to get a glimpse of the moviemaking process.

Despite the difficulties, Selig's *The Coming of Columbus* (1912) was completed and went on to phenomenal success. Audiences around the world flocked to see this cinematic reenactment. In a special showing for Pope Pius X, *The Coming of Columbus* earned a historical footnote of its own as the first movie to be screened at the Vatican. The Pope was highly impressed with Selig's film and awarded the Colonel an honorary medallion for his efforts.

Replicas of two of Columbus's ships in the Jackson Park Yacht Basin. *(From the collection of Michael and Kate Corcoran)*

Another Selig innovation was buying stories to adapt into movies. Convinced by 1905 that filmmakers would eventually run out of ideas, Selig began looking for a source of fresh material. He made an initial contact with Moses Koenigsberg, editor of the William Randolph Hearst–owned *Chicago American*, then began working with a New York publishing representative to obtain new stories.

Though Edison had pioneered the movie serial with *What Happened to Mary?* in 1912, Selig took the form a step further. In 1913, the Chicago newspaper world was in the midst of a circulation war. Seven papers were competing for daily readership. It was nothing for a newspaper to publish 17 editions in a single day in a desperate effort to stymie the competition. Selig, sensing opportunity, went to the *Chicago Tribune* with a proposal.

The result was *The Adventures of Kathlyn*, a 13-chapter serial for both film audiences and newspaper readers. Each week, the plucky Kathlyn, played by Selig actor Kathlyn Williams, went through a series of torrid events, leading up to a high-pitched cliff-hanging ending. The thin storyline revolved around an American woman who inherited a royal title in India. Debuting on December 29, 1913, *The Adventures of Kathlyn* was popular in both mediums. Viewers headed to the theaters week after week for another breathless installment, while simultaneously following Kathlyn's exploits in the *Tribune*. If figures are to be believed, *Tribune* circulation went up 10 percent as a direct result of *The Adventures of Kathlyn*.

Williams, who was known as "the Selig Girl," also appeared in Selig's best-known work, the first screen version of *The Spoilers*, in 1914. This tale of the Alaskan gold rush was based on a novel by then-popular author Rex Beach. Realizing the money to be made in the picture industry, Beach demanded a whopping sum of $2,500 for the rights to his story. Selig hammered out a compromise with the author, arranging a royalty payment while the Colonel maintained story rights—marking the first time royalties were given to an author on a movie project. Shot at the Western Avenue studio, *The Spoilers* featured Williams and Selig's top leading man, William Farnum. The film was remade on several occasions. A 1930 version featured Gary Cooper, and the best-known remake, released in 1942, starred John Wayne, Randolph Scott, and Marlene Dietrich.

As Chicago's wintry climate was not conducive to year-round filming, Selig started branching out to warmer locales. He opened one film studio in Jacksonville, Florida, and another on the outskirts of Los Angeles, at the corner of Eighth and Olive Streets, although he still maintained Chicago as his base of operations.

Selig's Chicago studio temporarily shut down in 1914 during an unexpected recession. Though he soon reopened, Selig's eyes remained on California, where his western studio was growing in size and stature, drawing such rising talents as Tom Mix and Roscoe "Fatty" Arbuckle. Short cartoons, dubbed "Seligettes," were another aspect of the facility. Sticking to his sense for showmanship, Selig launched a well-planned publicity stunt in the summer of 1915. The Colonel chartered a train—dubbed the "Selig Movie Special"—as part of a two-week excursion to the Panama Pacific Exposition in San Francisco and a tour through the Southern California studio. At the cost of $128 per person, the excursion was faithfully recorded every step of the way by Selig cameras.

Certainly the film industry had grown in California, with studios such as Biograph and Keystone doing a thriving business in the Los Angeles suburb of Hollywood. Realizing that the future of the movie business was California, Selig had all but shut down his Chicago operations by 1918. A few films were still made here, including the box office disaster *The Crisis* (1918). This Civil War drama was based on a novel by Winston Churchill, a cousin of the future British prime minister. *Pioneer Days* (1917), a recreation of the famed Fort Dearborn massacre shot on location in Wilmette, signaled the end of Selig's Chicago production.

Selig maintained an office at 3945 N. Western Avenue through 1919, but the move to California was permanent. Though he continued to dabble with independent production as late as 1922 and maintained a stable of exotic creatures for animal adventure films, Selig grew bored with the movie business. Instead, he earned a healthy profit by selling the rights to stories he had bought years before. Retired and rich, Selig lived in happy obscurity until his death in 1948.

Essanay Film Manufacturing Company (1907–1917)

501 N. Wells Street

1333–1345 W. Argyle Street

Between 1333 and 1345 W. Argyle Street is St. Augustine College. Occupying five acres in Uptown, St. Augustine's mission is to make higher learning accessible to nontraditional students, with its emphasis on Chicago's Hispanic community. The campus buildings have a unique history. A distinctive Indian-head logo, on top of an arched door at one entrance, is part of the reason these buildings have earned landmark status from the Chicago City Council. The college's Charlie Chaplin Auditorium also recalls the history of these buildings. Though an important educational resource today, this Argyle Street location was originally built as the headquarters for the Essanay Film Manufacturing Company.

Essanay was founded by George K. Spoor and William "Bronco Billy" Anderson. Spoor's entrance into the moving picture business was something of a fluke. In 1895, he owned a newspaper stand at the Chicago and North Western rail station at Kinzie Avenue and Wells Street. On occasion Spoor worked the box office of the Waukegan Opera House in downtown Waukegan.

Meanwhile, Edwin Hill Amet, a Waukegan employee of the Chicago Scale Works, was tinkering with a device for motion picture projection.

The entrance to Essanay Film Manufacturing (1345 W. Argyle), the most significant silent film studio in Chicago, now home to St. Augustine College. *(Photo by Kate Corcoran)*

His previous invention had been a penny scale that could print out a card telling a person's weight. Amet had bigger hopes with his motion picture projector but craved the advice of an expert.

Figuring someone at the Opera House would have inside knowledge of the entertainment industry, Amet approached box office manager Spoor with his experiments. Not letting on that his show business connections were limited to the ticket booth, Spoor agreed to look at Amet's invention. Impressed but broke, Spoor asked what it would take to complete the projector. Amet estimated his final cost to be $65. Though he barely had the capital, Spoor "advanced" Amet $25—almost all the money Spoor had at the moment.

Amet completed his projector, dubbed the "Magniscope," the following year. Yet when all was said and done, Amet decided the moving picture fad wouldn't last. He sold his share of interest in the invention to Spoor, who quickly established the National Film Renting Company at 62 N. Clark Street. This business distributed films and projectors to the burgeoning moving picture theater circuit nationwide. Before long, Spoor dumped the newspaper stand and began raking in profits from this new entertainment form.

For the most part, Spoor distributed simple films that documented the everyday life of late 19th- and early 20th-century America. Subjects like rushing streetcars, crowded city streets, or athletic events were popular with audiences craving to see something moving on the screen. Within 10 years of his original $25 investment, Spoor had built up a considerable corporation. Among his many employees were Donald J. Bell, who was in charge of film projector installation, and Albert S. Howell, who headed up the maintenance department. In 1907, the duo left Spoor's outfit to form their own motion picture equipment company, Bell and Howell.

Itching to develop as a film entrepreneur apart from Colonel Selig, in April 1907 Bronco Billy paid a visit to Spoor's offices. The two agreed that between Spoor's distribution talents and Anderson's filmmaking abilities, a production partnership could result in mutual benefits. Together they formed the Peerless Film Manufacturing Company. By August, the company had undergone a significant name change. Adopting their initials of S and A, the company was rechristened the Essanay Film Manufacturing Company and opened an office at 501 N. Wells Street.

The first Essanay release, *An Awful Skate, or the Hobo on Rollers*, was shot on the sidewalk outside the company's Wells Street home. Directed by

Anderson, this 1907 comedy starred a cross-eyed funnyman named Ben Turpin. Essentially the film was a mini-documentary as Turpin veered up and down the sidewalk, desperately trying not to smash into innocent pedestrians. Turpin, a vaudeville veteran, made $15 a week doing double duty as Essanay's house comedian and janitor. With his permanently crossed eyes and walrus mustache, Turpin's offbeat looks were made for comedy. He went on to great success as the ultimate second banana of silent slapstick comedies, working with everyone from Chaplin to Laurel and Hardy. As a joke, his eyes were insured for $1 million by the prestigious Lloyd's of London, should they ever come uncrossed.

TOP: Scene from *What Happened to Aunty*, a 1911 Essanay comedy. The hapless aunt of the family learns she's married a man of lesser means. *(Photo courtesy of Dave Drazin)*

BOTTOM: From the 1911 Essanay comedy *Oh You Teacher!* Notice the many men playing women's roles. This publicity still is captioned WE WILL SELECT THE HOMLIEST [sic] ONE. *(Photo courtesy of Dave Drazin)*

During Essanay's early years, slapstick was the stock in trade. "Home of Comedy Hits" was the studio motto, though Anderson was still churning out westerns. Like Selig Polyscope, Essanay made effective use of Chicago's prairie-strewn Rogers Park in such films as *The Life of Jesse James* (1908). Occasionally, Anderson would take a camera crew and his actors down to Starved Rock State Park to film within the rugged landscape. However, as Selig had learned, audiences were growing more sophisticated about the movies, and authentic backgrounds became a necessity.

As with his previous boss, Anderson made regular trips to Colorado to shoot film with authentic western landscapes. And again, following Selig's lead, Spoor and Anderson opened a California branch, the Essanay Western Company, headquartered in Niles Canyon, about 20 miles south of Oakland.

Still, Chicago remained Essanay's nerve center. With profits reaching record levels and the public demanding more films, Spoor and Anderson decided to construct a larger, more elaborate studio. They acquired property at 1333 W. Argyle Street on Chicago's North Side. Ultimately the studio stretched to 1345 W. Argyle as the complex grew. At its peak, the Essanay film factory housed three studios for shooting, a carpentry shop, prop and wardrobe storage, an area for film processing, a publicity department, and, of course, dressing rooms for the stars. The studio also possessed one of the most sophisticated movie lighting systems of the time, making effective use of both natural conditions and a complicated latticework of artificial lights. An Essanay employee, Alan Dwan (who later became a respected Hollywood director), created a mercury-vapor arc light system, a groundbreaking development in film production.

There was also an in-house publication, *Essanay News*, "published in the interest of Exhibitors and all Newspapers which use News of Photoplays and Players." In the publication's masthead was Essanay's Indian-head logo. This studio trademark was found on the doors, other studio publicity materials, and on title cards of every Essanay production. Based on the Indian-head penny (though for no specific reason), the emblem was

TOP: *On the Desert's Edge* (1911), one of the hundreds of westerns cranked out by Essanay Studios. *(Photo courtesy of Dave Drazin)*

MIDDLE: From *The Outlaw and the Child* (1911), one of Essanay's typical westerns. *(Photo courtesy of Dave Drazin)*

BOTTOM: *The Puncher's New Love* (1911), another typical Essanay western, with a good guy and his girl. *(Photo courtesy of Dave Drazin)*

designed by Spoor's sister, a student at the School of the Art Institute of Chicago.

Essanay, which coined the popular term "photoplay" to describe moving picture entertainments, developed a considerable stable of actors and film talent, led by handsome Francis X. Bushman. Bushman's pictures primarily were historical and dramatic romances, with such turgid titles as *His Friend's Wife* (1911), *The Mail Order Bride* (1912), *White Roses* (1912), *The House of Pride* (1912), and *When Soul Meets Soul* (1913). Another of Essanay's major players was Beverly Bayne. A 16-year-old Hyde Park High School student when she joined the studio, Bayne was often paired with Bushman as a love interest. Eventually the duo left Essanay for Metro Studios in California. They even married, though the nuptials were kept a secret for some time lest the Bushman/Bayne marital status affect their respective careers as matinee lovers.

Understanding the meaning of "clout" in Chicago years before the term came into use, Spoor and Anderson learned how to use public officials and facilities to their advantage. Anderson did get arrested at one point for setting off a false fire alarm so Essanay cameras could film Turpin on the run from the horse-drawn fire wagons. But civil disobedience gradually gave way to official cooperation between city officials and the studio. Mayor William Hale "Big Bill" Thompson became interested in greasing the wheels for Essanay after the studio offered to film Chicago's annual Prosperity Day Parade, a pet project of the mayor's. And it probably didn't hurt anything when Essanay hired Mayor Thompson's wife to write movie scenarios.

State government got in on the action as well. More than 500 members of the Illinois National Guard were featured as extras in Essanay's epic adventure *In the Palace of the King* (1915). The studio also got permission to film the drama *Power* (1916) at Starved Rock State Park; casting Illinois governor Edward Fitzgerald Dunne in a supporting part inevitably helped to ease the process.

In addition to Turpin, the Essanay comedy wing boasted the talents of Wallace Beery. Beginning his show business career in 1902 as an assistant to the elephant trainer of Ringling Brothers Circus, Beery turned to comic performance for Broadway and vaudeville shows. At Essanay, Beery's burly appearance was put to incongruous use by outfitting him in a blonde wig and long dress. In this drag getup, Beery starred in a series of comic misadventures as "Sweedie, the Swedish maid." With titles like *Sweedie the*

Swatter (1914), *Sweedie and Her Dog* (1915), and *Sweedie Goes to College* (1915), these silly photoplays were quite popular.

Essanay housed a considerable writing staff. Ring Lardner Sr. and George Ade came up with photoplay ideas for a scenario department run by Louella Parsons. Parsons hailed from Freeport, Illinois, and came to Chicago to become a writer. Eventually she relocated to Los Angeles, acted in a few pictures, and then went to work for the Hearst newspaper chain, where Parsons carved out her stake in the American cultural landscape as a nationally recognized gossip columnist. Another future writer, Katherine Anne Porter, worked as an extra in many Essanay productions. She later became an accomplished short story author and novelist; her best-known work, *Ship of Fools*, was turned into a 1965 film by director Stanley Kramer.

Porter often worked with another Essanay extra, a Chicago teenager named Gloria Swanson. Swanson's aunt was a friend of Spoor's, and in June 1914 she brought young Gloria to the Argyle Street complex. While touring the facilities, Swanson was noticed by the Essanay casting director. In a matter of days, she was cast in her first picture, playing the part of a guest at a wedding. For this less-than-remarkable cinematic debut, Swanson was paid a grand total of $3.25. After an undeserved chewing-out by a temperamental director on her third film, Swanson nearly quit the business.

Essanay had other plans. Swanson was offered a place in the studio's stock of extra players at a guaranteed salary of $13.25 per week, regardless of whether she worked one day or four. Saturday work increased her weekly salary to nearly $20.

Swanson wasn't just noticed by the casting people at Essanay. Beery was smitten with the beautiful young woman and often drove her home in his open-top Stutz Bearcat. Whispers of a liaison between the beefy comedian and another young woman ultimately forced Essanay to permanently exile Beery to their California branch. Two years later when Swanson was a rising star in California herself, Beery became the first of her six husbands.

By far the biggest name to work at the Essanay Chicago studio was Charlie Chaplin. In 1914, Chaplin was the most popular film star in the world, thanks to his work with Mack Sennett and his comedy film factory at Keystone Studios. When Chaplin's contract with Keystone ended, the British comic found himself in an enviable negotiation position.

Come autumn, the contract talks between Keystone and Chaplin disintegrated. Anderson, out west working on his *Bronco Billy* films, met with Chaplin to talk over future possibilities at Essanay. After some discussion, Anderson wired Spoor back in Chicago. He proposed they offer Chaplin the then-unheard-of salary of $1,000 per week. However, by the time Anderson heard back from Spoor, Chaplin's asking price had risen to $1,250 per week. Anderson agreed and even promised Chaplin a signing bonus of $10,000. With the deal settled, Anderson and Chaplin boarded a train in late December for the comic's Chicago debut.

Upon arrival, Chaplin was disappointed to learn that Spoor was out of town. He toasted New Year's of 1915 with Anderson and his family, and all appeared bright for the new Essanay sensation. Yet Chaplin's brief Chicago period ultimately proved to be an unhappy experience for the comic.

It turned out Spoor had deliberately missed Chaplin's Chicago arrival. Chaplin later discovered the real story: when Anderson first suggested hiring Keystone's sensation, Spoor claimed he never heard of the world's most popular comedian. This was an oddly out-of-touch response for someone so deeply involved in the film industry. However, at the recommendation of Essanay director Jess Robbins, Spoor agreed to hire Chaplin. Still, the $1,250 per week fee seemed excessive to Spoor, particularly when other studio comics were only making $75 per week. Consequently, when Chaplin was due to arrive, the penny-pinching Spoor made sure he wasn't around.

Chaplin also had difficulty getting his promised bonus out of Essanay. He was bounced from office to office in a fruitless search for the promised cash. Though the money eventually was paid, the brusque treatment gave Chaplin a strong indication of things to come.

The snub by Spoor and the withheld bonus were just part of Chaplin's dissatisfaction. He felt Essanay was too regimented as a business and ultimately not hospitable to creativity. Chaplin was horrified to learn Essanay routinely screened original negatives during the editing phase of filmmaking, rather than go to the added expense of making a positive work print. Bushman tried to smooth things over by telling Chaplin that the up-front operations were just the "antithesis" of how Essanay really worked. "But it wasn't," Chaplin wrote in his autobiography. "I didn't like the studio and I didn't like the word 'antithesis.'"

Chaplin moved into the penthouse suite at the Brewster Building at 2800 N. Pine Grove. His next stop was the shops on State Street to buy new baggy pants and oversized shoes, his trademark costume. Despite the turmoil at Essanay's business office, Chaplin was ready to work.

He got back on his creative track and shot his first comedy for the studio. Titled *His New Job*, the film was a tweak at his former Keystone employer Mack Sennett. The story revolves around a troublemaking handyman (Chaplin) who causes havoc when he is hired by "Lockstone Studios." (In retrospect, the picture might also have been an indication of Chaplin's unhappiness with Spoor.) Released in February 1915, *His New Job* was notable for introducing Chaplin to Ben Turpin. The two comics had good chemistry both on-screen and off and ended up making several films together. Also appearing in *His New Job* was Gloria Swanson. Chaplin had deliberately picked Swanson for the film, hoping the pretty bit player would add some comic sparkle to the film. Swanson, however, was unimpressed with Chaplin's slapstick. "All morning [during shooting] I felt like a cow trying to dance with a toy poodle," she later wrote in her autobiography, *Swanson on Swanson*. As a result, the disappointed Chaplin stuck Swanson in a smaller role, playing a secretary at a job placement office. Many years later, after she had achieved considerable success on her own, Swanson told Chaplin she had been deliberately obstinate during the making of *His New Job*. She had her sights set on a dramatic career and didn't want to be typecast as a lowly comic actress.

After *His New Job* was completed, Chaplin wanted to be as far from Spoor as he could. He demanded to work exclusively at Essanay's California studio. When the contract ended in 1916, Chaplin left Essanay for the Mutual Film Corporation.

Chaplin's defection was the beginning of the end for Essanay. A few years earlier, in 1908, Essanay, Selig Polyscope, and seven other production companies had banded together to form the Motion Picture Patents Company. This business alliance was designed to combat Thomas Edison's claim that other motion picture professionals were infringing on his patents. However, in the process of creating their coalition, the Motion Picture Patents Company put a stranglehold on other movie companies. They threatened to cancel contracts for raw film stock with George Eastman if he dared to sell film to any other motion picture business. Additionally, in order to control all aspects of distribution, the Motion Picture Patents Company formed the General Film Company, effectively giving the nine studios sole ability to distribute and control product. In 1915, the Supreme Court ruled that this confederation violated the Sherman Antitrust Act. Both the Motion Picture Patents Company and the

General Film Company were ordered disbanded, opening up immense opportunities to new film companies and distributors.

This legal decision and the defections of Chaplin, Bushman, Beery, and others to new film companies ultimately contributed to the studio's tailspin and end. Without a stock company of stars, Essanay pictures no longer raked in box office dollars. Other non-movie-related factors affected Essanay's bottom line, including a national coal shortage, a raging flu epidemic, and the ongoing war in Europe. Faced with mounting financial troubles, Spoor finally closed Essanay in 1917.

Having retained a good part of his personal fortune, Spoor sunk $4 million into a 3-D film process known as Natural Vision. However, with the advent of sound films, coupled with the Great Depression, Natural Vision flopped. Broke but not broken, Spoor left the film business altogether and later recouped his losses via a wise investment in Texas oil fields.

Anderson's post-Essanay career was a disaster. He tried producing Broadway shows with little success, then headed back to California in hopes of reviving his movie cowboy career. However, due to copyright laws, Anderson was forced to relinquish his Bronco Billy screen name. Metro Studios (a precursor of Metro-Goldwyn-Mayer) hired Anderson to direct a few comedy shorts starring an up-and-coming funnyman named Stan Laurel. Laurel eventually left Metro for Hal Roach Studios, where he entered into a career partnership with Oliver Hardy.

After his contract with Metro ended, Anderson was unable to find work in the film industry. Doomed to Hollywood oblivion, Anderson spent many years floating through a series of menial jobs, with occasional forays into the lowest levels of the movie business. However, the first screen cowboy star was not entirely forgotten. In 1957, Anderson was plucked from obscurity by the Academy of Motion Picture Arts and Sciences and awarded an honorary Oscar for "contributions to the development of motion pictures as an entertainment."

After Essanay's Chicago doors closed, Spoor sold the studio facilities to his former employees, Bell and Howell. In 1973, the Bell and Howell corporation donated part of Essanay to WTTW, the Chicago public television station. The buildings later became home to Essanay Stage and Lighting Company, one of Chicago's top rental houses for industrial film and commercial production.

The Argyle Street properties were next passed to St. Augustine College. Recognizing Essanay's importance to the city, on March 26, 1996, the

Commission on Chicago Landmarks
gave monument status to the Argyle
Street building. The students and
teachers at St. Augustine still walk
past the old Essanay entranceway. The
studio where Chaplin shot *His New
Job* has been rechristened the Charlie Chaplin Auditorium. Just above
the auditorium, the original catwalk,
where Essanay stagehands scurried
about during filming, remains unchanged. The staircase, located outside
the 1345 building, is another studio
vestige. And deep within the basement of the 1333 building, there are
two vaults, one of which is still labeled
with warnings on handling fragile
silent-era nitrate film.

One of two remaining Essanay film
vaults still stands in its original
location beneath the Essanay sound
stage, now the Charlie Chaplin Auditorium of St. Augustine College. *(Photo
by Kate Corcoran)*

The South Side: The Silent Era's Home to African American Filmmakers

While Selig and Essanay were producing films on the North Side, the
South Side also proved to be a fertile ground for moving picture entrepreneurs. As the silent era blossomed, movies reflected the culture of
the time—a society that was segregated and racist. African Americans
were usually relegated to playing jungle natives, comic buffoons, or sub-
servient positions of porters, maids, and domestic help—a trend that
continued well into the Hollywood sound era. Quite often in silent films,
Caucasian actors decked out in blackface played African Americans.

Consequently, entrepreneurs, eager to see an accurate reflection of
their people, began producing their own films known in African American communities as "Race pictures." Though hampered by low budgets
and crude technical aspects, Race filmmakers took on social issues facing
the African American community, including racial prejudice, poverty,
and interracial strife. Light skin tone versus darker skin tone was a recur-
rent theme in many Race pictures.

Race movies received enthusiastic support from the *Chicago Defender*.
Founded in 1905 by Robert S. Abbott, the *Chicago Defender* was a weekly

newspaper focusing on the concerns of Chicago's African American community. Pullman porters often carried the paper with them on their train routes, thus giving the young paper a quick national circulation. In the April 9, 1910, edition of the *Chicago Defender*, Sylvester Russell, the newspaper's "Foremost Drama Critic," wrote, "The moving picture craze has developed a wonderful stampede among the Negro . . . theater goers." Indeed, African American–operated studios popped up around the country, with regional filmmakers headquartered in such disparate sites as Los Angeles, Philadelphia, and Lincoln, Nebraska. As with the white studios, Chicago proved an ideal spot for enterprising African Americans. Many popular jazz acts and vaudeville performers either lived in or passed through the city, creating a diverse and accessible talent pool. Though the South Side film industry never approached the financial success of Selig Polyscope or Essanay, its impact was felt during the silent era.

Foster Photoplay Company (1913)

Grand Theater, 3110 S. State Street

3312 S. Wabash Street

As with Colonel Selig, William Foster's entertainment background served as his entry to the fledgling motion picture industry. Getting his start in New York City, Foster first entered show business as a publicity agent for the Cole and Johnson Company, a popular minstrel show of the late 19th and early 20th century. Intrigued by the possibilities vaudeville had to offer, by 1904 Foster was in Chicago, booking acts and serving as business representative for Robert Motts and the Pekin Theatre (a.k.a. the Pekin Inn and the Pekin Cafe), located at 2700 S. State Street. This landmark playhouse/nightclub on Chicago's South Side housed an orchestra and stock acting company. During this period, Foster also wrote articles for the *Chicago Defender* using the pseudonym Juli Jones Jr. The thrust of his reporting focused on entertainment, though Foster also dabbled in sportswriting.

In 1913, Foster struck out on his own. As an answer to the stereotypes of white filmmakers, Foster opened the Foster Photoplay Company, the first African American–owned and operated film production company in the United States. "Nothing has done so much to awaken race consciousness of the colored man in the United States as the motion picture," Foster wrote for the African American newspaper the *Indianapolis Freeman*. "It has made him hungry to see himself as he has come to be."

Foster headquartered his outfit at the Grand Theater, located at State and 31st Streets (which advertised itself in the *Chicago Defender* as "built for the colored people"), before moving to 3312 S. Wabash.

Foster's first picture was a two-reel comedy, *The Railroad Porter* (a.k.a. *The Pullman Porter*, 1912). This slapstick comedy featured Lottie Grady and Howard Kelly, two actors Foster knew from the Pekin Theatre. The innocuous plot followed the adventures of a Pullman porter, ending in a slapstick chase in the vein of Mack Sennett's Keystone comedies. Foster wrote and directed *The Railroad Porter* and released it with a companion newsreel, which featured a YMCA parade of African Americans. Foster's work was very successful in local theaters, as well as in New York and other eastern cities.

Heady with this initial success, Foster continued producing two-reel comedies and went in search of a national distributor. For a time, he even considered relocating to Jacksonville, Florida, where a number of white studios had set up operations.

By 1917, Foster's dream had withered. Shut out from film distribution channels by racism and unable to book his comedies into white-owned theaters, Foster closed up his production house. He rejoined the *Chicago Defender* as the circulation manager, only to leave a few years later to open a coffee distribution firm. However, Foster continued to show his films to South Side audiences. He even sent some of his movies overseas "to the boys in the trenches," the *Chicago Defender* told its readers, so African Americans fighting in World War I could have a small taste of home life.

Foster made a brief comeback in the movies at the close of the silent era. Relocating to Los Angeles, he was hired as an assistant to the director of Pathé Studios. Foster directed a few musical short subjects featuring African American performers, then tried to reestablish himself as a producer. Though he incorporated the second Foster Photoplay Company and opened up a Los Angeles office in 1928, the business folded before making a single film.

The Unique Film Company (1916)
3519 S. State Street

The Unique Film Company, formed by businessman Miles M. Webb, only produced one picture. *Shadowed by the Devil*, released in 1916, was based on a story by Webb's wife. The drama focused on three major characters, one a spoiled little rich girl and another a poor but hard-working young man. The third character was the devil-possessed son of an entrepreneur, hopelessly trying to free himself from Satan's grip. Beyond this meager description, not much is known about the film or how it was received. In any event, Unique folded after producing this single film.

Peter P. Jones Film Company (1916)

3704 S. Prairie Avenue

3849 S. State Street

Peter P. Jones came to filmmaking through portrait photography. Studio portraits by Jones, who hailed from Kalamazoo, Michigan, were considered some of the best in the country. He first came to Chicago in 1908. Jones's reputation quickly grew, and eventually he opened up a studio at 3519 S. State Street. "Pictures by Electric light—no more dark or cloudy days or even nights in the Peter P. Jones studio," read his advertisements. Many prestigious figures of the early 20th century sat before Jones's lens, including social activists W. E. B. DuBois and Booker T. Washington, artist Henry Tanner, and entertainer Bert Williams.

Jones made an important contribution to Chicago political history when in 1912, he became the first African American to run for the city council. Aiming for the office of alderman of the Second Ward, Jones's political ambitions were thwarted when his petitions for a spot on the ballot were officially denied. Undaunted, Jones continued his campaign. Pleading with Second Ward residents, Jones used the *Chicago Defender* to publicize a write-in campaign. The effort was for naught, and the would-be alderman went back to the portrait business.

Jones turned to moviemaking in 1914. The Peter P. Jones Film Company opened up at 3704 S. Prairie Avenue, then later moved to 3849 S. State Street. His first effort was *Sambo and Dinah* (1914), a forgettable two-reel comedy that relied on stereotyped characters to carry the humor. Jones's second film put him on the map. *For the Honor of the Eighth Illinois Regiment*, released in September 1914, was a documentary highlighting the exploits of the Eighth Illinois Regiment, an all–African American military unit based in Chicago. The film detailed their achievements during the 1898 Spanish-American War, including participation in Theodore Roosevelt's renowned charge at San Juan Hill. *For the Honor of the Eighth Illinois Regiment* opened at the Pekin Theatre, where it was a hit.

Jones continued making newsreels; then in 1916 he produced a five-reel comedy, *The Slacker*. The story revolves around a would-be draft dodger who desperately wants to avoid the Great War in Europe. After a dream in which he encounters a war veteran, the protagonist changes his mind and achieves glory on the battlefields of France.

Following *The Slacker*, Jones relocated to New York. He returned to still photography, and became the first African American hired by a major movie studio when Jones took a job with Selznick Film Laboratories, a facility run by movie pioneer Lewis J. Selznick. In 1922, Jones tried his hand again at film production in an abortive attempt to make a film with aviator Bessie Coleman. Coleman, the first African American woman to earn a pilot's license, was a well-known stunt flier and test pilot. The following year Jones produced a two-reel airplane comedy, *How High Is Up?* (1923), his last known effort at moviemaking.

Birth of a Race Photoplay Company (1917)
123 W. Madison Street
29 S. LaSalle Avenue

In 1915, the *Chicago Daily News* carried advertisements for D. W. Griffith's Civil War epic *The Birth of a Nation*, noting that seats were being sold four weeks in advance and patrons were asked to name two dates if possible. The full-page ad, which at one point trumpeted that the film had been shown "185 Times in Chicago Today and Not an Empty Seat Yet," also listed many of *The Birth of a Nation*'s highlights. Viewers were in store for a host of excitements previously unimaginable in moving pictures. The "gigantic spectacle" promised 3,000 horses, 18,000 people, and 5,000 scenes, put together for film audiences at the staggering cost of $500,000. The advertisement also heralded the film's many historical reenactments, including Sherman's march to the sea, the assassination of Abraham Lincoln, and the "rise of the Ku Klux Klan."

Others were less impressed with Griffith's depiction of the KKK. While *The Birth of a Nation* was a landmark achievement in American movies in its pioneering use of editing, epic storytelling, and rousing climax, it also was an appalling historical rewrite of the post–Civil War South. The film generated controversy throughout the United States, arguably the first time in the nation's history that racism in popular culture garnered open public debate. Though President Woodrow Wilson called the film "history written in lightning," other notable figures including novelist

Upton Sinclair and philanthropist George Foster Peabody condemned the production.

In Chicago, Mayor William Hale "Big Bill" Thompson managed to delay the opening of the film for some time. Eventually *The Birth of a Nation* was the subject of debate in the Illinois legislature, leading to a bill prohibiting racially inflammatory material from stage and screen. This bill passed by an overwhelming majority of 111 to 2.

Griffith, the son of a Confederate Army colonel, was shocked and dismayed over the outrage his film generated. Ultimately he was forced to cut and recut the picture, opening different versions around the country, often depending on what local attitudes would and would not tolerate on-screen. The controversy ultimately broke Griffith. He attempted to answer his critics with *Intolerance* (1916), an epic production examining fanaticism through the ages. The film, while today acknowledged as a masterpiece, was an expensive flop. Though Griffith continued working into the early sound era, he became an alcoholic, unable to shake the personal defeat he experienced with *The Birth of a Nation*.

At the time of *The Birth of a Nation*'s release, the *Chicago Defender* published a letter to the editor against the film, written by Booker T. Washington. The letter, which was later printed in African American newspapers throughout the country, read in part: "No matter how many other artistic and historic features the play may have, its ultimate result will be to intensify race prejudice and thereby do great, lasting harm to both races." Washington also considered what impact his own autobiography, *Up from Slavery*, might have if it were turned into a photoplay. Washington passed away on November 14, 1915, leaving it for others to take up that challenge.

Emmett J. Scott, Washington's confidential secretary since 1897, continued to pursue the project. Before Washington's death, the two had explored producing a film called *Lincoln's Dream*, a project that ultimately fell apart due to financial difficulties. This abortive attempt was an ominous prelude to what ultimately ensued.

By July 1916, Scott had regrouped. He incorporated the Birth of a Race Photoplay Corporation in Delaware, though the production was headquartered in Chicago. Such varied national figures as Booker T. Washington's widow, former president William Howard Taft, Illinois governor Frank Lowden, and noted Sears Roebuck executive and philanthropist Julius Rosenwald all endorsed the idea behind the proposed film. A brochure, inviting investors to buy stock in this new film corporation, stated that *The Birth of a Race* would show "the true story of the Negro, his life in Africa, his transportation to America, his enslavement, his freedom, his achievements, together with his past, present, and future relations with his white neighbor and to the world in which both live and labor."

The war in Europe slowed down fundraising, as Scott, concerned over issues facing African American draftees, became a special adviser to US Secretary of War Newton Diehl Baker. Yet stocks for the film continued to be sold and promises made on potential returns. The African American community of Chicago's South Side bought considerable shares. Sales then concentrated on the Jewish community, with scenes condemning anti-Semitism promised additions to the completed film.

The film was to be made in conjunction with the Selig Polyscope Corporation. After spending $140,000 on production, Selig dropped the project. It seemed that the stock sales had been grossly mismanaged, though this was carefully shielded from shareholders via a periodic newsletter trumpeting the continuing production. Dismayed at what was happening to the original concept, Rosenwald withdrew his support. Others who had previously endorsed the film also distanced themselves. Then, in the spring of 1918, Chicago stockbroker Giles P. Corey was arrested for fraudulently promoting the actual value and return on stock.

Down but not out, the production was acquired by Daniel Frohman of the New York–based Frohman Amusement Company. Things seemed to be picking up; after all, Frohman was a reputed show business producer and theatrical impresario. In conjunction with his brother Charles, Frohman controlled many theaters throughout the United States.

As the film changed hands, so did the nature of the story. It was now turning into a biblical epic, with recreations of Old and New Testament stories. Frohman moved the production to Tampa, Florida, to shoot biblical footage. The original concept of promoting racial tolerance and harmony fell to the wayside as anti-German propaganda was added to exploit wartime sentiments. Scott's name was also dropped as the film's scenarist.

The film was finally completed at Chicago's Rothacker Film Manufacturing Company, located at 1339 W. Diversey Parkway. In November 1918, an innocuous advertisement appeared in the back pages of *Variety* announcing the grand opening of *The Birth of a Race* at the Blackstone Theatre at 60 E. Balbo Avenue. (Then one of the world's most fashionable venues, today the theater is owned by DePaul University and has been rechristened the Merle Reskin Theatre.) Investors were asked to pay a hefty sum of $10 apiece for opening-night tickets.

The film finally opened in December 1918. What resulted after the many years of effort and controversy was a complete shambles. The biblical story and the war story lines in *The Birth of a Race* seemed like two different movies haphazardly stitched together. Promised scenes of racial harmony and enrichment were gone, replaced by a sequence in which a young white boy bullies an African American child. Some producers, knowing what they had on their hands, went to the trouble of inking out their names on the official program given to opening-night attendees.

Surprisingly, the film earned mixed reviews. Some pronounced the film "clean, sincere" and "worth seeing," if perhaps a bit on the long side. On the other hand, the show business publication *Moving Picture World* declared, "The names of three men are given as the authors of the scenario. It would be a deed of charity not to reveal their identity nor the names of the members of the cast. All have well-earned reputations and are probably anxious to live down their connection with the entire affair."

Historical Feature Film Company (1914)
105 W. Monroe Street
Ebony Film Corporation (1917)
608 S. Dearborn Street
2332 N. California Avenue

The Historical Feature Film Company was a white-owned company that produced two-reel comedies. Aimed at both African American and white audiences, the slapstick shorts relied heavily on black stereotypes of the era. The studio's films included *Black and White* (1914), *Money Talks in Darktown* (1916), and *A Natural Born Shooter* (1917).

In 1917, Ebony Film Corporation was founded by a group of white film investors. Run by Luther J. Pollard, an African American who served as Ebony's figurehead, the studio offices were located downtown on S. Dearborn, with production facilities on N. California Avenue. Ebony also had an outdoor studio located just outside Oshkosh, Wisconsin. The company of 40 players included Sam Robinson, a cousin of Bill "Bojangles" Robinson, who would be one of Hollywood's premier tap dancers in the

1930s. Another member of the Ebony stock company was Sam T. Jacks, who would become involved with the Royal Gardens Motion Picture Company in 1919.

As titular head of Ebony, Pollard espoused racial pride in the studio product. "We specialize in comedy, the same as the producers of Charles Chaplin . . . or any other producers of comedy," he wrote to a Los Angeles–based African American filmmaker. "You will find [our films] to be clean and without those situations which are usually attributed to the American Negro. We proved to the public that colored players can put over good comedy without any of that crap shooting, chicken stealing, razor display, water melon eating stuff that the colored people generally have been a little disgusted at seeing."

However, Ebony comedies—such as *Ghosts* (1917), *The Porters* (1918), *A Busted Romance* (1918), *The Bully* (1918), and *A Black Sherlock Holmes* (1918)—tended to be overacted and ham-fisted. The films were well received in white theaters, where stereotypes played as appealing lowbrow humor. African American audiences saw the Ebony films in a totally different light.

The *Chicago Defender* printed numerous editorials and letters to the editor, complaining about the nature of Ebony's films. "It was with abject humiliation that myself and many of my friends sat through the scenes of degradation shown on screen," wrote one angry viewer. "If [the films] were meant for comedy, the meaning certainly miscarried."

Part of the problem was that before Pollard and company actually produced films of their own, they released the Historical Feature Film Company movies under the Ebony name. The earlier films, which were more blatant in their racist stereotypes, resulted in a boycott of Ebony pictures. Led by the *Chicago Defender*, theaters catering to African American audiences gradually stopped booking the Ebony product. This inevitably resulted in financial difficulties for the company, and Ebony ultimately folded in 1919.

The Micheaux Film and Book Company (1918)
538 S. Dearborn Street, Suites 807–808
Ambitious and hard-driven, Oscar Micheaux was something of a spiritual predecessor to the American independent film movement of the 1990s. The child of former slaves, Micheaux was born in 1883. Raised in the small town of Metropolis, Illinois, at the very southern tip of the

state, Micheaux moved to Chicago in 1900. After working a series of odd jobs, he relocated to Wheaton, where he became a farm laborer. Though this low-paying job largely involved pitching hay, Micheaux lived simply and was able to open a bank account. After a couple of years, he took a job as a Pullman porter. His paycheck amounted to a lowly sum of $40 a week, but Micheaux again was able to save while traveling throughout the country.

In 1904, Micheaux put in to buy a plot of government land being sold by lottery in South Dakota. Though unsuccessful in this attempt, Micheaux became a landowner two years later when he was sold a portion of land near Gregory, South Dakota. Micheaux developed into a proficient farmer despite having no experience in agriculture. He built a sod house and taught himself the art of tilling soil and raising crops. Among his neighbors in Gregory, Micheaux's reputation was considerable, and he became a popular figure with business people and other farmers. In frequent business trips to Chicago, Micheaux extolled other African Americans to move west, though he had little luck in this campaign. However, Micheaux was still a much-respected figure in Chicago's African American community, and a visit by him often merited a few lines in the *Chicago Defender*.

Over the years, Micheaux corresponded with Orlean McCracken, a minister's daughter from his hometown. In 1910, the two were married at a church in Chicago. McCracken's father cared little for Micheaux and did not trust his headstrong son-in-law. Micheaux's marriage deteriorated when Orlean could not adapt to the sparse conditions of prairie life. In 1911, she gave birth to a stillborn child. Pressure from her parents, coupled with growing crop difficulties, led to Orlean leaving Micheaux for the more hospitable environs of Chicago.

A bad drought ultimately led to the end of Micheaux's life as a farmer. Ever the entrepreneur, Micheaux decided to turn his unique life experiences into fiction. In 1913, Woodruff Press, a company based in Lincoln, Nebraska, published Micheaux's thinly veiled autobiographical novel, *The Conquest*. Micheaux began traveling around the country, selling his book from town to town. This barnstorming sales technique was a pattern Micheaux would later carry over from his literary career to his life as a filmmaker.

Micheaux wrote his second novel, *The Forged Note*, in 1915. His third book, *The Homesteader*, published in 1917, was another roman a clef, detailing Micheaux's life as a homesteader and his failed marriage. It was this novel that led to the next phase of Micheaux's life.

The Homesteader was read by George P. Johnson, an executive with Lincoln Motion Picture Company, an African American film business with offices in Omaha, Nebraska, and Los Angeles, California. After a series of meetings between Micheaux, Johnson, and Johnson's brother Noble, negotiations to bring *The Homesteader* before the cameras broke down. The Johnsons saw Micheaux's story as a short, three-reel movie, whereas Micheaux felt the epic nature of his plot demanded much more significant screen time. (Noble Johnson later became an actor in numerous Hollywood films, including roles such as Queequeg in the 1930 adaptation of *Moby Dick* and a tribal chieftain in the original 1933 *King Kong*. He continued playing small supporting and uncredited parts well into the 1940s.)

To this end, Micheaux went into the moviemaking business himself. In 1918, he opened the Micheaux Film and Book Company with the express purpose of making a movie out of *The Homesteader*. Offices were opened in Sioux City, Iowa, and at 538 S. Dearborn Street in Chicago. Turning to old friends, Micheaux raised funds for the production by selling stock to the white businesspeople and farmers of Gregory.

Shooting much of the film outside of Sioux City, Micheaux utilized a cast of professional actors brought in from New York City. The story, which is overtly autobiographical, involves Jean-Baptiste, a young African American homesteader who is unhappily married to a woman named Orlean, the daughter of a tyrannical minister. After Orlean kills her father and commits suicide (perhaps Micheaux's wish fulfillment?), Jean-Baptiste meets Agnes, the daughter of a Scottish immigrant. Though at first their love seems doomed because of their racial difference, it eventually is learned that Agnes's late mother was black, thus freeing the couple to marry.

The Homesteader opened at Chicago's Eighth Regiment Armory on Thursday, February 20, 1919. The wordy advertisement for the film read, "Passed by the Censor Board despite the protests of three Chicago ministers who claimed that it was based upon the supposed hypocritical actions of a prominent colored preacher of this city!" Undoubtedly, this was a veiled reference by Micheaux aimed at his former father-in-law. Micheaux's photoplay clocked in at almost three hours, an unheard-of running time during the silent era. The *Chicago Defender* immediately dubbed it "the greatest of all Race productions."

Booking his film at numerous South Side movie venues and then at the-aters throughout the Midwest, Micheaux managed to turn a healthy profit. The success invigorated Micheaux as he plunged onward as a filmmaker.

One of the reasons Micheaux was able to earn back the investment on *The Homesteader* was his bargain-basement approach to filmmaking. While he was a natural storyteller, Micheaux's cinematic sensibility was crude at best. His films suffered from bad lighting, choppy editing, and a host of other technical blunders. Another criticism Micheaux faced early in his career was his casting of light-skinned African Americans in heroic roles and darker members of the race as villains. Micheaux even used light-skinned African Americans to play white characters.

Using his time-tested method of promotion and fundraising, he trav-eled extensively throughout the South to book his films and obtain money for new productions. At its height in Chicago, the Micheaux Film and Book Company turned out three films a year.

In 1920, Micheaux stirred up considerable controversy. The previous year, racial tensions in Chicago exploded into riots after Eugene Wil-liams, a young African American, was stoned and drowned by a group of whites after he accidentally drifted on a raft over to a "whites only" beach along 29th Street. From July 27 through 31, Chicago was a city under siege by its own citizens. African Americans battled white mobs in the streets. Ultimately, it took the National Guard and a timely rainstorm to quell the violence. When the violence was finally over, 23 African Ameri-cans and 15 whites were dead, while 537 people were reported injured. Hundreds more had lost their homes in numerous arson fires.

Tackling these still-raw emotions head-on, Micheaux released *Within Our Gates* (1920), a drama notable for a scene in which a white mob lynches an African American. Initially, the Chicago Board of Movie Cen-sors vetoed any plans to show *Within Our Gates*, fearing the film would incite a second riot. However, the board agreed to a second viewing of the film, this time inviting area officials and representatives of Chicago's African American community.

The results were mixed. Alderman Louis Anderson and Edward Wright, the corporation counsel for Chicago, believed that the film should be shown despite the unsettling lynch scene. In their view, it was an accurate portrait of some ugly truths. Others, including a coali-tion of African American and white clergy, believed that *Within Our Gates* would only cause more problems. At sermons throughout the city, ministers implored their congregations to protest the film. On the morning *Within Our Gates* was scheduled to open, the interracial Methodist and Episcopal Ministers Alliance appealed to Chicago's Mayor Thompson and chief of police John J. Garrity. Both officials refused to censor Micheaux's work.

Like any other "controversial" movie throughout cinematic history, *Within Our Gates* was suddenly *the* film to see. "8,000 feet of sensational realism," crowed advertisements. "Cost more than any 10 racial films ever made."

On Monday, January 12, 1920, *Within Our Gates* opened to a packed house at the Vendome Theater, 3145 S. State Street. The *Chicago Defender* called the film "the biggest protest against race prejudice [and] lynching . . . ever written or filmed."

Emboldened by his success, Micheaux returned to a lynching theme the following year with *The Gunsaulus Mystery*. This drama was loosely based on the case of Leo Frank, a Jewish man murdered in 1915 by an angry mob in Marietta, Georgia. *The Gunsaulus Mystery* was shot in New York, where Micheaux had relocated. Though the Chicago office remained open as a distribution wing for Micheaux Book and Film Company, by the early 1920s all production had shifted to New York City. His 1924 film *Body and Soul* marked the film debut of the noted African American actor, singer, and activist Paul Robeson.

In 1926, Micheaux finally closed what remained of the Chicago office, though he continued making films well into the sound era. Micheaux developed an ensemble of African American actors to correspond with popular Hollywood figures. Thus Lorenzo Tucker was billed as "the Black Valentino," Ethel Moses as "the Black Harlow," and Bee Freeman as "the Sepia Mae West." His 1939 film *Lying Lips* featured Robert Earl Jones, the father of noted actor James Earl Jones.

With the increasing sophistication of Hollywood productions, coupled with Micheaux's lack of technical panache, it became harder to find venues to show his work. Illness and financial difficulties forced him to leave the film business in 1948. Micheaux did what he knew best—hit the road and tried to sell his books. He died in 1951, seemingly relegated to the position of footnote in American film history.

In the mid-1980s, Micheaux was rediscovered by a new generation of moviemakers and film buffs. With the growth of independent cinema and the rise of such African American directors as Spike Lee and

Julie Dash, Micheaux was finally recognized as a cinematic pioneer. His surviving films, including *Within Our Gates*, were featured in retrospectives across the United States. In 1986, the Directors Guild of America gave Micheaux a posthumous honor with a Golden Jubilee Special Directorial Award, recognizing his efforts to bring African American stories to the screen. On February 13, 1987, Micheaux was given the ultimate in Hollywood honors: his own star on the Walk of Fame along Hollywood Boulevard.

The Royal Gardens Motion Picture Company (1919)

459 E. 31st Street

The Royal Gardens, run by Virgil L. Williams, was a popular nightclub and restaurant with Chicago's African American community. Clarence Muse, who went on to play supporting parts in numerous Hollywood features, including Jim to Jackie Coogan's *Huckleberry Finn* (1931) and Snoe in *The Black Stallion* (1979), was often hired by Williams to stage floorshows at the club. Another regular performer was jazz legend King Oliver. Between 1918 and 1921, the King Oliver Band—featuring trumpeter Louis Armstrong—was a steady attraction for the Royal Gardens.

In 1919, Williams attempted to pick up where William Foster had left off. Working with Sam T. Jacks, who had acted in several pictures for the Ebony Film Corporation, Williams entered the movie business by establishing a new branch of his entertainment ventures, the Royal Gardens Motion Picture Company. His intent was to create a center where African Americans could learn the craft of filmmaking.

Royal Gardens only produced one picture of note, *In the Depths of Our Hearts* (1920), with shooting taking place around the city and in rural Wisconsin. The story revolves around a light-skinned African American woman who disdains anyone with a darker complexion. Though her daughter agrees with these sentiments, the woman's son falls for a dark-skinned girl. Separated from her by his mother, the young man is sent to his uncle's farm, only to run off and eventually be reunited with his love. In the end, his mother and sister come to realize skin hue is not what makes a person's character.

Williams took particular pride in the technical qualities of his film, which he felt were better than most Race pictures showing in South Side theaters. Though the film is forgotten today, the *Chicago Defender* praised *In the Depths of Our Hearts* in 1920 for both its dramatic qualities as well as some "wonderful amount of action of the thrilling sort—hand to hand fights between red blooded men which will make you sit up and take notice." According to some sources, the Royal Gardens Motion Picture Company produced at least two other films, including a fairly well-received comedy. However, by 1920, Williams's dream succumbed to financial difficulties and the filmmaking operation folded.

Other African American Production Companies

Democracy Photoplay Corporation (circa 1918)

Delight Film Corporation (circa 1919)

Pyramid Picture Corporation (circa 1920)

Fife Productions Company (circa 1922)

Little is known about either the Democracy Photoplay Corporation or the Delight Film Corporation. Like Ebony Pictures, both companies were owned and operated by whites. Democracy produced at least one known film, titled *Injustice* (a.k.a. *Democracy or a Fight for Right*, 1918). Advertised as a "Smashing Virile Story of Our Race Heroes," the film was not well received.

Delight was another matter entirely. Rumored to be producing a version of Shakespeare's *Othello* using an entirely African American cast, the company proved to be something of a fly-by-night operation. Spied on by an agent from Lincoln Motion Picture Company, an African American photoplay operation located in Los Angeles, the Delight operation does not emerge from history with glowing credentials. According to the Lincoln agent, "the whole place looks like a swindling joint." The attitudes of the studio's white owners came through clearly in advertising campaigns that read, "Colored people are funny." In any event, the Delight Film Corporation, like so many of its peers, folded without making much of an impact.

There were at least two other Chicago-based African American production companies operating during the silent era. Other than their names, there is scant information on the Pyramid Picture Corporation (circa 1920) and Fife Productions Company (circa 1922).

More Early Film Landmarks

Other Silent Productions

There were a handful of other films shot in Chicago in the silent era. For a brief time, there was a third studio on the North Side, the American

Film Manufacturing Company, located at 6227 N. Broadway, with
offices at 207 S. State Street. Run by John Freuler, the studio was staffed
by former Essanay hands who left the larger studio after internal
squabbles. Among them was Alan Dwan, who got his first opportunity
to direct at American. However, most production was done in California, and the studio eventually became part of Mutual Film Corporation
in Hollywood.

The most notable major silent film to be made in Chicago was *That
Royle Girl*, a 1925 feature directed by D. W. Griffith and featuring W. C.
Fields in a rare dramatic role. At this point in his career, Griffith was
all but washed up. In the wake of the *Birth of a Nation* controversy and
the financial misfortunes of *Intolerance*, Griffith had fallen from his
august position as cinematic pioneer to studio hack. The slight story of
That Royle Girl revolves around a Chicago flapper, Joan Daisy Royle,
played by Carol Dempster. A fashion industry worker by day, Royle
pines for bandleader Fred Ketlar (played by silent film actor Harrison
Ford). When Ketlar is accused of murdering his estranged wife, Royle
seeks to clear his name. In the end, Royle marries an attorney, Ketlar
gets hitched with a chorus girl, and Fields has little to do in his role as
Royle's father.

That Royle Girl was produced by Paramount Pictures as Famous
Players-Lasky Corporation, which allowed Griffith to do some location
work in Chicago. Most notable were scenes of Carol Dempster shot
at the famed Augustus Saint-Gaudens statue of Abraham Lincoln, just
east of what is now the Chicago History Museum in Lincoln Park. In
typical Griffith sentimentality, Dempster's character believes she can
commune with the spirit of Lincoln emanating from the statue.

The film climaxes in a tornado destroying the hideout of the gangsters
who have killed Ketlar's wife. Griffith later explained this sequence as
"the only elemental thing I could use that could carry on and culminate
the fury of life in Chicago—the vortex of disordered . . . humanity."

That Royle Girl did little to impress either critics or moviegoers. By
1925, Griffith's brand of drama and overwrought emotion was passé.
The film died a quick death at the box office and was instantly forgotten. Since its release, all prints of *That Royle Girl* have disappeared.
Perhaps an errant copy is hidden in someone's attic or mislabeled and
buried inside a studio vault, but as of this writing, the film remains lost
in movie history. In 1980, *That Royle Girl* was added to the American

Film Institute's list of the "ten most wanted" lost films, determined by historical and/or artistic merits.

Other notable silent films shot in Chicago include a 1914 adaptation of *The Jungle*, the first dramatization of Upton Sinclair's muckraking novel about the city's meatpacking industry. Cowboy star William S. Hart came to Chicago in 1919 to film his western *Breed of Men*. A 1916 feature, *The Dumb Girl of Portici*, has some significance as well. Produced by Universal Pictures, this tale of a poor Italian girl in love with a Spanish nobleman in the midst of political upheaval is the only known film of the renowned Russian ballet star Anna Pavlova. Fire-damaged arches and columns, remainders of Frank Lloyd Wright designs at the Sans Souci Amusement Park at Cottage Grove and 60th Street, fill in the revolutionary background sets. The film also features an uncredited extra by the name of William Henry Pratt. Fifteen years later, Pratt—using the stage name Boris Karloff—would gain international acclaim as the Creature in Universal Pictures' 1931 horror classic *Frankenstein*.

David Drazin: A Modern Practitioner of a Silent Film Art

"Instead of reading notes off of a page, I'm reading the picture, the images. That in a sense tells you everything you need to know about what kind of music goes with a silent film. You can sort of approximate what kind of music the pictures say."
—*David Drazin*

From the earliest days of cinema, technicians experimented with methods of marrying image and sound; *The Jazz Singer*—released in 1927 and considered the first real "talkie"— was a culmination of many trials and errors. But silent films were never really "silent." Filmgoers in the early

Chicago-based pianist David Drazin, a modern master of silent film musical accompaniment. *(Photo by Mike Canale)*

20th century were used to musical accompaniment, be it a full-blown orchestra playing a grand score at one of Balaban and Katz's movie palaces or a solo piano player accompanying the movie showing at the neighborhood theater.

Chicago is fortunate when it comes to silent films: there are numerous venues for watching classics like *The General*, *Nosferatu*, *The Gold Rush*, or *Way Down East* as the films were meant to be seen. Every summer the Silent Film Society of Chicago (www.silentfilmchicago.com) holds a festival that routinely packs the house with sold-out shows. Live musical accompaniment in the form of pipe organ (and once each summer, a complete orchestra), is an integral part of the experience.

David Drazin is another stalwart on the silent film scene, known to Chicago audiences for his consummate piano work. He's the staff pianist at the Gene Siskel Film Center. Drazin also accompanies silent films for the Wilmette Theatre, the Silent Film Society of Chicago, and Doc Films at the University of Chicago, and for screenings at Argonne National Laboratory. He's played throughout the United States and was a guest pianist at the Silent Film Festival in Pordenone, Italy.

"I grew up with a love for this stuff," he says. His first taste of silent film was a clip from Charlie Chaplin's *The Adventurer* (1917), broadcast on the old 1960s children's program *Discovery*. "That made a huge impression on me. It was the most exciting thing I'd seen as a five-year-old." About the same time, Drazin started learning piano, though he never cared for the "book learning" part. "I just wanted to goof around on the keyboard. I could play a boogie-woogie when I was eight." Absorbing great jazz by listening to his father's collection of old 78 rpm records, Drazin quickly learned to emulate his heroes: Fats Waller, James P. Johnson, Mary Lou Williams, Kansas City Frank, Alex Hill, and other vanguard artists in blues and Harlem stride jazz. While his music skills grew, so did his exposure to silent film in his hometown of Cleveland, Ohio. Eventually he put together his two passions, playing for screenings at the local library.

When Drazin came to Chicago in the 1980s, he offered his talents to the Film Center of the School of the Art Institute at Columbus Drive and Jackson Street as an accompanist for their silent film programs. He made his debut in 1985 and has been playing for them ever since.

There is no school to learn how to "play for pictures," as Drazin says. It's a case of learning by doing. But silent movies naturally lend themselves to musical accompaniment, often providing "musical cues." Take, for example,

Charlie Chaplin's 1918 comedy *A Dog's Life*. Much of the film takes place in a cabaret, which features a hot burlesque dancer, a hyperkinetic jazz band, and a soloist (Chaplin's love interest, Edna Purviance) who brings the audience to tears with an emotional ballad. The musically based images and action inform Drazin what tempo to play and what sort of ambience should be underscored. Intertitles—the title cards between film shots—also provide Drazin with cues. As illustration, look at one of the intertitles in D. W. Griffith's epic *Intolerance*, which reads, "In the good old summertime." This reference to a 1902 parlor song by George Evans and Ren Shields naturally calls for this old standard.

"Circus Days," a typical vintage film score Drazin sometimes uses in his work. *(Image courtesy of Dave Drazin)*

There are other factors Drazin considers. "If I'm playing for a movie from 1909 it's not going to have fast cutting. The temptation is to play slowly when there's not a rapid alternation of shots. But that's not the case at all, because the emotional content of the actor's performance tells me how fast or slow the music should be."

Physical action is another important cue. If the action involves a cowboy fight scene or a comedy chase sequence, Drazin picks up the pace, playing in agitato, an Italian term that literally means "agitated."

With a movie lasting anywhere from a few minutes to an hour or more, Drazin has to pace himself throughout the screening. He is not just playing a song or supporting a larger piece; Drazin is a solo musician working in tandem with projected images. "If the picture is huge like *Ben Hur* [the original from 1925], you don't want to kill yourself at the beginning, because the chariot race is coming towards the end. I don't like to be bombastic to start, but give something light and gentle at the opening and let the audience drink it in. Audiences today generally aren't accustomed to hearing someone play on a piano at a movie. They're not used to hearing hammers hitting strings. With television and the Internet you

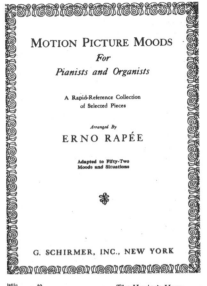

TOP: Books like *Motion Picture Moods* contained hundreds of standard songs silent film accompanists could adapt to just about any situation in dramas, comedies, westerns, and other movies. *(Image courtesy of Dave Drazin)*

BOTTOM: "The Hunter's Horn" from *Motion Picture Moods*. Note the many on-screen situations the editors suggest for this piece. *(Image courtesy of Dave Drazin)*

control volume, but when I play, I'm the volume control."

While Drazin's improv skills are an important tool in his repertoire, he does use vintage scores to provide an authentic experience. Fortunately, sheet music from the era survives. One book he uses was something of a musical bible from the silent days, *Motion Picture Moods for Pianists and Organists*. There is an apt subtitle to the volume: "A Rapid-Reference Collection of Selected Pieces." Compiled by a conductor and composer named Ernö Rapée, the book is packed with a myriad of styles, including tangos, classical standards, national anthems, and jazzier pieces. On the left-hand side of each page is a comprehensive index with suggestions as to what situations a pianist might want to use a particular burst of music in.

Just as today, songs were written in conjunction with movies, with sheet music sold to the public, an early-20th-century equivalent to today's soundtrack album. Drazin uses these songs when possible. One of his biggest career thrills was playing music written specifically for the child star Baby Peggy—with the now-90-plus former silent star in the audience.

Over the years, Drazin has developed a fondness for accompanying certain films. Buster Keaton's Civil War comedy The General (1927) is a particular favorite. "Every time Keaton is on-screen I can have fun with a different song. When he's not on-screen, the music is serious. When Keaton's on-screen the laughs are big, and

I've got to support that." Though the film was released some eight decades ago, modern audiences get caught up in the comic sweep of the action. "The audiences sometimes burst into applause when Keaton knocks off railroad ties as he's sitting on the train's cowcatcher. Really, it's a transcendent film," he says.

Drazin's work is available on CD; he's also provided music for DVD releases. You can hear him on *Charley's Aunt* (1925), which stars Syd Chaplin, Charlie Chaplin's brother; a collection of Roscoe "Fatty" Arbuckle shorts; and a set of silent baseball-themed films. Find out more about Drazin at www .kendavies.net/daviddrazin.

Sheet music used for a film starring silent movie star Baby Peggy. Drazin once played this piece with the elderly "Baby Peggy" in the audience. *(Image courtesy of Dave Drazin)*

Balaban and Katz Theaters

The movie business would not be the same in America had it not been for two entrepreneurs from Chicago. As photoplays evolved into a lucrative form of popular entertainment, Barney Balaban and Sam Katz operated a string of theaters throughout the city and suburbs that set the standard for motion picture exhibition.

Balaban, the son of Russian-Jewish immigrants, grew up on the Near West Side near the thriving Maxwell Street Market. In 1908, Balaban pooled financial resources with his brother Abe and purchased the Kedzie Theater at Kedzie Avenue and Roosevelt Road. The venture proved successful, and within a year the brothers added a second theater.

By 1915, Balaban acquired a new partner, Sam Katz. The duo hatched a plan to build a theater of their own, the Central Park Theatre. Located at 3535 W. Roosevelt Road, the building for many years after the demise of the theater was the home of the People's Church of God-Christ, a rather ironic evolution in the grand scheme of things. In the minds of the Balaban brothers and Sam Katz, the Central Park Theatre was a sanctuary for Chicago moviegoers. Designed by Cornelius and George Rapp, the Central Park featured 400 velour-covered seats, beautiful chandeliers, and hand-painted wall murals. The gorgeous interior had an added benefit: ice-cooled air that offered Chicagoans relief from the often grueling summer humidity. In addition to showing the latest movies from Hollywood, this picture palace also featured live entertainment.

The Balaban and Katz empire gradually expanded beyond its West Side roots. Their holdings included theaters on the North and South Sides, downtown, and in the suburbs. Some of their better-known playhouses included the Apollo on Randolph near Clark Street; the Belmont at 1635 W. Belmont Avenue (today a retail and condominium complex); the Belpark at 3231 N. Cicero Avenue (now the Golden Tiara bingo parlor); the Biltmore at 2046 W. Division Street (now demolished); the Century

Built in 1926, the Granada Theatre in Rogers Park used decorations from actual palaces, churches, and villas throughout Italy and Spain. It was demolished in 1990. *(Thomas G. Yanul, photographer, Library of Congress, Prints and Photographs Division, Historic American Buildings Survey, HABS ILL, 16-CHIG, 109-5)*

LEFT: Interior detail of Adler and Sullivan's 1891 Garrick Theatre (formerly the Schiller Building). Despite a court battle and support for its preservation initiated by Richard Nickel, the Garrick was demolished in early 1961. *(Richard Nickel, photographer, Library of Congress, Prints and Photographs Division, Historic American Buildings Survey, HABS ILL, 16-CHIG, 60-2)*

RIGHT: Balaban and Katz's opulent Paradise Theater opened in 1928 in Chicago's Garfield Park neighborhood. With the advent of the talkies, poor acoustics presumably cost the theater its attendance, and it was sold and then demolished in 1956–1958. *(Image from a postcard circa 1929, in the collection of Kate Corcoran)*

at 2828 N. Clark Street (today the Century Mall); the Congress at 2135 N. Milwaukee Avenue (today a multiuse concert hall); the Coronet on Chicago Avenue in Evanston (now occasionally used for theatrical productions); the Gateway at 5216 W. Lawrence Avenue (now part of the Polish community's Copernicus Cultural and Civic Center); the Granada at 6427 N. Sheridan Road (demolished despite a valiant effort to save this beautiful theater); the Howard in the 1600 block of W. Howard Street (retail and office space today, although the auditorium has been demolished); the Lakeside at 4730 N. Sheridan Road (which now houses the Mordine & Co. Dance Theater, among other businesses); the McVickers at 25 W. Madison Street (demolished); the Marbro at 4124 W. Madison Street (demolished); the Maryland at 855 E. 63rd Street (demolished); the Norshore at 1749 W. Howard Street (demolished); the Nortown at 6230 N. Western Avenue (demolished); the Paradise at 231 N. Pulaski Road (demolished); the original Regal at 4719 S. Parkway Boulevard (demolished); the Riviera at 4746 N. Broadway (now a popular live music venue); the Roosevelt at 110 N. State Street (demolished); the State-Lake at 190 N. State Street (now the home of WLS/ABC television and radio studios); the Tivoli at 6325 S. Cottage Grove Avenue (demolished); and the Tivoli at 5021 Highland Avenue in Downers Grove (still operating). In 1945, Balaban and Katz also purchased the Garrick Theatre at 64 W. Randolph Street. Formerly known as the Schiller Building, this Adler and Sullivan–designed complex was demolished in 1961 and replaced with a parking garage. Two other Balaban and Katz showcases were the Chicago and Uptown Theatres (see separate entries on pages 93 and 200, respectively).

Balaban and Katz theaters were the original "movie palaces," often with grand auditoriums that could seat anywhere from 500 to 2,000 customers. Lobby chandeliers, of course, were a prerequisite. Ushers wore spiffy red uniforms, complemented by spotless white gloves.

Ultimately, Barney Balaban and his smart business acumen attracted the attention of Hollywood, and in 1936 Paramount Studios came calling. Balaban sold Paramount two-thirds of his theater chain and eventually became president of the studio. But in 1948, with the case of *United States v. Paramount Pictures, Inc.*, the Supreme Court ruled that film studios unfairly had a stranglehold on film distribution. In essence, by supplying top-notch entertainment only to the Paramount-owned Balaban and Katz theaters, executives had conspired with theater owners to control the movie distribution market. Paramount and other major studios had to release control of their theater chains, a move that ultimately led in part to the downfall of the classic Hollywood system.

Balaban retained his position as Paramount's president until his retirement in 1967. Subsequently named honorary chairman of the board, he held that title until his death in 1971. (His nephew, Bob Balaban, continues working in the "family business" as an actor and director.) The Balaban and Katz theater chain was renamed ABC–Great States in the late 1960s and was sold to Plitt Theatres in 1974. Eventually the chain was bought by Canadian-based Cineplex Odeon.

And therein lies another irony in the Balaban and Katz legacy. In their heyday of the 1920s and early 1930s, a Balaban and Katz theater meant a night of elegant moviegoing. From the moment you arrived at one of their many movie palaces, you knew it was special. Grand architecture, the curtains parting from the screen as the film began, and the snappily dressed theater personnel all pointed to one thing: moviegoing was something special, and all patrons deserved royal treatment. Compare that ideal to what is offered today by the legal inheritors of the Balaban and Katz tradition. The next time you're at an anonymous movie complex with its small screens, thin walls, and shopping mall atmosphere, close your eyes and imagine attending a show at the old Central Park Theatre.

It must have been a slice of moviegoing heaven.

Film Row

800 S. Wabash Avenue to Wabash and
  15th Street

Once upon a time, this strip of South Wabash—now part of the Burnham Park neighborhood—was a hotbed of wheeling and dealing for film exhibitors in the lucrative Midwest markets. During its heyday between the 1920s and the 1940s, theater owners would run from building to building, looking for the latest Hollywood features, cartoons, and newsreels. Posters and press materials, movie projectors, candy and popcorn for the concession stands, screening rooms, and even a place to repair damaged films could all be found along this hustler's paradise. The mile-long string of offices was affectionately known by its denizens as "Film Row."

All the major studios, including Paramount, Metro-Goldwyn-Mayer, Columbia, and Warner Bros. had offices along the strip. Carl Laemmle, who got his start as a movie exhibitor, moved up to distribution by taking an office on the 800 S. Wabash block. Laemmle eventually pulled up stakes and moved out west to make the

TOP: The Universal logo is still visible in the concrete of this building at 1234 S. Michigan Avenue, built in 1945. *(Photo by Kate Corcoran)*

BOTTOM: With its simple curved brick and glass block construction, 1301 S. Wabash Avenue was originally the Chicago headquarters for Universal Studios. Since this photo was taken, the entrance has been completely redone; the building now houses the Scout Waterhouse and Kitchen, an upscale sports bar. *(Photo by Kate Corcoran)*

LEFT: Formerly the Paramount Pictures Film Exchange (completed in 1930), 1306 S. Michigan Avenue is now the home of the Columbia College Dance Center. *(Photo by Kate Corcoran)*

RIGHT: Original art deco entrance details are still visible at the 1307 S. Wabash Avenue address that once housed the Warner Bros. Film Exchange (constructed in 1929), currently the Film Exchange Lofts condominiums. *(Photo by Kate Corcoran)*

product himself. His new company, Universal Pictures, eventually rented an office along Film Row, this time to peddle its own films.

With over one million theater seats to fill throughout the Midwest, owners of theaters ranging from downtown movie palaces to small-town houses flocked to Film Row (or "the Avenue," as it was also known). Naturally, parties on both the distribution and exhibition ends wanted the best deal they could get for their money. Competition was fierce, so it wasn't unusual to see bargains being struck on the sidewalk. Why let a theater owner venture into someone else's office when you could sell your movies right on the street? In the 1950s, companies like American International Pictures, which specialized in cheap juvenile delinquent and horror films, ruled the roost along Film Row. During this era, David F. Friedman, who later partnered with Herschell Gordon Lewis on many exploitation features, got his cinematic start working for a film distributor on S. Wabash.

With the changing face of the neighborhood in the 1960s, however, the cacophony of Film Row was eventually muzzled. As S. Wabash degenerated into a crime-infested area, studio representatives scattered to safer parts of the city.

Today, the neighborhood is on a roll, with fashionable stores and restaurants that serve the residents of the glut of new condos and lofts that have arisen in the South Loop, taking root along the block. The presence of Columbia College, including, appropriately enough, its new film school facility at 1415 S. Wabash Avenue, has given old Film Row a new luster.

Call Northside 777: When Hollywood Embraced the Dark Streets of Chicago

In the first week of December 1932, Chicago seemed to have gone crazy. Though the gangster heyday of Al Capone and his ilk seemed like a bad memory, the city saw six murders in those early winter days. The bloody spree came to a head on December 9, when police officer William Lundy was gunned down while trying to prevent the holdup of a delicatessen at 4312 S. Ashland Avenue.

The pressure was on to solve this brutal murder. The Century of Progress World's Fair was less than six months away and Mayor Anton Cermak wanted the killing solved—and solved quickly.

Deli owner Vera Walush fingered two local men as the killers. Joseph Majczek and Theodore Marcinkiewicz were brought to trial in 1933 and quickly found guilty. They were sentenced to 99 years each and sent to Stateville Prison in Joliet.

Flash forward 11 years.

On October 10, 1944, city editor Karin Walsh of the *Chicago Daily Times* (a forerunner of the *Chicago Sun-Times*) found an advertisement buried in the classifieds: "$5,000 reward for killers of Officer Lundy on December 9, 1932. Call GRO-1758, 12 to 7 PM." Walsh assigned reporter James McGuire, a former private investigator, to check out the story. What he found was an amazing tale of perseverance.

Majczek's mother Tillie, a Polish immigrant from the Back of the Yards neighborhood, firmly believed in her son's innocence. To raise the $5,000 reward, she spent the next 11 years on the night shift, scrubbing floors at Commonwealth Edison's downtown offices.

As a human interest story, Tillie Majczek had the potential to sell a few papers. McGuire passed his notes on to reporter Jack McPhaul. Readers hung on every word as McGuire and McPhaul pumped out story after story. Eventually the twisted truth came out: Vera Walush wasn't just running a delicatessen—her place of business was fronting for an illegal speakeasy. Walush claimed she had hidden in a closet during the robbery, but threatened with arrest for brewing black market hooch, she suddenly changed her story.

Initially, Walush hadn't been able to identify either Majczek or Marcinkiewicz as the murder suspects. In fact, Walush was twice given the opportunity to pick Majczek out of a police lineup. Word got out that Vera Walush was about to finger a neighborhood kid named Ted. Fearing he was the target, Marcinkiewicz hid out in the home of his old friends, the Majczeks. When the police came to the door, Joe Majczek told them to come in. "I have nothing to hide," he declared at the time.

Majczek and Marcinkiewicz were arrested and put on trial for Lundy's murder. Their defense attorney, an ex–mob lawyer who had survived a gangland hit, had turned to drink to relieve chronic pain; by the time of the Lundy case he was a raging alcoholic. His drunken courtroom demeanor was pointed out by Majczek, the court bailiff, and even presiding judge Charles P. Molthrop.

It didn't help. Majczek and Marcinkiewicz were sent to jail, and an appeal, written by the defense attorney in the midst of an alcoholic haze, was quickly dismissed. Unbeknownst to the two convicted men, however, new information had been provided to Judge Molthrop.

An anonymous detective informed the judge about some of the shifty tactics used to obtain the guilty verdict. Among other things, Majczek had been held for more than a day before Walush decided to change her story. Hearing this, Molthrop was enraged. He vowed to bring Walush in for perjury charges and rehear the case even if he had to pay for it himself. The state's attorney's office, fearing backlash from an already outraged public, as well as the police force, took Molthrop aside. The judge was "advised" to drop the case unless he wanted to see his career come to a premature end.

As the story unfolded, Illinois governor Dwight H. Green became interested. Majczek was granted a full and unconditional pardon and was released from prison on August 14, 1945. Eventually it was determined that Marcinkiewicz also had been denied the constitutional right to a fair trial, though his release came five years later.

In Los Angeles, the heart-wrenching story of Tillie Majczek had not gone unnoticed. Darryl F. Zanuck, the legendary producer at 20th Century Fox, was enamored with the story. In the fall of 1947, a crew of 70, including director Henry Hathaway and star James Stewart, came to Chicago. In classic Hollywood tradition, the original story was streamlined, characters combined, and certain plot elements left out. Titled *Call Northside 777* (1948), the film sees the two reporters changed to a single character, played by Stewart. McGuire, who did the majority of the street work for the story, was hired as a technical advisor for a fee of $2,500, which also included compensation for the rights to the story. McGuire recreated his investigation, personally taking Stewart on a tour of Chicago's mean streets. Director Hathaway filmed the story in a stark, documentary-like style, bringing his cameras to many of the actual locations where the original story unfolded.

Filming took place over 10 weeks and made extensive use of South Side neighborhoods. Stewart does much of his investigation at the New City police station, 3501 S. Lowe Avenue, the department's ninth precinct, where McGuire uncovered arrest records. Actor Richard Conte, who plays Majczek's screen counterpart Frank Wiecek, is interrogated at the Criminal Courts building. Saloons throughout the Back of the Yards neighborhood become darkened pits where Stewart asks questions, eventually leading him to "Wanda Skutnik" (Betty Garde), the Vera Walush character. One of the film's most gripping scenes was actually shot at Walush's apartment at 725 S. Honore Street. Other scenes were shot along Michigan Avenue, at downtown police headquarters, and along the Chicago River.

Call Northside 777 wasn't just limited to Chicago locations. Hathaway was given permission to shoot inside Stateville Penitentiary in Joliet, where Stewart looks up Conte for his side of the story. Additional material was filmed in Springfield, including scenes at the old State Capitol building.

The result is a stark, often riveting drama. Stewart's performance is low-key, allowing his character to slowly realize that the truth isn't always cut and dried. Hathaway's direction is enhanced by Joseph MacDonald's moody cinematography, capturing Chicago at a unique point in its history.

The climactic resolution, in which a photograph must be sent by wire from Chicago to Springfield, is another of the film's many highlights. Considering today's technologies of fax machines and e-mail, we have become accustomed to instantaneous information. Hathaway builds genuine suspense as Stewart awaits the precious photograph that may clear Conte—while modern audiences are amazed at the crude machinery the scene hangs on. Another powerful moment is when Conte submits to a lie detector test to prove his innocence. Administering the test is actual polygraph developer Leonarde Keeler in his only screen role.

And the other real-life players? Majczek remarried his wife, whom he had divorced after his arrest. After becoming an insurance broker and moving to Oak Lawn, Majczek was involved in a car wreck in 1979 that resulted in massive head trauma. He spent his remaining years in a nursing home and died in 1983.

After his release from prison, Marcinkiewicz changed his name to Marcin and relocated to California. In 1982, he suffered from debilitating eye problems; fearing blindness, he committed suicide rather than be admitted to a nursing home.

McGuire died in the 1950s. McPhaul, whose reporting also inspired the film *I Am a Fugitive from a Chain Gang* (1932), never got a dime from Hollywood for either film. He continued writing for the *Times* and its successor, the *Chicago Sun-Times*, and retired in the early 1970s. In 1983, McPhaul died of cancer. Tillie Majczek died in 1964.

Officer Lundy's murder was never solved.

2

Downtown

River North and North Michigan Avenue

Rush Street and Division Street Area

Although it's now dismissed by the youngsters, who've dubbed it "the Viagra Triangle," anybody who was hip and happening in the 1970s inevitably found themselves gravitating toward the allure of the bars along Rush Street and Division Street: Faces, BBC, and many more. That dizzying nightlife center was faithfully captured in *Looking for Mr. Good-bar* (1977), an adaptation of Judith Rossner's novel. The story revolves around a naive Catholic woman (Diane Keaton) whose double life as teacher of the deaf and party girl comes to a violent end when she picks up the wrong guy on a fateful New Year's Eve.

The film is definitely a product of its time. Hairstyles and clothing on some characters must truly be seen to be believed. Ultimately, *Looking for Mr. Goodbar*, at its best, is a morass of turgid movie clichés. Gay men are flaming queens (keep in mind, this is eight years after 1969's ground-breaking *Midnight Cowboy*), women suffer from the Madonna/whore complex, and straight men are psychopaths ready to boil over.

Yet within this mass of stereotypes, director Richard Brooks manages to provide a fairly intriguing documentary look at Chicago's nightlife in the mid-1970s.

Mother's

26 W. Division Street

A mecca among singles bars, Mother's played a prominent role in the yuppie romance *About Last Night . . .* (1986). Have a drink here and you can pretend to see where Demi Moore and Rob Lowe loved and fought. In reality only the exterior of Mother's was used in the film; the bar's decor was faithfully recreated on a Hollywood soundstage!

The sister bar of Mother's, Shenanigans (16 W. Division Street), is another popular Division Street watering hole. It had a small part in *Nothing in Common* (1986), a Tom Hanks comedy/drama about the difficulties faced by a man whose parents are divorcing. *Nothing in Common* turned Shenanigans (normally a singles nightspot) into the favorite neighborhood watering hole of Hanks's curmudgeon father, played by Jackie Gleason.

Tim Kazurinsky: Windy City Wordsmith

This photo of Tim Kazurinsky was taken by his dear friend the late and much lamented Dick Cusack, father of actors John and Joan Cusack. *(Photo by Dick Cusack)*

Tim Kazurinsky was born in the United States, but his mother returned the family to her native Australia when he was only two months old. He was raised in a very rough part of Sydney, then returned to the United States at age 16. After living in Johnstown, Pennsylvania, he moved to Chicago and attended Wright Junior College. Following studies at the University of Pittsburgh and the University of Illinois, Kazurinsky returned to Johnstown, where he became a newspaper reporter. "But I didn't want to be a starving writer," he says, "so I switched to advertising." For a while he worked in St. Louis doing ad work for a department store, then came back to Chicago and got a job with Leo Burnett. "I was a lousy presenter of commercials," says Kazurinsky, "so I took classes at Second City." The idea, in Kazurinsky's mind anyway, was to improve his presentation skills through improvisational comedy techniques. Instead, he found himself getting more involved in Second City and eventually joined the main-stage company.

While at Second City, he became friends with ex-journalist Denise DeClue. When director Tony Bill needed a drastic rewrite of a movie he was filming in Chicago, *My Bodyguard* (1980), he went to Second City owner Bernie Sahlins, who put out an open call to the company for someone to doctor up Bill's script. Kazurinsky and DeClue teamed up for the project. "Well, eight to ten weeks later, we'd pretty much rewritten every word of the movie," says Kazurinsky. "That was our first exposure to screenwriting." The film featured several Chicago-area high schoolers in the cast, including Joan Cusack of Evanston Township High School and Jenevive (later Jennifer) Beals of Francis Parker. Cast in the title role was New Trier East student Adam Baldwin.

The movie became a huge hit, and their excellent script had much to do with the film's success. But due to the bizarre nature of Hollywood screenwriting rules, Tim and Denise were never given screen credit for their work. Nonetheless, that project forged a creative bond between them and they became a writing team.

Their next major project, *About Last Night . . .* (1986), starred Rob Lowe and Demi Moore and was an adaptation of David Mamet's thorny stage play *Sexual Perversity in Chicago*. Of course, rewriting David Mamet is in and of itself a considerable task. "It was pretty scary, because he's such a hallowed figure," says DeClue. Kazurinsky concurs. "It's impossible [to rewrite Mamet]. You just go, OK, this is a different beast." It took several years for the pair to complete the script and for the movie to become a reality.

In between getting the assignment and completing the final draft, Kazurinsky was hired for *Saturday Night Live*. All the while, he and DeClue continued working on the script. Kazurinsky's run as an SNL cast member lasted from 1981 through 1984, and when it was over, he returned to Chicago.

Following the success of *About Last Night . . .*, Kazurinsky and DeClue penned another comically poignant adolescent film, *For Keeps* (1988). Starring Molly Ringwald, the film is a sensitively told tale of how teenagers learn to cope with an unexpected pregnancy. In 1997, their offbeat western *The Cherokee Kid* became an HBO telefilm with comedian Sinbad in the title role. In addition to writing the script, Kazurinsky and DeClue also served as producers on the project. Falling into a groove as a writing duo, the two collaborated on more than 30 television and film scripts.

In the late 1990s, however, a long bout of ill health for Kazurinsky, a lull in both their careers, and the strain of working so closely together for so long combined to take its toll on the pair, and their relationship began to fray.

Desperate to continue the partnership that had served them both so well for so long, the pair even went into couple's therapy. "I had to tell my wife, 'I'm going to a marriage counselor with my writing partner.' Which was a little freaky." Tim's wife, Marcia (who performed on Broadway for many years), was very understanding and encouraged them to attend the sessions.

Unfortunately, what Kazurinsky and DeClue discovered over the next several months of sessions was that their working relationship was damaged beyond repair. "Nineteen years of sitting at a chair next to someone and staring at the same screen, arguing over commas and dashes and punch lines" is how Kazurinsky describes the cumulative effect of too many years in the emotionally draining and often volatile world of a serious writing partnership. They both agreed that their working relationship needed to come to an end, and although they remain dear friends to this day, Tim and Denise never wrote together again.

Denise went on to write and produce various projects for public television and other clients, and Tim continued with his writing and performing. He had already done a great deal of acting on his own: several *Police Academy* films, supporting roles in television programs like *Married . . . with Children* and *Early Edition*, and other films including *Somewhere in Time* (1980), *Neighbors* (1981), *Continental Divide* (1981), *Hot to Trot* (1988), and Bobcat Goldthwaite's cult comedy *Shakes the Clown* (1992). He was still in demand for his acting abilities, but Kazurinsky wondered if he could ever write something as good as his best work with Denise.

That question was answered in the affirmative when he completed and sold a script for a movie that was produced for television, titled *Strange Relations* (a.k.a. *My Beautiful Son*, 2002). *Strange Relations* stars Paul Reiser (best known for the 1990s TV show *Mad About You*) as Dr. Jerry Lipman, a successful New York psychiatrist who is diagnosed with leukemia and is informed that he will die unless he receives a bone marrow transplant from a suitable donor. Since the donor has to be a sibling, this amounts to a death sentence for Jerry, who is an only child.

He shares the bad news with his mother, played by Olympia Dukakis. She drops a bombshell by informing him that he was adopted as an infant and that his biological mother is still alive in England. Jerry then travels to England to seek out his mother and any siblings who might be able to provide a life-saving marrow donation. He arrives in England and tracks down his birth mother, who lives in a tiny Spartan hovel in the slums of Liverpool (modeled after Tim's boyhood home in the slums of Sydney). Reiser introduces himself to her and the movie really takes off, as Reiser becomes acquainted with the family he never knew he had and the person he never knew he was. Initially aghast at the poverty and crude manners of his newfound kin, he learns to cast his prejudices aside and accept them for who they are (as they do for him).

Profoundly touching and life-affirming, *Strange Relations* maintains its unique tone throughout the film. Whenever it threatens to sink into "disease of the week" drama or "fish out of water" comedy clichés, Kazurinsky's script heads in unexpected and satisfying new directions. It's no wonder that he was nominated for a Writer's Guild of America Award for best original long-form script. Actress Julie Walters won a BAFTA Award (British equivalent of an Oscar) for Best Actress for her performance as Reiser's birth mother. ("We couldn't afford Julie," Kazurinsky notes, "but someone slipped her the script. Turns out her daughter had leukemia at 16 and beat it—and Julie wanted to do the film.") Making the movie was an experience that Tim treasures. "All in all, four of the best weeks of my life, on that set."

Aside from his writing, Kazurinsky has continued what he is best known for: crazy offbeat cameos in quirky independent comedies, such as *Poor White Trash* (2000), *Roll Bounce* (2005), *I Want Someone to Eat Cheese With* (2006), *Stash* (2008), and *Scrooge & Marley* (2012); and TV shows including *Curb Your Enthusiasm*, *According to Jim*, and *Still Standing*. He has also returned to live performing, something he had not done since his Second City/*SNL* days, appearing in a Chicago Shakespeare Theater production of *A Midsummer Night's Dream*, playing Wilbur Turnblad in *Hairspray* at the Drury Lane, and portraying Felix in *The Odd Couple* at the Northlight Theatre.

Tim and Marcia live in Evanston, and their two children, Pete and Zoe, are now grown. Tim is thankful that he and Marcia were able to raise them in the Chicago region. "I'm glad they got to grow up here. I think it's hard to raise kids anywhere, but I think it's a little easier around here."

The Drake Hotel
140 E. Walton Place

One of Chicago's most elegant hotels, the Drake opened its doors on New Year's Eve 1920. The hotel was conceived by John Burroughs Drake, a well-known hotelier of the era, as a place for his sons John and Tracy to manage. Quickly gaining a reputation as a place to see and be seen, the Drake attracted guests from around the globe. In the 1930s, the Gold Coast Room was home to big band radio broadcasts heard over WGN radio.

In its many decades of operation, the Drake has been an overnight home to an eclectic collection of Hollywood celebrities, world leaders, and other noted individuals. Movie-wise, the Drake Hotel always rates high on the posh meter. In *Mission: Impossible* (1996), a simple mention of "a room at the Drake" is all it takes for secret agent Jon Voight to impress his colleagues in the international spy game—no mean shakes in a cinematic profession known for impeccably high standards.

New York food critic Julia Roberts stays at the Drake while plotting the downfall of rival Cameron Diaz in *My Best Friend's Wedding* (1997). In the dark social satire *Risky Business* (1983), Tom Cruise and Curtis Armstrong drink pricey hot chocolates in the Drake's Palm Court while waiting to confront high-priced call girl Rebecca DeMornay. Unfortunately for the three of them, Guido the killer pimp (Joe Pantoliano) is also there, flashing his nasty smile and a nastier gun. Scenes from the bland basketball drama *Heaven Is a Playground* (1991) were also shot here, as well as footage for *The Blues Brothers* (1980) and the made-for-television movie *Man Against the Mob* (1988).

The Drake played a climactic role in *Hero* (1992). It was here where Andy Garcia, a homeless man turned accidental hero, decides to jump off a ledge rather than face the truth and his love interest, reporter Geena Davis. As a teeming mob watches from below, Garcia is ultimately bullied back inside by Dustin Hoffman, an off-kilter crank with real hero credentials.

The epic Clint Eastwood Iwo Jima saga *Flags of Our Fathers* (2006) uses the Gold Coast Room for a crucial sequence that occurs during yet another war bond rally the unfortunate heroes are forced to attend, as well as other hotel and common rooms for various sequences.

Four Seasons Hotel
120 E. Delaware Place (at 900 N. Michigan Avenue)
Located in the heart of Michigan Avenue's shopping district, the Four Seasons Hotel has shown up in a handful of films. The opening reception in *The Fugitive* (1993) takes place at the Four Seasons, and in fact, Harrison Ford, the film's star, stayed here while the production was in Chicago. *Chain Reaction* (1996) and *Miracle on 34th Street* (1994) also shot scenes here.

The John Hancock Center
875 N. Michigan Avenue
Towering over North Michigan Avenue since 1969, the John Hancock Center is one of Chicago's signature skyscrapers; it ranks as the fourth-tallest in Chicago, just behind the Sears Tower, Trump Tower Chicago,

and the Aon Center. Its 100 stories hold offices, condominiums, and a variety of shops. Counting the antennas atop the building, the Hancock checks in at 1,127 feet tall. The 94th-floor viewing deck offers a spectacular view of Lake Michigan and many points beyond, while the building's Signature Room is one of the city's more chichi eateries.

Movie-wise, the Hancock is another of those characteristic "Chicago" buildings filmmakers love to use in opening shots. A few (very few) directors have also ventured through the doors to take advantage of the Hancock's interior.

With the completion of Trump Tower, the 100-story Hancock Center is Chicago's fourth-tallest building. *(Photo by Kate Corcoran)*

The Hancock Center is turned into a haunted house of sorts for *Poltergeist III* (1988), as poor Heather O'Rourke is followed by spooks for a third outing while aunt Nancy Allen and uncle Tom Skerritt do a lot of helpless screaming. On a less melodramatic note, Tom Cruise and Rebecca DeMornay have a poignant final scene over drinks at the 95th-floor Signature Room in *Risky Business* (1983).

It took *The Blues Brothers* to exploit the Hancock's status as one of the world's tallest buildings. As part of the climactic chase sequence, Jake and Elwood Blues (John Belushi and Dan Aykroyd) lead neo-Nazi Henry Gibson and one of his henchmen on a wild ride through expressway construction. A quick turn saves the Blues Brothers but sends Gibson's vehicle hurtling off an unfinished ramp. Soaring into the air, we see the car hit its peak, then rapidly descend with the John Hancock Center in the background to provide scale.

To accomplish this shot, the automobile was hoisted some 1,200 feet into the air via helicopter and then dropped into a vacant lot along the Chicago River. Incidentally, the chase leading up to this bizarre sight was a fine example of geography by editing. Though portions of the scene were shot along Chicago expressways, director John Landis used an unfinished Milwaukee expressway as the launching pad for Gibson's car. Look carefully in the background and you'll see a distinctively non-Chicago skyline in some shots.

Sadly, the John Hancock Center gained fame as the final crash pad for one of Chicago's favorite funny guys. In December 1997, the body of Chris Farley was found in the comedian's Hancock condo. Official cause of death was later determined to be a combination of drugs, alcohol, and Farley's weight.

For information on the John Hancock Observation Deck call (888) 875-VIEW. To make reservations at the 95th floor, call (312) 787-9596. Or for more details on the building itself, visit www.johnhancockcenterchicago.com.

Water Tower Place

835 N. Michigan Avenue

The Magnificent Mile's shining shopping mall is anchored by Macy's and boasts many terrific shops and dining options. Movies shot here include *Poltergeist III* (1988) and *Mo' Money* (1992). The remake of *Miracle on 34th Street* (1994), a tale of a young lady who learns a few things about Christmas and Kris Kringle, makes obvious use of Water Tower Place for its wonderful shopping atmosphere. However, the most memorable movie moment for Water Tower Place is in the minor comedy *Class* (1983). Prep student Andrew McCarthy enters Water Tower Place's trademark glass elevators as a naive innocent but exits a little wiser after he's seduced in the vertical see-through people-mover by Jacqueline Bisset, the mother of a school chum. Certainly one of the most preposterous movie scenes ever shot in Chicago, but oddly memorable nonetheless!

A hilarious movie scene was set on the Magnificent Mile a bit down the street from Water Tower Place, involving hustler Vince Vaughn's attempts to score some holiday cash by impersonating a Salvation Army Santa in the holiday comedy *Fred Claus* (2007). Vaughn's scheme crashes when a "real" Santa confronts him. When Vaughn tries to flee, he is chased down Michigan Avenue by a mob of enraged Santas and pummeled senseless by the crazed Kringles.

NBC Tower

455 N. Cityfront Plaza Drive

Home to WMAQ-TV, Chicago's NBC affiliate, the NBC Tower is an art deco–style building created by the architectural firm of Skidmore, Owings, and Merrill. At the top of this 38-story limestone structure is a shiny spire decorated with the NBC peacock logo. Opened in 1989, the

NBC Tower looks almost like something out of the Manhattan skyline, moved west and plunked down along Chicago's lakefront.

In the movies, the NBC Tower was the headquarters for television news reporter Geena Davis in *Hero* (1992). One scene shot outside the tower required literally hundreds of extras, which ultimately whipped an overwhelmed NBC security force into a lather.

The most infamous show to emanate from the NBC Tower studios was the long-running trash fest *The Jerry Springer Show*, which was taped there until the show's relocation to Connecticut in 2009. NBC security was again worked into a lather several years back when a pack of "out-of-control teenage daughters" (a popular Springer theme) began flashing their breasts to passing drivers, which caused a huge traffic snarl in the cul-de-sac behind the building once word was broadcast to cab drivers all around the downtown area.

Billy Goat Tavern

430 N. Michigan Avenue

"Cheezborga! Cheezborga! Cheeps! No Coke, Pepsi!" The cry was made famous by John Belushi on *Saturday Night Live* in the mid-1970s in a series of sketches revolving around a grimy little diner. Of course, Belushi didn't create this catch phrase out of thin air—he picked it up while hanging out at the famed Billy Goat Tavern, located beneath Michigan Avenue just off Hubbard Street. With its handy location near the Tribune Tower and the Sun-Times Building (the latter of which has since been replaced by the Trump Tower), Billy Goat's has long been a favorite of Chicago journalists, most notably the late, great Mike Royko.

Royko was a friend of Belushi's family from way back. Years later, Chicago's curmudgeon laureate became the model for Belushi's "Ernie Souchak" character in the film *Continental Divide* (1981). Comparing

The Billy Goat Tavern below Michigan Avenue. *(Photo by Kate Corcoran)*

real life to reel life in one of his columns, Royko opined, "As to the plot of the movie itself, I had mixed reactions. Some of it was realistic and some of it was ridiculous. . . . When the beautiful birdwatcher [Blair Brown] turns up in Chicago . . . [Belushi] takes her to eat in the restaurant on the 95th floor of the John Hancock. That's unrealistic. At that joint's prices, she'd have to eat cheeseburgers in Billy Goat's."

The Goat opened around 1934. The original tavern was located on the West Side, near the old Chicago Stadium, before eventually moving to its present location. Of course, everyone in Chicago knows the story about the original owner, Sam Sianis, who attempted to bring his billy goat to the 1945 World Series in Wrigley Field. Kicked out by Cubs ownership, Sianis put a hex on the team as his vengeance, claiming they would never be in another World Series. 'Nuff said.

Once you enter the Billy Goat, it's hard not to think you've stepped into a 1940s movie. The tavern is dimly lit, and the bar is littered with photos of famous and infamous elbow benders who've called the Goat their home away from home. Yes, you'll hear the order taker loudly shouting that joyful "Cheezborga! Cheezborga!" refrain, but you're in for a big surprise if you ask for Pepsi. To the shock of many, the Billy Goat Tavern serves "Coke, no Pepsi!"

Surprisingly, other than the *SNL* connection, the Billy Goat Tavern hasn't been used much by Hollywood. The short-lived television shows *Jack and Mike* and *Missing Persons* both shot scenes here, but the most screen time the Goat has ever seen is probably in the delightfully quirky comedy/drama/suspense romp *Unconditional Love* (2002), when it's visited by Kathy Bates and her daughter-in-law (hilariously played by Meredith Eaton).

The original Billy Goat Tavern can be reached at (312) 222-1525. Contact information on the other six locations around Chicago (and the one in Washington, DC) can be found at www.billygoattavern.com. The cheeseburgers are just as good, but none of these locations have the same goofy energy that permeates the Michigan Avenue Goat.

The Wrigley Building
400 and 410 N. Michigan Avenue

If ever a location defined Chicago in the movies, it's the Wrigley Building. Situated on Michigan Avenue along the north bank of the Chicago River, the distinctive terra cotta exterior and two-story, four-faced clock tower is wonderfully photogenic. Illuminated at night by powerful lamps installed along the south bank of the river, the Wrigley Building's regal presence has been a filmmaker favorite for decades.

Over the years, it has become a cinematic keynote to establish that "we're in Chicago." The structure serves this purpose in such varied movies as *Native Son* (the original 1951 version, with Richard Wright playing his fictional creation Bigger Thomas) and the science fiction thriller *The Relic* (1997). The building was also a regular on television's *Early Edition*.

Having the Wrigley Building appear in a window is always a sign you're dealing with high-powered characters. This is best exemplified by Tommy Lee Jones's investigation room with a clock tower view in *The Fugitive* (1993) and Vanessa L. Williams's legal office in *Soul Food* (1997). Will Ferrell's hospital room in the wonderfully unique comedy *Stranger Than Fiction* (2006) also has a clock tower vista.

The Wrigley Plaza at the base of the building is one of the city's best locations for people-watching. This scenic walkway is also the starting point of one of the many action sequences in the slam-bang thriller *Mercury Rising* (1998), and where Tom Hanks's character emerges from the marble stairway leading

TOP: The facade of the Wrigley Building, former headquarters of the chewing gum empire, is composed of six increasingly brighter shades of white terra cotta as you approach the top, which gives the entire structure the appearance of a uniform hue. *(Photo by Kate Corcoran)*

BOTTOM: The landmark Wrigley Building is a revered Chicago icon. *(Photo by Kate Corcoran)*

down to the river on his way to visit with Frank Nitti in *Road to Perdition* (2002).

In *Call Northside 777* (1948), the Wrigley Building itself is vital to the plot. It is here that reporter James Stewart meets Kasia Orzazewski, a proud Polish woman who cleans offices at night in an effort to free her son from prison. It's hard to forget the haunting scene where the two first meet, with Stewart's heels echoing through the darkened hallway as Orzazewski quietly scrubs the floor.

Gore flick disciples must come to the Wrigley Building if they want to tread the former stomping grounds of their lord and master, Herschell Gordon Lewis. In the late 1960s and early 1970s, Lewis's ad agency and filmmaking headquarters occupied a suite of offices here. (For more information, see Lewis's profile on page 249.)

With the release of *Safety Last* (1923), Harold Lloyd's thrill comedy about a "human fly" who scales a towering structure, the Wrigley Building hosted a rather bizarre publicity stunt. The high point of *Safety Last*, literally and figuratively, is the famous sequence where Lloyd dangles from the hands of a tower clock, numerous stories above terrified onlookers. To promote the feature, Lloyd was scheduled to break a bottle of champagne on the Wrigley Building clock tower. Though wary of the idea, Lloyd didn't have much choice in the matter. With 10,000 fans gathered in the Wrigley Plaza, the reluctant comedy star was brought to the top of the building. There he was greeted by a steeplejack dressed in Lloyd's signature coat and glasses.

According to plan, the double was to be lowered to the clock face while sitting on a boatswain's seat attached to a rope. This being the Windy City, the gales whipping around the clock tower, 425 feet above Michigan Avenue, weren't exactly the most favorable for such a flimsy device. The faux Lloyd, an expert on safety in high places, took one look at his working conditions and announced, "Gentlemen, I need the money but I don't want to commit suicide." With the double out of the picture, promoters wondered if Lloyd himself could be lowered to the clock face. Fortunately, Lloyd's insurance, and good common sense, prevented him from taking any chances.

Yet all was not lost, at least from a movie publicist's perspective. Returning to the street, the bespectacled comic took a megaphone and jumped onto the roof of a nearby taxicab. "I told them exactly what had happened," Lloyd later recalled. "I told them I didn't want to commit suicide and had no intention. Of course, it became a big joke. We got tremendous play in the Chicago papers, more than if we had gone through with the stunt."

Trump Tower and Chicago Sun-Times Building
401 N. Wabash Avenue (at the Chicago River)

A recent addition to Chicago's skyline, Trump Tower is the second-tallest building in the city at 1,362 feet. Before the building was even finished, the uncompleted upper floors served as the scene of Batman's final confrontation with the Joker in *The Dark Knight* (2008).

But years before the tower was even a gleam in the Donald's eye, the building it replaced, the Chicago Sun-Times Building, had played host to several feature films, often playing itself (or the newspaper company contained within it, to be precise). While the exterior of the building appeared squat and somewhat ugly on film, interior shots of the immense newsroom with its rabbit warren of desks and cubicles and huge windows overlooking the river screamed, "We are at an important newspaper!" to the moviegoer.

Numerous Hollywood productions have incorporated the *Chicago Sun-Times* in one form or another, including *While You Were Sleeping* (1995), *I Love Trouble* (1994), *Straight Talk* (1992), and *Never Been Kissed* (1999). *I Love Trouble* features Julia Roberts as a *Sun-Times* writer who falls for Nick Nolte, a competitor at the *Tribune*. *Straight Talk*, another *Sun-Times*-based movie, features an even more preposterous romance. James Woods, looking painfully uncomfortable, plays a hard-bitten *Sun-Times* columnist trying to learn the real story behind sweet-natured radio talk-show host Dolly Parton. Brilliant actor John C. Reilly looks even more painfully uncomfortable as a crabby *Sun-Times* editor in the unfathomably unfunny Drew Barrymore comedy *Never Been Kissed*.

Another film takes its inspiration from one of the paper's best-known writers. *Continental Divide* (1981) features John Belushi as a Mike Royko–esque columnist who digs up political dirt for the *Sun-Times*. The film's story revolves around another unlikely romance, this one involving Belushi and Blair Brown, a reclusive ornithologist the Belushi character is sent to interview. Brown lives at the top of a Colorado mountain, which means the Chicago-bred scribe has to make some considerable personal compromises to get his story.

After the film opened, Royko was besieged by colleagues and fans, all wanting to know how much of *Continental Divide* was real and how much was fiction. Hoping to answer these questions, Royko wrote a tongue-in-cheek column, saying, among other things, "On the way up the mountain, the columnist loses his supply of liquor and cigarettes and is heartbroken. That's stunningly realistic. In fact, I wept during that part of the film."

When Belushi died of a drug overdose the following year, Royko printed a tribute column to the boy he saw grow up into a movie star. "I learned a long time ago that life isn't always fair," wrote Royko. "But it shouldn't cheat that much."

In addition to the building, the *Sun-Times* newspaper often showed up in feature films when a note of Chicago realism was necessary. The paper makes for a great punch line in *Ferris Bueller's Day Off* (1986), with its headline story about the movie's title character.

The paper is virtually a character in the Chicago-set television show *Early Edition*, as the whole plot of the show revolves around an enchanted copy of the *Sun-Times* containing the next day's news, which appears every morning at the protagonist's front door. *Early Edition* ran for four seasons from 1996 to 2000, during which dozens of Chicago locations were showcased and numerous Chicago actors appeared. Even though it was canceled more than a decade ago, *Early Edition* still maintains a small but rabid fan base.

The Chicago River and Its Bridges

One of the city's most enduring symbols is the Chicago River. The Main Branch runs about a mile from the lakefront to Wolf Point (the meeting point of the three branches), the North Branch runs from Wolf Point for 34 miles out to Lake County, while the South Branch is four miles long to its end at the Chicago Sanitary and Ship Canal. Between 1882 and 1900, as motion picture technology was being developed inland, another major feat of engineering was taking place along the mouth of the Chicago River. To prevent the polluted river from further fouling the city's drinking-water supply drawn from Lake Michigan, it was decided to reverse the river flow away from the lake. It took some $40 million and the efforts of more than 8,500 workers, but eventually this audacious task was completed.

Filmmakers have been drawn to the river since cameras started turning in Chicago. And why not? As a location it provides a wealth of

opportunity. Do you want romance?
Check out Julia Roberts and Dermot
Mulroney's slow dance on a tour boat
in *My Best Friend's Wedding* (1997).
Male bonding? Check out the scene
in *About Last Night* . . . (1986) as
James Belushi and Rob Lowe stum-
ble stone drunk along the riverside
arguing about women. Danger? *V. I.
Warshawski* (1991) stages a speed-
boat chase down the Chicago River.
The television series *Chicago Fire*
(2012–) uses the downtown as the
backdrop for an elaborate river rescue scene. And that Windy City
tradition, dyeing the Chicago River
green for St. Patrick's Day, is faithfully
documented in *The Fugitive* (1993).

There are about 20 movable bridges over the Chicago River System in the downtown area; each takes about eight minutes to raise and lower. *(Photo by Kate Corcoran)*

The many bridges spanning the river offer filmmakers a different viewpoint and a certain ambiance that's hard to resist. Each one provides a
unique perspective. Jean Reno teaches Christina Applegate the finer
points of swordplay on the Lake Street Bridge in the comedy/fantasy
romp *Just Visiting* (2001). Of course, you'll never find a bunch of garbage
just sitting on the sidewalk in Chicago like they have in the movie, as the
city's extensive alley system precludes the need for curbside collection.

In a breathless chase sequence in *Chain Reaction* (1996), Keanu Reeves
scrambles up a raised Michigan Avenue Bridge to escape his pursuers. It's
certainly a hair-raising stunt and not one that was easily accomplished.
Shooting required five nights in which the bridge had to be raised and lowered numerous times. To make those five nights productive, six months
of preparation work went into the scene. Bridge engineering, stunt chore-
ography, lighting the set, and actor and crew safety were among the many
variables that had to be taken into account before cameras could roll.

A similar but more comical chase up the raised Michigan Avenue Bridge
occurs toward the end of *Unconditional Love* (2002), when Kathy Bates,
Rupert Everett, and Meredith Eaton are pursued by a crazed crossbow-
wielding serial killer. The unraised Michigan Avenue Bridge is also the site
of a chase sequence in the 1998 Bruce Willis action feature *Mercury Rising*.

Detail of deck truss, Michigan Avenue Bridge, 1987. *(Jet Lowe, photographer, Library of Congress, Prints and Photographs Division, Historic American Buildings Survey, HAER ILL, 16-CHIG, 129-3)*

On a more cerebral note, one of the key moments in *The Untouchables* (1987) takes place on the Michigan Avenue Bridge. Kevin Costner, playing no-nonsense cop Eliot Ness, stands alone on the bridge, dejected over his inability to stop gangster Al Capone (Robert DeNiro). As he silently sulks, Costner is confronted by a streetwise beat officer played by Sean Connery. This slightly tense exchange leads to Costner later seeking out Connery to enlist him in his battle against Capone's forces.

Director Michael Bay's effects-heavy blockbuster *Transformers: Dark of the Moon* (2011) also utilizes the Michigan Avenue Bridge and the whole surrounding area in the climactic battle scene.

A great stunt took place off the Wells Street Bridge. In *Code of Silence* (1985), cop Chuck Norris struggles with a bad guy atop a moving CTA "L" train. As the train crosses the Wells Street Bridge, both criminal and hero take a dive from the moving train into the river below.

The Wells Street Bridge also plays a crucial role in *The Fugitive*. Harrison Ford, as the fleeing Dr. Richard Kimble, uses a phone booth to call the office of Tommy Lee Jones, the US marshal who has been trying to find him. Analyzing a tape of the call, Jones and company detect the sound of a train as well as bridge warning bells in the background. It doesn't take them long to realize exactly where Ford placed his call from.

The Franklin Street Bridge appears in *Batman Begins* (2005) as the bridge between downtown Gotham City and the Narrows, a frightfully fetid criminal-infested island. During the climactic action sequence that closes the film, the Batmobile comes careening across the bridge on its way to assist in the fight against evil.

Other films to use Chicago River bridges include *Prelude to a Kiss* (1992, Kinzie Street), *The Package* (1989, Kinzie Street), *Blues Brothers 2000* (1998, Roosevelt Road and Courtland Street), *Hope Floats* (1998, Roosevelt Road and Kinzie Street), *Hoodlum* (1997, Courtland Street), *The Negotiator* (1998, Clark Street), and *Soul Food* (1997, Roosevelt Road).

Nicholas Cage's apartment in *The Weather Man* (2005) has a commanding view of the Main Branch of the river and its stunning series of drawbridges. The view was courtesy of the RiverBend condominium building, which was completed in 2002 and sits at the intersection of the three branches of the river. The view from the apartment was so amazing that the filmmakers worried that people would just think it was faked in a studio, and the attention of everyone involved in the scenes shot there would wander toward the view. More recently, the Starz cable network series *Boss* made prominent use of a RiverBend unit.

For a scenic trip along the Chicago River, take a Wendella boat ride, which launches from the northwest corner of the Michigan Avenue Bridge at the Wrigley Building. Phone (312) 337-1446 for more information or visit their website at www.wendellaboats.com.

An integral part of any exterior shot of the downtown river since its construction in 1983, the 333 W. Wacker building's distinctive 365-foot glass facade is never the same twice, as it reflects all aspects of its surroundings. The southeast sides facing the Loop are flat and angular, providing transition between the curvilinear forms of nature (river and clouds) and the rectangular geometry of human construction (streets and buildings). *(Photos by Michael Corcoran)*

Chicago Filmmakers on the Chicago River

In 1997, Chicago filmmaker D. P. Carlson conjured up an idea for a documentary on the creative process that offers a great deal of complexity
within its simple setup. *Chicago Filmmakers on the Chicago River* places
Chicago-bred directors on boats, sends these personalities on a journey
down one of our town's most enduring symbols, and lets them talk about
their work.

"Basically, *Chicago Filmmakers on the Chicago River* kind of came out
of a conversation my buddies and I were having one night," says Carlson.
"We were talking about how the Chicago River has never been used as a
character in a film. You see it as a backdrop, you see it as an establishing
shot, you'll see a scene on the river, but you never see it as a recurring
character. We threw around some narrative ideas to do a fiction-type film
and joked that it might be fun to get in a boat one day and float around with
a camera, take a few beers, and monkey around.

"Then it occurred to me that it might be kind of cool to touch base with
different filmmakers I knew and ask them about the river. The idea was to just
throw them on different boats and do a documentary about film directors
from Chicago. The river would be used as a kind of metaphor for the creative
process because it was the big transportation route in Chicago history with
early settlers coming up the river and carving out different waterways.

"So I started asking certain people who I knew to be in it, mostly independent filmmakers. Then I decided maybe I should get a Hollywood-type
guy, and I went after Andy Davis [director of *The Fugitive* (1993)]. I thought
I'd do a short film, maybe a half-hour movie about this creative process
and have it build up to Davis, our most successful, most true-to-form kind
of Chicago filmmaker in that he brings films back here all the time."

Once Davis agreed to do the film, Carlson decided to ask other former
Chicagoans now working in Hollywood to participate. "I was trying to stay
specific to people who were from the Midwest and from Chicago. I got
Haskell Wexler to climb on board and Harold Ramis, and all of a sudden my
idea of having one character represent the Hollywood side of things turned
into a handful of guys and the project got bigger."

In addition to Davis, Hollywood stalwart John Landis went along for the
ride. Other filmmakers who've gone down the river for Carlson's camera
are Stuart Gordon and Michael Mann (also representing the established
"Hollywood" crowd) and all levels of independent filmmakers, including

John McNaughton, Steven A. Jones, Jerry Blumenthal, Gordon Quinn, Tom Palazzolo, Louis Antonelli, and a handful of local indie filmmakers of the late 1990s who have since gone on to other professions and locales.

In addition to being a fascinating portrait of Chicago filmmaking in the late 1990s, *Chicago Filmmakers on the Chicago River* also works on another level, as a record of the river circa 1998, before the real estate development boom and the resurgence of interest in the river for recreation changed its landscape and look so drastically. This is a rougher, more industrial river, yet it's also a wilder one, with wildlife cavorting in overgrown areas that now feature high-end condos and manicured, antiseptic "riverwalks."

The IBM Building

330 N. Wabash Avenue

Now officially known by its address since the departure of the computer giant from the building, this structure was designed by famed modernist architect Ludwig Mies van der Rohe, who fled the Nazis in the late 1930s to become head of the architecture department at the Illinois Institute of Technology on the South Side of Chicago. The IBM Building was completed in 1972 and was his last and largest building in the United States.

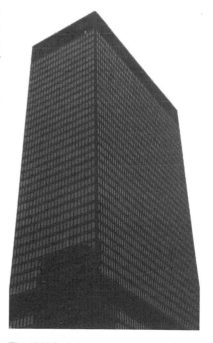

After Wayne Manor was destroyed in *Batman Begins* (2005), in *The Dark Knight* (2008) the IBM Building becomes the new home of Bruce Wayne, who has a swinging penthouse dwelling there.

The roof of the building was replicated in an L.A. soundstage for the final rooftop action sequence of *Mercury Rising* (1998). The background that moviegoers see in that scene is an amalgam of views from the top of the IBM Building, Aon Center, and Sears Tower. Joan Cusack, who

The IBM Building at 330 N. Wabash.
(Photo by Kate Corcoran)

played the fictional sibling to her real brother John in the movie *High Fidelity* (2000), had her office in the building as well.

Marina City
300 N. State Street
Built in 1964, Marina City was considered the ultimate in efficient architecture, despite the buildings' resemblance to corncobs sprouting along

the Chicago River. Designed by Bertrand Goldberg Associates, each of the two towers is 62 stories tall. The first 18 floors of each building are for parking; the remaining floors hold offices, shops, and a bank as well as apartments. Depending on where the apartment is situated, the view from the semicircular balconies of a Marina City residence can be spectacular. A former ground-level movie theater has been transformed into the House of Blues.

With its unusual design, Marina City is one of many visual clichés moviemakers use to signify a Chicago location. The Marina City parking lot serves as a home away from home for the Jeep of yuppie prince Tom Hanks in *Nothing in Common* (1986). But

Bertrand Goldberg's corncob-shaped Marina City. *(Photo by Kate Corcoran)*

the ultimate use of these lots belongs to Steve McQueen's 1980 action-thriller *The Hunter*.

In the film's most compelling sequence, McQueen drives a tow truck pell-mell through the serpentine Marina City lots in fevered pursuit of a dangerous bond jumper. The crazed criminal leads the chase in a green 1980 Pontiac Grand Prix but takes a wrong turn at the 15th floor, hurling the car through the protective cable fence of the garage and plunging it into the Chicago River.

Setting up a stunt like this took considerable planning on the part of the filmmakers in cooperation with Chicago police. Paramount Pictures, making sure nothing would be missed, set up six cameras, including one stowed in a helicopter above the Dearborn Street Bridge, to film the plunge. A stuntman started the engine then quickly left the driving to a well-placed dummy as the Pontiac went charging over the edge at 40 miles per hour. Some 1,500 spectators had gathered at street level to watch this bizarre commuter nightmare.

Three cars had been prepared in case anything went wrong, but happily the first take was right on the money. The car hit the water, floated for a moment, then sank to the mucky river bottom. That last part actually changed the course of the film: in the original script, the driver survived and was taken into custody, but when the car sank, it forced McQueen's character to bring the man back to California dead rather than alive. In an unlikely homage, the scene was recreated for an Allstate commercial in 2006.

For a more surreal look at the towers, check out *Mickey One* (1965). Warren Beatty and Alexandra Stewart join a crowd gathered at the base of Marina City, where an eccentric artist has set up a Rube Goldberg contraption. After setting his creation in motion, the artist lights up his opus in a fiery blaze of creative glory. The Chicago Fire Department rushes to the scene and douses the burning artwork with chemical foam. In the dreamlike sequence, Marina City glows like two eerie candles while gobs of white foam float through the air toward the camera.

The towers' distinctive look was also featured on the cover of legendary alt-country band Wilco's much-celebrated *Yankee Hotel Foxtrot* album, the creation of which was chronicled (along with several lovely shots of Chicago) in the documentary film *I Am Trying to Break Your Heart* (2002). It even graces the skyline in a futuristic Chicago circa 2035 in the Will Smith sci-fi flick *I, Robot* (2004), based on the Isaac Asimov novel.

Merchandise Mart

350 N. Wells Street (at the Chicago River)

Designed by Graham, Anderson, Probst, and White and opened in 1930, the Merchandise Mart has about four million square feet of floor space, which technically makes

Often used in films to establish that you are "in Chicago," the imposing Merchandise Mart became Hudsucker Industries in the Coen Brothers' delectable satire *The Hudsucker Proxy* (1994). *(Photo by Kate Corcoran)*

it one of Chicago's largest buildings. What it lacks in height, it makes up for in volume. Until the construction of the Pentagon, this was the world's largest building by floor area.

The Merchandise Mart is situated on the Chicago River and is home to one of the city's busiest "L" stops as well. More than 5,000 manufacturers and designers use the Mart to house furniture and other interior decorating wares. Once owned by the Marshall Field family, the Merchandise Mart was purchased by Joseph P. Kennedy in 1945. Since then, many Kennedy family members have been ensconced in powerful positions at the Mart. In 1998, the Mart was sold to Vornado Realty Trust.

Its imposing size worked well for brothers Joel and Ethan Coen in their dizzy satire *The Hudsucker Proxy* (1994). The building, which spans two city blocks, serves as the exterior of Hudsucker Industries, the mammoth company run by Paul Newman's character. The Mart exterior has also shown up in countless other films in background and establishing shots to let everyone know we're in downtown Chicago.

The Loop

The "L"

"As a kid I always lived near and used the 'L'. It represented the arteries and veins of the city to me." —*Director Andrew Davis*

Snaking through the city and stretching out into the northern and western suburbs, the Chicago Transit Authority's elevated train and subway system is commonly referred to as the "L" (the CTA's new officially mandated spelling). Since the 1890s, commuters have been depending on the city's train system, which was consolidated under the CTA's authority in 1945. And filmmakers love the "L." It's the mother lode of Chicago locations, having been used in over 150 feature films and in countless television programs and commercials.

Hollywood has shown us all aspects of the "L." Consider that staple of action films, the chase sequence. In *The Hunter* (1980), Steve McQueen is shot at while clinging to the roof of a train. In the Andrew Davis picture *Code of Silence* (1985), Chuck Norris dukes it out with a bad guy along the top of a moving train, before both take a dive into the Chicago River off the Wells Street Bridge. A few years later, Davis used the "L" for a tense game

Intersection of "L" tracks at Wabash Avenue and Van Buren Street. *(Photo by Kate Corcoran)*

of cat and mouse in *The Fugitive* (1993). Billy Crystal and Gregory Hines go on an unlikely but wildly entertaining chase in *Running Scared* (1986), driving their battered automobile down the elevated tracks in pursuit of criminals. And would-be superhero Damon Wayans creates a special vehicle to ride the rails at maximum velocity in the comedy *Blankman* (1994).

How about romance? In *While You Were Sleeping* (1995), Sandra Bullock plays a fetching Randolph Street station CTA clerk. She fantasizes over one of the station regulars, handsome Peter Gallagher. Ultimately this obsession leads Bullock into a contrived movie love story. The comedy begins when Gallagher falls off the platform into the path of an oncoming train. Bullock leaps from her post, saves Gallagher's life, and quickly finds herself intertwined with Gallagher's family—and his equally handsome brother, Bill Pullman. In the sweetly satisfying ballroom dance romance *Shall We Dance?* (2004), weary lawyer Richard Gere looks up through the window of his stopped train and spies a pensive Jennifer Lopez standing in the window of a dance school.

In *Risky Business* (1983), high school student and future business leader Joel Goodson (Tom Cruise) makes love to his girlfriend-for-a-night, Lana (Rebecca DeMornay), while aboard a CTA train. This encounter takes the duo around the city, above ground and below, in a passionate tour of Chicago's many "L" stops.

The television program *ER* (1994–2009) made extensive use of the "L," particularly the Chicago-Wells station. Located just north of the Loop, the curving tracks of this "L" stop provide a marvelous view of the downtown skyline. Couple that with station signs reading "Chicago," and a director couldn't ask for a nicer shot to establish location.

The series *Chicago Hope* (1994–2000) also used this stop, as did the movie *Blink* (1994) and a host of others.

As some of the "L" stops are still adorned with their vintage design elements, they provide a wonderful opportunity for period filmmakers. The Oscar-winning *The Sting* (1973) is a good example of this, using the old station at 43rd and Calumet for a scene where Robert Redford has to go on the lam. Incidentally, this sequence also points out one of *The Sting*'s historical errors. Station signs indicate the stop is for *A* and *B* trains, a service that wasn't instituted by the CTA until after World War II, well past the early-1930s era of *The Sting*. (The *A* and *B* stop system was subsequently dropped in 1995.) A more recent period use of the "L" along Wabash Avenue is in *Public Enemies* (2009), where the tracks outside the windows of the Gothic / art deco Pittsfield Building are done up in 1930s regalia and an antique gangster-era train is run past the window.

The eclectic face of the "L" system is another boon to filmmakers. Though much of the system runs through the inner city, portions of the "L" tracks run along both the Kennedy and Dan Ryan Expressways. This helped producers of the action thriller *Mercury Rising* (1998) when it came to creating one action sequence.

Disgraced FBI agent Bruce Willis is protecting a 10-year-old autistic boy from the nefarious clutches of shadowy government agents. In one scene, Willis is forced to pull over on the Kennedy Expressway, alongside the "L" tracks near the Addison Street stop. Jumping over the retaining wall between the expressway and the train tracks, Willis sees the boy wander onto the tracks into the path of an oncoming CTA train and runs to the child as another train heading the opposite direction comes screaming down the line. Willis has to leap with the boy into a tiny ditch between the two high-speed trains, pulling off this gymnastic maneuver in the nick of time.

When the Chicago portion of the production came to an end, the *Mercury Rising* team bought a train car from the CTA. The rest of the sequence, which involved a gunfight aboard the train and a bad guy getting thrown onto the tracks, was shot on a Hollywood soundstage.

Spider-Man 2 (2004) features an insanely frenetic and special effects–laden chase/fight scene between Spidey and Doc Ock on the downtown "L" tracks, standing in for a New York City elevated line.

By far the most elaborately goofy use of the "L" has to be the romantic comic fantasy *Just Visiting* (2001), where Jean Reno and Christina

Applegate ride a horse up the stairs of the Madison Street "L" stop and onto a crowded train car.

The comic book shoot-'em-up *Wanted* (2008), with James McAvoy and Angelina Jolie, uses the "L" for some hair-raising stunts and intense gunplay (although why do movie people think that someone could ride around the city in broad daylight atop a train car like it's a Shetland pony and nobody would notice?). The pulse-pounding techno thriller *Eagle Eye* (2008) has an intense stunt sequence in which Shia LaBeouf falls several stories from a crane, bounces off an "L" platform awning, and lands smack in the middle of the tracks just as a train is approaching.

Other films that have used the "L" include *About Last Night . . .* (1986), *Ali* (2001), *Backdraft* (1991), *Columbiana* (2011), *Flatliners* (1990), *Go Fish* (1994), *High Fidelity* (2000), *Medium Cool* (1969), *Michael* (1996), *Mickey One* (1965), *Native Son* (1986), *The Promotion* (2008), *Red Heat* (1988), and *U.S. Marshals* (1998). Now if only some filmmaker would take advantage of the stretches of the Brown and Pink Lines that are at street level!

Bob Janz: The CTA Manager Who First Helped Hollywood Catch a Train

When Hollywood productions returned in earnest to Chicago in the late 1970s, of course the first place they wanted to shoot was on the city's awesomely photogenic "L" lines. But CTA officials were a bit flummoxed. Who among them could work with these Hollywood types, with all their fancy equipment and odd requests? Who knew the CTA system, infrastructure, and proper safety procedures so well that they could make the movie people happy while also keeping everyone involved safe and still not inconveniencing regular commuters?

The man they turned to was Bob Janz, and he became the "go-to guy" for CTA filming for the next 17 years. Janz (along with his colleagues Bob

Bob Janz. *(Photo by Pat Mglej, SpiritImages Photography)*

Heinlein, Bruce Moffat, Sid Edwards, and several others) orchestrated the use of CTA equipment and facilities for countless film and television productions, including such tricky and train-intensive shoots as *The Hunter* (1980), *Risky Business* (1983), *Code of Silence* (1985), *Running Scared* (1986), and *Planes, Trains & Automobiles* (1987).

Janz, who has the easygoing manner and deep voice of a born storyteller, began with the CTA in 1960 and worked his way up through the ranks, eventually becoming director of rail service, in charge of the entire system. In the mid-1970s, he was the head of a department called Methods and Standards, which dealt with safety issues. As he tells it, "One day my boss called me in to his office and asked me, 'How'd you like to make a movie?' I said, 'Sure, waddaya need?' He said, 'Just go down the hall and see this guy, Bob Heinlein'"—one of the CTA's public relations representatives.

The first production Janz and Heinlein worked with was *The Million Dollar Ripoff* (1976), a made-for-TV caper flick that starred comedian Freddie Prinze (the late father of turn-of-the-millennium heartthrob Freddie Prinze Jr.). Janz and Heinlein were such a successful team that they became the permanent liaisons for Hollywood productions shooting on the CTA. "We would always have a meeting with the filmmakers before shooting to figure out what the costs would be," says Janz. "My boss came to one of them, listened for a while, then looked at me and said, 'Can you do all this stuff?' I said, 'Sure, it's all fake, it's all smoke and mirrors.' He said, 'Great, I'm leaving,' and he left me totally in charge of those meetings from then on."

TOP: If this photo of Gary Coleman on the set of the movie *On the Right Track* (1981) were in color, you would see that the bodysuit he is wearing is bright pink. And you would be very frightened. *(Photo by Bob Janz)*

BOTTOM: *Diff'rent Strokes* star Gary Coleman relaxes on an "L" platform between takes. *(Photo by Bob Janz)*

Janz and his team were presented with a huge task when the production of *The Hunter* came into town to shoot a long and complicated chase

TOP LEFT: Final discussions before the camera rolls on a scene from *The Million Dollar Ripoff* (1976). *(Photo by Bob Janz)*

TOP RIGHT: Camera and sound equipment being set up underneath the Quincy "L" station. *(Photo by Bob Janz)*

MIDDLE LEFT: CTA employees Bob Janz (left) and Bob Heinlein (center) hanging out on the "L" with a heavily disguised Freddie Prinze during shooting of *The Million Dollar Ripoff*. *(Photo by Bob Janz)*

MIDDLE RIGHT: Freddie Prinze inside an "L" station in the heist/caper film *The Million Dollar Ripoff*. *(Photo by Bob Janz)*

BOTTOM: The camera crew for *The Million Dollar Ripoff* confers before shooting a scene on the "L" tracks. *(Photo by Bob Janz)*

TOP LEFT: Actor/stuntman Tom Rosales Jr. behind the wheel of the auto that will plummet into the Chicago river from the Marina City parking garage. *(Photo by Bob Janz)*

TOP RIGHT: Screen legend Steve McQueen and director Buzz Kulik discuss an upcoming scene on the set of *The Hunter*. *(Photo by Bob Janz)*

BOTTOM LEFT: The crew of *The Hunter* (1980) prepares to shoot part of the famous Marina City car chase scene. *(Photo by Bob Janz)*

BOTTOM RIGHT: Some of the equipment used to shoot the elaborate chase sequence on board a CTA train in *The Hunter*. *(Photo by Bob Janz)*

sequence on a CTA train. Janz himself even appeared in the movie as a train engineer accosted by a crazed gunman. "There's a shot with a guy who's in the way of Bernardo [the gunman, played by actor/stuntman Tom Rosales Jr.], and Bernardo points the gun at him and screams, "Get outta the way!" and he really looks scared. So at lunchtime, I said to him, "You know, you really looked scared," and he said, "Yeah, and tomorrow they're gonna point that gun at you. And 'Is it or isn't it loaded?' is all that's gonna be going through your head!"

The Hunter, based on the life of bounty hunter Ralph "Papa" Thorson, was screen legend Steve McQueen's last film. While it doesn't hold up well as a film, it's worth catching for the Chicago sequences near the end of the movie that feature the extended chase scene on the "L," leading up to the famed shot of a car careening through the guardrail of the Marina

City parking garage and plunging into the Chicago River (although you'll probably end up doing a lot of fast-forwarding to get there).

Janz and company spent six weeks with the film crew shooting the chase scene, which used almost all of the North Side Red Line tracks as well as the subway and parts of what is now the Pink Line. In the sequence, McQueen chases dangerous fugitive Bernardo through the Uptown neighborhood and onto a train at the Wilson Avenue Red Line stop. Most of the onboard action involves McQueen on the roof of the train, being shot at by the desperate Bernardo. The train enters the subway with McQueen still on the roof (a stunt the star performed himself) until it finally stops in the tunnel. McQueen pursues the mad miscreant down the tracks, up an emergency exit to street level, and into the Marina City parking garage.

The famous train sequence for *Risky Business*, in which Tom Cruise and Rebecca DeMornay furiously faux-hump aboard a seemingly magical train that travels the entire CTA track system (elevated and subway) without any other passengers boarding, was, Janz says, "a *huge* pain in the butt" because of all the time involved and the extent of the system used.

The most involved CTA scene that Janz worked on was for *Running Scared*. In the scene, a limo carrying an evil drug kingpin (played by Jimmy Smits) flees a pair of detectives (Billy Crystal and Gregory Hines) who are in hot pursuit. The chase takes an insane turn when the limo driver lurches the vehicle onto the Skokie Swift tracks in the near north suburbs, and suddenly (by the miracle of film) they are on the downtown elevated tracks. The drivers weave and careen around the Loop elevated tracks until the limo crashes head-on with an oncoming train and flips up and over.

The first two cars of the train that smashes into the limo were destined for the scrap heap and purchased by the production company for the scene. All engines, electronics, and equipment were removed, and the train was being run by Janz from the third car in the rear. He was unable to see where he was going and relied on a signal from the director as to when to move forward. The car and limo were actually riding on the tracks, with no special equipment on the undercarriage, and had been lifted onto the "L" tracks by a crane.

The incredibly long workday involved in shooting the crash itself led to a humorous and slightly awkward situation with Janz and the female production assistant who was stationed back in the cab with him. Everyone had been on the set since 4 AM, and it was now midafternoon. While waiting a particularly long time for the next take to begin, Janz and the PA both nodded off in the cozy train. "The director called for action, *'Train!'*; the train didn't move. So he tried again. Still the train didn't move. So he sent the assistant director, and he came back and looked in the cab window, and there we were, both napping away. So he gets on the radio and yells, 'Hey! They're back here *sleeping together!'"*

Janz and the embarrassed assistant both jolted awake as the entire crew erupted in laughter.

Despite the good ribbing the director and crew gave Janz about the incident, they were very impressed with his ability to coordinate action sequences and even asked him to help out with the film's climactic showdown scene at the Thompson Center. In that scene, Gregory Hines's character climbs several stories up the outside wall of the building using just a rope and window washer's harness, then crashes through the glass and rappels down while blasting away with a machine gun. A very exciting stunt, and one that none of the regular stuntpeople for the film were willing to perform. So Janz had one of the actual window washers from the building (who was more than happy to comply) double as Hines and climb the sheer glass walls of the building (a stuntman handled the interior crashing portion, which was done in a studio).

Janz regularly received kudos not just for his ability to coordinate sequences and quickly arrange cars and equipment to suit the constantly changing needs of the filmmakers, but also for his steady hand at the

The aftermath of the limo vs. train collision from *Running Scared* (1986). *(Photo by Bob Janz)*

controls of a train. A smooth ride was pivotal for any cameras shooting on the train and for the safety of the stuntmen precariously perched on the outside. For instance, the Chuck Norris movie *Code of Silence* has a sequence in which two stuntmen wrestle aboard the roof of an "L" car before both finally leap from the roof into the river while the train crosses the Wells Street Bridge. Although the men were actually jumping into a net below the camera frame, the stunt was quite tricky and dangerous. One of the stuntmen was so pleased with Bob's piloting skills that he came up to Janz and hugged him after the stunt, crying out, "You've got golden fingers."

Aside from earning the love and loyalty of stunt performers, Bob recalls bonding with many stars during his career. Sharing lunch and conversation with the late John Candy on the set of *Planes, Trains & Automobiles* (1987), having a great time with Danny DeVito while he was in town directing a pilot for a short-lived Mary Tyler Moore TV series (in which she played a Chicago news columnist), and chatting with Kirk Douglas for a few hours during the shooting of CTA scenes for his film *The Fury* (1978) are among the highlights.

Bob Janz and Danny DeVito relax during a break in filming on the pilot for a short-lived series starring Mary Tyler Moore. *(Collection of Bob Janz)*

The shoot for *The Fury* also yielded a hilariously surreal story (and one for the "dumb crook" files), when an unobservant criminal attempted to mug an actress (playing a nun!) right on the set. The offender was able to take about one step before being grabbed by plainclothes Chicago detectives assigned to guard the production.

Bob retired from the CTA in 1992 and now lives with his wife Pat in the far western suburb of Yorkville. He remains active in several railroad-related organizations and writes articles for rail fan publications.

Gene Siskel Film Center

164 N. State Street

Founded in 1971 as the Film Center of the School of the Art Institute of Chicago, the Film Center was renamed in honor of legendary Chicago film critic Gene Siskel in 2000. Dedicated to an ambitiously eclectic mission from its inception, the Film Center's first two retrospectives, presented in 1972, were of influential French director Jean Renoir and American slapstick master Buster Keaton. "Anything in the realm of the motion picture is within our mission," according to director of programming Barbara Scharres. Edgy independent comedies share the screen with international and art house offerings. Annual events include an Iranian film festival and the acclaimed Black Harvest Festival, which celebrates the African American experience on film with a special emphasis on premiering midwestern and Chicago movies.

Another important part of the Film Center's mission is to provide opportunities for filmmakers to speak with their audiences in person through lectures and panel discussions. The center features over 100 guest artists per year.

In 2001, they moved into their state-of-the-art facilities at 164 N. State Street. World-renowned projection booth designer James Bond (his real name) was hired to create the most technically excellent environment possible in which to view films. Sight lines, acoustics, proper lenses, and projection booth layout were taken into consideration. The attention to detail even extended to special projectors with variable speed motors that can show old silent films at the speed at which they were intended (silent films were often hand-cranked and meant to be seen at a much slower speed) without the manic, herky-jerky movements people have unfortunately grown used to. The larger of the two theaters even has a baby grand piano for live music accompaniment of silent films!

The Gene Siskel Film Center shows films "from emerging filmmakers to the great masters" seven days a week on two screens, presenting approximately 1,500 screenings to over 65,000 film enthusiasts per year. For more information call (312) 846-2600 or visit www.siskelfilmcenter.org.

Marshall Field's (now Macy's)
111 N. State Street

Marshall Field's was a Chicago shopping institution that predated the Chicago Fire of 1871. The store underwent countless changes after its founder Marshall Field first came to Chicago in 1856. After going into partnership with Potter Palmer and accountant Levi Z. Leiter, Field opened his first State Street store in 1868. Like much of the downtown retail area, the six-story building was destroyed in the Great Chicago Fire. Field rebuilt on the same site two years later, only to see that building burn to the ground as well in 1877.

But Field refused to quit. Once more, he erected a department store on the corner of State and Washington, and the result was a manor house for consumers. Designed by Daniel Burnham, the store went up in 1892, with additional facilities added in 1904 and 1907. The interior is marked by wide courts, grilled railings, and wonderful skylights. Outside you'll find beautifully ornate clocks at State and Washington and State and Randolph. These timepieces are State Street landmarks, and the phrase "Meet me under the clock" has been a motto for many Marshall Field's tag-team shoppers. Even today the store's windows are gaily decorated with holiday scenes. Visiting this display, gazing at the enormous Christmas tree inside the store, and a visit to the Field's Santa have been annual traditions for countless Chicago-area families.

In a tragic blow for lovers of Chicago tradition, the Marshall Field's chain was purchased by a large conglomerate in 2006, and all the stores, even this historic flagship, were changed to Macy's. This enraged many Chicagoans, who still occasionally mount street protests to rail against this affront to Chicago's identity. Others still try to follow the old traditions as best they can, making the yearly pilgrimage to see the Christmas windows despite their relative lack of opulence compared to bygone days.

Regardless of what sign may sit on the exterior, the holiday traditions surrounding this location will continue to live on in many films. Judge Reinhold (inhabited with the personality of his preteen son, Fred Savage) worked here in *Vice Versa* (1988). *Curly Sue* (1991) and *Straight Talk* (1992) also shot scenes here. *Looking for Mr. Goodbar* (1977) staged a misfired fantasy sequence with the Field's Christmas windows, having Diane Keaton imagining herself a star figure skater while gazing at the holiday display.

Looking for some good dining in between cash registers? Check out the Walnut Room and see where Julia Roberts had a bite to eat in *My Best Friend's Wedding* (1997).

Then there's *Baby's Day Out* (1994). A slapstick comedy in the tradition of *Home Alone* (1990) and the Three Stooges, the film revolves around a group of bumbling kidnappers who can't keep track of the baby they've snatched. The baby has a wild day on the town, the trio (led by Joe Mantegna) gets knocked around, and everyone lives happily, if improbably, ever after.

The basic joke of the movie hinges on the premise that absolutely no one would possibly notice a happy baby crawling around Chicago by himself. In the fantasy world of Hollywood that might be all right, but within the realistic environs of the Loop, a lone baby would definitely be noticed. One scene in *Baby's Day Out* called for the youngster to crawl out of Field's and accidentally end up in a taxicab while Mantegna and company watch in comic horror. The scene was shot on a Saturday afternoon, a busy time for the store. Enormous crowds had gathered to watch a 27-inch-tall man (actor Verne Troyer, who played Mini-Me in the *Austin Powers* sequels), outfitted with a latex baby head and hands, crawl his way from the store to the street. As with many movie locations, the Chicago Police Department had set up barricades around Field's to prevent onlookers from interfering with the 180-person movie crew. Of course the inevitable happened.

The "baby" crawled out of Field's. With a large crowd, including many of Chicago's finest, watching, one hapless couple, unaware the scene was fictional, broke through the police line to rescue the roving tot. From beneath his latex baby head, the little man screamed, "Put me down!" The couple, terrified by this bizarre child whose lips didn't move though he screamed like a rabid trucker, totally freaked out. Whether this well-meaning pair chose to play Good Samaritans ever again is unknown, but the incident has become a legend among Chicago film crews.

Nathan Crowley: The Architect of Gotham City

Nathan Crowley is a production designer. Born in England, Crowley now lives in California. But work on four consecutive movies filmed in Chicago over the course of almost five years—*Batman Begins* (2005), *The Lake House* (2006), *The Dark Knight* (2008), and *Public Enemies* (2009)—has conveyed the status of honorary Chicagoan upon him.

Before we explore what Crowley has been up to during his tenure in our city, he first makes clear what a production designer does: "The production designer is in charge of the feel and the look of the entire picture, from locations to the set, the physical sets, the film sets, props, the set dressing, and into postproduction in terms of visual effects for the entire look. It's done in conjunction with the director of photography and the director themselves. Really, it's about creating a world for the story to inhabit."

Possessing the keen eye and creative powers of a serious visual artist, combined with the unbridled enthusiasm of a kid who's been set loose in the world's largest toy store, Crowley has transformed Chicago into Gotham City, designed and supervised the construction of a modernist glass house over a lake in a Cook County forest preserve, created all of Batman's futuristic vehicles (the Batmobile, the Batpod, and even the flying vehicle from *The Dark Knight Rises*, dubbed "the Bat"), and turned the clock back on an entire

Nathan Crowley in his home office, decorated with scale models of various Batman vehicles he designed. *(Photo by Nathan Crowley)*

block of Lincoln Avenue outside the Biograph Theater to make it look almost exactly like it did the day John Dillinger was gunned down in 1934.

Crowley earned a degree in three-dimensional design in England, then came to live in America in 1990. He found a job drafting for a film studio and "it kind of went from there." In 2001, Crowley met director/writer Christopher Nolan and worked for him on *Insomnia* (2002), a thriller starring Al Pacino and Robin Williams. The two men hit it off and developed a close working relationship that has led to them making three more films together (with more on the way).

The next project the pair collaborated on, *Batman Begins*, was the film that first brought Crowley to Chicago. Although the production did relatively little location shooting in Chicago, Crowley spent weeks prowling the city, studying it and getting ideas for a giant model of Gotham City that he and Nolan would build together back in Los Angeles. Falling in love with the city's beautiful and unique architecture, Crowley combined key elements of Chicago's buildings and infrastructure with his own fertile imagination to create the dark, hallucinatory dreamscape that is Gotham City in their first Batman film.

The model was crucial to their vision of Gotham City and to the film, because one thing Nolan and Crowley agreed on when they first set out to revive the Batman story was to keep the use of computer-generated effects to a minimum. "We have this policy of realism. Trying to not play the

The base of the dome of 35 E. Wacker Drive (originally known as the Jewelers Building) was where Batman first revealed himself in *Batman Begins* (2005). *(Photo by Kate Corcoran)*

audience out. The essence of Batman is that he has no superpowers, so you really have to ground him in hard reality and things we know and cities we know to make him not invulnerable."

Another thing that soon became obvious to them was that Chicago would play a larger part in the film: "We knew we liked Chicago a lot. We went there on the first film primarily to do the car chase on Lower Wacker, because it's so fantastic, and then ended up shooting more stuff there. We were on top of the Jewelers Building shooting the scene when Batman initially reveals himself in *Batman Begins*. After we shot that scene it became very clear that Chicago had a lot more to offer than we realized."

Crowley became even more enamored of Chicago on his next film, *The Lake House*, in which architecture and the love of architecture is an integral part of the story. *The Lake House*, which stars Keanu Reeves and Sandra Bullock, is a romantic fantasy revolving around a stunning glass house that sits on poles above a small bucolic lake (hence the title of the film). Reeves plays an architect who moves into the eponymous lake house, which was his boyhood home and was designed by his cold and distant father, a famous modernist architect, played by veteran film actor Christopher Plummer.

As Reeves moves back into the house, which has been abandoned since his mother died many years before, he discovers a letter in the mailbox from the previous tenant, played by Bullock. Confused by this note, as the house has been deserted, Reeves sends a return letter asking Bullock what she is talking about. As their correspondence continues, they gradually realize that

Bullock is actually occupying the house two years after Reeves, and that some sort of mysterious power embedded in the mailbox is allowing them to correspond through time. They soon fall in love and try to unravel the mystery of the mailbox in order to allow themselves to meet in "real time" and consummate their newfound love.

Many critics have derided the film, but if you buy into the premise (Hey, it's a romantic fantasy, people; it doesn't have to make sense!), *The Lake House* is a very sweet and tender film that features beautiful cinematography, extensive use of Chicago locations, and Keanu Reeves's best performance to date as an actual non-computer-generated human being.

And even the movie's harshest detractors will agree that the lake house itself is a fantastic piece of architecture—one that Crowley designed himself and a set construction team built in a little over two months on a small lake in a forest preserve near the suburb of Palos Hills. The house was built on pylons on the shore of the lake; then the area underneath the structure was excavated so that it then sat above the water.

It was an arduous process that Crowley felt was important for the sake of the film: "Early on I decided to expend most of my portion of the budget entirely on building the house, and I'd rely on Chicago to provide me with the rest of the film as a location, because there's plenty of great locations and great architecture to complement the design of the house. So we built in Maple Lake, which is in a forest preserve. It was a complicated process to build a house, and we didn't have much time—we had about nine weeks to build it. It was a large undertaking, but the whole film revolved around this house, so it was very necessary."

After filming was completed, Crowley and crew dismantled the house and returned the lake to its previous state. The task of building the house and the entire story of the film had an especially surreal resonance with Crowley, whose father and grandfather were both architects. "It was strange to read the script because my father still has a glass house in London that we lived in when I grew up. I grew up in a glass house! I mean, we have a great relationship, but it was an interesting parallel in terms of modernism. . . . And we had to create this book for his [Keanu Reeves's] father, so I tried to persuade my father to give me all of his work so I could create the book, but my father didn't want that kind of involvement. I think he kind of regrets it now."

The wide range of Chicago's architectural styles was also a great help to Crowley as he created the look of the film. "I always call Chicago 'the Rome of the US,' because it's got such a wide variety of architecture done by a varied assortment of great architects in such a small area, so you get to observe the great history of the last century's architecture."

Crowley's next Chicago project was the celebrated blockbuster *The Dark Knight*, on which he continued his journey of discovery through Chicago architecture, focusing even more intently on the city's wide array of modernist structures. This aesthetic break from *Batman Begins* (and all previous Batman films) was brought about by the continuing evolution of the Batman story. "In *Batman Begins*, we'd obviously taken on this whole franchise, and we kind of saw a way into it in terms of an origin story. Chicago seemed like a logical place, and we relied on some of the old architecture. The city of Gotham had, like most cities, a broad range of historic architecture up through the modern. So in *The Dark Knight* we really wanted to make a continuation of that story. We really wanted to describe Gotham [visually] and that maybe we should not feature some of the old architecture, that we should play it more clean and stick with Modernism. We thought we should use these buildings that say, 'This is a modern city, this is a thriving modern city' and really take the Gothic out of Gotham."

The first way that Crowley and Nolan took "the Gothic out of Gotham" was by relocating Wayne Industries into the Daley Center and Bruce Wayne's residence into the IBM Building, a classic Ludwig Mies van der Rohe design. Nathan first noticed the IBM Building the night when they were filming *Batman Begins* on the top of the Jewelers Building. "When you look at it at night it looks like it's floating, especially from high above." Another change from the look of the first film was that in *The Dark Knight*, most of the action takes place during the day. "The whole thing about *Batman Begins* is that some of the best scenes are when he doesn't reveal himself, and night is very useful for that. So in *The Dark Knight*, once we started down the path where we knew we were making a film about the workings of a city, there was a conscious push to say, 'Look, if we're gonna reveal Gotham, we've got to find a city and we've got to push the city and use the city, and shoot during daylight and really reveal it in that sense.'"

This revealing of Gotham required them to do much more location filming in Chicago, shooting in the city a total of 13 weeks as opposed to just three for *Batman Begins*. *The Dark Knight* was the largest film shoot ever in Chicago.

Cooperation of the city, businesses, and local citizens is an area where Chicago really shines. This was reinforced to Crowley during the shooting of the fourth film he worked on here, the period action drama *Public Enemies*, a retelling of the John Dillinger story with Johnny Depp as Dillinger and Christian Bale as FBI man Melvin Purvis. During that shoot, Crowley and set decorator Rosemary Brandenburg worked to transform Lincoln Avenue outside of the Biograph Theater back to how it appeared in 1934, and then they had to completely abandon the elaborate set during a holiday weekend in busy Lincoln Park. "We had to open up the street to traffic, close down the center lane, and put all our stuff in the center. You know how many hundreds and thousands of people walked past the set? Because we had to open up the set so people could walk through it, but no one destroyed it. It was pretty impressive, you know. And hats off to the location department, the city, and the police for making that work."

Despite the effort involved in the transformation and the risks in leaving it open to the public for that weekend, Crowley felt that the needs of the film required it to be done: "Historically, we really can't fake the Biograph. It's not the place to do it in the John Dillinger story. You kind of have to take a couple places that big things happened in his life, the Biograph being one of them, and film there. We looked at options like faking it in Milwaukee, but it's an injustice to the Dillinger story to start faking stuff like the Biograph; if you do, you've kind of sold out at that point."

Once Crowley and Brandenburg had resolved that morphing the street outside the Biograph was necessary, the big job became how to bring it about. That block of Lincoln was in one of the trendiest and busiest shopping districts in the city, teeming with high-end retail and high-volume bars and restaurants.

"We really thought, We're going to have to somehow turn this street back in time," Crowley recalls. "We and the city worked out a way of doing lane closures so we could facade half the street! We did all of the buildings around the alley where he was shot, the exterior of the Biograph, and the interior lobby. We put cobblestones down, we put the tram lines in, we had to take out the lamp posts; we had to do all this stuff—the traffic lights, there was a McDonald's there, we had to cover that up. I'm astonished that everyone went along with it. I guess people who work on that street really understood where we were trying to go with it. It was definitely an inconvenience, but I think they were excited. There is a sort of excitement in the [Chicago] community that allows us to work in these places."

In addition to being responsible for the overall look of exterior and interior sets and locations, the production designer also has dominion over the props and other set pieces. For some movies, this can prove to be a huge task, such as in the Batman films, when Crowley had to design and arrange for the fabrication of all of Batman's vehicles. "Probably the hardest things to do in those Batman films, as far as taking the most time, [were] designing the Batpod and the Batmobile, because you've got to design them, model them, and then you've got to build them from the ground up as a working vehicle. And they're fast, they really do go a hundred miles an hour, and you want that reality. You don't want a digital car. That's very important to us."

Not that playing with models and designing the kind of fantasy vehicles you dreamt about and drooled over as a kid is a punishment or anything. "It's also great fun," Crowley says. "You get to design the Batmobile first, and then you persuade some crazy engineers to build it, and then you get to drive it [*laughs*]. Yeah, some of the funnest things are the cars and bikes, although you can't drive that bike [the Batpod from *The Dark Knight*]; it's impossible. . . . No one else would go near it apart from that French stunt driver [Jean-Pierre Goy], and he spent six months with it learning how to handle it. It might look good, but in terms of a bike design I don't think anyone should copy it."

And if the proceedings didn't have enough of the aforementioned "little kid loose in the toy store" vibe, Crowley mentions where the balance of this work took place: in Chris Nolan's garage. "When we first started *Batman Begins*, we converted his old two-car garage with a washer and dryer in it, and we just put some workbenches in there. Because he was still writing the script, we wanted to get going on the Batmobile, so we just started building models in there. And the garage was a pretty rotten place back then. It didn't have heat or air-conditioning. When the maid had to do the laundry, we had to go out for the afternoon. Then, after *Batman Begins*, he spent some money on it and turned it into an art studio, and now it's lovely. It's got fans, it's got a kitchenette. It's all fantastic now, but it started out with bare concrete and drywall and it was a moldy place to make models."

So the Batmobile was born in a musty garage? "Oh, yeah, it's great. We did *The Prestige* in there too. It's good because he likes to work in a hurry and he has a big family. He also likes doing a lot of rewrites, so his office is right next to the garage and we can communicate and it's kind of private."

His tenure in Chicago has definitely endeared the city to Crowley. "I love Chicago. If I have big-city work to do in a film, it'll definitely be one of my first stops." One of the many reasons why Crowley is so enamored of working here is that the best film locations are often rather close to each other, and the congestion is relatively minimal. "I love Chicago because I can walk to work, and I know everyone in Chicago likes to complain about the traffic, but compared to other cities it's fantastic." One thing Crowley won't miss about our fair city? The same thing Chicagoans themselves decry. "I've been here for four years in a row running. I don't like the winter; I'm fed up with the winter here."

Although the third installment of the Batman franchise used locations other than Chicago, given Chicago's prominence in the film industry, Crowley may still have to brave our chilly temps yet again.

Chicago Theatre
162 N. State Street

On October 26, 1921, Barney Balaban and Sam Katz opened the doors to the flagship of their movie theater empire, the Chicago Theatre. Though it may not have quite lived up to its nickname "the Wonder Theatre of the World," the Chicago Theatre set the standard for other film palaces.

Designed by Cornelius and George Rapp, who created many of Balaban and Katz's theaters, the Chicago Theatre featured a five-story lobby. The grand staircase, modeled after that of the Paris Opera, took guests to balcony seats of the seven-story auditorium. Crystal chandeliers hung from the ceiling. The orchestra pit was outfitted for up to 50 musicians, as well as a mighty Wurlitzer pipe organ. The marquee was just as grand, featuring a sculpted mini-replica of Paris's Arc de Triomphe.

The opening-night show was *A Sign on the Door*, starring Norma Talmadge, one of the era's most popular stars. Talmadge's brother-in-law, Buster Keaton (then married to Natalie Talmadge), provided live entertainment, while the Chicago Plan Commission chair, Charles H. Wacker, served as the evening's host.

Over the next four decades, the Chicago Theatre was the place to see great films and live entertainment. John Philip Sousa, Duke Ellington, Benny Goodman, Jack Benny, Will Rogers, Al Jolson, Sophie Tucker, Eddie Cantor, Frank Sinatra, Milton Berle, Bob Hope, the team of Dean Martin and Jerry Lewis, Sid Caesar, Sally Rand, and many other headline entertainers all trod the Chicago Theatre boards.

The influence of television and the decline of the city's downtown theater district, however, provided a double whammy to the Chicago Theatre. By the 1970s, this once-shining palace had deteriorated into a

LEFT: View of the west elevation of the theater, showing the sign and adjacent Page Brothers Building, looking to the southeast, circa 1997. *(Library of Congress, Prints and Photographs Division, Historic American Buildings Survey, HABS ILL, 16-CHIG, 165-5)*

RIGHT TOP: View of the Chicago Theatre and vertical sign, looking to the northeast, circa 1996. *(Library of Congress, Prints and Photographs Division, Historic American Buildings Survey, HABS ILL, 16-CHIG, 165-2)*

RIGHT BOTTOM: The Chicago Theatre's distinctive Balaban and Katz logo window. *(Photo by Kate Corcoran)*

third-rate movie house. Eventually its owners, the Plitt Theatres chain, decided it would be more cost-effective in the long run to simply close up shop. On September 19, 1985, the once-bright lights of the Chicago Theatre marquee were dimmed, seemingly for the last time.

The fate of this building became a cause célèbre. A committee of concerned businesses and citizens, calling itself the Chicago Theatre Restoration Associates, was formed. With some help from city officials, the Chicago Theatre was purchased from Plitt and some $25 million put forth toward its reconstruction.

In less than a year, the miracle was complete. With hard work on the part of Daniel P. Coffey and Associates and A. T. Heinsbergen and Company, the Chicago Theatre was restored to its former grandeur. In a move that was symbolic of the theater's rich history, Frank Sinatra was booked as the new theater's opening act. The Chairman of the Board sang to a sold-out crowd on September 10, 1986.

Though the theater had its ups and downs after the much-ballyhooed opening, the Chicago Theatre hit the jackpot when it booked the Andrew Lloyd Webber–Tim Rice musical *Joseph and the Amazing Technicolor Dreamcoat*. Featuring former teen heartthrob Donny Osmond in a sparkling performance, this biblically based musical comedy played to record crowds. The Chicago Theatre was truly reborn as an exciting new venue for live downtown performance.

Once Donny and company moved on, the Chicago Theatre transformed into a top-rate live music venue; what's more, the restoration inevitably attracted film production. Charles Grodin and Robert DeNiro shared some aggravation here in the cross-country caper *Midnight Run* (1988). DeNiro later returned to film some scenes for *The Untouchables* (1987). For *Blues Brothers 2000* (1998), some stuff was shot in front of the theater as well.

Tours of the theater are available some weekdays and on Saturdays; visit www.thechicagotheatre.com/tour.html for details and to purchase tickets.

Leo Burnett Building

35 W. Wacker Drive

At the corner of Wacker Drive and Dearborn Street stands the mighty Leo Burnett Building, a towering homage to the power of advertising. The agency itself was founded by Burnett, a former police reporter, in 1935. Beginning with just eight employees, Burnett's ad agency grew into a corporate giant. Today Leo Burnett has offices around the world and more than 7,500 employees. The business has always been headquartered in the Windy City, and the Leo Burnett Building, designed by Kevin Roche, gives the company a magnificent home.

The talent at Burnett is second to none—several former Burnett creatives have gone on to work in Hollywood. Among the alumni are Tim Kazurinsky and the team of Jeffrey Price and Peter S. Seaman, who wrote the screenplays for *Who Framed Roger Rabbit?* (1988) and *Doc Hollywood* (1991).

The Leo Burnett Building, home of the renowned advertising agency, is the birthplace of such important cultural icons as the Pillsbury Doughboy, Tony the Tiger, and the Keebler Elves. *(Photo by Kate Corcoran)*

The Leo Burnett Building is a rather versatile movie location. Kevin Bacon works in its offices in *She's Having a Baby* (1988), and Kelly Lynch keeps her law practice here in *Curly Sue* (1991). It has also showed up in *Midnight Run* (1988) and *Betrayed* (1988) and impersonated a ritzy Manhattan location for *Home Alone 2: Lost in New York* (1992).

Old State of Illinois Building
160 N. LaSalle Street

Built in 1924 by the Burnham Brothers (sons of architect / city planner Daniel Burnham), this building was originally named after its architects. In 1946, the Burnham Building was bought by the state government as its Chicago headquarters and subsequently was known as the State of Illinois Building. When the Thompson Center was opened in the mid-1980s, Illinois government offices moved out.

Though eclipsed by the gaudy glass and steel of the new state headquarters, the old State of Illinois Building still had one brief, shining moment— it became Cole's Department Store in the remake of *Miracle on 34th Street* (1994). Ironically, the new Thompson Center served as its competitor.

The R. R. Donnelley Building (now the United Building)
77 W. Wacker Drive

Before the new headquarters of R. R. Donnelley (they have since departed, and the building is now known as the United Building or simply referred to by its address) was completed, it made for an intriguing film set.

It's here where white supremacist Tom Berenger and undercover FBI agent Debra Winger face off in *Betrayed* (1988). The scene has Berenger and Winger sneaking onto the construction site with the purpose of shooting a human target on the street below. Winger prevents the assassination, only to learn there's a lot more to the situation than it would appear.

Ten years later, the Donnelley building became the focal point of *The Negotiator* (1998). Samuel L. Jackson, playing a top police negotiator, enters the tower (which, for the purposes of the film, became a government building) to prove his innocence when he's accused of masterminding a labyrinthine money-laundering scheme. Taking hostages within an office suite, Jackson ultimately squares off in a battle of wits with his peer negotiator, Kevin Spacey. While the two play cat-and-mouse games, Wacker Drive is choked with police cars, barricades, and countless extras; police snipers are poised on surrounding buildings; and helicop-

Samuel L. Jackson takes hostages in this building at 77 W. Wacker Drive in the movie *The Negotiator* (1998). *(Photo by Kate Corcoran)*

ters buzz around like oversized mosquitoes. The interior office scenes were shot on a soundstage in L.A., with a 40-foot-by-160-foot poster simulating the view out the window.

Downtown Randolph Street
Randolph Street between Michigan Avenue and Wells Street

If you take a walk down Randolph Street between Michigan Avenue and Wells Street, you'll find yourself in a bustling throng. Between the businesspeople, bike messengers, and tourists, downtown Randolph is a great place for people-watching.

If you're looking for movie locations along Randolph, you'll find plenty. The Chicago Cultural Center, the former Marshall Field's, and the Thompson Center are among the most prominent landmarks (see individual entries). Yet the Randolph Street we know today is very different from what this thoroughfare was just a few years ago.

During the 1940s, Randolph Street was the heart of Chicago's big-ticket theater district. Huge neon marquees flashed movies, plays, and special celebrity appearances for theaters like the Apollo, the Garrick, the Oriental, the Palace, the United Artists, and the Woods. The Showman's League, an organization for people in the entertainment business, maintained its headquarters at the corner of Randolph and Wells.

On a hot Saturday night, Randolph Street was the place to be. Slowly, however, the luster of this thriving district began to fade. By the 1970s, blockbuster movies no longer played exclusively at downtown theaters. Randolph's once-proud movie palaces were reduced to playing karate movies, exploitation action flicks, and the more-than-occasional pornographic film. By the mid-1980s, most of the theaters were demolished, though the Oriental and the Palace merely shut their doors.

Although today this downtown street is largely composed of business and government buildings, it has made a cultural comeback of sorts. The Oriental (renamed the Ford Center for the Performing Arts) has undergone extensive renovation and now caters to big-ticket musicals and other theatrical productions. Combined with the resurgence of the (Cadillac) Palace Theatre, the new Goodman Theatre on Dearborn (formerly the Harris and Selwyn theaters), State Street's majestic Chicago Theatre, and the lovingly restored Bank of America Theatre (formerly the Shubert) around the corner on Monroe Street, the movie palaces of Chicago's theater district have been reborn as live venues.

If you're nostalgic or just plain curious about old Randolph Street, there are a few films that will give you a glimpse of the theater district's decaying glory. In *Mickey One* (1965), Warren Beatty cruises the street in search of a booking agent. Michael Mann's *Thief* (1981) features an interesting shot of James Caan driving past the glowing Randolph Street marquees. The neon signs are seen as reflections off the hood of Caan's car, creating a feverish, dreamlike ambiance.

Matt Dillon played a small-town gambler who comes to Chicago during the 1950s-era drama *The Big Town* (1987). When the production came to town, Randolph Street was on its last legs as a theater district.

What showed up on-screen was a nice period look, giving the right ambiance to Dillon's world of low-life excitement.

The Illinois Film Office
100 W. Randolph Street, Suite 3-400

Established in 1976 as Hollywood was gradually rediscovering the beauty of Chicago, the Illinois Film Office (IFO) was set up by Governor Jim Thompson as a way of creating new revenue streams for Illinois. The IFO is ground zero for any producer thinking about bringing a production to Illinois.

Veteran line producer Christina Varotsis describes the agency's integral role: "The Illinois Film Office is a resource for our location team. They have a database with pictures, and a lot of times the location manager will put a call in to the Film Office to ask stuff like, 'Hey, what cemeteries are user-friendly right now?' or to see if they have pictures of some specific location. They're a good resource for identifying locations. They're also the place that every filmmaker talks to when they are taking care of their tax credit applications when they are in preproduction. They are the entity that handles receiving and processing the applications. They also provide you with the guidelines for accounting procedures and all the practical aspects of the tax credit."

The tax incentives are paramount to attracting productions to Illinois, as the state has recently learned the hard way. With not only Chicago's traditional movie-shooting competitor, Canada, vying for filmmakers' attention, but Iowa, Wisconsin, and Michigan building production facilities and offering large tax incentives as well, Illinois cannot afford to be left behind.

The competition is fierce, as Varotsis will attest to. Often when she prepares a budget for a film to be set in Chicago or elsewhere in the state, Christina will also be asked by the penny-pinching production to provide one for Iowa, Detroit, or even various European locations. "One time I was asked to do a budget for Detroit for a film set in Ireland, which I thought was a bit of a stretch," she laughs.

This is the reason why in late 2008, the Illinois Legislature passed a 30 percent tax incentive to film productions that shoot in Illinois. While tax rebates to large corporations can result in the money being pocketed by greedy CEOs and the company leaving the state for greener pastures, film productions recycle the money directly back into the local economy via payments to food and equipment vendors, union crew members, and other various and sundry entities and persons.

The Chicago Film Office

1 N. LaSalle Street, Suite 2165

A division of the Mayor's Office of Special Events, the major part of the Chicago Film Office's job is to coordinate filmmaking needs with city concerns. "The office is the focal point of concerns regarding city services so a production company doesn't have to get involved in bureaucracy," says CFO director Richard Moskal. "It's the city's way of saying we can accommodate the movie business in a quick and efficient fashion." The CFO also works closely with communities where films are being shot.

"We work closely with the Illinois Film Office," says Moskal. "They're dealing with economic development and marketing. They encourage film producers to do work here, and they do a lot of the initial legwork, hooking them up with resources. The Chicago Film Office gets down to streets. We're an advocate for the industry in terms of getting the films made, but we're also watching out for the city and the communities so that neighborhoods don't necessarily get taken advantage of by what can be very huge demands and challenges."

Christina Varotsis praises the work of the CFO: "The Chicago Film Office really works with filmmakers to make sure things go as smoothly as possible. Another thing is that compared to other major cities, the permit process is so easy. It's affordable, and they really encourage you and work to make it easy for film crews by arranging for street closures as well."

Jeff Garlin, the costar and executive producer of the hit HBO series *Curb Your Enthusiasm*, raves about how the CFO helped him out when he shot his independent comedy *I Want Someone to Eat Cheese With* (2006) in the city. "The Chicago Film Office couldn't have been better. They were fantastic. They bent over backwards for me, and they made shooting in Millennium Park easy, easy, easy!"

Production designer Nathan Crowley describes how integral the cooperation of the city and CFO was to the success of the blockbuster *The Dark Knight* (2008) by helping to facilitate large-scale chases and stunts in the downtown area: "The Chicago Film Office is incredibly helpful for filming. They arranged for huge parts of the downtown to basically be shut down at night and on the weekends. It's phenomenal!" The city went so far as to allow the filmmakers to blow up an entire factory (which was slated for demolition) for a scene in the film.

Transformers: Dark of the Moon (2011) also received massive amounts of support from the Film Office, which helped coordinate the closing of one of the city's busiest streets, N. Michigan Avenue, for almost four days. The movie also shut down Wacker Drive and Wabash, Lake, and LaSalle Streets for long stints.

James R. Thompson Center / State of Illinois Building
100 W. Randolph Street

To some it's a beautiful postmodern palace. To others, it's a glass-and-steel nightmare representing the worst modern architecture can belch up. Take it or leave it, if you live in Chicago, inevitably you'll have some kind of business here at the James R. Thompson Center, also known as the State of Illinois Building.

The building, opened in 1985, was designed by architect Helmut Jahn, well known for his forays into glass-and-steel construction. Jahn was personally chosen by then–Illinois governor James Thompson to design the edifice, inspiring one local wag to dub the completed building "Thompsonland." Indeed, with its expansive atrium, towering escalators, glass elevators, and always-buzzing food court, the James

The James R. Thompson Center, also known as the State of Illinois Building (1985) was designed by architect Helmut Jahn. *(Photo by Kate Corcoran)*

R. Thompson Center does have the look and feel of a low-rent carnival inside a life-sized Lego structure. While the design may be attractive to some, it also has a rather significant drawback: the building suffers from perennial heating and air-conditioning trouble.

In *Music Box* (1990), Costa-Gavras's story about the trial of a long-hidden Nazi war criminal, federal prosecutors have offices in the Thompson Center. The building's mall-like environment is neatly exploited in *Miracle on 34th Street* (1994), turning the Thompson Center into a Christmas-festooned department store. *Switching Channels* (1988), a sort of broadcast remake of the famed Chicago newspaper play *The Front Page*, by Charles MacArthur and Ben Hecht, also has some fun with the building, making good use of its futuristic ambiance. Sullen serial killer Keanu Reeves stalks one of his victims in the Thompson Center, again reimagined as a shopping mall, in the tepid thriller *The Watcher* (2000).

The playhouse qualities of Jahn's architecture are pushed to the limits in the Billy Crystal–Gregory Hines cop-buddy picture *Running Scared* (1986). In the film's climactic sequence, Crystal and Hines and the bad guys engage in a massive shootout, which includes Hines rappelling from the roof and scads of shattered glass.

Cook County Building / City Hall
118 N. Clark Street/121 N. LaSalle Street

"Hut! Hut!" That's not the cry of pigeons but the regimented yell of tethered SWAT team members scrambling down the City Hall columns in *The Blues Brothers* (1980). That film's frenzied climax ends here, with scores of cops and national guardsmen pouring through the hallways to the county assessor's office, where Joliet Jake (John Belushi) and Elwood (Dan Aykroyd) complete their mission from God and pay off an orphanage tax bill to mild-mannered clerk Steven Spielberg. Of course, that's the film's biggest joke, since in real life the orphanage would be a tax-exempt organization!

The Cook County Building was built between 1906 and 1907, and City Hall came shortly thereafter, with ground-breaking in 1909 and a grand opening in 1911. Those Corinthian columns the *Blues Brothers* SWAT team hop down are the tallest on any city building, towering at 75 feet apiece.

Aside from Jake and Elwood, City Hall has been visited by characters in *Miracle on 34th Street* (1994) and *A Family Thing* (1996), among other films. The old coal tunnels deep beneath the structure double as underground passageways beneath the Field Museum in *The Relic* (1997), when City Hall tunnels proved to be an easier place to film.

Apparently there's something about the Cook County Building/City Hall that attracts movie men on the run. In addition to Jake and Elwood's County Building encounters, poor Dr. Richard Kimble (Harrison Ford) is nearly captured here by US Marshal Sam Gerard (Tommy Lee Jones) in *The Fugitive* (1993). Of course, in real life, Harrison Ford wouldn't be looking up prisoners in the Cook County Building, as he does in *The Fugitive*. On the other hand, the bulletproof glass doors that nearly stop Ford dead in his tracks don't exist here, either.

Love, however, does spring eternal in the building's basement. Though often referred to as a "City Hall wedding," marriages are actually a function of Cook County government. So head downstairs, where you and your intended can be married by a Cook County judge, and while you're there, take a few puffs on a good cigar in honor of Groucho Marx. On February 4, 1920, Groucho (a.k.a. Julius Henry Marx) and his first wife, Ruth Johnson, took their vows in a Cook County judge's chambers. This being a Marx Brother's marriage, appropriate chaos ensued. A potted plant appeared to blissfully walk around on its own throughout the room during the ceremony, courtesy of a carefully hidden Harpo. And when the justice of the peace solemnly intoned, "We are gathered here to join this couple in holy matrimony," Groucho replied in his superlative fashion, "It may be holy to you, Judge, but we have other ideas."

Most recently, the building has served as the focal point of the excellent Starz Cable Network original series *Boss*, starring Kelsey Grammer, Connie Nielsen, and a slew of Chicago's finest actors. The show depicts Grammer as a fictitious Chicago mayor (sort of a mixture of ex-mayors Richard J. and Richard M. Daley, current mayor Rahm Emmanuel, and Vladimir Putin) dealing with a degenerative brain disease and the possible dissolution of his political empire.

Richard J. Daley Civic Center and Plaza
50 W. Washington Street

One of the best places in the city for people-watching, the Richard J. Daley Civic Center and Plaza is a quintessential Chicago site that can't be duplicated. The towering 31-story building, which houses many courts and offices, was opened in 1965 and overlooks Daley Plaza, home to one of the city's most universally recognized symbols, the rust-red Picasso statue.

Movie-wise, Daley Plaza's scenic beauty is a natural location for film-makers looking to add a distinctive splash of local color. It's been seen on-screen in one form or another in films like *Adventures in Babysitting* (1987), *Baby's Day Out* (1994), *Backdraft* (1991), *Blink* (1994), *Ferris Bueller's Day Off* (1986), *The Fugitive* (1993), *The Lake House* (2006), *Mercury Rising* (1998), *Stranger Than Fiction* (2006), and *The Dark Knight* (2008), which used the Daley Center as Wayne Industries headquarters. Still, none of these films can compete with the ultimate Daley Center location shoot in *The Blues Brothers* (1980).

The scene has everything: national guardsmen by the truckload, cops on foot and horseback, fire trucks, tanks, antiaircraft guns, and helicopters all crammed on the plaza in hot pursuit of Blues Brothers Jake (John Belushi) and Elwood (Dan Aykroyd). Shot over Labor Day weekend in 1979, the scene used more than 500 extras and cost $3.5 million to film. Breakable plate glass was installed in the building, allowing Belushi and Aykroyd (or, more properly, a stunt driver) to blast the Bluesmobile through a window on the Washington Street side of the building, down corridors, and past a bank of elevators, and then to make a quick exit via another obliterated window on the Randolph Street side.

Calder's *Flamingo* at the Federal Plaza
Dearborn and Adams Streets

The Federal Plaza is surrounded by the Dirksen, Kluczynski, and Metcalfe Federal Buildings, with the United States Post Office–Loop Station off to one side. While these glass-and-steel towers present an imposing visual picture, what really captures the eye is the abstract sculpture that anchors the plaza, Alexander Calder's 53-foot-tall *Flamingo*.

It is in the shadows of the *Flamingo* that Adam Baldwin and Chris Makepeace have a celebratory ride on Baldwin's motorbike in *My Bodyguard* (1980). The joy felt by these two awkward teens is a wonderfully exuberant moment to behold. Baldwin and Makepeace practically radiate energy from the screen.

Ferris Bueller's Day Off (1986) also uses it as a backdrop in the scene where Ferris jumps a German Day Parade float to sing "Danke Schoen" to an adoring crowd (although hopping a parade float in the "real" Chicago would probably result in a hospital stay).

On a less poetic note, Debra Winger's FBI office headquarters in *Betrayed* (1988) are located in the Dirksen Building, and Larry the Cable Guy's joyous celebration of redneck ineptitude, *Witless Protection* (2008), also makes use of the plaza.

The Rookery

209 S. LaSalle Street

Without a doubt, this is one of downtown's most beautiful buildings. Built in 1885 by Daniel Burnham and John Wellborn Root, with interior work done by Frank Lloyd Wright in 1907

Alexander Calder's 1973 stabile sculpture *Flamingo* is located in Federal Plaza in front of the Kluczynski Federal Building and Loop Station Post Office. *(Photo by Kate Corcoran)*

and others through the years, the Rookery is glimmering with historical beauty. The building is 11 stories tall, with a dark red facade and elegant window designs framed by stone columns. A stone arch serves as the main entrance on LaSalle Street. If you look along the granite columns on either side of this entrance, you'll notice a pair of birds carved into the stone. These are rooks, a European relation to the American crow, from which the building gets its name.

The arched entrance on LaSalle Street stands in for Chicago Police headquarters in the big-screen version of *The Untouchables* (1987). Scenes from *Folks!* (1992), a laughless Tom Selleck comedy, were shot here, as were a few moments of *Kissing a Fool* (1998), starring David Schwimmer. The fatuous Mel Gibson comedy vehicle *What Women Want* (2000) used the exterior of the Rookery as his fictional office, but the interior was shot in a Canadian soundstage and resembles a Frank Lloyd Wright–influenced Williams-Sonoma store more than the Rookery's luscious interior.

Perhaps Hollywood's most careful use of the building was in *Home Alone 2: Lost in New York* (1992). The Rookery's exterior served as the entrance for Duncan's Toy Chest, a faux New York emporium. The film was shot during the final stages of the Rookery's restoration, with a scene calling for a large three-dimensional sign to be attached to the building. Not wanting to deface the intensive work that had gone into refurbishing the building, a special sign was created that would stay up yet not be anchored to the Rookery's stone exteriors.

Duncan's Toy Chest is another case of one on-screen place using two real-life sets. When actors passed through the Rookery doors, they found themselves, through the magic of editing, transported to the Uptown Theatre on North Broadway near Lawrence Avenue. The beautiful lobby of this former Balaban and Katz palace was the toy store's interior.

Chicago Board of Trade / LaSalle Street Canyon

141 W. Jackson Boulevard

At the corner of Jackson Boulevard and LaSalle Street stands the mighty Chicago Board of Trade. Designed by the architectural firm of Holabird and Root, the building was opened in 1930 as the center for commodities trading in the Midwest. A classic example of the art deco style, a 36-story tower juts out from the Board of Trade's nine-story base. The building is finished in limestone and capped by a pyramid-shaped roof. Looking out on LaSalle Street from the rooftop is a 31-foot-tall statue of Ceres, the Roman goddess of grain and harvest. Along the building's northern face are carvings of a Native American and a Mesopotamian, representing the

LEFT: The Chicago Board of Trade (1930) is one of the best examples of art deco architecture in the city and dramatically completes the LaSalle Street Canyon. *(Photo by Kate Corcoran)*

RIGHT: LaSalle Street Canyon, shown here from the north side of the LaSalle Street Bridge. A similar scene appears in *Road to Perdition* (2002) as Michael Sullivan and Michael Jr. arrive in Chicago. *(Photo by Kate Corcoran)*

corn and wheat that were the original stocks in trade here. Between the two reliefs are a clock and an eagle carved into the limestone.

South LaSalle Street is nicknamed "the Canyon," and for good reason. With tall buildings lining either side of the street and the looming Chicago Board of Trade serving as an anchor, this corridor is the very essence of an urban canyon. It's a visually striking conglomeration of Chicago architecture, stretching between Adams Street and Jackson Boulevard. Crawling with traders, bankers, and businesspeople during the day, the LaSalle Street Canyon has become a playground for filmmakers in recent decades. South LaSalle has been seen in *The Untouchables* (1987), *Mad Dog and Glory* (1993), *Folks!* (1992), and *Limit Up* (1989), a lame comedy set among Board of Trade employees.

In those films, South LaSalle Street is clearly identified as a Chicago location. Yet the two most interesting uses of the Canyon on-screen transformed these environs from the Windy City to the Big Apple. *Hoodlum* (1997) features Laurence Fishburne as Ellsworth "Bumpy" Johnson, a real-life figure from the New York gang wars of the 1920s and 1930s. He'd previously played the character as a supporting part in Francis Ford Coppola's drama *The Cotton Club* (1984), but in *Hoodlum*, directed by Bill Duke, this Harlem-based gangster is at the center of action.

One of *Hoodlum*'s biggest set pieces is a shootout between Johnson and thugs sent by his Manhattan rival Dutch Schultz (Tim Roth) outside the New York City Opera House. Director Duke chose the LaSalle Street Canyon for this sequence, exploiting the block's period look. The Board of Trade became the Opera House, old-fashioned streetlights and WPA banners were affixed to light poles, and for one brief, bloody moment, LaSalle was transported back in time and location.

Though problems inevitably hit film sets, the *Hoodlum* production crew faced a rather unusal concern when it came to filming this sequence. The LaSalle Street shootout, which included gunfire and explosions, was scheduled for production the same week as the 1996 Democratic National Convention, which was being held a few miles west at the United Center. In anticipation of the event, Secret Service agents had scoped out the city from top to bottom to make sure nothing could possibly endanger President Clinton or any of the other top government and political figures visiting the city during convention week. When word came that *Hoodlum* was planning to film a violent, albeit fictional, confrontation, the Secret Service quickly nixed the idea. Negotiations between the production and officials ensued and included Secret Service interviews with many of the movie team's principal behind-the-scenes people. Finally, a compromise was reached, fake bullets and blood were allowed to fly through the air, and the Democrats renominated Bill Clinton without a hitch.

Speaking of presidential threats, *Death of a President* (2006), a controversial faux-documentary that features a fictional assassination of George W. Bush, staged an elaborate antiwar protest on LaSalle Street that included over 400 extras and culminated in the "presidential motorcade" being surrounded by furious demonstrators (one of whom almost is able to jump on the "president's" limo). As luck would have it, the real Secret Service (which was guarding ex-president Clinton during an appearance at McCormick Place), got wind that there was another motorcade in the city and began inquiring as to the identity of the dignitary in question (worried someone was in town they weren't aware of) until being informed that it was for a movie that was filming. This inquiry caused a bit of consternation to those involved in the production, as they were trying to keep the incendiary nature of the plot confidential, particularly from the Secret Service.

U.S. Marshals (1998), a sequel of sorts to the made-in-Chicago thriller *The Fugitive* (1993), takes place in a variety of locations, including downstate Illinois, Chicago, and New York. One key sequence involves a briefcase being handed off between two shadowy contacts in the midst of a crowded Manhattan lunch crowd. Through creative set decoration and quick editing, the LaSalle Street Canyon was transformed into its Lower Manhattan counterpart, Wall Street. Chicago street signs were camouflaged, New York newspaper boxes were placed on the sidewalk, and a horde of extras was utilized to recreate the madness of Wall Street at lunchtime. The result is a realistic-looking New York location, filmed entirely in Chicago.

The most memorable and bombastic uses of the LaSalle Street Canyon are in Christopher Nolan's first two celebrated reinterpretations of the Batman myth, *Batman Begins* (2005) and *The Dark Knight* (2008). *The Dark Knight* features a game of chicken in the middle of LaSalle Street between Christian Bale's Batman piloting the Batpod and the late Heath Ledger as the Joker at the wheel of a semitruck, resulting in the 18-wheeler doing a cartwheel in the middle of the street. *Batman Begins* climaxes with an elevated train running down the middle of LaSalle (courtesy of production designer Nathan Crowley's ingenious model-making abilities) being blown up before it can crash into the

"Wayne Industries Building" (a.k.a. the Board of Trade).

Sears Tower (now Willis Tower)

233 S. Wacker Drive

Bounded by Wacker Drive, Franklin and Adams Streets, and Jackson Boulevard, the Sears Tower was completed in 1973. Designed by the firm of Skidmore, Owings & Merrill, the building has 110 stories, is 1,453 feet tall, and has over 104 elevators. It was originally built as the headquarters for Sears, Roebuck, and Company; however, 20 years later Sears relocated its corporate offices to Hoffman Estates, Illinois. In 2009, insurance broker Willis Group Holdings leased a portion of the building and obtained the naming rights.

As one of the Windy City's iconic buildings, the Sears Tower has been used in countless films to establish that "we're in Chicago." It's another case of Hollywood taking a local landmark and turning it into a very tall visual cliché, as in *The Package* (1989) and *Michael* (1996).

Thankfully, the Chicago-based John Hughes understood the Sears Tower's appeal to Chicagoans and highlighted the spectacular view from its Skydeck in *Ferris Bueller's Day Off* (1986). It's here where Ferris (Matthew Broderick), his girlfriend Sloane (Mia Sara), and their neurotic pal Cameron (Alan Ruck) lean against the windows and soak up all Chicago has to offer.

TOP: The magnificent Sears/Willis Tower looms above the Chicago skyline. *(Photo by Kate Corcoran)*

BOTTOM: Twenty-eight acres of black aluminum panels and over 16,000 windows compose the massive exterior of the Sears/Willis Tower; 2.5 million cubic feet of concrete were used in its construction. *(Photo by Kate Corcoran)*

Probably the most dramatic use of the Sears Tower is scene in *The Dark Knight* (2008) when Batman stands looking over Gotham from the corner of the roof of one of the lower sections. Actor Christian Bale actually did that scene, held only by two wires connected to a harness and anchored in the roof. Location manager James McAllister recalls the fear of the crew: "He was in a harness that they put him in and he literally went right to the edge. If you can imagine the 90-degree angle that's on the corner of the building, he was standing right on that edge up off of the roof. Then the helicopter came in to film it. One of the best helicopter pilots in the business, Fred Hoskins, came in, and he was probably about 15 feet from Christian when they shot it. If you've ever been near a helicopter you know the force, and there he was however many stories in the air with this helicopter 15 feet away. It was incredible, and I really have to take my hat off to Christian for doing that. It was unnerving to even be out walking on the roof with all that wind, but to be right up on that cornice. And it was kind of a hazy night, so everybody thought we were going to have to do it again, because it was kind of soupy, but it ended up being a fantastic shot."

For ticket information on Skydeck Chicago, call (312) 875-9447 or visit www.theskydeck.com.

Chicago's still-magnificent Union Station waiting room, designed in 1917 by Graham, Burnham, and Co. *(Photo by Kate Corcoran)*

Union Station
210 S. Canal Street

Bordered by Jackson Boulevard and Adams, Canal, and Clinton Streets, Union Station was designed by famed Chicago architect Daniel Burnham and was completed after his death by Graham, Anderson, Probst, and White, in 1925. The name comes from the "union" of four major rail companies that converged on this important hub. Though rail use has declined with the rise of air traffic, Union Station is still a busy hive of activity. Commuter services and Amtrak passenger trains serve the thousands of passengers who pass through Union Station on a daily basis.

The centerpiece of this building is a gorgeous waiting room. The waiting room's wooden benches are surrounded by fluted columns, and overhead is an immense skylight. On either side of the waiting room you'll see two bird statues. One is a rooster, representing morning travel; the other is an owl, symbolizing the nighttime voyager.

Union Station's visual appeal was made for the movies. *Chain Reaction* (1996), *Code of Silence* (1985), *I Love Trouble* (1994), *Love Jones* (1997), *Midnight Run* (1988), *My Best Friend's Wedding* (1997), *The Package* (1989), *Prelude to a Kiss* (1992), *Red Heat* (1988), and *Vice Versa* (1988) all staged scenes here. *The Sting* (1973), set in 1930s-era Chicago, made effective use of the station's period look. The television shows *ER* and *Early Edition* also shot scenes here.

Yet one Union Station film stands above them all. With *The Untouchables* (1987), director Brian DePalma, actors Kevin Costner and Andy Garcia, and one teetering baby carriage staged what can either be called a brilliant homage or a glossy rip-off, depending on your view of film history.

The scene has Costner, as Eliot Ness, and Garcia, as a member of the fabled cop squad, facing off with some of Al Capone's henchmen on a Union Station staircase. Enter a mother innocently pushing her baby carriage. Amidst all the hullabaloo, the baby carriage breaks free from Mommy and begins a slow-motion roll down the stairs.

Sharp-eyed film buffs immediately recognized the source of this scene. In 1925, Russian director Sergei Eisenstein filmed *Battleship Potemkin*, a fictionalized account of a 1905 sailors' revolt. The most dramatic sequence involves a mob of Czarist soldiers attacking the people of Odessa on a public flight of steps. Amidst all the fireworks, a dying mother releases a baby carriage, sending her infant plummeting down the steps.

Unlike *Potemkin's* unlucky infant, *The Untouchables'* baby is rescued by Costner and company. A bit unrealistic? Well, of course, but this is still a fun set piece, combining flashy editing and camera work for a nicely choreographed sequence.

Union Station is where the title train of *Silver Streak* (1976) supposedly crashes in the slam-bang finish of a Los Angeles–to–Chicago run. In reality, the station's interior was recreated at an airplane hangar at Lockheed Aircraft in Los Angeles, and a train was sent barreling through the phony set.

Michael Mann's retelling of the John Dillinger story, *Public Enemies* (2009), which stars Johnny Depp as the famed bank robber, made extensive use of Union Station, even using the now-abandoned art deco–style Amtrak offices above the station as G-Man Melvin Purvis's Washington, DC, headquarters. They also shot a scene on one of the station's older platforms (which still has the old steam vents) for a dramatic sequence in which a group of Texas Rangers, whom Purvis (played by Christian Bale) enlists to help him in his battle against Dillinger, arrive at the station. Production designer Nathan Crowley insisted the studio bring in the largest still-working steam locomotive engine in the world for the shot, and "it just barely fit in Union Station." The gunmen alight from the train and march through the ornate lobby of the station "like the Cavalry arriving."

The Lakefront, Michigan Avenue, and Grant Park

Navy Pier
600 E. Grand Avenue

As an on-screen location, Navy Pier once ranked as Chicago's foremost seedy waterfront. Shoot-outs, drug deals, car chases, and murders have all been a part of this landmark site's movie history. Following its mid-1990s makeover, Navy Pier's cinematic representations have evolved from nightmare alley to dream-date location. And with its enormous IMAX theater, this is also one of the best places in town to watch movies as they were meant to be seen.

The pier was designed by Charles Sumner Frost in 1914. After two years of construction, Municipal Pier (as it was originally known) opened as a recreational spot for Chicagoans, complete with shopping, restaurants, and its dazzling Grand Ballroom. The city even extended streetcar lines for the convenience of pier visitors. During World War I, Municipal Pier was temporary home to numerous military recruits and Red Cross units. By the war's end, the pier's status as a tourist spot was reinstated. A theater was opened, restaurants flourished, and throughout the 1920s it was a thriving center for Chicago culture and entertainment.

Chicago's picturesque Navy Pier is the most visited tourist attraction in Illinois. It doubled as a ferry dock in the blockbuster action film *The Dark Knight* (2008). *(Photo by Michael Corcoran)*

Renamed Navy Pier in 1927 as a tribute to navy personnel who had served in the war, the pier also was used as a dock for freight and passenger boats. Though the stock market crash took its toll on attendance, Navy Pier remained open throughout the 1930s. By the end of the decade, however, fewer boats used this lakefront dock.

After the start of World War II, Navy Pier closed as a tourist site. It was leased to the United States Navy for training, which lasted through 1947. Two aircraft carriers were docked alongside the pier, and at one time a young navy pilot named George Herbert Walker Bush trained here.

Following the war, Navy Pier was used as a branch of the University of Illinois until Circle Campus was built in 1965. Some docking still went on, as well as occasional conventions and city festivals. For the most part, however, the pier was underused until its rehabilitation in the mid-1990s.

The empty pier, while a ghost of its former self, was a filmmakers' paradise. The empty Grand Ballroom could serve as just about anything, from warehouse to soundstage, and the lengthy pier run was ideal for a variety of situations. Couple that with the wonderful skyline view and access to the lake, and Hollywood just couldn't resist.

The cops and robbers films *Thief* (1981) and *Running Scared* (1986), *Raw Deal* (1986), *Cooley High* (1975), and even the offbeat romantic comedy *Touch and Go* (1986) all staged some of their chase sequences here. The low-budget comedy *Monkey Hustle* (1977) also used Navy Pier for a few nefarious dealings.

Director Brian DePalma brought a Cadillac, a load of guns, and several twisted government agents to Navy Pier for *The Fury* (1978). The idea was to have good guys and bad guys blast away at each other, with the $11,000 Caddie taking a climactic plunge into Lake Michigan. The scene, while full of action, wasn't a complicated shoot until an unforeseen glitch appeared in the form of two news crews, eager to capture this wild chase for their own viewers.

What resulted was a war of camera crews. When asked to leave, a team of German newspeople graciously picked up their equipment and split. However, a local television outlet stayed, determined to grab some action footage for broadcast. Splitting from the pier for a boat they had hired for the evening, the cameramen and reporter set up offshore, waiting for DePalma to shout "Action!" Instead, the producer, Frank Yablans, ordered his people to flash high-powered movie lights at the vessel in order to ruin any television camera footage. Eventually the police marine unit was called in, sending the boat and its passengers packing. Finally, after a delay of 45 minutes (which cost *The Fury* production some $2,250), the movie cameras rolled and the Cadillac was sent into the drink.

In *The Color of Money* (1986), director Martin Scorsese used Navy Pier for a different sort of shoot-out. The Grand Ballroom was transformed into an Atlantic City casino, where pool legend Eddie Felson (Paul Newman) faces his former protégé, table hustler Tom Cruise.

Meanwhile, Navy Pier was on the verge of rebirth. With the success of ChicagoFest in the late 1970s, the site was once more looked at as a viable cultural center. After some years of negotiation, the Illinois State Legislature authorized creation of the Metropolitan Pier and Exposition Authority. Under this consortium's leadership, Navy Pier underwent a $150 million redevelopment. When all was said and done, the pier was brighter than ever. Now boasting an auditorium, a Ferris wheel, and a walkway of shops and restaurants, Navy Pier became one of Chicago's hot spots. The days of seedy waterfront filming were gone.

Hollywood's car chases and shoot-outs were replaced by film crews looking for Chicago color. *Straight Talk* (1992), *I Love Trouble* (1994), and *Losing Isaiah* (1995) all shot scenes at the pier. The television people came, too, as *ER* and *Chicago Hope* took breaks from their California hospital sets for location work at Navy Pier. More recently, the front entrance of Navy Pier filled in as the exterior of the fancy North Side roller rink in the African American teen skate movie *Roll Bounce* (2005) and was used for a dramatic evacuation-via-ferryboat scene in Christopher Nolan's *The Dark Knight* (2008).

For more information about Navy Pier activities, call (800) 595-7437 or visit www.navypier.com. For tickets to the Navy Pier IMAX theater, call (312) 595-5629.

Lower Wacker Drive

Wacker Drive runs along the south bank of the Chicago River and provides a unique two-level street, which comes in handy for drivers trying to negotiate downtown traffic. Though David Letterman once told a Chicago audience that "Wacker" was really his college nickname, this drive was named after Charles H. Wacker a onetime president of the Chicago Plan Commission (CPC). The CPC was instrumental in developing Wacker Drive in the 1920s.

Be careful when you're on Lower Wacker. If we are to believe Hollywood, this underground drive is a haven for car chases. *Thief* (1981), *Primal Fear*

(1996), and *Red Heat* (1988) are just some of the films that have exploited Lower Wacker's twists and turns for some action-packed excitement.

In fact, the *Red Heat* chase sequence ultimately led to a change in regulations for filmmakers using Lower Wacker. Before shooting a chase sequence involving a CTA bus, production team members hosed down Lower Wacker so it would have a wet look on-screen. Wetting down a street is a popular practice for movies. Apparently the soaked pavement makes for a better street look, at least in the eyes of Hollywood. It's a case of artistic license and movie logic—city streets around the world never stay dry at night.

The lower deck of Wacker Drive along the Chicago River. The location of numerous car chases, Wacker Drive is the only street in Chicago with both north-south and east-west addresses as it curves along two sides of Chicago's Loop. *(Photo by Kate Corcoran)*

Unfortunately for the *Red Heat* crew, no one calculated how much oil and grit had accumulated over the years on Lower Wacker. When water hit the pavement, this dry gunk turned to slime, making for extremely dangerous driving conditions. During the first rehearsal of the film's chase sequence, the bus lost control on the slippery asphalt and went careening into a support column. To make matters worse, two minutes later a drunk driver picked the wrong time to head down Lower Wacker. The combination of a boozed-up motorist and street ooze were uncontrollable. The car smashed through a barricade and onto the film set. Though ultimately the chase sequence was filmed a few nights later, new rules were established forbidding filmmakers from ever again wetting down Lower Wacker.

Another terrifying Lower Wacker scene was in *Henry: Portrait of a Serial Killer* (1987). Tag-team killers Henry (Michael Rooker) and Otis (Tom Towles) pull over, pretending to have car trouble. When a Good Samaritan stops to help, Otis pulls out a gun and murders the ill-fated benefactor.

Both of Christopher Nolan's first two Batman films feature chase scenes on this subterranean thoroughfare, the more elaborate one in the mega-blockbuster *The Dark Knight*, which features some incredibly hair-raising stunts.

Wacker Drive is actually just one of a whole array of streets in Chicago that have a "lower" version. Lower Randolph, Michigan, Columbus, and numerous other streets, byways, and subterranean loading docks combine with pedways and tunnels to create a vast labyrinthine (and often frighteningly foreboding) "underground Chicago."

Oddly enough, the only film to really showcase the catacombs of the Windy City has been *Unconditional Love* (2002), a quirky, eclectic, and extremely entertaining film starring Oscar winner Kathy Bates and Rupert Everett. Shelved by its studio for several years, then released directly to the Starz Cable Network with virtually no mention, *Unconditional Love* is one of those gems that has fallen through the cracks of the capricious Hollywood distribution system. Bates stars as a frumpy Chicago housewife, Grace Beasley, who idolizes a cheesy love crooner, Victor Fox, played with manic glee by Jonathan Pryce. When her husband (played by Dan Aykroyd) leaves her just before her idol is murdered in the caverns below Chicago (coincidently right before a television appearance where Grace was to finally meet him in person), Grace is inspired to hop a flight to England to attend his funeral. In a bizarre turn of events (few things in this film aren't bizarre), she bonds with Victor's grieving gay lover, Dirk Simpson, played by Rupert Everett. Grace and Dirk return to Chicago to solve Victor's murder and bring his killer to justice, which leads them on an odyssey through the bowels of downtown Chicago in pursuit of the "Crossbow Killer" (Did I mention that Victor was killed by a serial killer?). *Citizen Kane* it ain't, but it's definitely unique and interesting, and often side-splittingly funny. And if all that isn't enough, Julie Andrews does a cameo that will forever change the way you look at her.

A Chicago landmark, the Carbon and Carbide Building (Hard Rock Hotel) presumably got its distinctive green and gold colors based on a gold-foil-covered champagne bottle. The building's rooftop serves as the location of the exciting opening of *Wanted* (2008). *(Photo by Kate Corcoran)*

Outer Drive East

400 E. Randolph Street

This 40-story high-rise, built in 1963, is well known for its ground-floor swimming pool, which is covered by a geodesic dome. Movies filmed at this unique poolside location include *Medium Cool* (1969), *Mickey One* (1965), and *Nothing in Common* (1986).

The Smurfit-Stone Building (now Crain Communications Building)

150 N. Michigan Avenue

With its giant, mirrored diamond top sloping across the Chicago skyline, this building certainly isn't for all architectural tastes. Designed by A. Epstein and Sons, this unusually designed building has been a part of Michigan Avenue's diverse scenery since the early 1980s.

Movie fans will instantly recognize the Smurfit-Stone Building for its climactic role in the slapstick comedy *Adventures in Babysitting* (1987). It is here that Elisabeth Shue's wild night comes to its over-the-top conclusion. Stick around after the closing credits—the film ends with a punch line atop this structure's sloping roof.

The distinctively sloped roof of the Smurfit-Stone (now Crain Communications) Building was designed to provide a lake view for the maximum amount of offices and to resemble a boat sail. *(Photo by Kate Corcoran)*

Chicago Cultural Center

78 E. Washington Street

The interior of the Chicago Cultural Center boasts the world's largest Tiffany dome, elegant mosaics, marble staircases, and a constantly changing series of art exhibits and concerts. The exterior resembles a palace, with tall columns, graceful arches, and sun-filled windows. Opened as the Chicago Public Library in 1897, the center has been a favorite site of Hollywood filmmakers. This visually rich location has doubled as an opera house, a government building, a courthouse, and much more.

The Tiffany Dome in Preston Bradley Hall, Chicago Cultural Center, formerly the Chicago Public Library. *(Photo by Kate Corcoran)*

For more than 70 years, the building served as Chicago's central library. By the mid-1970s, however, the building had become too small for such a purpose. The holdings were moved to a book warehouse on N. Michigan Avenue, and in 1991 the Harold Washington Library at State Street and Congress Parkway became their permanent home. As for the original library building, it was revamped as a performance and art space and dubbed the Chicago Cultural Center. Dance troupes, theater companies, lecturers, exhibiting artists, and many others provided a renewed energy to the stately architectural monument.

The moviemakers followed.

Code of Silence (1985) used the Cultural Center as an art gallery, where tough cop Chuck Norris follows a young woman to protect her from bloodthirsty mobsters. The building's Romanesque facade served as various New York City period buildings in *The Public Eye* (1992), *The Babe* (1992), the remake of *Miracle on 34th Street* (1994), and *Hoodlum* (1997). It's also been seen on the television programs *Early Edition* and *ER* and the British television film *March in Windy City* (1998), where it housed a political rally for a nefarious office-seeker.

It was also used as a community center in a climactic scene in *Barbershop 2: Back in Business* (2004), where Ice Cube's character makes an impassioned plea for his business to be spared from the developers who are gentrifying his neighborhood. However, its period look is best captured in Brian DePalma's gangster drama *The Untouchables* (1987), where Preston Bradley Hall and its gorgeous stairway double as an opera house.

If you want to retrace the steps of straight-jawed Eliot Ness (Kevin Costner) tracking down Capone henchman Frank Nitti (Billy Drago), head to the north staircase. Of course, you won't be able to get to the roof, where Nitti takes his fatal (and totally fictional) plunge, but head out to Randolph Street and you'll see where he goes splat.

Once you're outside, take a look at the steps and dramatic entrance. Now imagine the space as seen through whirling camera angles, mixed film stocks, and a decidedly edgy point of view. That's what Oliver Stone did when he shot the frenzied courthouse scene of *Natural Born Killers* (1994) at the Cultural Center's north entrance, filling Randolph Street with a mob of starstruck fans, tabloid reporters, cops, and one smug, sunglasses-festooned killer. As Woody Harrelson's psychopathic killer Mickey Knox declares to the camera, "You ain't seen nothing yet!"

Millennium Park
Michigan Avenue between Randolph and
     Monroe Streets

Frank Gehry's initial design for the Pritzker Pavilion was rejected because it "wasn't Gehry enough." He went back to the drawing board and incorporated more of his trademark flourishes and sweeping ornamentation into the structure. *(Photo by Kate Corcoran)*

The idea for what became Millennium Park was born in the mid-1990s in the unlikely setting of Mayor Richard M. Daley's dentist's office, which overlooked the northern end of Grant Park. Dismayed by the contrast of Chicago's beautiful "front yard" (as Grant Park is known) with what then was an ugly rail yard and collection of vacant lots between Monroe and Randolph streets, His Honor resolved to remove this blight by constructing a little park to honor the impending new millennium.

The original plan called for a modest park with a band shell at a cost of about $150 million. Those plans were rejected, however, and world-famous architect Frank Gehry was hired to design a new structure,

TOP: At 110 tons, Anish Kapoor's *Cloud Gate* sculpture (a.k.a. "the Bean") is in the only spot in Millennium Park it could be safely ensconced, near a load-bearing wall. Be sure to walk under it for the full effect. *(Photo by Kate Corcoran)*

BOTTOM: The ice rink at Millennium Park, the scene of a father/daughter bonding attempt gone horribly awry in *The Weather Man* (2005), is transformed into an outdoor cafe in the summer. *(Photo by Kate Corcoran)*

but he wasn't available until 2001. A snowball effect occurred during the delay, whereby the scope and expense of the new park were massively expanded. Millennium Park ended up costing $475 million ($270 million of which came from the city). Construction delays stretched into 2004, and the cries from the park's many critics grew deafening.

Those cries were all but silenced when Millennium Park was opened to the public in July 2004 and folks got to see all the wonders now ensconced on this 24.5-acre site. Anish Kapoor's 110-ton sculpture *Cloud Gate* became an instant sensation among Chicagoans, who dubbed it "the Bean." Jaume Plensa's brilliant postmodern take on gargoyles, Crown Fountain, is a water park and avant-garde art installation in one, with a pair of 50-foot-tall video towers alternating the visages of 1,000 ordinary Chicagoans on their screens (just watch out when they purse their lips!). The Lurie Gardens were a revelation, combining theatrical lighting with world-class landscape architecture and horticultural skills. And the long-awaited Gehry band shell, the Jay Pritzker Pavilion, is a stunning fusion of wondrous sculpture and perfect acoustics. Gehry also created the sensuously serpentine BP Pedestrian Bridge, the only bridge he has ever designed. The park became a worldwide destination for fans of art and architecture, bringing a level of recognition to Chicago not seen since the World's Columbian Exposition of 1893.

Since its opening, several feature films and TV programs have utilized Millennium Park's sumptuous vistas. In *The Break-Up* (2006), Vince Vaughn, who plays a tour guide, expounds in front of the park from atop a double-decker bus. (On a side note: his character is supposedly "the best tour guide in the city," but real Chicago tour guides who watch the film are either amused or frustrated by the fact that almost every word out of his mouth in the guiding scenes is either inaccurate, exaggerated, or just plain BS.)

The pilot episode of the late Patrick Swayze's 2009 cable series *The Beast* (his final project) has a fabulous swirling crane shot of the Pritzker Pavilion and surrounding buildings during a brief scene there, and the first season of *Prison Break* from 2005 to 2006 uses Crown Fountain as a backdrop for a meeting between two characters. The TV shows *Boss* and *Leverage* have also visited.

The picturesque ice rink that faces Michigan Avenue has been the most filmed portion of the park. *The Weather Man* (2005) utilized the rink for a lengthy scene in which Nicholas Cage's character has an attempted bonding session with his daughter that goes horribly awry at a company celebration. In *Nothing Like the Holidays* (2008), Vanessa Ferlito and an old flame share a tender moment while by the rink.

Shattered, a 2007 thriller starring Pierce Brosnan and Maria Bello, also used the park (for about three seconds), as have *The Lake House* (2006), *The Vow* (2012), the mind-bending sci-fi suspense thriller *Source Code* (2011), and the gratuitously brutal yuppie fear-fest *Derailed* (2005), with Jennifer Aniston and Clive Owen.

Jeff Garlin claims to be the first director to shoot in Millennium Park, but his indie comedy *I Want Someone to Eat Cheese With* (2006) sat on the shelf for almost two years before its release. "I knew the first time I went to Millennium Park that I was going to shoot that scene there. It was something I had to do; I love that place." Regardless of whether he was the first to shoot there, his delightfully dry comic offering definitely lingered in the park longer than most productions, with an extended scene where Garlin and comedy goddess Sarah Silverman share a heart-to-heart chat.

Millennium Station
151 E. Randolph Street (beneath Millennium Park)
Originally an Illinois Central Railroad terminal, the underground station now serves the Metra Electric and South Shore commuter lines. Its

smooth, black-floored hallways with gold stripes running through them were shown to great effect in *The Dark Knight* (2008) in a scene where actor Christian Bale (actually stunt driver Jean-Pierre Goy) pilots the Batpod through the station.

The Art Institute of Chicago
Michigan Avenue and Adams Street

In *Ferris Bueller's Day Off* (1986), Matthew Broderick leads girlfriend Mia Sara and hypochondriac pal Alan Ruck on a glorious tour of the Art Institute. Director John Hughes juxtaposes his cast with museum artwork, creating what amounts to a visual poem that sticks out amidst the rest of the film's controlled chaos. Best moments? A quiet kiss shared between Broderick and Sara, framed by the stained glass windows of Marc Chagall, and a stare-off between Ruck and Georges Seurat's *A Sunday on La Grande Jatte*, with Ruck becoming at one with the pointillist masterpiece. (This painting, the most popular attraction at the Art Institute, also inspired the Stephen Sondheim musical *Sunday in the Park with George*.)

Founded in 1879 as the Academy of the Fine Arts, the museum was formally renamed the Art Institute of Chicago in 1882. Surprisingly, only one other feature film has taken advantage of the magnificent settings within the museum—the little-seen independent film *Watch It* (1993).

For more information on the Art Institute, call (312) 443-3600.

Chicago Symphony Center (formerly Orchestra Hall)
220 S. Michigan Avenue

If you want to catch one of the great orchestras of the world, head to S. Michigan Avenue and the Chicago Symphony Center (formerly the Orchestra Hall Building). This magnificent concert hall, designed by D. H. Burnham and Company, first opened its doors in 1905. It is home to the Chicago Symphony Orchestra, considered one of the finest classical ensembles in the world.

On-screen, the Symphony Center is one of the city's most neglected sites. Some films shot along Michigan Avenue provide a glimpse of the building and its entranceway, which is carved with the names of Bach, Mozart, Beethoven, and other composers. The only picture in recent memory to go through the doors and shoot inside is *Home Alone 2: Lost in New York* (1992). Even then, Orchestra Hall didn't get to play itself—it doubled for New York's Carnegie Hall!

For more information on Chicago Symphony Center and the Chicago Symphony Orchestra, visit their website at www.cso.org.

Fine Arts Building
410 S. Michigan Avenue
Fine Arts Theater
418 S. Michigan Avenue

Designed by S. S. Beman, the same architect responsible for the community of Pullman on the far South Side, the Studebaker Building was built in 1884 as a carriage factory and showroom. You can still see the name "Studebaker" etched in the facade above the sign for the famed Artist's Snack Shop. When the Studebaker Company left town and started making those bloody motorcars (a fad that will soon blow over), the new owner had Beman add three stories and converted the building into studios, galleries, and offices for artists, writers, and others, renaming it the Fine Arts Building. Supposedly L. Frank Baum wrote some of his *Wizard of Oz* books in an office he rented here; at the time he was also on the payroll as a scenarist for Selig Polyscope, which filmed the earliest screen versions of Baum's Oz stories (see page 10). Another important

The Fine Arts Building was originally built for the Studebaker Company to assemble and showcase their wagons and carriages. Converted in 1898 into studios and theaters, this exterior detail still shows a remnant of that remodeling. *(Photo by Kate Corcoran)*

tenant was the Little Theatre, a dramatic group that was a harbinger of Chicago's modern off-Loop theater community, as well as *Poetry* magazine, which had offices there for several years.

The Fine Arts Building later housed a theater named after the building's original owners. For many years, the Studebaker Theatre was a venue for live performances, before switching over to movies. The theater fell into disuse in the 1960s and for a time served as an outlet for pornographic films. In 1981, this changed when the auditoriums were overhauled and the theater was rechristened the Fine Arts Theater.

The Fine Arts Theater then had a 20-year run as an art film theater, but competition from the Siskel Film Center and other new art film venues eventually took its toll, and the theater closed in 2003. A glimmer of hope remains for this august institution, however, as the new owners have vowed to revive it (perhaps returning it to its original role as a live theater).

The Auditorium Theatre
50 E. Congress Parkway
Roosevelt University
430 S. Michigan Avenue
Officially opened by President Benjamin Harrison on December 9, 1889, the Auditorium Building is a historic work of Chicago architecture designed by the team of Dankmar Adler and Louis Sullivan. At the time of its construction, the Auditorium was Chicago's tallest building and was one of the first multipurpose constructions to be wired for electrical lighting. Theatergoers also had the option of staying a while—the top floors housed hotel rooms and a restaurant.

Following the stock market crash of 1929, the Auditorium fell into disuse and disrepair, finally closing its doors in 1941. During World War II, soldiers in transit were housed at the Auditorium, and the stage, designed for perfect acoustics by Adler, was turned into a GI bowling alley! Once the war ended, the building was acquired by the newly founded Roosevelt University. Though much of Adler and Sullivan's work was maintained throughout the entire building, the actual theater remained shut. Restoration of the Auditorium proved too costly for the fledgling educational facility.

In 1960, however, a consortium was formed to bring the Auditorium Theatre back to its former glory. Three million dollars and seven years later, the theater doors were reopened as a performance venue. Going to the Auditorium today is like stepping, ever briefly, back in time. Sullivan's refurbished sweeping staircases and gorgeous mosaics are still awe-inspiring, recalling a grand era when this theater was Chicago's cultural mecca.

With its consummate 19th-century design, the Auditorium has done a fine job for filmmakers who need a period look. *Gaily, Gaily* (1969), Norman Jewison's cliché-ridden adaptation of the memoirs of Chicago journalist Ben Hecht, features a few scenes shot in the upper balconies.

TOP LEFT: Exterior of the Auditorium Building from the southeast, July 1963. *(Cervin Robinson, photographer, Library of Congress, Prints and Photographs Division, Historic American Buildings Survey, HABS ILL, 16-CHIG, 39-1)*

BOTTOM LEFT: The lush Sullivan-designed staircase and lobby of Roosevelt University served as the Lexington Hotel, home to Al Capone (Robert DeNiro) in the big-screen version of *The Untouchables* (1987). *(Photo by Kate Corcoran)*

RIGHT: Auditorium Hotel office, looking toward the reading room, showing columns, circa 1890. *(J. W. Taylor, photographer, Library of Congress, Prints and Photographs Division, Historic American Buildings Survey, HABS ILL, 16-CHIG, 39-96)*

The Joan Jett and Michael J. Fox rock musical *Light of Day* (1987) includes some footage shot here, as do the Joe Mantegna comedy *Baby's Day Out* (1994) and the syndicated television remake of *The Untouchables* (1993–1994). Around the corner on Michigan Avenue, be sure to stop at Roosevelt University. The school's magnificent lobby and lush Sullivan staircase double for the Lexington Hotel, home to gangster king Al Capone, in the big-screen version of *The Untouchables* (1987).

If you'd like to take a tour of the Auditorium Building, call (312) 922-2110.

Columbia College

Main Building, 600 S. Michigan Avenue
Film and Video Department, 1415 S. Wabash Avenue
Dance Center, 1306 S. Michigan Avenue
Ludington Building, 1104 S. Wabash Avenue
Music School, 1014 S. Michigan Avenue
Getz Theater, 72 E. 11th Street
Brunswick Building, 623 S. Wabash Avenue
Torco Building, 624 S. Michigan Avenue

Founded in 1890 as the Columbia School of Oratory, Columbia College has been around Chicago even longer than the movies. Originally begun as a school for women's speech studies, today Columbia offers a multi-faceted arts curriculum, including undergraduate and graduate programs in fiction writing, dance, theater, graphic design, advertising, public relations, photography, and journalism. What's more, with almost 200 specialized undergraduate and graduate courses offered by its Department of Film and Video, Columbia College ranks as the world's largest film school.

The film schools at New York University, UCLA, and USC are higher profile, but Columbia College alumni have developed a solid reputation in Hollywood. Janusz Kaminski, who won an Oscar for his cinematography on Steven Spielberg's *Schindler's List* (1993), graduated from Columbia. So did George Tillman Jr. and Bob Teitel, the writer/director and producer behind *Soul Food* (1997) and several other hit films. Another Columbia grad, Theodore Witcher, hit it big with *Love Jones* (1997). Declan Quinn (actor Aidan's brother, by the way) did the dreamlike cinematography for

FACING PAGE: Some of the Columbia College buildings of the South Loop Campus. In 2004, Columbia received a $150,000 Campus Heritage Grant from the J. Paul Getty Foundation to develop a Campus Preservation Plan and Historic Building Restoration Guidelines for nine of its buildings in the South Loop area. *(Photos by Kate Corcoran)*

TOP LEFT: Detail of the 1014 S. Michigan cornice.

TOP RIGHT: 1104 S. Wabash entrance (Ludington Building).

MIDDLE LEFT: 600 S. Michigan (Alexandroff Campus Center, former the headquarters of International Harvester).

MIDDLE RIGHT: 623 S. Wabash (originally designed by Solon S. Beman, architect of Pullman, for the Studebaker Brothers Carriage Company).

BOTTOM: Detail of entrance, 72 E. 11th Street (Getz Theater, formerly the Chicago Women's Club).

the critically acclaimed *Leaving Las Vegas* (1996). Peter Teschner edited *Doctor Doolittle* (1998), *Howard Stern's Private Parts* (1997), the HBO film *The Late Shift* (1996), and *The Brady Bunch Movie* (1995), all of which were directed by another former Chicagoan, Betty Thomas. Columbia grads Carl Seaton and Kenny Young made the amusing independent comedy *One Week* (2000). John McNaughton, director of *Henry: Portrait of a Serial Killer* (1987) took classes here too. And these are just some of the better-known Columbia students.

The Columbia faculty includes many film professionals with significant professional credits in directing, cinematography, editing, producing, sound, and other areas of specialization. International filmmakers often come in for a semester or two, providing cinematic perspectives of different cultures. Such well-known figures as Spike Lee and Michael Apted have given guest lectures, and successful alumni periodically return to give current students an added incentive. (Interestingly enough, when the film school was in its infancy, Herschell Gordon Lewis taught movie production classes at Columbia.)

Though the Film and Video Department has produced a healthy share of working professionals, Columbia graduates from other disciplines have also made their mark in the film and television industry. Most notable are television actors Andy Dick and Isabella Hofmann, as well as Conan O'Brien sidekick Andy Richter.

For more information about Columbia College, check out the school's website at www.colum.edu.

Blackstone Hotel
636 S. Michigan Avenue

Built in 1909, the Blackstone Hotel was designed by Benjamin Marshall and named after Timothy Blackstone, a Chicago railroad magnate whose mansion once stood at this site. The hotel is 22 stories tall with a three-story limestone base.

The Blackstone has particular historical significance in the annals of American politics. In 1920, when the Republican Convention whooped it up in Chicago, top honchos locked themselves in suite 804–805, lit their cigars, and debated over who would be their party's next presidential nominee. When the team finally emerged, Warren G. Harding was their anointed candidate, and the "smoke-filled room" became part of the American vernacular.

There is also some notoriety to the Blackstone. Many years ago, there was a murder in a room that today is permanently closed to guests. Rumor has it this killing was a gangland hit. Apparently the victim wasn't so eager to shed his mortal coil and stuck around to haunt the joint. Strange things supposedly happened to anyone who stayed in the room. In fact, New York mob boss Lucky Luciano refused to stay at the Blackstone whenever he was in town because of this specter.

When the film *Hoodlum* (1997), which featured Luciano as a major character, was looking for 1930s period locations, a location scout checked out possibilities at the Blackstone. He asked to take pictures of this room and hotel officials reluctantly allowed him. The scout, however, was warned that his photographs of this room, probably wouldn't turn out. When the pictures were finally developed, a strange white blur appeared in every image.

TOP: The Blackstone Hotel, with its distinctively shaped green roof, has recently been renovated and returned to a world-class hostelry. *(Photo by Kate Corcoran)*

BOTTOM: The recently remodeled "smoke-filled room" at the Blackstone Hotel. *(Photo by Kate Corcoran)*

The tourist theater crowd aren't the only out-of-towners who like the Blackstone. Hollywood filmmakers have been using this classic old hotel for quite some time. Andrew Davis, a hometown boy made good, came here for *Above the Law* (1988) and *The Package* (1989). *Only the Lonely* (1991), *Rent-a-Cop* (1988), *The Babe* (1992), and *My Best Friend's Wedding* (1997) also used the Blackstone, as did the television series *Early Edition*.

The hotel's elegant Crystal Ballroom was used for some scenes in the offbeat satire *The Hudsucker Proxy* (1994). The same ballroom was the site of the exuberant dance scene in *Love Jones* (1997). This charming romantic tale marked the directorial debut of Theodore Witcher, a graduate of Columbia College, which is just down the street.

The Blackstone also stood in for an Atlantic City hotel for Martin Scorsese's *The Color of Money* (1986). It's here where the cute but dumb pool hustler played by Tom Cruise checks in while waiting for his chance to play in a major national tournament.

The Blackstone fell prey to massive neglect after being purchased by the Maharishi Mahesh Yogi in the 1980s (the Maharishi's aversion to alcohol also drove the venerated Jazz Showcase to move out) and was closed down in 2000 after a failed inspection. A failed plan to convert the building into luxury condos left it empty until 2005, when the Blackstone underwent a $128 million restoration and reopened as a Renaissance Hotel (Marriott's boutique chain of hotels). For more information or reservations at the Blackstone Hotel, call (312) 447-0955.

The Chicago Hilton and Towers was originally the Stevens Hotel, the largest hotel in the world when it was built in 1927. The hotel stood in for the Lexington Hotel (Capone headquarters) in *Road to Perdition* (2002) and New York's Downtown Athletic Club in *The Express* (2008). *(Photo by Kate Corcoran)*

Chicago Hilton and Towers
720 S. Michigan Avenue

Designed by the firm of Holabird and Roche for hotelier James W. Stevens, this Chicago landmark was once the largest hotel in the world. When it opened its 3,000 guest rooms in 1927, the Stevens Hotel (as it was first named) boasted such amenities as an 18-hole rooftop golf course complete with real grass, a private library with more than 25,000 books, a five-lane bowling alley, an indoor ice rink, a 27-seat barber shop, and a 1,200-seat theater featuring the latest in "talking picture equipment."

In 1942, as part of the war effort, the Stevens was purchased by the United States Army for a mere $5 million, a real bargain considering that construction alone cost $30 million. By 1945, the hotel had changed hands again and took on the name of its new owner, Conrad Hilton. Significant renovations reduced guest rooms to 2,200 and later to 1,543, but the hotel lost none of its glamour. Over the years, the Hilton added a pair of Imperial Suites, a fully equipped athletic room, an International Ballroom, and five restaurants. In 1985, at a cost of $185 million, the hotel was completely renovated for modern standards and rechristened the Chicago Hilton and Towers.

The Hilton and Towers was featured in the opening scene of *Primal Fear* (1996), in which Richard Gere makes his entrance at a Catholic Charities event. It doubled as New York's Plaza in *Home Alone 2: Lost in New York* (1992), providing a home away from home for Macaulay Culkin. Julia Roberts shared a claustrophobic moment in Hilton elevators with Cameron Diaz in *My Best Friend's Wedding* (1997). The hotel has also been featured in the syndicated television remake of *The Untouchables* (1993–1994), *The Fugitive's* sequel *U.S. Marshals* (1998), and *Little Fockers* (2010).

Director Andrew Davis first used the Chicago Hilton and Towers in *The Package* (1989). Shooting in the midst of a brutally cold Chicago winter, Davis staged an outdoor rally across the street on the edge of Grant Park, where protesters decried a visiting Soviet premier. This scene was shot on one of the coldest days of the year, with a biting wind sweeping off the lake.

The Package also featured the hotel's Grand Ballroom as the site of a presidential dinner. A magnificent 12,640-square-foot space, the ballroom is trimmed with 22-karat gold leafing, original frescoes, and crystal chandeliers.

Davis revisited the Grand Ballroom in *The Fugitive* (1993). It is here where wrongly convicted Dr. Richard Kimble (Harrison Ford) bursts in on shocked conventioneers and untangles Dr. Charles Nichols's (Jeroen Krabbe) twisted trail of corporate corruption and murder. The hotel then transforms into an action-packed labyrinth as Ford, Krabbe, and lawman Samuel Gerard (Tommy Lee Jones) dovetail into a thrilling chase through the Hilton and Towers promenade roof, elevator shaft, and laundry room.

While there's some deliberate confusion amidst the sheets, steam, and flying metal I-beams of the climactic laundry room sequence, the crates labeled "Palmer House" shouldn't throw sharp-eyed viewers. No, the sequence wasn't shot at different hotels and then edited together. Rather, the elaborate Chicago Hilton and Towers laundry takes up three stories of the hotel, making it one of the largest industrial laundries in the country. Not only does this facility handle the many sheets slept on by Hilton and Towers guests, but they also take in wash from the nearby Palmer House Hilton at State and Monroe.

To book a room, make dinner reservations, or inquire about banquet facilities at the Chicago Hilton and Towers, call (312) 922-4400.

Grant Park
Michigan Avenue between Randolph Street and Roosevelt Road

Stretching roughly from Randolph Street on the north to Roosevelt Road on the south and bordered by Michigan Avenue and the lake, Grant Park is another of those great places that visually declares "Chicago and nowhere else" on screen. With its wide assortment of summer music programs at the Petrillo Music Shell (Columbus Drive and Jackson Boulevard), the annual Taste of Chicago food fest in July, and acres of park space, Grant Park provides filmmakers with a rich diversity of settings. To the west, Chicago's downtown buildings majestically rise, and the panoramic view at sunset can't be beat.

For a historical viewpoint, check out Haskell Wexler's *Medium Cool*. Shot documentary-style in the midst of the upheaval surrounding the 1968 Democratic National Convention, *Medium Cool* accurately portrays the madness of the time as a pivotal scene occurs during the actual riots, when members of the Chicago Police Department brutally confront Vietnam War protesters.

Joe Mantegna, Joe Pantoliano, and Brian Haley tromp through the park in their hapless kidnapping efforts in *Baby's Day Out* (1994), while Demi Moore and Rob Lowe pitch woo and softballs here in *About Last Night* . . . (1986). The latter film, a romantic comedy based on David Mamet's acerbic play *Sexual Perversity in Chicago*, was originally scheduled for a summer production. "The play ends with Jim Belushi's character describing girls on the beach," says coscreenwriter Denise DeClue. "By the time we were shooting it was fall and we couldn't do beach. So we decided to do softball in Grant Park. The production company had to put leaves on the trees because all the real leaves had already fallen."

The Petrillo Music Shell, the center of Chicago's slew of free summertime music festivals, was the site of an explosion-filled declaration of personal independence by everyone's favorite 12-stepper, Stuart Smalley

(Al Franken), in *Stuart Saves His Family* (1995). The Robert Altman–directed film *The Company* (2003), which features the Joffrey Ballet, used it for a pivotal performance scene, and the band shell can also be seen in the slight yuppie coming-of-age picture *Windy City* (1984).

Studs Terkel on *Medium Cool*

In 2008, Chicago lost one of its greatest cultural icons: celebrated author, interviewer, storyteller, actor, activist, and all-around wonderful human being Studs Terkel. Terkel was interviewed for the first edition of *Hollywood on Lake Michigan*, and he talked about the filming of *Medium Cool* (1969).

During the filming of *Medium Cool*, director and native Chicagoan Haskell Wexler turned to Terkel for advice on Chicago neighborhoods. "I knew Haskell from when he was going to Francis Parker High School," Terkel recalled. "He'd been away for a while, and he wanted certain things [in the movie]. I showed him different things here and there, certain people that he met. I was sort of his cicerone, you might say; I was his guide around town, but Haskell's so good he would have done it without me." Regardless, Wexler expressed his gratitude by giving Terkel screen credit as "Our Man in Chicago."

Medium Cool is a landmark film, shot in the midst of the turmoil surrounding the 1968 Democratic National Convention. The scanty plot follows television cameraman Robert Forster (later seen in 1997's *Jackie Brown*) and his soundman Peter Bonerz (who later became familiar to audiences as "Jerry the dentist" on the Chicago-based television sitcom *The Bob Newhart Show*) as they examine the social chaos of the times. In the process, Forster meets Verna Bloom's character, an immigrant from Appalachia now living in an Uptown apartment with her 13-year-old son.

What gives the film its sense of immediacy is the documentary-style shooting and incorporation of footage from inside the International Amphitheatre, where the Democratic Convention was held. Wexler heightened the realism by actually shooting scenes in the middle of the Grant Park riots. Bloom wore a bright yellow dress during filming, which was a stark contrast to the dark colors worn by the Daley cops as they squared off against the Yippies and their followers.

"Nelson Algren said that never has he seen such a scene with the fusion of reality and fantasy together," said Terkel. "The yellow dress, the mother running through [the riots], as an actress, an actress running through a scene in which an actual scene is occurring at that moment. "It wasn't a documentary in that sense. This is an actress playing a role in a plot, such that it is, with an actual moment and the cops beating the crap out [of people] and the actress is seen in it running through, which is a remarkable moment, I think. And there's the moment when Jonathan Hayes, the associate producer, shouts, 'Look out Haskell, it's real!' You have a crazy combination of Haskell doing a documentary at the same time he wants a story line. I've never seen anything quite like it before.

"I find it tremendously exciting. Haskell himself . . . he is unique. He's a marvelous cinematographer, he's a committed man, of course, but that isn't it, either. He's a certain kind of revolutionary, in the good sense—revolutionary in technique. He'd done something no one quite did before."

Buckingham Fountain

Congress Parkway and Lake Shore Drive

Buckingham Fountain, located on the eastern edge of Grant Park, is one of the city's splendors. Modeled after the Latona Fountain at Ver-

Buckingham Fountain, which opened in 1927, recently benefited from a major restoration. *(Photo by Kate Corcoran)*

sailles, this memorial display of shooting water and colored lights was dedicated on August 26, 1927, by Chicago socialite Kate Buckingham in honor of her late brother Clarence. The basin holds 1.5 million gallons of water, and 133 jets can blast up to 14,000 gallons per minute through the fountain.

Nia Long and Larenz Tate shared a sweet moment at Buckingham Fountain in the must-see romantic comedy *Love Jones* (1997). Shot on a fog-shrouded night, the fountain provides an ethereal backdrop as the two lovers nuzzle in the mist. It's one of the most romantic scenes in any Chicago movie, from perhaps the best romantic comedy ever filmed here.

In another fine African American indie film, Tyler Perry's *Meet The Browns* (2008), Angela Bassett and Rick Fox cavort around the fountain. Just make sure you are getting the *Meet the Browns* that is a feature film, not the video of Perry's almost unwatchable stage musical of the same name (recorded at a theater in Cleveland), which actually features some of the same actors and a similar plot.

For a less idealized view, consider the popular Fox television sitcom *Married . . . with Children*. The opening credits of this obnoxiously funny Chicago-based series begin with the Buckingham Fountain shooting water high in the air to the sounds of Frank Sinatra's hit "Love and Marriage." The weekly tales of Al and Peg Bundy and their two children, Bud and Kelly, brutally savaged sitcom-family stereotypes and was a surprise hit that lasted for 10 seasons, from 1987 to 1996. *Married . . . with Children* wasn't just popular with Americans; foreign viewers, particularly German audiences, were enthralled by the show. In 1994, when World Cup soccer came to Chicago, city tourist officials quickly learned to steer TV-mad European visitors to Congress Parkway and Lake Shore Drive, where they could make a pilgrimage to what is known overseas as "Bundy Fountain."

Buckingham Fountain runs from 8:00 AM to 11:00 PM daily, with a 20-minute water display on the hour and light and music shows after dusk, typically from May to mid-October, depending on weather. Times are subject to change when large events take place in or around Grant Park.

Native Son (1951 and 1986)

Richard Wright's 1940 landmark novel about a young African American caught in a trap between social forces and his own deadly mistakes has been filmed twice. The first version, released in 1951, stars Wright himself as his antihero Bigger Thomas; the second, released in 1986, features Victor Love in the role.

Native Son is an emotionally charged story, fueled by racism, classism, radical politics, and sexuality. Hollywood circa 1950 clearly wasn't ready for such powerhouse material. Yet European director Pierre Chenal was a great admirer of the book and was determined to capture it on film. Wright himself was enlisted by Chenal to play his own fictional creation, though the author was much too old for the part. Though the majority of the production was shot in Argentina, Chenal did some location work in Chicago, the setting of *Native Son*.

The film's opening sequence includes shots of the Wrigley Building, Buckingham Fountain, State Street, and the legendary Riverview amusement park. Chenal contrasts these shiny exteriors with the bleak world of Chicago's South Side "Black Belt," where Bigger lives with his family. Ultimately, this first version of *Native Son*, while ambitious, falls well short of its good intentions. Still, it remains an interesting, if flawed, historical curio and is definitely worthy of a viewing.

The second screen version of *Native Son* was made as part of the Public Broadcasting System's *American Playhouse* series. Released theatrically before appearing on PBS, this *Native Son* boasts a strong cast: Matt Dillon as the radical Jan, Elizabeth McGovern as Mary Dalton, Carroll Baker as Mary's mother, Geraldine Page as the Daltons' maid, Oprah Winfrey as Mrs. Thomas, and newcomer Victor Love as Bigger. In a small role, as one of Bigger's buddies, was Ving Rhames, who would develop into a powerful film actor with his role as mob boss Marcellus Wallace in Quentin Tarantino's *Pulp Fiction* (1994).

While the ensemble works well together, the script unfortunately was much less than the sum of the cast's collective talents. At some points the film lurches unevenly from scene to scene. Choppy transitions also work against the compelling nature of the story.

The 1986 *Native Son* did make good use of Chicago locations to achieve a 1930s period look. Scenes of Bigger's neighborhood were shot around the 6300 blocks of South Martin Luther King Drive and South Greenwood Avenue. In contrast, the opulence of the Daltons' lifestyle was captured in the Hyde Park area. Some scenes were also shot in Logan Square, around the 3100 block of West Logan Boulevard.

The Dalton residence was located at 49th Street and South Drexel. A Gothic-style mansion, designed in a similar style to many of the buildings at the neighboring University of Chicago campus, this house is actually the living quarters for a group of Serbo-Croatian Greek Orthodox priests.

Lake Shore Drive

Starting at 5700 North, where Sheridan Road and Hollywood Avenue connect, and heading south to 67th Street, Lake Shore Drive (a.k.a. LSD or the Drive) offers a spectacular view of both Lake Michigan and the city's skyline, taking drivers past universities, posh condominiums, museums, beaches, Navy Pier, and much more. During the day, it's an entertaining drive (as long as it's not rush hour), but at night it's a spectacular panorama of Chicago's light and color. Needless to say, Lake Shore Drive is a very attractive location for filmmaking.

If you want to see what the Drive has looked like over the years, head to the video store. One of John Wayne's few non-western/war films, *Brannigan* (1975), features the Duke as a Chicago cop who ends up tailing some bad guys to England. Though the local scenes barely last five minutes, the opening credits feature a ride down the long-gone S curve, a severely serpentine stretch of LSD that both bedeviled and entranced Chicagoans for many years until being straightened in the 1980s. *Medium Cool* (1969) also gives a glimpse of the S curve, as well as other parts of the Drive in its opening credits, as the camera follows a motorcycle courier rushing news film to a television station.

Because of its uninterrupted length, the Drive is ideal for movie chases. The grand finale of *The Blues Brothers* (1980) begins its downtown demolition derby at a stretch of the Drive along the McCormick Place convention center. LSD also is the starting point for the high-octane chase sequence in *Risky Business* (1983). Driving his dad's purloined Porsche containing a high-priced call girl (Rebecca DeMornay) and his very nervous friend Miles (Curtis Armstrong), future enterpriser Joel Goodson (Tom Cruise) leads pissed-off pimp Guido (Joe Pantoliano) on a wild ride extending all the way to the suburb of Highland Park. "I don't believe this," moans Armstrong. "I've got a trig midterm tomorrow and I'm being chased by Guido the killer pimp."

Apparently the Drive has an attraction to North Shore movie teens with heisted parental automobiles. The indomitable Ferris Bueller (Matthew Broderick) "borrows" a red Ferrari from the father of his neurotic friend Cameron (Alan Ruck), then picks up girlfriend Sloan (Mia Sara) and enjoys an energetic drive up and down the Drive in *Ferris Bueller's Day Off* (1986). Had they been there 12 years earlier, the intrepid trio might have seen one of LSD's more unusual movie sites: a gun-toting, bicycling priest in the action-packed *Three the Hard Way* (1974), which featured a threesome of a different sort: Jim Brown, Fred "the Hammer" Williamson, and Jim Kelly.

Still, the real winners of Hollywood's "how to creatively use Lake Shore Drive" derby are inevitably *When Harry Met Sally* (1989) and *My*

Best Friend's Wedding (1997). Chicagoans couldn't help but smirk when University of Chicago graduates Billy Crystal and Meg Ryan leave the campus on a road trip for New York City and somehow wind up several dozen blocks out of their way as they cruise south along N. Lake Shore Drive. It may have been an unexplained bad turn on the part of the characters, though director Rob Reiner undoubtedly wanted to capture the scenic skyline of North LSD.

My Best Friend's Wedding's cinematic reconstruction of the Drive is even more blatant. In one sequence Julia Roberts is seen entering the northbound lanes of LSD near McCormick Place, then pulling off the Drive in the southbound lane around Delaware Street. Just how Roberts is able to pull off this incredible maneuver is probably best left to a bemused Chicagoan's imagination.

The Field Museum of Natural History
Roosevelt Road and Lake Shore Drive

Following the World's Columbian Exposition of 1893, the building that served as the Palace of Fine Arts (which was rebuilt as the Museum of Science and Industry in 1933) became the repository of tens of thousands of objects and artifacts from the fair. Rechristened the Field Columbian Museum, it remained in Jackson Park until reopening as the Field Museum of Natural History at its current location in the Museum Campus area (where it sits alongside the Shedd Aquarium, Adler Planetarium, and the remodeled Soldier Field).

The Field Museum of Natural History has been a versatile location for filmmakers. *The Package* (1989) utilizes the building's Romanesque columns as a stand-in for a government building in Washington, DC. A pivotal scene from the first season of *Boss* takes place at an event held in the spacious lobby. *Music Box* (1990) and *She's Having a Baby* (1988) also features scenes at the Field Museum, as does *Continental Divide* (1981).

Originally founded to house biology and anthropology collections amassed for the 1893 World's Columbian Exposition, in 1921 the Field Museum of Natural History moved from Jackson Park to its present location. *(Photo by Kate Corcoran)*

A fine example of cinematic magic occurs at the Field Museum in the 1996 feature *Chain Reaction*. Keanu Reeves begins a chase sequence on the second floor of the Field Museum, then dashes through the airline exhibit of the Museum of Science and Industry before ending up back at the Field. How Reeves gets from Roosevelt Road to 57th Street and back again so quickly is one of *Chain Reaction's* biggest mysteries (along with how Keanu Reeves could play a character who understands physics).

The biggest Field Museum production is the surprise 1996 box office hit *The Relic*. Based on a novel by Douglas Preston and Lincoln Child, *The Relic* turns the Field Museum into a veritable spook house, complete with labyrinth hallways and staircases, slamming doors, icky bugs, and one vicious monster with a taste for human brain matter holed up in the tunnels beneath the museum.

The Field museum was renamed the Museum of History for the 2001 Christina Applegate/Jean Reno romp *Just Visiting*. Actually a remake of a hit French film *Les Visiteurs* (1993), which Reno made many years earlier, *Just Visiting* is a time-travel fantasy/comedy. Reno plays a medieval French knight who is magically transported in error to contemporary Chicago by a sorcerer (played by Malcolm McDowell). Reno ends up meeting Applegate, who bears a striking resemblance to his wife but is actually his much-later descendent. Reno enlists Applegate's help in returning him, along with McDowell and Reno's vassal (played by French actor Christian Clavier), back to their own time to avert a horrible tragedy. Lighter and fluffier than a meringue, *Just Visiting* is an amusing little comedy that makes great use of Chicago locations, especially the "L" (see page 76).

South Loop

Old Van Buren Street
Van Buren Street between State Street and Clark Street

Take a walk down Van Buren Street between State and Clark. It's an impressive stretch of downtown, with its clean streets right in the shadow of the Harold Washington Public Library at State and Congress.

It doesn't seem that long ago that downtown along Van Buren was a haven for cheap bars and single-room-occupancy hotels. Down-and-outers roamed the streets—guys like Joliet Jake and Elwood Blues. Before Van Buren cleaned up its act, the street's down-and-out look was a favorite among Hollywood filmmakers.

Circular bay windows of the Old Colony Building provide a view into "Visionary Vanguard," a fictional architect's office in *The Lake House* (2006). *(Photo by Kate Corcoran)*

One of the most popular locations on the strip was the Stag Hotel. This cheap men-only flophouse was the home of Dan Aykroyd and John Belushi in *The Blues Brothers* (1980). With its proximity to the "L" tracks, the Stag Hotel was ideal for a great comic setup. The production rented a pair of CTA "L" cars, then played with them like a giant train set. As Aykroyd stares out his window, the "L" zips back and forth to the point of absurdity. Look carefully next time you watch *The Blues Brothers* and you'll notice those train cars are sans passengers.

When *The Blues Brothers* was done shooting, Belushi took a can of shaving cream and signed his name on the wall of Jake and Elwood's supposed room. No one wanted to touch this unique autograph, and ultimately the shaving cream petrified into a rock-hard signature. When the walls of the Stag Hotel came tumbling down in the late 1980s, Belushi's wall-sized autograph ended up as part of the rubble.

The Stag was where Kirk Douglas holed up while searching for his missing son in Brian DePalma's misfired horror film *The Fury* (1978). John Travolta was also a movie Stag resident. In *Eyes of an Angel* (1991), a forgettable flick made before his *Pulp Fiction* career rebirth, Travolta played a single father down on his luck and living at the Stag. His daughter befriends an abused dog, a turn of events that eventually leads Travolta out of Chicago.

The Big Town (1987), a look at illegal gambling in the 1950s, and *A Night in the Life of Jimmy Reardon* (1988), William Richert's autobiographical film starring the late River Phoenix, are two other films that capture the decadent beauty of Van Buren's squalor. Both productions were in Chicago during the fall of 1986 and ended up shooting on Van Buren during the same week.

Independent Feature Project/Chicago

1104 S. Wabash Avenue, Suite 403

One of the best resources for Chicago-based moviemakers is the Independent Feature Project (IFP)/Chicago. A not-for-profit organization, the IFP brings together directors, writers, camerapeople, editors, and other movie technicians for education, socializing, and—most important—advice and assistance in taking your independent film from concept to screen.

The IFP/Chicago is part of the national IFP network, which includes chapters in New York, Los Angeles, Minneapolis, Miami, and other cities. The group is devoted to helping independent filmmakers through seminars, special programming, and screening opportunities. The organization is now also responsible for presenting the acclaimed Chicago Underground Film Festival.

For membership information, contact the Independent Feature Project/ Chicago at (312) 506-4699 or visit www.ifpchicago.org.

The Roosevelt Hotel

1152 S. Wabash Avenue

Although today it's a luxury apartment building with rents starting at $1,100 a month, not too long ago the Roosevelt Hotel was a fleabag single-room-occupancy hotel where you could crash for a few bucks a night if you didn't mind rubbing elbows with a motley assortment of refugees from a Tom Waits song.

Despite its lack of amenities—or, actually, because of it—the Roosevelt has been a popular place for movie characters. Matt Dillon stays here in *The Big Town* (1987). In *Primal Fear* (1996), a scuffle breaks out at the Roosevelt between defense attorneys and a possible eyewitness to murder.

The Roosevelt Hotel is Dolly Parton's dwelling in *Straight Talk* (1992), a dimwitted romantic comedy starring the country music icon. One of the many riders in *Chicago Cab* (1998), a fine independent offering adapted from the hit Chicago stage play *Hellcab*, is also a Roosevelt Hotel resident.

3

North

The City

North Avenue Beach
1600 N. Lake Shore Drive
One of the most popular lakefront gathering spots in the summertime, this is also a favorite site with film and television producers. *About Last Night* . . . (1986) and *End of the Line* (1987) both had scenes here, as did episodes of *Chicago Hope, Crime Story, ER,* and *Amerika,* the 1986 television miniseries about a Soviet takeover of the United States. Even the party-happy programming of MTV has brought its cameras to North Avenue Beach.

Lou Gilbert begins his journey through Chicago after emerging from North Avenue Beach in *Goldstein* (1964). Brian DePalma also took advantage of this lakefront location in his thriller *The Fury* (1978). Look quickly among the extras as teenage Amy Irving strolls along the North Avenue Beach bicycle path: James Belushi, then a fledgling member of Second City, can briefly be spotted in the crowd. Nearby Oak Street Beach is visited by Don Ameche and Joe Mantegna near the conclusion of David Mamet's gem *Things Change* (1988). The lakefront at a spot further north serves as a meeting place in the indie film *Qwerty* (2012), a relationship comedy whose main character participates in the National Scrabble Tournament.

Ambassador East (now the Public Chicago)
1301 N. State Parkway
Simply put, the Ambassador East was one of Chicago's premier movie sites. It was a place where, if your timing was right, you were apt to bump into Cary Grant, either on the set of Alfred Hitchcock's escapist thriller *North by Northwest* (1959) or perhaps dining in the hotel's fabled Pump Room.

142

The hotel opened its doors in October 1926. Originally built as a swanky residential and travelers' hotel, the Ambassador East was nearly out of business some six years later when the Depression deeply cut into owner Ernest Byfield's profits. Fortunately, the end of Prohibition and revamping of the hotel's sister building, the Ambassador West, brought this elegant edifice back from the brink of disaster. The addition of the Pump Room in 1938 sealed the hotel's status as a place for people to see and be seen.

Taking his cue from the spa in Booth Tarkington's novel *Monsieur Beaucaire*, Byfield hired Chicago architect Sam Marx to design a unique dining spot. The result was the Pump Room, an almost ethereal restaurant with crystal chandeliers, murals, blue sapphire walls, and white leather booths. From its opening day, with waitstaff wearing scarlet swallowtails and feathered headpieces, the place was a hit.

In the 1930s and 1940s, movie stars traveling between New York and Hollywood routinely had a three-hour layover in Chicago. Eager to exploit this high-profile clientele, Byfield arranged for personalized limousine service to shuttle celebrities from Union Station to the Pump Room. As a result, the Pump Room quickly became the Chicago restaurant of choice for many famous names. While the celebrities sat along the eastern portion of the restaurant, captivated movie fans took up the western side for food and the opportunity to watch screen idols eat.

Anybody who was anybody was automatically seated in the Pump Room's legendary Booth Number One. Booth Number One has seen a veritable who's who of celebrity grace its seats. John Barrymore, Judy Garland and Liza Minnelli, Humphrey Bogart and Lauren Bacall, Jack Benny, Natalie Wood, Lassie, Joan Crawford, Zsa Zsa Gabor, Cary Grant, Mickey Rooney, Frank Sinatra, and Ronald Reagan are just a few of the many Booth Number One guests. During the filming of *The Sting* (1973), Robert Redford and Paul Newman spent every lunch at Booth Number One, never varying from a meal of ham sandwiches washed down with Pilsner.

After Byfield's death in 1950, the hotel passed through a series of hands until it was finally bought by the Omni Corporation in 1986. The Pump Room also changed ownership more than once and spent 22 years with Chicago restaurateur Rich Melman's Lettuce Entertain You Enterprises. The Ambassador East—now known as the Public Chicago—and the Pump Room are now owned by Ian Schrager.

On the big screen, room 463 of the Ambassador East is where Cary Grant, having survived an attack by a machine-gun-wielding crop duster, catches up with Eva Marie Saint in *North by Northwest* (1959). The hotel plays a pivotal role in *My Bodyguard*; the charming 1980 coming-of-age story features Chris Makepeace as the son of the Ambassador East's live-in manager, played by comedian Martin Mull. Stealing the show is Ruth Gordon as Mull's eccentric mother, who provides unending trouble for the hotel's staff and guests. The Ambassador East also pinch-hits as a Los Angeles hotel for the traveling Chicago Cubs in *Rookie of the Year* (1993). The Pump Room has been in its share of films as well, including the moment where shy cop John Candy introduces girlfriend Ally Sheedy to his inflexible mother in *Only the Lonely* (1991) and the first date between Dolly Parton and James Woods in *Straight Talk* (1992).

To book room 463 or any other room at the Public Chicago Hotel, call (312) 787-3700. Dinner reservations at the Pump Room can be made by calling (312) 229-6740.

Edwin G. Cooley Vocational High School ("Cooley High")
1225 N. Sedgwick Street
Though the building has been torn down, this address was once the location of Edwin G. Cooley Vocational High School, the inspiration for the 1975 comedy *Cooley High*. Starring Lawrence Hilton-Jacobs, Glynn Turman, and Garrett Morris, *Cooley High* depicts the lives of inner-city high school kids circa the early 1960s.

The film is based on the life of screenwriter Eric Monte, a former Cooley High student who grew up in the nearby Cabrini-Green housing project. Monte, who moved to California after serving in the military, wrote for the 1970s television sitcom *Good Times*, which was also set in Cabrini-Green. *Cooley High* served as inspiration for another sitcom, *What's Happening!!*

Cabrini-Green
Division and Halsted Streets
The Cabrini-Green housing complex was a case of good intentions gone horribly wrong. Originally built in 1942, this public housing project was intended to provide inexpensive apartments for Chicago's poor. It was named after Mother Cabrini, a nun later elevated to sainthood

for her work with the underprivileged. In 1962, the Chicago Housing Authority added another set of buildings to the area, the William Green Homes. Consequently, the complex became known as Cabrini-Green. Over time, the Cabrini-Green housing project also became synonymous with gang crime and drugs. The apartments were poorly maintained by the CHA, and elevators were constantly breaking down. Though originally meant to help the city's underprivileged, Cabrini-Green became a testament to urban despondency and remained so for years, until beginning in the late 1990s, almost all of it (except for a scant few low-rise buildings) was razed.

Yet even during its nefarious heyday there were glimmers of hope that existed in pockets beneath Cabrini-Green's ugly facade. The Cabrini Connections Film Festival provided children living in the complex an opportunity to make and publicly exhibit their own videos and films. One such film, *The Real Cabrini* by Jimmy Biggs, won first place for documentary at the 1997 Chicago Children's Film Festival. And in February 1994, independent director Joel Goodman brought a camera crew to shoot rock videos for the Slick Boys. This trio of Chicago cops—Eric Davis, Randy Holcomb, and James Martin—used rap music as a way of connecting with kids and offering an alternative to the uglier sides of Cabrini. "When we were out there shooting," says Goodman, "Cabrini-Green residents came up to us, rapping positive lyrics, and it was an incredible sight to see. It was 15 below, but everyone came out, eyes wide open to see in their backyard an independent production using some of their own residences. It really gave these young kids hope that there's something more out there than the problems of Cabrini-Green."

Hollywood also came to Cabrini-Green. The 1970s CBS television sitcom *Good Times* was set there and featured shots of the housing complex in the opening credits, and the basketball drama *Heaven Is a Playground* (1991) made extensive use of Cabrini-Green locations.

The cult horror film *Candyman* (1992) was likewise shot inside the housing complex. In this low-rent thriller, an anthropologist studying urban legends makes her way through the elaborate tunnel system of the ominous Cabrini-Green towers. There is a kernel of truth to the movie's premise, as several Cabrini high-rises had crawl spaces in the walls between the bathrooms that made residents' apartments accessible to criminals, who removed the bathroom mirrors of vacant units in order to enter the tunnels and then made their way into the bathrooms of other apartments. Terrified residents often had to barricade their bathroom doors at night to avoid being attacked in their sleep.

More recently, the movie *Hardball* (2001), with Keanu Reeves, was set in Cabrini-Green, although it was actually filmed in the ABLA Homes project on the West Side. The movie is very loosely based on a book about a real youth baseball league that thrived in the development—so loosely based that there was a storm of controversy when *Hardball* was released. Many folks affiliated with the league were unhappy because of the foul language used by the young actors (cursing is strictly forbidden and severely punished in the Near North Little League, as is any symbol of gang involvement), and one of the league's founders, Bob Muzikowski, actually sued the film's producers for defamation of character for the way he was portrayed.

Although Cabrini-Green is gone for all practical purposes, its memory will live on, not only in movies like *Cooley High* (1975) but also in the minds of the former residents, who occasionally have organized reunions to get together and reminisce about the old days. Because as hard as things were in the shadow of the towers, people still raised families and built lives there; and it's just human nature to remember more of the good times than the bad.

Chicago Filmmakers
5233 N. Clark Street

Whether you are interested in highly personal, noncommercial movies, want to learn more about the filmmaking process, or need to rent equipment, Chicago Filmmakers has what you're looking for. Founded in 1973 by three students from the School of the Art Institute, the organization has grown into one of the city's most important resources for independent filmmakers.

Chicago Filmmakers offers Chicagoans an alternative to the usual commercial fare of your local multiscreen commercial theater complex. Chicago Filmmakers provides a local outlet for short experimental films, avant-garde work, and documentaries. They also do copresentations with other local film entities, including the School of the Art Institute, the Goethe Institute, and Facets Multimedia. One of Chicago Filmmakers' most important contributions to the local movie scene is its sponsorship of Reeling: The Chicago Lesbian & Gay International Film Festival.

Classes at Filmmakers cover a wide range of cinema production, including sound, editing, screenwriting, producing, and camera work.

Selections range from one-night seminars to full 10-week courses. Equipment rental and editing facilities are also available for noncommercial moviemakers. Additionally, Chicago Filmmakers has membership options and volunteer opportunities for everyone from students to professionals to plain old film lovers. Membership privileges include discounts on class tuition and supplies, equipment access, special rates for a wide variety of movie magazines, and, perhaps most important, technical consulting on film projects from the talented Filmmakers staff.

For more information, contact Chicago Filmmakers by phone at (773) 293-1447, or visit their website at www.chicagofilmmakers.org.

Twin Anchors Restaurant
1655 N. Sedgwick Street
This is the restaurant where Minnie Driver works in the superb romantic comedy *Return to Me* (2000), which was directed and cowritten by Chicago icon Bonnie Hunt. Driver plays a woman who receives a desperately needed heart transplant, and David Duchovny is the grieving husband of the woman who donated Driver's new heart. A coincidence brings them together and they haltingly begin a romance that is greatly complicated when they find out each other's identities. Carroll O'Connor, Robert Loggia, David Alan Grier, Jim Belushi, and Hunt herself make up the core of the terrific supporting cast. Smart and funny with a heart of gold, this is the kind of simple yet sophisticated romantic comedy that people complain "they don't make anymore."

Flat Iron Building and Wicker Park
1579 N. Milwaukee Avenue
Milwaukee, North, and Damen Avenues converge to form one of the city's busiest corners in the thriving Wicker Park neighborhood. Once upon a time, this area was the stomping grounds of writer Nelson Algren; today it's home to an attractive mix of pierced punks, artists, yuppies, and the vestiges of a once-thriving Latino community. Restaurants, galleries, funky little coffee shops, music stores, bars, and clubs dot the area, though operations come and go, changing names and management with surprising regularity.

Maybe that ongoing change has something to do with this area's uncanny popularity with movie companies. One area location scout recalled a three-week period in which the short-lived television series

EZ Streets, the pilot for TV's *Early Edition*, another television pilot called *For the People*, and the movie *Michael*, starring John Travolta, all shot scenes in this Wicker Park area. *Soul Food* (1997), *Love Jones* (1997), and the eponymous, not-so-thrilling thriller *Wicker Park* (2004) also used the neighborhood environs as a background for dramatic action.

In *Red Heat* (1988), made before the area was a hip-happening mecca, Soviet cop Arnold Schwarzenegger and wiseguy Chicago detective James

Belushi hole up in their car just outside the Flat Iron Building, 1579 N. Milwaukee Avenue, while tailing some bad guys through this area. The Flat Iron Building, which normally houses art galleries and office space, became an apartment building in *Blink* (1994), home to Madeleine Stowe's character.

The old dive bars from the Nelson Algren days are showcased in the films of 1990s-era independent filmmaker Jim Sikora, who shot the shoestring-budget features *Walls in the City* (1994) and *Bullet on a Wire* (1998) in the many gin joints, taverns, and taprooms of Wicker Park and Bucktown.

The most notable film set in Wicker Park/Bucktown, however, is the Stephen Frears–directed *High Fidelity* (2000), which stars John Cusack (who also coproduced and cowrote the screenplay) as a hip Wicker Park record store owner who spends the film decrying his all-time worst rela-

Tower of Chicago's Flat Iron Building, 1579 N. Milwaukee Avenue, which has been used as a background for several movies, including *Red Heat* (1988) and *Blink* (1994). *(Photo by Kate Corcoran)*

tionship failures while in the midst of yet another. He traces his insecurities and difficulties with women back to his early adolescence, blaming much of his misery on all the tragic pop songs of his youth. Jack Black is fabulous as a bitter, snobbish slacker store clerk, and local actor Todd Louiso shines as Cusack's other employee, a delightfully awkward and obsessive music geek. Iben Hjejle, Lisa Bonet, Sara Gilbert, Catherine Zeta-Jones, Lili Taylor, Tim Robbins, and Cusack's sister Joan round out the excellent supporting cast. The film is based on a novel of the same name by Nick Hornby. The book is set in London, but Cusack and his collaborators were seasoned habitués of the Chicago music/culture scene and knew just how to transpose the London locales into their Chicago counterparts. Although the record store itself was created in an empty storefront at Milwaukee and Honore, the production used such tried-and-true Chicago venues as the Double Door, Earwax Cafe, Rainbo Club, and the Green Mill. The end result is an energetic celebration of music geekdom that doesn't shrink from pointing out the fatal flaws of the rock 'n' roll myth in regards to living an emotionally sustainable life.

Go Fish: Breaking Ground and Making Careers

Years before Ellen and Rosie came out of the closet, and long before *The L Word*, a smart and sweet lesbian romantic comedy shot on a less-than-bare-bones budget in Wicker Park and other North Side locations shocked the independent film community (and the filmmakers themselves) by becoming an international hit and paving the way for other lesbian films to reach a mainstream audience.

Go Fish (1994) began as a creative project between University of Illinois–Chicago alumna Rose Troche and her significant other, Guinevere Turner. "We were going out," says Turner. "Rose had just graduated [from UIC] and I had graduated from Sarah Lawrence in New York. She had a BFA in Film/Video/Photography and I had my little, useless bachelor of arts degree—not useless, but not practical. We just started talking about how we wanted to make a film together. I said, 'Well let me write something and you can shoot it.' At that point it was an idea for a 15-minute film. The more we talked about it and the more we talked to other people, it just sort of grew to the point of becoming an hour long and we said, 'Hell, if we're going to make an hour-long movie, why not just make a feature?'"

Through a network of friends, Troche and Turner found Ann Rosetti, a local cinematographer "who was happy to suffer through the whole process with us for free," says Turner. "We shot it on weekends and after work. I would come home to my apartment, which would be full of c-stands and wires and everything, make the phone calls and make sure the food was coming and get in front of the camera." In addition to co-writing and coproducing *Go Fish* with Troche, Turner also played one of the two romantic leads.

"All together we shot for about 45 days, but that was over a two-year period," Turner recalls. "It started out [with us] buying film stock, which is like 60 bucks for 12 minutes of black-and-white film. When we had film, the rest of the [production] was very much thanks to the Chicago university system—Rose was at UIC (since she was still working there so she could borrow equipment), we had someone at Northwestern, we had someone at the Art Institute, someone at Columbia. We would ask everyone if we could use their privileges to borrow equipment, and it would be this crazy, mad 'Take the van around these colleges, and gather all the equipment, get it to wherever we're shooting.'

"It was a crazy way to [make a movie], but it was free! I think we actually rented equipment only twice. Our basic strategy for raising money was never doing anything but just talking about this movie. Part of our strategy of having benefits was as a way of letting people know what's going on. We had never made more than $1,000 at a benefit.

"About three-quarters of the way through shooting we really ran out of money and were about to get evicted."

At this point, Troche hooked up with New York producer Christine Vachon and her partner, Tom Kalin, a School of the Art Institute graduate who had directed *Swoon* (1992), a retelling of the Leopold and Loeb murder case. Vachon passed the word to John Pierson, the moneyed guru of the modern independent film movement. "Pierson eventually gave us the $50,000 we needed to finish, which to us was a million," says Turner.

Once completed, *Go Fish* was entered into the prestigious Sundance Film Festival. The offbeat story of lesbian romance was an instant audience hit, and Troche and Turner's labor of love was picked up for distribution by Samuel Goldwyn. "After Sundance, we were like, 'What the hell? How did this happen?'" says Turner.

Though the strain of making the film broke Troche and Turner's collective wallet, as well as their personal relationship, the duo found themselves in the enviable position of being independent film darlings. What's more, *Go Fish* was becoming an international phenomenon.

"We really thought we were going to make a film that was going to go to gay and lesbian festivals in America if we were lucky, and we ended up all over the world," Turner recalls. "We went out of our minds. We used to laugh all the time, because we'd have a limo coming to pick us up to bring us to the airport to fly us to Spain and we wouldn't even have three dollars to tip the driver. We went to Germany (where *Go Fish* won the Best Feature Award at the 1994 Berlin International Film Festival), Spain, England. Rose went to Italy, Ireland, and Australia. We both went to Israel and Japan."

The popularity of *Go Fish* launched successful careers for both of its creators. Troche went on to direct a pair of feature films, *Bedrooms and Hallways* (1998) and *The Safety of Objects* (2001), before directing an episode of HBO's monumental series *Six Feet Under* and becoming a regular director/producer on the hit lesbian-themed Showtime series *The L Word* (a show that the success of *Go Fish* made possible). Turner has been in demand both as a writer and actress, appearing in films such as *Chasing Amy* (1997) and *American Psycho* (2000) (she also cowrote the screenplay for the latter), and writing several screenplays including *The Notorious Bettie Page* (2005) and *BloodRayne* (2005). She's also written a script for and played a recurring character on *The L Word*.

Despite having moved away from the Windy City, Turner credits Chicago with providing a special environment in which creative people can learn their craft and work with a community of like-minded artists. "*Go Fish* is truly a product of Chicago. There's a spirit in Chicago of people: when you say, 'Oh, we're going to do this and this,' everyone's like, 'Oh, can I come and help?' whereas in New York everyone is like, 'Fuck that, I've got my own shit to do. I've moved to New York to do my thing.' I feel like the film is the product of a certain kind of working-class ethic, family oriented, 'Let's all do something together' kind of spirit that to me is really a part of what Chicago is."

And no matter where her path leads her, Turner will always remember the tiny project that started it all. "Basically, *Go Fish* completely, radically changed my life and gave me a career."

The Second City
1616 N. Wells Street

In the mid–20th century at an abandoned second-floor chop suey place at North and LaSalle, comedy was forever changed. A group of friends—including Paul Sills, Mike Nichols, Elaine May, and Sheldon Patinkin—split from their classes at the University of Chicago, took over

The Second City, home to improvisation, has produced numerous writers, directors, and actors who have had a major influence on television and film. *(Photo by Kate Corcoran)*

the former restaurant, and turned it into a theater called the Playwrights Theatre Club. Along with pals David Shepherd, Barbara Harris, Ed Asner, Zohra Lampert, Eugene Troobnick, and Byrne and Joyce Piven, the group threw together production after production.

By 1955, the company had regrouped both in name and technique. Under the banner "the Compass Players," this troupe, aided by newcomers Severn Darden, Shelly Berman, Roger Bowen, Jerry Stiller, Anne Meara, and Alan Arkin, hurled themselves into Chicago nightclubs. In their invigorating freestyle theater known as "improvisation," the Compass gang took theater games developed by Sills's mother, Viola Spolin, and staged rollicking comedy revues. No subject was too sacred, no person too revered, to escape the satirical skewer of the group. Their home base was the Hi-Hat, a bar at 1152 E. 52nd Street, then the Dock at 6472 S. Lake Park Avenue, and finally the Off-Beat Room at 6344 N. Broadway. All these venues have since disappeared, but what was spawned on those dirty stages has become an international phenomenon.

A second Compass group, including Del Close, Nancy Ponder, Jo Henderson, and Theodore J. Flicker, played St. Louis for a while. Back in Chicago, Sills hooked up with newcomers Bernie Sahlins and Howard Alk and began the troupe's next phase. Throwing together a cast including Sahlins, Alk, Bowen, Darden, Andrew Duncan, Harris, Troobnick, and Mina Kolb, the gang took over an abandoned Chinese laundry at 1842 N. Wells Street, then tossed in a piano, a rudimentary stage, a few tables, and some chairs. Rechristened "the Second City" (the title of a *New Yorker* magazine piece about Chicago written by legendary journalist A. J. Liebling), the group staged its first show on December 16, 1959.

"I consider it a halcyon period for creative acting," says Avery Schreiber, a member of the troupe during the early 1960s. Indeed, this little storefront theater was quickly attracting national attention. New York–based magazines ranging from the *Nation* to *Time* sent writers to Chicago to see what the hell was going on in the Second City. Out of those sketch comedy revues grew a mighty cultural force. Soon Nichols and May were doing Broadway. Shelly Berman's comedy routines were laid down on vinyl and sold in record stores across the country. Alan Arkin began doing movies. Stiller and Meara took the foibles of their marriage to comedy clubs. Theodore J. Flicker wrote Elvis pictures and directed *The President's Analyst* (1967), which quickly became a cult classic. Nichols won an Oscar for directing *The Graduate* (1967). And things were just beginning!

As the 1960s expanded the American political, social, and cultural consciousness, the Second City grew from a scrappy Chicago-based theater into an American institution. Needing more room than before, during 1967's "summer of love," the troupe moved into a built-to-order home at 1616 N. Wells, the heart of Old Town.

Throughout the late 1960s and into the 1970s, the Second City's reputation for scat-of-your-pants sketch comedy expanded. Companies were opened in Los Angeles, Toronto, and Detroit. Second City played New York and developed a touring company that traveled from Podunk town to Podunk town like old-time vaudevillians.

Over the years, Second City troupes rose and fell on the strength of their versatile casts. The overall roll call reads like a who's who of American comedy, a veritable checklist of top stage, television, and film talents: Alan Alda, Dan Aykroyd, John and James Belushi, Peter Boyle, Jack Burns, John Candy, Steve Carell, Dan Castellaneta, Del Close, Stephen Colbert, Bill Cusack, Melinda Dillon, Paul Dooley, Brian Doyle-Murray, Robin Duke, Chris Farley, Tina Fey, Joe Flaherty, Aaron Freeman, Valerie Harper, Bonnie Hunt, Henry Jaglom, Tim Kazurinsky, Robert Klein, Linda Lavin, Eugene Levy, Shelley Long, Andrea Martin, Tim Meadows, Bill Murray, Mike Myers, Mick Napier, Bob Odenkirk, Catherine O'Hara, Gilda Radner, Harold Ramis, Joan Rivers, Paul Sand, Avery Schreiber, Amy Sedaris, Martin Short, David Steinberg, Betty Thomas, Dave Thomas, George Wendt, and Fred Willard. And that's just a sampling.

TOP LEFT: Bonnie Hunt and Rick Hall from Second City main stage, 1987. *(Photo courtesy of JenniferGirard.com)*

TOP RIGHT: Chris Farley, Jill Talley, Bob Odenkirk, Holly Wortell, and Tim Meadows, Second City main stage, July 1990. *(Photo courtesy of JenniferGirard.com)*

MIDDLE LEFT: Amy Sedaris and Steve Carell onstage together in the Second City revue *Truth, Justice, or the American Way*, circa 1993. *(Photo courtesy of JenniferGirard.com)*

MIDDLE RIGHT: Steve Carell, Paul Dinello, Stephen Colbert, and David Razowsky, Second City, March 1994 production of *Are You Now, or Have You Ever Been Mellow?* *(Photo courtesy of JenniferGirard.com)*

BOTTOM: Tina Fey, Scott Allman, and Rachel Dratch bring the sexy in Second City's 1996 revue *Citizen Gates*. *(Photo courtesy of JenniferGirard.com)*

Now owned and operated by Andrew Alexander, who helped develop the original Toronto troupe, the Second City has evolved into a theatrical institution. Its influence can be felt at many levels, from the numerous improvisational comedy troupes playing Chicago bars on any given night to the highs and lows of television's comedy warhorse *Saturday Night Live*. Homer Simpson of *The Simpsons* is voiced by Dan Castellaneta, a former Second City player. Betty Thomas gained national attention on the television ensemble drama *Hill Street Blues*, then came into her own as a film director with such features as HBO's *The Late Shift* (1996) and *Howard Stern's Private Parts* (1997). Bill Murray became America's favorite wiseguy. Bob Odenkirk revitalized sketch comedy on HBO with *Mr. Show*. Bonnie Hunt built an impressive film resume that included work with Tom Cruise, Harrison Ford, Tom Hanks, and Steve Martin, and then brought her sharp wit and improv skills to the daytime talk-show game. Tina Fey climbed the ladder at the SNL boys' club to become a television comedy powerhouse. Amy Sedaris brought her wickedly twisted sense of humor to the Comedy Central hit *Strangers with Candy*. Steve Carell went from *Daily Show* correspondent to movie and television stardom, and another *Daily Show* correspondent, Stephen Colbert, parlayed his faux right-wing blowhard persona into a basic cable empire. The list of alumni accomplishments is as offbeat and varied as any Second City revue.

The September 11, 2001, attacks brought America to a standstill and shocked the country to its core. It also presented a huge challenge to comedy troupes around the nation to try and glean laughter from such horrid events. Second City responded with *Holy War, Batman!*, a clever and thoughtful piece of work that was well received, even by those who had personally experienced 9/11. Andrew Alexander elaborates: "One particular night was very gratifying. A friend of mine who's a fireman had actually worked at Ground Zero for a few weeks after the attacks and had befriended a bunch of New York City firemen. They all came to Chicago one night about two weeks after the opening. There were about 30 of them in the audience, and they all stood up after the show and gave it a standing ovation. That was a real special night."

Having celebrated its 50th anniversary in 2009, Second City is now a multimillion-dollar world entertainment/media empire, with theaters and training centers in Chicago, Toronto, Los Angeles, and Detroit (they also offer a "Comedy Studies Program" through Columbia College);

eight touring companies that travel the entire globe with a wide variety of revues; films, TV and radio shows, blogs, streaming videos, and podcasts; and a corporate division that creates made-to-order industrial films and corporate entertainments. They've even teamed up with Norwegian Cruise Lines to offer shows and free improv workshops on four of their cruise ships!

Alexander says that the Norwegian Cruise Lines partnership has worked out well for both parties. "It's great for us. It's great for the talent; they get to go all over the world. It's kind of become an extension of our touring business, and with a 'captive audience' you don't have the stress of having to sell tickets. The feedback from the cruise line is that the free workshops are one of the most popular entertainment activities they have."

Reflecting on the changes in Second City over five decades, Alexander is upbeat. "I think even though we've expanded in a whole bunch of different areas, we've held on to the core values. What we do on those stages is still the most important thing, but we've been able to manage expansion in a way that doesn't denigrate the process or the work. I think we've built on it."

The thousands of people across the globe who enjoy the cornucopia of hilarious offerings put forth by the Second City each year would undoubtedly agree.

For ticket information, contact the Second City at (312) 337-3992. If you're interested in Second City classes call (312) 664-3959. The Second City website is at www.secondcity.com.

Steppenwolf Theatre
1650 N. Halsted Street

In the world of Chicago theater, where storefront troupes come and go with Darwinian regularity, the Steppenwolf Theatre Company is legendary. This scrappy ensemble, famous for bringing a pugnacious sensibility to the stage, has nailed something all fledgling Chicago companies dream of: unbridled success that has become world renowned. And in recent years, Steppenwolf has stepped beyond its role as a theater company to become a cultural institution.

To look over the list of ensemble members is to understand Steppenwolf's importance not only to theater but also to film and television production. People like John Malkovich, Gary Sinise, John Mahoney, and Joan Allen are household names to movie fans around the world. The film, television, and stage work of Steppenwolf members have earned Oscar nominations, Emmy awards, and Tony awards.

Steppenwolf got its start in north suburban Highland Park. In 1974, Sinise and his old high school pal Jeff Perry, along with Perry's Illinois State University (ISU) comrade Terry Kinney, slapped together a theater company. The company name was nabbed from a handy copy of Herman Hesse's novel someone happened to have. Later, after incorporating as Steppenwolf Theatre Company, the trio found it too expensive to switch monikers. For better or worse, they were Steppenwolf.

Within a couple of years, other ISU graduates migrated north and joined the company. Malkovich, Laurie Metcalf, and Moira Harris were among this group. They staged their shows at Highland Park's Immaculate Conception Church, 770 Deerfield Road, in a minuscule basement theater. Rent was 10 bucks a month, the ideal price for a group of starving actors.

From the start, Steppenwolf was committed to the ideal of ensemble acting. The collective developed a muscular approach to production, emphasizing emotional dynamics in their performances. Moving to the Jane Addams Hull House Center, 3212 N. Broadway, in the city, Steppenwolf grew in size and reputation. Allen, Mahoney, Glenne Headly, and Rondi Reed were among the new members. The enhanced ensemble tackled such meaty works as Harold Pinter's *The Caretaker*, Samuel Beckett's *Krapp's Last Tape*, and Eugene Ionesco's *Exit the King*. In just six years, the company had evolved into a considerable theatrical force.

As the collective became more renowned, Steppenwolf's approach to acting was adopted by other local companies, such as the Wisdom Bridge Theatre and the Remains Theatre (the latter founded by William Petersen, Gary Cole, and Amy Morton—all current Steppenwolf ensemble members), and eventually became known informally as the "Chicago style" of acting. Steppenwolf creative director Martha Lavey elaborates: "A highly visceral, energized style that was heavily influenced by the films of the time [of Steppenwolf's founding], particularly John Cassavetes. A very truthful style driven by the whole notion of an ensemble, which means it was less about the particular star turn that any one actor was doing but rather the highest level of power, which is derived from a group of people in close and intimate response to each other on stage."

Steppenwolf acquired its own space in 1982, moving into a 211-seat theater at 2851 N. Halsted Street. Shows that opened in Chicago played in

New York at prestigious venues like the Lincoln Center for the Performing Arts and the Circle Repertory Theatre. In 1985, the troupe was given a Tony Award for Regional Theatre Excellence. Three years later, John Steinbeck's estate gave permission for Steppenwolf to adapt *The Grapes of Wrath* for the stage. This groundbreaking production took Chicago by storm, then moved to the LaJolla Playhouse in California and the Royal National Theatre in London. Eventually *The Grapes of Wrath* moved to Broadway; it won Tony Awards for Best Play and Best Director for the 1989–1990 season.

When ensemble members hit Hollywood in the early 1980s, their impact resounded at all levels of the industry. Malkovich's big-screen debut, as a blind man in *Places in the Heart* (1984) earned him an Oscar nomination. The intensity he brought to his roles, whether in an art film like *The Object of Beauty* (1991) or something as blatantly commercial as *Con Air* (1997), was pure Steppenwolf. Writer Charlie Kaufman was so taken with Malkovich's acting ability and highly refined public persona that he wrote an entire screenplay that revolved around a magical crawl space that allowed a person to experience the world as John Malkovich. The resultant film, *Being John Malkovich* (1999), is a surreal romp through the deepest recesses of the human psyche and desires. It stars John Cusack, Cameron Diaz, indie film stalwart Catherine Keener, and of course, Malkovich himself, who obviously had a wonderful time lampooning his own artsy image and the bizarre conceits of fame itself. The success of that film elevated Malkovich to a pop-culture icon, and his continued high quality of work has maintained that status.

Other members quickly followed. Laurie Metcalf won several Emmys for her supporting role on the sitcom *Roseanne*. Sinise developed into a screen chameleon, easily switching from regular guy to historical figure to boiling madman. He also directed a remake of John Steinbeck's *Of Mice and Men* (1992), starring as George opposite Malkovich's Lenny. His yeoman work in films has continued over the years, and he currently stars in the hit CBS television series *CSI: New York*. Joan Allen has become one of the finest actors in Hollywood, with standout performances in such films as *Nixon* (1995), *The Ice Storm* (1997), *The Contender* (2000), *The Bourne Supremacy* (2004), and *The Bourne Ultimatum* (2007). Jim True-Frost appeared as "Buzz the Elevator Operator" in the Coen Brothers comedy *The Hudsucker Proxy* (1994) and in several television series, including a recurring role in the fabulous beyond description HBO series *The Wire*.

Perry, Headly, Mahoney, Kinney, and others also became well-known figures to movie and television audiences worldwide.

In 1991, the Steppenwolf Theatre Company moved into a specially built complex at 1650 N. Halsted Street. The building holds a main stage with a seating of 510, while a studio theater seats between 100 to 300, depending on the show. As the company grew into their space and continued to excel, Steppenwolf slowly began to evolve from a theater company into a cultural institution with a much wider scope. They launched several programs designed to expand the organization's relationship to the greater community and to go far beyond the original mission. As Lavey puts it, "When we started, it was just about producing five plays a year."

One such program has been the Visiting Company Initiative, where fellow Chicago ensembles are invited to come in and mount their productions in Steppenwolf's space.

Steppenwolf Theatre, home to many acclaimed actors, playwrights, and directors. *(Photo by Kate Corcoran)*

Lookingglass, Teatro Vista, 500 Clown, About Face, and Congo Square are but a handful of the theater companies that Steppenwolf has hosted. They have also opened the theater up to other types of performance, such as music (the Art Ensemble of Chicago, the Roches, Ramblin' Jack Elliott), performance art (the Pajama Men, Sandra Bernhard), and monologists/raconteurs (David Sedaris, Sarah Vowell, Garrison Keillor).

Another extremely important program is Steppenwolf's initiative for the youth of Chicago. This consists of the Steppenwolf for Young Adults program, which mounts two productions per year for high school–age youth, and the Young Adult Council, a group of about a dozen high school students who have an ongoing relationship with Steppenwolf and learn about all aspects of the theater. According to Lavey, these programs are now an integral part of Steppenwolf: "Those activities are part of what we regard as our 'platform as a public square,' and when we think about our work as a whole, we really want to be a place where the work on our stage activates a public discourse about how live now and what we think about our future. Having all these artists and a range of really eclectic skills, performances, and modalities keeps us in line with the energy of this city and contemporary American life. By bringing in these wonderful artists and a mix of audiences young and old, it really keeps the 'three-ring circus' energy that's so right for Steppenwolf and so right for our city."

Steppenwolf also began providing for its own needs by establishing a program for creating and developing new plays to mount in its theaters. The New Plays Initiative, begun in 1995, has borne fruit, with over 40 new plays developed and produced since its inception. This has been a boon not only to Steppenwolf, but for the entire infrastructure of live theater throughout the world.

A recent Steppenwolf megahit production was *August: Osage County*, a blistering semiautobiographical play written by ensemble member Tracy Letts (although not part of the New Plays Initiative). *August: Osage County* was an instant hit when it premiered in Chicago, then it took Broadway by storm and in late 2008 traveled to London, where it wowed audiences and critics alike. Letts has written several plays, one of which, the profoundly creepy and claustrophobic *Bug* (2006), was made into a film directed by William Friedkin and starring Ashley Judd. A film version of *August: Osage County* is also in the works, with a projected release in late 2013.

Sinise, Kinney, Perry, and Chicago theater veteran Tim Evans have teamed up to create a spin-off of the original theater company, Steppenwolf Films. The new film production company is a separate fiduciary entity but still shares the same name and artistic goals as the parent organization. Steppenwolf Films' first feature, *Diminished Capacity* (2008), starred Matthew Broderick and Alan Alda. Its next production, *The Last Rites of Joe May* (2011), starred Dennis Farina as an aging con man facing the possible end of his larcenous career.

Despite their global reach and immense success, the ensemble remains committed to Chicago and their home theater. Members routinely plan their film schedules to allow for Steppenwolf productions and periodically hold movie previews in Chicago as fundraisers for the theater. And the ensemble keeps growing: in late 2008, veteran actor William Petersen left his starring role on the long-running, wildly popular TV series *CSI: Crime Scene Investigation* to return to Chicago and join the Steppenwolf ensemble as its 42nd member, bringing his career full circle from his days at the Remains Theatre.

For more information, contact Steppenwolf Theatre's switchboard at
(312) 335-1650 or check out its website at www.steppenwolf.org.

Ora Jones: Immersed in the Chicago Stage

**"I don't know much about film at all. I don't have any great desire to go out
to L.A. I like the stage, that's where I like to be."**   —*Ora Jones*

Ora Jones is almost sheepish about
her small cameos in several films over
the years. "I think it might take longer
for me to talk about the scenes I was
in than it would to watch them. Just
one little moment here and there and
if you blink you'll miss me."

Ora Jones. *(Photo courtesy of Ora Jones)*

Despite her reticence, she's still managed to create a couple of memorable
moments in some of the best movies
ever made in Chicago. Her turn as the
bemused front desk person at Emma
Thompson's fictional publishing house
in *Stranger Than Fiction* (2006), con-
fronted by a seemingly unbalanced Will Ferrell ("I'm a character in her new
book and I think she's going to kill me") is pure comedy gold; understated yet
absolutely hilarious—just about the best performance you can do with two
minutes of screen time. And her slightly larger role as the "Trust Counselor"
for Nicholas Cage and Hope Davis in Gore Verbinski's brilliant seriocomic
gem *The Weather Man* (2005) drives what is one of the funniest segments in
the movie, bringing welcome comic relief to what is at times a painful look
into a man's worst foibles and life's trials and tribulations.

Feeling compelled to act ever since the age of six, Jones studied theater
at Notre Dame University. She spent a summer working at a theater in
Vermont after graduation, then went to visit a friend in Chicago who was
involved in the local theater scene. "I was going to be here for five days.
That was 20-some-odd years ago!" she laughs. "I just sort of stayed."

More than two decades later, she has appeared in countless stage productions around Chicago and the rest of the nation, even earning a Joseph

Jefferson Award (Chicago's version of a Tony Award) for her work in Steppenwolf's production of *The Violet Hour*. Jones has been appearing in Steppenwolf shows for more than a decade and was recently invited to become an ensemble member.

The anything-goes nature of Chicago theater appeals to Jones. "There are so many different kinds of theater here," she says. "And it's all permissible, it's all allowed. I call it 'the theater allscape.' Any kind of theater you can think about doing, someday you'll get a chance to do it. Someday, somehow you're going to get a chance to tell your story. Good theater and bad theater in Chicago has nothing to do with how much money you spent, whether you're in a union, whether you have a resident company, whether you even have four walls and a roof that you can call your own. The theater in Chicago is just about good storytelling and that is where it rises and falls. It doesn't matter what you did with it, if the story is no good it's no good, and if the story is great you can tell it on the street corner."

Chicago's theater scene is a close-knit community, which Jones feels is at the heart of the theatrical experience. "There's no reason to do theater if you're not going to be part of a community." This cooperative spirit and cross-pollination between companies is one of the reasons she feels the city is such a hotbed for acting talent and imaginative productions. "There isn't a lot of competition or fighting. There's this great idea of just getting the work done and that the story is the most important character in the show. That leads to actors generating more opportunity for each other and themselves to tell their stories. People in Chicago write and they teach, they direct, they produce. You may be a resident member of one theater company and you work for another. There's a lot of people jumping from theater to theater in the course of a day, and it gives a lot of opportunity for community and conversation."

Communication with the audience is essential in live theater. As Jones explains, "It's not just about standing on a stage and shouting, 'Everybody shut up, I have something really important to say.'" That partnership between audience and performer is key to Chicago theater and can be a magical experience for both parties. "Chicago theater really invites the audience to come along with them, and as an audience member, it's an invitation to a very wonderful dance. It's about taking the trip together."

Jones's first stint in front of the camera came in 1994, when she appeared in an episode of the TV show *Missing Persons*. That was followed by a cameo as a day care worker in *Losing Isaiah* (1995), a powerful drama starring Jessica Lange and Halle Berry, then as a woman about to give birth in the independent feature *Chicago Cab*. Appearances in several films and television episodes ensued, and 2005 marked her spot in *The Weather Man*, with her *Stranger Than Fiction* moment happening the next year.

The *Stranger Than Fiction* shoot is now a near legend amongst the Chicago film community for the almost blissful atmosphere that surrounded the production, something that Ora noticed herself in the day she spent filming her part. "It was a creative atmosphere; it was a lot of fun. Everyone I had to deal with in the crew, from hair and makeup, the sound people, the lighting people, craft services, whatever, even the people who drove me back and forth to the set. It was just a lot of fun, and they were so relaxed and having a good time. Which just puts you so at ease and helps you be creative as far as what you're going to do."

Jones credits the director, Marc Forster, and star Will Ferrell as the key players in creating this nurturing vibe. "Mr. Ferrell and Mr. Forster were very encouraging. And I don't think you get to have these experiences too much when you're the day player. You're just there to say 'yes' or 'no' or just have a small moment with them. If I could have one day a year like that, I'd put up with a lot of junk."

Despite her obvious acumen for film work, Ora insists she is still mystified by the process. "I don't really understand film a lot, so I'm really happy to have these smaller roles. Because I look at that camera and I know that it can take in the entire room and myself with it, but looking at that little lens—there are days when I just look at it and say, 'Hmmm, how do I tell a story to this piece of equipment as opposed to a living, breathing human being who's going to come along on the journey?'"

But as scores of theatergoers and film lovers will attest, with Ora Jones at the helm, it will always be a journey worth taking.

Kartemquin Films: Documenting Society

"To foster understanding, change thinking, and build support for social change."

These words from the mission statement of Kartemquin Films sum up an organization that has not only shined a light into how we live our lives but has also illustrated ways in which those lives could be better lived. Though it's most well known as the company that made *Hoop Dreams* (1994) a reality, Kartemquin Films is a long-standing Chicago institution. Since its inception in the late 1960s, Kartemquin has been a thriving hub for socially conscious documentary filmmakers. In 1998, the Chicago Film Critics Association presented Kartemquin partners Gordon Quinn and Jerry Blumenthal with the Big Shoulders Award, honoring their "ongoing efforts to promote filmmaking [that] best exemplifies the bold, innovative, and independent spirit of Chicago." And in 2007, Kartemquin received one of eight international MacArthur Awards for Creative and Effective Institutions.

"I came to school at the University of Chicago in 1960," recalls Quinn. "I got involved in the Documentary Film Group [which held screenings of documentary films] there and met a guy named Jerry Temaner. At that time there was no film department at the University. Then it was a 'God forbid you should do anything with your hands!' kind of attitude."

Gordon Quinn (left) and Jerry Blumenthal at Kartemquin studios. *(Photo courtesy of Kartemquin Films)*

Following graduation, Quinn worked in New York, then returned to Chicago after Temaner called with the possibility of doing a film with fellow U of C alum Stan Carter about an old-age home. The result was a documentary called *Home for Life*. The trio formed their own film company, Kartemquin, which took its moniker from a conglomeration of the names "Carter," "Temaner," and "Quinn."

"We formed Kartemquin in 1966 with the original concept to make films about social issues," says Quinn. "What we found very quickly was you had to do more than just show people the problems. You also had to have the political forces and the power to actually change things."

Carter left the following year, and Jerry Blumenthal joined Kartemquin. The company offices moved from Hyde Park to 1901 W. Wellington Avenue on the North Side, but Kartemquin's mission remained the same. "Gradually we became politicized and our films became more political," says Quinn. "We made a series of films sponsored by Catholic Adult Education, including *Inquiring Nuns* (1968) and *Thumbs Down* (1968). There were a few other films, and we took on a more anti–Vietnam War flavor."

Inquiring Nuns is a particularly moving experience, based on a simple but profound idea. Shot in 1967, the film follows two nuns through the streets of the city as they ask people, "Are you happy?" The responses provide a unique snapshot of Chicago and the mood of the country as tensions were mounting over the Vietnam War and the resultant civil unrest.

By the late 1960s and early 1970s, Kartemquin had evolved into a collective of about 12 members. People from the labor movement, teachers, and other socially concerned individuals all lent a hand to produce films that spoke to, rather than about, issues. Yet in order to survive as a company, Kartemquin also produced industrial and educational films. "We realized if we were going to survive and be independent, we needed to have a way of also doing things that paid," says Quinn.

"The collective was a group of people that we gathered around us in 1972," says Blumenthal. "Basically, the idea of the collective was that you bring together people from a variety of backgrounds, all of whom shared this notion that film, the kind of documentaries that we were interested in, ought not to be produced in a vacuum by people who were just filmmakers. The films ought to be produced in a context where the relationship between the filmmaker and the subject had some real teeth to it. This way the subject that we worked with and the ultimate distribution and use of the film were all tied together from the very beginning."

Through the 1970s and 1980s, Kartemquin produced a series of social portraits, looking at the problems of Chicago's inner city through the eyes of children, in such films as *Winnie Wright, Age 11* (1974) and *Now We Live on Clifton* (1974). In 1981, when the Pullman railcar factory threatened to close, the Kartemquin cameras documented the struggles between labor and management. "In *The Last Pullman Car* (1983) we went back and told a hundred-year history," says Blumenthal. "What we did was follow a steelworkers local that was trying to save its jobs. Pullman was closing and going into another business. In order to understand what was happening to them, we had to go back and include 100 years of labor relations and the industrial history of what happened at Pullman.

"That was a very important thread in our work during the 1970s and early 1980s, a desire to use film as a way of providing some sort of historical, political, and economic analysis to underlie the stories we were telling. But we never stopped telling the stories—the human story was always up front, and that's why we made a film."

Kartemquin's next big project was *Golub* (1988), a study of artist Leon Golub. "It just so happened that the Leon Golub retrospective was at the Museum of Contemporary Art," Blumenthal recalls. "We sort of knew Leon from way back when he was a Chicago artist. I went down to see the exhibit

Gordon Quinn and Jerry Blumenthal shooting the documentary *Golub* (1988) with museum visitors. *(Photo courtesy of Kartemquin Films)*

and I said, 'Hey, why don't we do a film about this?' Everybody thought that was not such a bad idea, because of Leon's political interests and because he's such a powerful artist. His art seemed to us to have the capacity to really move people to think about what was going on around them outside the museum. Leon brought the real world into the museum in a particularly compelling way, a very aggressive way.

"We began the project back in 1985. It took us three and a half years to finish, and it was not so much because of funding. We had money from the Focus Infinity Fund and eventually got a series of grants from various funds and arts councils. We got a big grant from the National Endowment for the Arts. But we were sort of setting out into new territory, making a film about art and trying to figure out how to tell that story in a way that would really involve the film audience in the same way that the spectators in the gallery are involved in Leon's paintings. We had to use all kinds of devices to fold it all together—how to use music and archival footage in a way that was very different from our earlier films.

"In those earlier films, when we did historical passages they were very separate from the passages in the present; in other words, the film would sort of stop and we would say, 'Now we have to look at one hundred years of history.' You would do that 10- or 15-minute passage, then come back to the story in the present. But when you've got Golub painting about mercenaries, about death squads, about stuff that's going on around you on television every night, how do you convey that sense of the present, the presence of all this information and all this kind of incredible political, moral turmoil and brutality? How do you tie that all together and make it seamless? That was a pretty intense experience for us, those three and a half years.

"I think that we succeeded in solving that problem and making a good movie. It was very different from anything we had done prior to that."

Thirteen years later, Kartemquin released *Golub: The Late Works Are the Catastrophes* (2004), which revisits Golub. Kartemquin has also done two films on Golub's wife, artist Nancy Spero.

Of course, the film that brought the Kartemquin collective's work to a much wider audience was the Chicago-set documentary *Hoop Dreams*, a fascinating study of how basketball impacts the lives of two African American high school players and how the dream of NBA riches is used to manipulate and exploit young black men. *Hoop Dreams* was a hit at Sundance and other festivals and was considered a shoo-in to win the Oscar for Best Documentary, perhaps even to become the first documentary to garner a Best Picture nomination. But *Hoop Dreams* ended up not getting nominated at all, which ironically provided the film much more attention. Steve James, director/coproducer/coeditor of *Hoop Dreams*, explains: "The next best thing to us getting a Best Picture nomination was what happened, which was to get nothing, because it created this big firestorm of controversy. It became the lead of a lot of articles, it became the headline: *'Hoop Dreams* Slighted!' instead of *'Forrest Gump* Gets 10 Nominations!' If we had gotten the nomination, it would have been buried in the stories, because that was expected."

All that publicity resulted in *Hoop Dreams* being released in many more theaters and provided the film with larger box office revenues than any previous documentary. The three collaborators on the film—Steve James (director/coproducer/coeditor), Peter Gilbert (director of photography/coproducer), and Frederick Marx (coproducer/coeditor)—have done several other projects in the intervening years, both together and separately.

Marx followed up *Hoop Dreams* with *Saving the Sphinx* (1998), a documentary about a team of individuals attempting to (as you might imagine) save and conserve the deteriorating Sphinx. He then tried his hand at a fictional feature film, the languid and beautifully filmed *The Unspoken* (1999).

The experience of making *Hoop Dreams* attuned Marx to the struggles faced by young men, inspiring him to make a pair of films exploring this subject, *Boys to Men?* (2004) and *New American Heroes*, which is still in production. *Boys to Men?* deals with the problems and obstacles encountered by teenage boys as they attempt the transition to manhood; *New American Heroes* is the sequel and posits that mentorship and initiation can be used to combat the adverse effects of negative role models and lack of guidance.

Another documentary, *17 Paths to Enlightenment*, is also in production. Marx can be reached through his website at www.warriorfilms.org.

In the wake of their post–*Hoop Dreams* success, James and Gilbert formed their own production company, Longshot Films, through a deal with Disney studios. In 1997, James and Gilbert made *Prefontaine* (1997), a feature film for Disney's Hollywood Pictures division about the late Olympic runner Steve Prefontaine. In 1998, Gilbert and Kartemquin's Gordon Quinn went to Vietnam to film a documentary for network television. *Vietnam: Long Time Coming* follows a group of American veterans returning to Vietnam for a cross-country bicycle race.

Stevie (2003), a film about James reconnecting with a troubled youth he had mentored in the "Big Brother" program 10 years previously, was coproduced and directed by James, with coproducer Quinn and Gilbert sharing camera duties with Dana Kupper. What was supposed to be a small piece about James reuniting with "Stevie" (who had become a bitter and dysfunctional adult) evolved into a four-year project when Stevie was arrested for a major crime. The resultant film examines not only the effect of Stevie's bad life choices on himself, but also on his family and upon James, who finds himself drawn into the story as the film progresses.

PBS aired Kartemquin's seven-hour miniseries *The New Americans* (2004), which showcases the lives of immigrant families from five different countries (India, Mexico, Nigeria, Palestine, and the Dominican Republic) over a four-year period, from before they leave their homelands through their first years in America. James and Quinn were executive producers, and a slew of great documentarians, including Peter Gilbert and Jerry Blumenthal, worked on this landmark miniseries.

In 2008, James and Gilbert shared both coproducer and codirector duties on another brilliant collaboration, *At the Death House Door*, which has garnered the same sort of attention that *Hoop Dreams* received. *At the Death House Door* tells the story of Carroll Pickett, a prison chaplain in Huntsville, Texas, who presided over 95 executions during a 15-year period. Having no one he could share his emotional burden with, Pickett made cassette-tape recordings of his thoughts and impressions of each individual execution, describing the entire day (which Pickett would spend with each condemned man from 6 AM until they were killed at midnight) in vivid detail.

Several interconnected threads tie the film together: footage of Pickett recounting his life and experiences to the camera; shots of him listening to

his tapes (none of which he had heard
since recording them); Pickett's visit to
the prison cemetery where all the condemned men were buried; interviews
with his adult children, friends, and colleagues; and a birthday party for Pickett
attended by his children. Also woven
into the narrative are two *Chicago Tribune* reporters investigating a story
about Carlos De Luna, an executed
man who was almost undoubtedly
innocent (a sentiment shared by Pickett
at the time, which he reveals in a meeting with the two journalists), and the
story of De Luna's sister, who becomes
inspired by the injustice foisted upon
her brother to become an activist
against the death penalty.

All of these elements are artfully
combined into what is one of the
most powerful documentary films
(or any other category of film or narrative form) ever made. And despite
the fact that one can't watch this film
without becoming convinced that
there is something seriously wrong
with America's prison system in gen-

Top: Peter Gilbert (left) and Steve
James at the prison cemetery in
Huntsville, Texas. *(Photo courtesy of
Steve James)*

Bottom: Peter Gilbert and Steve
James filming Rev. Carroll Pickett in
his office. *(Photo courtesy of Steve James)*

eral and the death penalty in particular, all political issues are superseded
by the story of Carroll Pickett, a man who willingly endured unspeakable
emotional agony and torment because of his ministerial calling and strong
religious faith. A man who is undoubtedly a Christian in the purest sense.

In 2011, James partnered with Alex Kotlowitz (known for such books as
There Are No Children Here and *Never a City So Real*) to create another
riveting documentary, *The Interrupters* (2011), which follows the lives of
three "violence interrupters" who work for the antiviolence organization
CeaseFire (later renamed Cure Violence) and spend their time attempting to head off gang conflicts in the most dangerous and poverty-plagued
areas of Chicago.

Although Kartemquin's films have been receiving worldwide attention for decades, the collective's 2008 offering *Milking the Rhino* expands Kartemquin's narrative scope to a global level. *Milking the Rhino* was filmed in Kenya and Namibia and deals with efforts to convince rural African tribesmen in these areas (who have previously been excluded from the conversation) to engage in what is

known as "community conservation," a strategy that involves these tribes replacing their centuries-old cattle-based culture with one that relies on ecotourism and finding sources of income from wildlife other than simply killing the animals for meat, ivory, or other products.

Different from most wildlife conservation documentaries, which either ignore the natives or cast them as the enemy, *Milking the Rhino* seriously examines the greater issues surrounding the controversy. The film follows several groups attempting to find a way to save Africa's wild areas without displacing the locals or depriving them of a means to survive. It is a riveting and fascinating narrative that is also beautifully shot and hypnotically paced.

TOP: Kaparo, a community game guard at the Il Ngwesi Lodge in Kenya, with a black rhino named Omni. *(Photo by David E. Simpson)*

BOTTOM: Director David E. Simpson checks playback with James Ole Kinyaga, senior host of Il Ngwesi. *(Photo by Jason Longo)*

While their scope and reach may be global, the Kartemquin collective intends to remain in Chicago. "There are a lot of good synergies between different groups and people in Chicago," says Quinn. "There's a certain amount of support for each other. Chicago is a very good climate to remain independent but not have to compete so hard for your survival."

Kartemquin's documentary work is available for rent or sale at Facets Multimedia and is often broadcast on public television. You can also order Kartemquin's films through its website at www.kartemquin.com.

Facets Multimedia

1517 W. Fullerton Avenue

Originally founded as a screening alternative to bring foreign works to Chicago, Facets Multimedia has blossomed into one of the nation's premier film resources. It's the only place in town where you can catch a Rainer Werner Fassbinder retrospective, rent a Herschell Gordon Lewis flick, create your own Eastern European film festival for the DVD player, take appreciation classes like "Ideology and the Body in Pasolini's Cinema" or "Film Noir and the Hol-lywood Blacklist," and even bring the kids to see the best children's films from around the world. Roger Ebert wasn't hyperbolizing when he called Facets "a temple of great cinema . . . an amazing place."

Facets Multimedia, where the end of America is only a movie. *(Photo by Kate Corcoran)*

Facets Multimedia is the brainchild of Milos Stehlik, a Czechoslovakian native who came to Chicago in 1962. Eager to create a showcase for Eastern European film in Chicago, Stehlik and a partner started showing films at a rented theater on the corner of Halsted and Armitage. "It was kind of a strange situation," Stehlik remembers. "Even though the films were quite successful at this theater, [the owners] were kind of jealous of it, so we decided to come up with a theater on our own. Our first location was at the Resurrection Lutheran Church in Lakeview."

Forced to find a new location, Facets eventually found a permanent home at 1517 W. Fullerton. The building was originally a department store, then served as headquarters to *Die Hausfrau*, a German-language journal "with a big circulation in Argentina!" Stehlik notes. Facets bought the building and took up residence in May 1977, using volunteer construction to transform the space into a movie theater.

Over the years, Facets' reputation has grown considerably. Today it houses two theaters, one for film screenings and the other for video projections. As venues for foreign films disappear, Facets thrives as a showcase for international cinema. Fans of independent, low-budget films have also found a haven at Facets.

As part of its commitment to comprehensive filmgoing for Chicago, Facets brings in guest lecturers who represent many aspects of contemporary filmmaking. Werner Herzog, Claude Chabrol, Louis Malle, Robert Altman, Errol Morris, and Dušan Makavejev have all spoken at Facets, giving midwesterners a unique opportunity to speak with world-renowned directors.

In 1982, the nonprofit institution took a huge leap of faith into the slowly growing market of home video rental. The video experiment proved to be a huge success, as was its upgrade into DVD production and distribution several years later. The institution now stocks over 65,000 films on DVD, many of them even digitally restored by Facets. It also carries a variety of film-related books and, in association with Academy Press, has also published guides for gay/lesbian, African American, and nonviolent/nonsexist children's videos. Be sure to pick up a copy of Facets' thick catalog; the rich offerings within go far beyond the fare found in other places, even the vaunted Netflix. It's no wonder that Facets' repeat customers include directors Martin Scorsese and Jonathan Demme.

The expansion into DVD and video has been an asset to another important part of Facets: its many film appreciation classes. "Oddly enough, what made classes possible was video," Stehlik says. Facets held classes off and on for a few years, but the high cost of film rental often made tuition costs prohibitive. Owning an extensive video library essentially allowed Facets to bring down class fees. The classes in film history and aesthetics consider an expansive range of topics. Viewing includes works from the silent era, world cinema, American independent films, and Hollywood blockbusters—sometimes all of which are represented in a single thematic course.

Unlike many film institutions, Facets recognizes the importance of films for children. If you're looking for an alternative to Disney pictures or endless Barney videos, Facets has what you're looking for. Facets also holds an annual children's film festival every autumn.

Since those first screenings at Halsted and Armitage, Facets Multimedia has become an important resource for local filmmakers and institutions. Its commitment to Chicago's filmmaking community is reflected through ongoing relationships, screenings, and film distribution. The work of local documentary stalwarts Kartemquin Films and Tom Palazzolo can both be rented through Facets Video. Additionally, Facets has cosponsored a number of programs with the Siskel Film Center, Chicago Filmmakers, and the Goethe Institute.

For membership information, film schedules, rental/sales and work-shop information at Facets Multimedia, call (800) 331-6197 or visit www.facets.org.

Ruth Ratny and ReelChicago.com: The Website of Record

The website we now know (and love) as ReelChicago.com began its life as *Screen* 30 years ago. "I was not new to trade-paper writing when I started *Screen*," explains founder Ruth Ratny. "Earlier, I was a freelance columnist for New York–based *Backstage*, and my Chicago Report column was the only blip on the flyover zone. When I quit, there was a total national black-out of Chicago production news."

Ratny founded *Screen* as a four-page, 8-by-10, typewritten newsletter, which debuted inauspiciously in 1979 during the Screen Actors Guild's first commercials strike in 23 years. "My first lead story was about the SAG strike. I earned the unforgiving enmity of the director of the local SAG chapter when my story noted how advertisers said they would continue to produce com-mercials by going overseas and by using—eek!—nonunion talent."

Ratny determined at the start that *Screen* was going to be all the things that the *Chicago Unlimited Digest* newsletter, the only connective trade tissue at the time, was not. "The weekly *Digest*, whose mission was to promote actors who had opted to work in Chicago, didn't convey much information," she says. "I determined that *Screen*'s information would be precise and detailed, that we would spotlight interesting but unsung indi-viduals, that we would demonstrate the depth of creative talent and dispel the evil 'Second City Syndrome' (SCS) that held that everyplace and every-one else was better than Chicago. SCS sufferers would see that Chicago was bigger and better than they ever imagined."

During her 23 years editing and publishing *Screen*, Ratny was honored with numerous awards: Advertising Woman of the Year and Midwest Advertising Woman of the Year, 1979, the same year she founded *Screen*; Chicago Coalition Recognition Award in 1985; Women in Film Recognition Award in 1989; and membership in *Today's Chicago Woman*'s 100 Women Hall of Fame.

ReelChicago.com began in 2002, a year after Ratny left *Screen*. "Leaving *Screen*—a long story—was one of the worst disasters of my life. Two other disasters that followed in short order were a freak accident, from which I was still recovering when I left *Screen*, and shortly thereafter, a bout of cancer. Still, throughout the cancer treatment trauma, I was able to maintain ReelChicago."

"Issues" of Reel contain news stories, current indie film projects, listings of screenings and events, and columns contributed by experts in their fields. Ratny says, "With the last 'e-lert' of 2008, we had published 46 'issues,' almost twice as many as the current *Screen*'s 25 issues, and all of it original content. I'm always thinking about the reader's need to know, focusing on targeted, detailed, and exclusive news stories not found anywhere else—my specialty. Also, strictly Chicago content, although we now include Wisconsin and Michigan stories, since they affect or pertain to Chicago. What's different is the instant delivery, viral wins over print, low overhead, instant posting and updates, infinitely greater readership and potential. Reel is read throughout the world."

But as always, Ratny will never shy away from printing the ugly truth when it needs to be revealed. "We've never hesitated to expose the scandals and chicanery of individuals and companies who tried to get away with something illegal or immoral. We've exposed all kinds of scams and crooked deals and people. Bookkeepers who embezzled from their employers and put them out of business. Individuals going behind their partners' backs to open their own company with pirated clients. Directors' kickbacks, rigged bids, conflicts of interest, hidden ownerships of companies revealed, and so on.

"So when a taxpayer-funded state agency goes out of state for commercials targeted to Illinois residents and then gives phony reasons to justify their actions, we took—and still take—great pleasure in exposing them. In November 2008, the [Illinois State] Lottery's Chicago agency hired a local sales rep's 'production' company to produce a $500,000 package of holiday spots. In turn, the rep's company hired an L.A. director, L.A. editorial house, and music house it also just happened to represent. What troubled me was that both the lottery director and its long-time ad agency knew the rules about spending state money for state projects in the state. They brazenly flouted the rules, assuming their deals would remain private, and then responded with 'Who me?' false innocence."

Although the issue of tax incentives for film/video producers tends to grab all the headlines whenever the issue of attracting more business to Illinois is discussed, Ratny says that "good incentives are a good start, a door opener, but incentives alone cannot sell a state. We're engaged in what Illinois Production Alliance president Lars Ullberg calls 'the incentives arms race,' the competition among states for their share of an industry that generates $9.3 billion in American salaries each year, according to the US Census. The new kick to 30 percent from the 20 percent incentives we've had since 2005 will be more helpful, but in order to successfully compete, Chicago, i.e., the filmmakers who benefit from Hollywood business, must raise the funds, apart from or in collaboration with the government, to create and maintain sales and promotion strategies to successfully compete with brutal and better competitors. We shouldn't put all our eggs in the one basket of tax incentives; we have to find a way to stem the unending exodus of talent to Los Angeles; we need a well-funded, well-organized industry marketing and publicity campaign to publicize city/state advantages and keep the legislators charged up."

Tom Palazzolo: Blazing His Own Trail

"If you were to put together Tom Palazzolo's complete works, you would have an interesting underground record of Chicago over the last 30 years."

—Roger Ebert

Combining the urban realism of documentary with the poetic grit of Nelson Algren's writing, Tom Palazzolo has carved out a unique niche among Chicago-based filmmakers. "I really like Chicago, doing documentaries on Chicago and people in Chicago," he says. "Urban settings are where I'm the most comfortable."

Palazzolo came to Chicago in 1960 for studies at the School of the Art Institute. "I got interested in photo and film and got into the underground and experimental film scene." He began making his own experimental documentaries and was a regular at the legendary Aardvark Cinematheque in the late 1960s. In 1968, Palazzolo went to the Mideast with a group of independent filmmakers as part of a government program to show other cultures how much freedom Americans have. After returning home, he was hired to teach at the City Colleges of Chicago. Over the years, Palazzolo established himself as one of the premier documentary filmmakers working in the city.

"I like the margins of things," he says today. "I don't make shocking films, but I do like the humanity of people sort of on the out-there, the lower end of society. I like marginal people and places like Riverview."

Palazzolo's subjects cover a wide spectrum of fringe culture. His wonderful documentary *I Married a Munchkin* (1994) is a warmhearted portrait of a married pair of little people, one of whom played a Munchkin in MGM's classic musical *The Wizard of Oz*. Another of Palazzolo's works, *Marquette Park II* (1978), looks at the ragtag National Socialist Party of Frank Colin as they plan a march through the heavily Jewish suburb of Skokie. These neo-Nazis "were more pathetic and sad than anything else," Palazzolo observes. "I try to make [my films] as personal to me as I can and as personal as I can. I've also done a couple of experimental films, which in a way are documentaries. I used some performance artists and did *Caligari's Cure* (1983), a sort of a funny remake of the silent German expressionist film *The Cabinet of Dr. Caligari*. Because I'm in this art environment, I did these weird painted sets. It really was kind of an 'art comedy.'"

Palazzolo's work has been shown at many prestigious venues, including New York's Whitney Museum and Museum of Modern Art. Locally, Chicago Filmmakers and the Siskel Film Center also screen his films, and Facets sells compilation videos of Palazzolo movies. Perhaps the best place to catch his work is on WTTW–Channel 11's popular show *Image Union*, which features Palazzolo's work on a regular basis.

Biograph Theater
2433 N. Lincoln Avenue

The best action to play at the Biograph Theater didn't happen on-screen. On July 22, 1934, the notorious bank robber John Dillinger stepped out of the Biograph doors into a hail of FBI bullets.

Dillinger's story has been told often, sometimes right, sometimes wrong, and more often than not in a mixture of fact, fiction, and fantasy. What follows is a thumbnail sketch of the Dillinger saga.

Dillinger was born in Indiana, on June 28, 1902. In 1923, Dillinger joined the United States Navy but soon went AWOL with no intention of returning. The following year he turned to crime, trying to hold up a store in his hometown of Mooresville, Indiana.

Dillinger was caught and thrown in the slammer. Paroled in 1933, he gathered a few like-minded individuals and started robbing banks.

By 1934, the Federal Bureau of Investigation was hot on the Dillinger case. Certainly killing two cops and two FBI agents along the way made the hardened criminal an especially favored target for the Feds, who listed him as Public Enemy Number One. Though Dillinger tried to change his looks through plastic surgery, he couldn't evade the law.

On July 22, 1934, Dillinger went to the Biograph with his girlfriend of a few weeks, Polly Hamilton, and Hamilton's landlord, a Romanian immigrant named Anna Sage.

The Lincoln Avenue Biograph Theater being dressed in period style for filming of *Public Enemies* (2009). *(Photo by Brian Carstens)*

Unbeknownst to Dillinger or Hamilton, Sage was facing deportation for helping run a prostitution ring. When Sage met Hamilton's new beau, a guy named "Jimmy Lawrence," she instantly realized he was the notorious bank robber. Despite plastic surgery, Dillinger was still recognizable.

Hoping to cash in on the substantial reward, as well as block the deportation charges against her, Sage went to a police officer who had been investigating her case. On July 20, 1934, she promised she could deliver Dillinger to the FBI. On the morning of July 22, Sage informed the local FBI office that she, Dillinger, and Hamilton would be going to either the Marbro Theatre at 4124 W. Madison or the Biograph that evening. Two teams of agents were dispatched to stake out the theaters.

That night, the threesome went to the Biograph. On the bill was *Manhattan Melodrama*, a gangster drama starring Clark Gable as racketeer Blackie Gallagher (Mickey Rooney also has a small role, playing the young Gallagher). At 10:30 PM, Dillinger and company exited the theater, and FBI agent Melvin Purvis, along with other Feds and some Chicago cops, were waiting. Dillinger ran down the alley next to the theater but was cut down in a shower of bullets.

The next morning, the story was all over the newswires. Sage was singled out as the mysterious "woman in red" who had betrayed America's most vicious bank robber.

The story of Dillinger's demise has been told numerous times onscreen. Tough guy Lawrence Tierney plays the title role in the 1945 film

Dillinger. The FBI Story (1959) portrays the FBI's point of view. *Appointment with Destiny: The Last Days of John Dillinger* was released in 1971. The 1973 *Dillinger* features Warren Oates as the notorious bank robber, while Robert Conrad essays the role in *The Lady in Red* (1979). Baby-faced Mark Harmon starred in a made-for-television *Dillinger* in 1991. The most unlikely spin on the story was the 1995 feature *Dillinger and Capone,* starring Martin Sheen as John Dillinger and Oscar winner F. Murray Abraham as Al Capone. Apparently some producer got the wise idea of pairing Chicago's two most notorious gangsters together on-screen, a partnership that never existed in real life.

Public Enemies (2009), the most recent retelling of the Dillinger tale, stars Johnny Depp as Dillinger and Christian Bale as Melvin Purvis and was directed by Michael Mann. The 2400 block of Lincoln Avenue around the Biograph was restored to appear almost exactly as it did on that day in 1934, with fake cobblestones, vintage automobiles, streetlights, signs, and remodeling jobs on the nearby storefronts helping to create the illusion (read more in the Nathan Crowley section, page 91).

The Biograph is now home to the Victory Gardens Theater Company. For more information, visit www.victorygardens.org.

Lincoln Park Zoo
2200 N. Cannon Drive

The Lincoln Park Zoo, one of the city's most popular attractions, was founded in 1868 with the gift of two white swans courtesy of the folks running New York City's Central Park. Today the zoo has more than 1,000 animals and provides visitors with one of the best walks the city has to offer.

The movies have also had a good time at Lincoln Park Zoo, where Joe Mantegna, Joe Pantoliano, and Brian Haley square off with a gorilla in 1994's *Baby's Day Out* (although their encounter was actually filmed on a soundstage). Chuck Norris takes a stroll through the zoo in *Code of Silence* (1985); so do David Schwimmer in *Kissing a Fool* (1998), David Duchovny in *Return to Me* (2000), and Pete Jones in *Outing Riley* (2004). A recent indie coming-of-age film, *Sin Bin* (2012), also has a scene at the zoo.

Head a little bit north across Fullerton Avenue to the Lincoln Park Lagoon and you'll find the site where high school bully Matt Dillon shoves around Adam Baldwin before receiving his comeuppance from Chris Makepeace in *My Bodyguard* (1980). The performances in this film are wonderfully natural, marked by the easy stylings of then-unknown Chicago actors Baldwin and Joan Cusack.

The Lincoln Park Zoo website is www.lpzoo.org. The zoo is open 365 days a year, and admission is free. For more information, call (312) 742-2000.

The Theatre School–DePaul University

2135 N. Kenmore Avenue

Founded as the Goodman School of Drama in 1925, the Theatre School became part of DePaul University in 1978 and is the oldest theater conservatory in the Midwest. The curriculum relies on a simple philosophy: "learn by doing." To this end, the school puts on over 35 productions a year in its wide array of performance spaces, the largest being the lavish 1,325-seat Merle Reskin Theatre, downtown near the Blackstone Hotel. The 14 specialized areas of study include acting, costume design, lighting design, scenic design, theater technology, playwriting, dramaturgy/criticism, and theater arts.

Stranger Than Fiction (2006) scriptwriter Zach Helm is a Theatre School graduate, as are Gillian Anderson, Kevin Anderson, Bruce Boxleitner, Melinda Dillon, Judy Greer, Gloria Foster, Linda Hunt, Harvey Korman, Karl Malden, Joe Mantegna, Lanny Meyers, Kevin J. O'Connor, Geraldine Page, Elizabeth Perkins, Amy Pietz, Aidan Quinn, John C. Reilly, Michael Rooker, Carrie Snodgress, and Adrian Zmed.

You can learn more about the Theatre School by calling (773) 325-7917 or visiting http://theatreschool.depaul.edu.

Robert DeNiro's Apartment in *Mad Dog and Glory*

635 W. Belden Avenue

Mild-mannered police photographer Wayne "Mad Dog" Dobie (Robert DeNiro) leads a pretty quiet life on this pretty quiet stretch of Belden until he inadvertently saves the life of mob boss/fledgling stand-up comic Frank Milo (Bill Murray) in 1993's offbeat comedy *Mad Dog and Glory*. The second half of the title comes in the form of Uma Thurman, a sort of feminine "gratuity" Murray passes on to the reluctant DeNiro for a week.

Pay close attention to the climactic fight scene outside this apartment and you'll notice a few subtle differences. Extras don't quite look the same from shot to shot, and DeNiro manages to get his hair cut, then grow it back, in between shots. You can credit this mysterious movie magic to that unique Hollywood convention, the test screening. This practice, designed to make all films everything to all potential viewers, is a standard for major movie studios. Unreleased films are trotted out before select audiences, responses are tallied, and alterations are made based on these reactions.

The original ending to *Mad Dog and Glory* had Murray's character beating the living daylights out of DeNiro's character. Defeated, DeNiro goes back into his apartment and sits on his couch. Thurman, who disappeared during the fight, comes walking in the door and sits down next to DeNiro—their fledgling love appears to have hope.

That's not what you see in the final cut, of course.

"Nobody liked that ending in the test screenings," recalls *Mad Dog and Glory* producer Steven A. Jones. "Audiences hated the fact that the Raging Bull got his ass kicked by Bill Murray. We kept saying, 'It's not the Raging Bull!' But it didn't matter.

"So we added a second half to the fight. The DeNiro character gets in a whole bunch of licks. We shot it literally a year later. DeNiro's hair had been cut down for *This Boy's Life* (1994), Bill had gotten bigger, and we couldn't get back some of the guys who were in Murray's gang. If you look really closely at all of the extras, after DeNiro throws that punch, they're all different extras. Look at the people across the street, see what they're wearing, they're all completely different. DeNiro throws a punch one year and it lands the next."

Steven A. Jones: Portrait of a Chicago Producer

"People will ask me, 'What kind of producer are you?' I always say, 'I'm the producer that's there every single day.'" —*Steven A. Jones*

Born in Syracuse, New York, and raised in Brooklyn, Steven A. Jones has managed not only to become a successful feature film producer, but also has been able to do it while based completely in Chicago, something almost unheard of in the L.A.-centric world of film.

Jones first came to Chicago in 1967 to study design and filmmaking at the now-defunct Institute of Design at the Illinois Institute of Technology ("an arty little part of a rigid technical college"). A self-taught drummer who was into underground music, Jones quickly fell in with the freewheeling Chicago music scene of the 1960s.

After two years, he began studying animation and took to it with gusto. His musical proficiency increased as well. "By the time I graduated I was a rock 'n' roll musician who dabbled in animation on the side in order to make a living." Music became a more serious part of his life, however, and Jones left for L.A. to become a professional musician. He lived and worked there for several years until growing weary of the scene and moving back to Chicago.

Upon his return, he ran into an old school friend. The friend convinced him to run his new company, which was doing animation sequences for commercials. Jones agreed, but only if he could remain a freelancer. He began a frenetic several-year period where he directed animation and continued his music career, often jetting back and forth to L.A. and touring between commercial assignments. Among the commercials he created were spots for Gatorade, McDonald's, and virtually all the animated Cap'n Crunch ads of the 1980s.

Jones's career as a feature film producer began in 1985 when a client of his, the Oak Forest–based video company Maljack Productions Incorporated (MPI), got on a roll. Formed by Waleed and Malik Ali, the sons of a Lebanese immigrant, MPI got into the video-releasing business in the early 1980s, just as the great home video boom was about to take off, and made a killing.

Having gotten a handle on video distribution, the brothers decided to take a leap into the production end of the business. John McNaughton, a freelance video director who worked with MPI, suggested a film based on the crimes of Henry Lee Lucas, a notorious serial killer McNaughton had seen profiled on television. The Alis liked the idea; after all, serial killer horror films like *Friday the 13th* (1980) and *Nightmare on Elm Street* (1984) had been immensely successful. McNaughton brought in Jones, who had designed the MPI logo as a freelance job. The duo was provided with $100,000, McNaughton wrote a script with the Organic Theatre's Richard Fire, and a trio of unknown actors was hired.

Playing Henry was Michael Rooker, an intense, handsome Chicago actor. Tom Towles was Henry's dimwitted friend Otis, and Tracy Arnold played Otis's sister Becky. McNaughton used a documentary style to explore the ugly world of these three characters. No moral judgment is made on Henry's actions. If anything, the audience looks over his shoulder. The result is terrifying. *Henry* wasn't the cartoonish violence of the *Friday the 13th* movies. We see the aftermath of Henry's work in stark reality.

"The people we made it for thought it was too arty, and the people who were artists thought it was too gory," says Jones. "We ended up in this no-man's-land."

Part of the film's terrible beauty comes from Rooker's chilling performance. Henry could be anybody. He is the guy with a broken-down car you try to help. He is the jerk you try to sell a hot TV to. You could take his order at a restaurant and smile when he flirts with you. He is the man at the door who's come to fumigate your house. No matter what your relationship is, he'll kill you.

In an age where serial killers are glorified on film, television, and in countless cheap paperbacks, *Henry* pulled no punches. The Alis didn't know what to make of McNaughton and Jones's work. They'd been expecting a standard shock-thriller: Teens head out for fun. Slowly the group gets picked off by an unseen murderer. Audience jumps at prerequisite scene of victim scared by cat . . . then killer strikes. Last member of the group manages to escape . . . but so does psychopathic fiend. Watch the whole formula again in numerous sequels.

Henry, on the other hand, was stark and brutal, and got under your skin. It was also an undeniable work of art. It played at the 1986 Chicago Film Festival to critical acclaim. Audiences recoiled in horror and praised the film's artistic merits.

Shocked by the realistic nature of *Henry*, the MPAA ratings board slapped the film with an X. That meant no distributor would touch *Henry*. Essentially, the film had been blackballed before it had a chance. "But then," says Jones, "Errol Morris, who made *The Thin Blue Line* (1988), guest-directed the 1989 Telluride Film Festival. He chose *Henry* as one of his three movies that the audience sort of had to see. When Morris stood up and said, 'This is a great work,' everybody looked at *Henry* in a different light, and it sort of took off from there."

Three years after it was completed, *Henry* had become a cult hit. Suddenly other theaters around the country wanted to show the film. New York critics put *Henry* in their annual Best Films of the Year lists. *Time* magazine decried *Henry*'s MPAA X rating, boldly stating, "This movie rates an X as in excellent."

Among the legion of new fans was Martin Scorsese, who gave the Chicago outsiders a chance at the mainstream with 1993's *Mad Dog and Glory*.

"Scorsese called John and said, 'I've got this idea for a screenplay. Maybe you want to do it,'" says Jones.

"*Mad Dog and Glory* was a great screenplay. John and I said, 'Yeah, we'll do it.' Then Scorsese asked, 'What do you think if I offer it to my friend Bob?' 'Bob?' 'Yeah, Bob DeNiro.' We said, 'Well, yeah, if you want to, go ahead.' Like we're going to tell Marty 'No!'

"Up until that point, *Mad Dog and Glory* was supposed to be an $8 or $9 million movie. We were thinking of casting guys like Joe Mantegna. Once DeNiro got involved, it changed considerably. The budget doubled. DeNiro was the guy who suggested casting Bill Murray. You know, the more money you bring into a picture, the more people you have telling you how to spend it. It became much more of a studio picture once DeNiro got involved, but on the other hand we got to work with him!

"We started *Mad Dog and Glory* in New York. We did preproduction work, but then Scorsese had to deliver a picture to Universal after Stephen Frears backed out of doing *Cape Fear* (1991) with DeNiro. Marty took over that picture and they put us on hold. The producer came over to our office and said, 'You know that movie you were going to do? Well, you're not going to do it now. You'll do it next year.' We said, 'Yeah, sure.' The head of production at Universal said, 'No, no, I'm telling you, you'll make this movie next year.' As things turned out, they told us the truth.

"But we were out of business at this point. Since we had nothing to do, John and I decided to call back one of the guys who'd called us up. One of them was Eric Bogosian, who had sent John a fan letter about *Henry*. We were talking to him and he said, 'You know, I'm trying to do a movie of my live show, but I don't want to talk to you guys about that.' We said, 'Talk to us, we just lost our job!'

"We ended up filming his live show in Boston with Ernest Dickerson, who was Spike Lee's cinematographer at the time. We did a big version of what he was doing onstage in New York City. John and I left what Bogosian was doing completely alone. We said, 'You do what you do, and we'll make the set a little bigger.'

"So we did our interpretation of what Bogosian did for a company called Avenue Pictures," which released the film in 1991 as *Sex, Drugs, Rock & Roll*. "[The company] even advertised the release for about 200 theaters. It got released in 20 and then Avenue Pictures went out of business! Once again, we had a picture that didn't get seen very much, but we got some good reviews and had some good times.

"Because of union labor charges, Universal decided to move *Mad Dog and Glory* to Chicago, which was fine for us. We got to stay home! We changed everything in the script to Chicago locations. John and I got to pick locations, like the water sculpture down on the river, so we had a little more fun.

"While we were editing *Mad Dog*, I picked up a *Chicago Tribune* magazine article about Jeff and Jill Erickson. They were this couple who robbed banks and then Jill had killed herself when they got caught. I said, 'Look at this, this is a great story.' I called the woman who wrote the article but she wouldn't return my calls.

"We went back to New York to finish *Mad Dog* and I saw a headline in the *New York Times*: 'Jeff Erickson Killed in a Shootout.' I started calling the writer again, but she wouldn't return my calls and I couldn't figure out why. It turned out somebody else had already optioned her material.

"A year later somebody sent us a screenplay [based on the option for Erickson's story]. It was really good. We didn't have another picture, and John was doing television. Finally, people at William Morris said, 'If you are willing to work with Luke Perry, we can probably raise enough money to make this movie.' John and I looked at Luke's rodeo movie, *8 Seconds* (1994), and agreed that he'd be fine. Luke's an innocuous, suburban guy.

"Then they said, 'By the way, you can have this newcomer, Ashley Judd.' John and I said, 'OK, let's go!' Once again, we got to work here. We shot in the O'Hare area, in just about every suburb around the airport. Hanover Park, Hoffman Estates, River Grove—these were all the places that Erickson actually went. We were in the actual bank that he held up. When we captured him in the movie, it was the same parking lot that they really captured him in. That was kind of interesting.

"We used Triton College in River Grove for the rehab scenes and Triton's Cernan Space Center for the planetarium. We had so little money that whenever we shot someplace, we'd have two more scenes that we could shoot real close by.

"*Normal Life* (1996) was made for theatrical release—or so we thought! But meanwhile, the money people said, 'Oh well, you know, we don't want to bother putting it out in theaters. We'll just sell it to HBO.' John yelled and screamed a lot and got them to release it in New York and Chicago.

"Once again, we just seemed to have this string of pictures that would never get released and then we'd get these great reviews. *Henry*; *Sex, Drugs, Rock & Roll*; and *Normal Life* all got incredible reviews!"

The next project the duo worked on, the sexy noirish thriller *Wild Things* (1998), needed no help from reviewers, as it was widely released and became a hit. Ironically, Jones and McNaughton had planned to part ways before this film. "What happened was that John and I did *Normal Life*, and we had gotten to a point that, from a personal and working relationship standpoint, we needed a breather. I think that John had really become his own man as far as directing goes, and we really needed to go our separate ways and see what we could do."

Jones left for England to develop a script for James Bond producer Barbara Broccoli, and McNaughton went to work on *Wild Things*. "A few months later," Jones recalls, "out of the blue, John calls me and says, 'I'm in Miami and we can't make a deal with this other producer; you need to come down here and help me make this movie.' I called the studio that was making the movie, Mandalay, and they said, 'Oh we met you last year. Don't even bother to come out to L.A. to meet us, just go to Miami and get to work.'"

Steve immediately jetted to Miami and rejoined McNaughton on the set. "It was interesting when I went down there, because I had to figure out what my job was, because it had changed. John was now a solo director, and that was fine, but what was I gonna do?" The duo quickly worked out their new roles. "I became more involved in the physical production and running interference with the production company, studio, and actors and less involved in the minute-by-minute creative decision-making," and *Wild Things* became a hit. "This was the biggest budget we'd had, which was over $30 million, and lots of movie stars [Kevin Bacon, Matt Dillon, Neve Campbell, Denise Richards, and Theresa Russell]. It was all in all a lot of fun, and it really did turn out well."

Unfortunately, the next film they worked on together, *Speaking of Sex* (2001), did not fare well at all. Despite having a $12 million budget and several stars (James Spader, Lara Flynn Boyle, Megan Mullally), *Speaking of Sex* fell prey (as many films have) to the vicissitudes of international high finance. StudioCanal, who financed the picture, was owned by Vivendi, a large, multibillion-dollar operation that had recently undergone massive expansion and then faced a massive collapse (with the requisite allegations of wrongdoing). The billions of dollars involved in the resulting financial imbroglio eclipsed any concern about a little $12 million film sitting on a shelf, so *Speaking of Sex* was never released theatrically (although it is now available on home video).

The unfortunate circumstances surrounding *Speaking of Sex* took its toll on two fronts. First, it pushed Jones and McNaughton onto separate paths such that, although they remain good friends and are trying to collaborate again, the pair have yet to work on another film together. Sadder still is the fact that, although McNaughton has since had much success as a director on several popular television shows (including *Without a Trace* and the acclaimed HBO series *John from Cincinnati*), the shelving of *Speaking of Sex* stunted the momentum he had achieved with *Wild Things* and prevented him from jumping into the top tier of feature film directors.

With his good friend John's film directing career stalled, Jones, now fully committed to being a feature film producer, began looking for other collaborators. He had already worked with fledgling director Tanya Wexler (daughter of real estate kingpin Jerry Wexler and niece of legendary cinematographer/director Haskell Wexler) on the quirky and moving indie film *Finding North* (1998) and was confident he could get other projects moving. One day, an executive from Mandalay named Todd Black introduced him to Chicago writer Steve Conrad, whom Black had worked with on *Wrestling Ernest Hemingway* (1993) and who was looking to write and direct a feature film. "We sort of hit it off and began conceptualizing and working on some things."

The first thing that came out of Jones's and Conrad's partnership was *Lawrence Melm* (2004). Although it was never released—"Too long to be a short and too short to be a feature"—it allowed Jones and Conrad to develop a working relationship and assemble the core of the team that they used on *The Promotion* (2008).

The Promotion, set in a fictitious Chicago grocery store named "Donaldson's," won the Best Film Award at the 2008 Midwest Film Fest. It's a low-key yet hilarious comedy in the tradition of *Office Space* (1999) and is steadily working its way toward cult status. It stars Seann William Scott of the *American Pie* films and veteran actor John C. Reilly as two assistant managers vying for a coveted manager spot in a new, yet-to-be-constructed Donaldson's store. The dirty tricks and extraordinary efforts they both undertake in pursuit of the promotion are humorous yet also poignant, as they underscore the huge struggles ordinary people must undertake in order to achieve their dreams in the face of a dehumanizing corporate oligarchy. It also features *The Office*'s Jenna Fischer as Scott's wife, Lili Taylor as Reilly's wife, and a sidesplitting cameo by Jason Bateman as a "team-building" retreat leader.

As Jones has gone through his career as a film producer, his role has evolved, much as the role of the producer itself has changed over the years. "In the old days, a producer would come up with an idea and hire everyone to execute it. A writer to write the script, director and crew to shoot, actors to act, composers, musicians, and editors to score and edit it—which just doesn't happen anymore unless you're Jerry Bruckheimer or someone like that."

After the demise of the old studio system, the role of the producer became much more segmented and specialized, as evidenced by the various types one sees listed in movie credits (producer, executive producer, associate producer, etc). "Some producers are liaisons for the money and rarely come to the set," explains Jones. "Others do creative overview, overseeing the process every single day from beginning to end. They call me a creative producer, because I'm not involved in finding the money, I'm involved in spending it and deciding how it gets spent in the budgeting process. People will ask me, 'What kind of producer are you?' I always say, 'I'm the producer that's there every single day.'"

Sometimes a producer's job is to attempt to heal rifts that develop between different factions of the creative team (such as the director and the studio, or between various sets of producers) over decisions on the final cut of the film. "So the producer's job is to negotiate between those two ends and reach an end where everyone is in agreement," Jones says. "What you'd really like is for everyone to be happy." Despite the producer's efforts, these disputes can often escalate and result in a film's release being delayed, sometimes indefinitely. "Everybody has good intentions, but then it just starts to become this tug-of-war. One camp sees things one way, the other camp sees it another way, and it's hard to get a consensus on how to get the movie finished."

This very sort of factionalism delayed the release of another Jones-produced film, *The Merry Gentleman* (2008), which sat in limbo until finally gaining a limited theatrical release in late 2009. This caused an extremely fine dramatic film (also Michael Keaton's directorial debut) to not receive the attention it deserved. And still another understated drama produced by Jones and which starred John Malkovich, *Drunkboat* (2010), was shelved for several years due to similar creative strife before being released straight to video.

Sometimes these differences occur because of the tenuous relationship between art and commerce that is at the core of the filmmaking industry.

Jones is well aware of this dichotomy and strives to overcome it: "You have to allow your artists as much leeway as possible and give them all the tools they can have to do what they want to do—that's why you hired them—but on the other hand you're still responsible to the guys who put the money up, because it's a commercial enterprise. For as much as it is an artistic enterprise, it's still a commercial one."

Jones has both advice and a warning for those who totally refuse to compromise their vision when making a film. "If you want to do a purely artistic enterprise then take your Super 8 or HD camera and knock yourself out; but as soon as you've got a partner who's paying the bills, you've got to start to think differently."

Though he's been a feature film producer for over 25 years now, one thing has always been clear to him: it was important to remain based in Chicago. "By the time *Henry* came out, I had already been to L.A. once as a musician and was about 40 years old, and I was thinking about starting a family. So the idea of moving to L.A. to become a filmmaker just had no appeal to me whatsoever, so I really didn't give it much thought. Then once my son was born, I knew I didn't want to raise him in that L.A. culture, where every waking moment of your existence is devoted to the industry."

Aside from seeming like a better place to raise his family, Jones had other personal reasons not to head west: "If you're in a bar in L.A., 95 percent of the people would be talking about movies. The other 5 percent would be talking about the music industry. I prefer to live in a place that's a little more real. There's no such thing as working-class L.A." The genuine nature of the city helps when making movies as well. "The fact that Chicago is not a film industry town makes people here want to really work extra hard, really be craftsmen at what they do."

Always looking to keep busy, Jones is developing several projects. But no matter what projects may come and go, Steven A. Jones will continue to produce films the way he has always lived his life—on his own terms.

Francis J. Dewes House
503 W. Wrightwood Avenue

A stately former mansion (and former home to the Swedish Engineers Society of Chicago), this wonderful Lincoln Park building is notable for the male and female statues beneath the wrought iron balcony. The period look of the Dewes House served *The Babe* (1992) and *Hoodlum*

(1997) well. It has also shown up in such contrasting pictures as Patrick Swayze's cop action flick *Next of Kin* (1989) and the Julia Roberts comedy *My Best Friend's Wedding* (1997).

"O'Neils" From *Only the Lonely*
3369 N. Clark Street

It changes names and themes every few years, but it will likely remain a bar for all eternity, as it sits in a prime location between two hot North Side drinking areas, the clubs of Lakeview/Boystown and the boozeries of Wrigleyville. In *Only the Lonely* (1991), this hangout at the corner of Roscoe and Clark became O'Neils, the neighborhood Irish pub. Maureen O'Hara, mom of shy cop John Candy, lifts her drink in salute to Candy's girlfriend, Ally Sheedy, here. In another drinking scene, one with a bit more edge to it, Candy and his uniformed colleagues bring in a deceased pal for one last round.

For Brian DePalma's big-screen version of *The Untouchables* (1987), the whole block was redressed as 1920s storefronts.

Brew & View at the Vic Theatre
3145 N. Sheffield Avenue

Looking for a combo of a late-night movie and cheap eats? Then check out Brew & View, one of the city's most entertaining spots for both movie- and people-watching. Brew & View is actually an offshoot of the Vic Theatre. When not hosting rock concerts or comedy shows, the Vic turns into a movie theater, albeit one that serves beer and pizza. What's more, this is one venue where talking during the show isn't a faux pas. Patrons tend to be on the rowdy side (late-night movies and beer . . . go figure), which makes this an ideal place to watch action flicks or robust comedies.

For a schedule of upcoming Brew & View movies, call (773) 929-6713 or visit www.brewview.com.

The Streets of Boston in *The Babe*
3400–3459 N. Southport Avenue (between Roscoe Street and Cornelia Avenue)

Today, Southport Avenue is a trendy stretch of coffee bars, nightclubs, shops, and restaurants. But for a few days in 1991, this stretch of Southport was transformed into 1916 Boston for the baseball biography *The Babe*, starring John Goodman as Babe Ruth.

But how do you get businesses to close up shop, induce the CTA to reroute buses and trains, and transform video stores into early-20th-century establishments? *The Babe* production company had to complete 65 different contracts with the many businesses and private residences on Southport to cover loss of clientele, parking problems, and other factors of daily living in this busy neighborhood.

Once this was completed, facades were built in front of businesses to establish a period look. Nearly 20 truckloads of mud and hay covered the street between Roscoe and Cornelia, while transportation was reduced to a few vintage automobiles and some horse-drawn wagons.

The on-screen result was terrific. For a few moments, Southport did become that busy 1916 Boston neighborhood where Ruth swaggered down the street.

The Music Box Theatre
3733 N. Southport Avenue

The Music Box Theatre opened in 1929 as a neighborhood alternative to the more palatial downtown movie houses. It was intended as a "second-run" theater, meaning that once a film had completed its run in the bigger Loop theaters it would be recycled to local movie houses. It was considered relatively small in comparison to downtown houses, with the capacity for 800 patrons. Though the Music Box was built with new sound technology in mind, it was equipped with room for an orchestra as well as a pipe organ should the talkies go bust. The ceiling, which remains a notable feature to this day, was painted dark blue and outfitted with twinkling lights and moving clouds.

Also a popular location for movie filming, the Music Box has appeared in *Only the Lonely* (1991), *Curly Sue* (1991), *Solstice* (1993), *High Fidelity* (2000), and *I Want Someone to Eat Cheese With* (2006).

Today, the Music Box is a prime destination for those looking to enjoy art films, foreign films, and rarely seen documentaries, both first-run and revivals. The theater's parent company, the Southport Music Box Corporation, also owns Music Box Films, which distributes foreign and independent films in the theatrical, DVD, and television markets throughout the United States. Among the most noteworthy are a documentary about performance artist Marina Abramovic titled *The Artist Is Present* (2012) and the original foreign-language version of *The Girl with the Dragon Tattoo* (2009).

For more information, call the Music Box Theatre at (773) 871-6604 or visit its website at www.musicboxtheatre.com.

iO Theater
3541 N. Clark Street

Known for years as the Improv Olympic until they were sued by lawyers from a certain quadrennial international sporting event (as if people were getting the two confused), iO was founded in 1981 by Charna Halpern. In 1984, the late improv guru Del Close came on board. Close, who was an early member of the Compass Players and Second City, blazed a brilliant trail across the landscapes of theater and popular culture.

iO is dedicated to the improv technique invented by Close known as the Harold, which is a complex long form of improvisation that relies on multiple themes and a series of recurring characters, phrases, and images that evolve as the themes progress. The Harold completely revolutionized improvisation, creating an immense new universe for actors to inhabit, one that is still being explored.

Alumni include Matt Besser, Mo Collins, Andy Dick, Rachel Dratch, Chris Farley, Tina Fey, Kate Flannery, Tim Meadows, Seth Meyers, Mike Myers, Amy Poehler, Andy Richter, and Matt Walsh. It is not uncommon for famous alums to drop in and perform here.

Call (773) 880-0199 for more info or visit http://ioimprov.com/chicago. Check out http://ioimprov.com/chicago/about/about for a great synopsis of the amazing life and career of Del Close.

Metro
3730 N. Clark Street

Looking for the Next Big Thing in pop music? Then check out Metro, the Midwest's premier showcase for cutting-edge bands. The Smashing Pumpkins, Ministry, and Liz Phair all learned their chops on the Metro stage before moving on to national fame and glory. Countless indie rock heavyweights such as Modest Mouse, Spoon, Sonic Youth, Luna, Stereolab, Deerhoof, the Fiery Furnaces, and R.E.M. (the club's first show ever, in 1982) have also played there.

When Hollywood has needed a nightclub scene, Metro's darkened ambiance nicely fills the bill. Joan Jett (ex-member of the Runaways and leader of the Blackhearts) and her movie brother Michael J. Fox play here in *Light of Day* (1987), a look at the day-to-day world of struggling rock bands. Supposedly set in Cleveland, a good chunk of the film was actually shot in Chi-town.

In *Blink* (1994), Madeleine Stowe plays a member of the Drovers, a real-life Chicago band that brings a Celtic lilt to their music. Metro is where Stowe sees a wanted killer in the audience (perhaps).

For more information about Metro, visit www.metrochicago.com or call (773) 549-4140.

Brewster Building

2800 N. Pine Grove Avenue (at Diversey Parkway)

This is one of the North Side's most beautiful condominium apartment buildings. Built in 1893, the Brewster Building was designed by R. H. Turnock. Its stately elegance is marked by polished red marble moldings on the windows and doorways and the beautiful grillwork of the cage elevator and stairway banisters. Overall, this is a visually stunning edifice—perfect for all kinds of films.

The Brewster has seen it all, from action films like *Running Scared* (1986) to the comic romance of *She's Having a Baby* (1988), to the over-the-top horror of *Child's Play* (1988). *Hoodlum* (1997) effectively used the building's vintage look to help recreate Chicago as 1920s New York City.

The Brewster briefly housed one of cinema's greatest names. Legend has it that when Charlie Chaplin worked at Essanay Studios during the early months of 1915, he stayed in the Brewster Building's luxurious penthouse suite.

Chicago Cemeteries in the Movies

Graceland Cemetery, 4001 N. Clark Street
Jewish Graceland Cemetery, 3919 N. Clark Street
Rosehill Cemetery, 5800 N. Ravenswood Avenue
Bohemian National Cemetery, 5300 N. Pulaski Road
Oak Woods Cemetery, 1035 E. 67th Street
Burr Oak Cemetery, 471 E. 31st Street

Cemeteries make great film locations. Shooting in a necropolis, with its ornate artwork and the inherent drama of the grave, amidst mausoleums and memorials, offers a wealth of possibilities for moviemakers.

On the North Side, Graceland Cemetery, 4001 N. Clark Street, is the location for the fireman's funeral in *Backdraft* (1991). Don't look in Graceland for the Volunteer Firefighters Memorial where the funeral is

TOP LEFT: The chapel and mausoleum of Bohemian National Cemetery, site of a big shootout in *U.S. Marshals* (1998). *(Photo by Kate Corcoran)*

MIDDLE LEFT: The Palmer Mausoleum in Graceland Cemetery. *(Photo by Kate Corcoran)*

BOTTOM LEFT: Lake of Reverence in Oak Woods Cemetery. *(Photo by Kate Corcoran)*

RIGHT: The real Volunteer Firefighters Memorial in Rosehill Cemetery. *(Photo by Kate Corcoran)*

held; that memorial is actually part of Rosehill Cemetery, north and west of Graceland. A replica of this memorial was created specifically for the film and temporarily installed at Graceland.

Another movie funeral shot in Graceland was for the low-rent horror flick *Damien: Omen II* (1978). That burial ceremony took place just north of the Potter and Bertha Palmer grave site, one of Graceland's landmark monuments. The Roger Moore thriller *The Naked Face* (1984),

The Negotiator (1998), and the television series *Early Edition* have also made use of Graceland.

Just south of Graceland, on the other side of Irving Park Road at 3919 N. Clark Street, is a smaller cemetery known as Jewish Graceland. Made up of four separate cemeteries, Jewish Graceland ironically served as the site of a Catholic burial in *Running Scared* (1986). Fake snow had to be strategically placed around the cemetery plots to cover Hebrew lettering and the six-pointed Stars of David carved into many of the graveyard's tombstones. *Flatliners* (1990), a surreal examination of life after death, also did some shooting at Jewish Graceland.

Rosehill Cemetery, 5800 N. Ravenswood Avenue, was used at the end of a chase/shootout in *U.S. Marshals* (1998) that was otherwise filmed in Bohemian National Cemetery. The combined cemeteries stood in for the Queens borough of New York.

Bohemian National Cemetery, 5300 N. Pulaski, is where Tommy Lee Jones, Wesley Snipes, and a mini-militia of good guys and bad guys exchange gunfire in *U.S. Marshals* before Snipes is magically transported to the eastern wall of Rosehill and makes his escape. The beautiful dome of Bohemian's crematorium and chapel is shown to great effect during the melee. Bohemian is also where Tom Hanks's murdered wife and son are buried in *Road to Perdition* (2002). In real life, former Chicago mayor Anton Cermak is interned there, as are several victims of the 1915 East-land Disaster, a horrible ferryboat mishap near the Clark Street Bridge on the Chicago River in which over 800 General Electric employees en route to a company picnic in Michigan were drowned when the boat capsized.

On the South Side, Oak Woods Cemetery was the place where *Next of Kin* (1989) staged its shoot-'em-up finale, where Mama Joe is buried in *Soul Food* (1997), where Katherine Erbe and son have a paranormal experience in *Stir of Echoes* (1999), and where Nicholas Cage's father is laid to rest in a raging rainstorm in *The Weather Man* (2005). Located at 1035 E. 67th Street, Oak Woods is one of the city's oldest graveyards. For history buffs, Oak Woods is an outstanding place to take a stroll. The graves here range from physicist Enrico Fermi to athletes Jesse Owens and Cap Anson. Roland Burris's enormous and yet-to-be-occupied monument (complete with a list of his achievements that still had room for "Senator") received much national attention when disgraced Illinois governor Rod Blagojevich nominated him to fill President Obama's vacant Senate seat. Oak Woods is also the final resting place of two Chicago mayors: William Hale "Big Bill" Thompson and Harold Washington, the city's first African American mayor. Washington died in the fall of 1987. Bernard Epton, who ran as the Republican candidate against Washington in 1983, died a few weeks later and is buried not far from his former rival.

Finally, there is Burr Oak Cemetery at 471 E. 31st Street. It's here, at this South Side burial ground, that the funeral scene of *Cooley High* (1975) takes place.

For more information on Chicago cemeteries, check out Matt Hucke's wonderful Graveyards of Illinois website at www.graveyards.com.

Lane Technical High School

2501 W. Addison Street

In *Wildcats* (1986), a football comedy starring Goldie Hawn, Lane Technical High School did double duty. In the film's thin story, Hawn loses her teaching job at "Prescott High," a suburban institution, then, improbably enough, becomes head football coach at the inner-city "Central High." Both schools are played by Lane Tech. Incidentally, look carefully at Hawn's players. Two of her athletes are Wesley Snipes and Woody Harrelson, who moved from supporting parts to star status, teaming up in *White Men Can't Jump* (1992) and *Money Train* (1995).

The retro look of Lane Tech's football field was perfect for the period drama *The Express* (2008), a biopic of Ernie Davis, the first African American to win the Heisman Trophy. The field was used extensively in the film's many football sequences.

Portage Theater

4050 N. Milwaukee Avenue

Opening in 1920, the Portage was a movie mainstay of the neighborhood throughout the 20th century. It was chopped into two theaters in the 1980s and eventually fell on hard times before shutting its doors in 2001.

It was reopened in 2006 after extensive renovations, which returned it to being a single-screen movie palace. Now a mainstay for the classic, sci-fi/horror, and indie film community of the entire Chicago area, the Portage hosts a yearly Silent Summer Film Festival (it also boasts a restored 1927 Kimball pipe organ) as well as several other niche festivals and low-budget indie film screenings and premiers. Its interior even doubled as that of the Biograph in 2009's *Public Enemies.*

Threatened with closure in 2011, the theater managed to survive due to an outpouring of community support from throughout the Midwest—but like all small independent theaters, it continuously faces threats from developers and a tight economy.

To learn more about the Portage's wonderfully eclectic array of programming and how you can help keep a cultural gem afloat, go to www.portagetheater.org.

The Pool Halls of *The Color of Money*
FitzGerald's at 6615 Roosevelt Road
Chicago's Finest Billiards at 6414 S. Cottage Grove Avenue
The Ginger Man at 3740 N. Clark Street
Chris's Billiards at 4637 N. Milwaukee Avenue

In 1986, Martin Scorsese, Paul Newman, and Tom Cruise came to town to film *The Color of Money*, a sequel of sorts to the classic 1961 film *The Hustler*. Newman won an Oscar for recreating the role of "Fast Eddie" Felson, a retired pool shark now taking young hustler Vincent Lauria under his wing. The premise has the duo traveling the Midwest, with Cruise gaining experience in various poolrooms before moving on to bigger stakes in Atlantic City. On-screen, we see a road trip. In reality, you can recreate *The Color of Money* journey with only one foray outside Chicago city limits. Unfortunately, a few of the pool halls featured in the film have gone belly-up, but you can still check out these places.

Start at FitzGerald's, the popular Berwyn nightspot at 6615 Roosevelt Road. That's where Newman first spies Cruise and sees potential in this talented, hopelessly cocky pool player. (FitzGerald's also shows up as the "Tear Drop Lounge" in the 1987 comedy *Adventures in Babysitting*.) Chicago's Finest Billiards at 6414 S. Cottage Grove is on the South Side. Up north, *The Color of Money* shot scenes in the Ginger Man at 3740 N. Clark and Chris's Billiards at 4637 N. Milwaukee.

Green Mill
4802 N. Broadway
The history of the Green Mill is packed with stories that rival Hollywood's fictional creations. This popular jazz club opened in 1907 under the name Pop Morse's Roadhouse. The establishment changed hands three years later and was given a new name: the Green Mill Gardens. With Essanay Studios just a few blocks north on Argyle Street, the

Green Mill became a popular place for actors to congregate. Western star and studio co-owner Bronco Billy Anderson was known to ride his horse to the Mill after a day's shooting, tie the steed to a hitching post, and head inside for a few drinks. Wallace Beery was another Green Mill regular from the Essanay lot; legend has it that Charlie Chaplin stepped in a time or two during his brief Chicago stay as well.

Aside from the Essanay gang, vaudeville performers passing through town would stop by the Green Mill in between their shows at the nearby Uptown and Riviera Theatres. Al Jolson, Eddie Cantor, and Sophie Tucker were among the many stars who frequented the Green Mill during this era.

The 1920s ushered in the brave new world of Prohibition. Though alcohol was now banned from coast to coast, the new teetotaling culture had little effect on Green Mill business when Al Capone's henchman "Machine Gun" Jack McGurn bought a partial ownership of the club. Capone and company held court in a booth past the end of the bar, affording them a good view of the entertainment onstage as well as both entrances. A trapdoor behind the bar led through the basement to an underground tunnel system, providing an escape route if needed. The trapdoor still remains, although the tunnel has been sealed off.

TOP: The Green Mill's exterior sign is still there, as only a replica was destroyed during the filming of *Thief* (1981). *(Photo by Kate Corcoran)*

MIDDLE: The velvety fabric of the curved booths and ornately framed murals make visiting the Green Mill an exquisite visual as well as aural experience. *(Photo by Kate Corcoran)*

BOTTOM: Al Capone's original booth—with excellent views of both doors and quick access to basement escape tunnels. *(Photo by Kate Corcoran)*

At the end of Prohibition and the Capone era in Chicago, the Green Mill once more became a legal operation. From the 1930s to the 1960s, it was a popular nightclub, boasting big-name jazz acts on its small stage. In the 1970s, the club slipped in stature, relegated to "dive" status and inhabited by assorted barflies and down-and-outers. Then in 1986, the Green Mill was bought by Dave Jemilo, who sunk money and hard work into restoring the club to its former grandeur.

Jemilo's efforts paid off. Today the Green Mill is one of the hottest nightspots in town—and definitely the coolest. Jazz acts here range from Ken Vandermark and Ed Petersen to the swinging retro sounds of the Mighty Blue Kings. Sunday nights include the Uptown Poetry Slam, still hosted by its originator, Marc Smith. It's an interactive, competitive form of live poetry in which contestants get on-stage and read poetry (sometimes written on the spot) to the cheers and jeers of the audience.

The Green Mill is also renowned for its Friday Night Open Jam, which begins at 1 AM and features up-and-coming young musicians sharing the stage with seasoned pros. Saturday late nights begin at midnight with the smoking-hot sounds of the Sabertooth Quartet, who play until 5 AM. As the morning progresses, jazz players from all over town show up after their shows to sit in with Sabertooth, and you never know who might walk in. Although not for the faint of heart (or liver), there's nothing quite like the feeling of walking out of the Green Mill at 5 AM (especially in the summer, when the sun is up and birds are chirping) and staggering over to get some well-needed breakfast to make you feel like a true urbanite.

For filmmakers, the club's picturesque interior and cool vibe are a cinematic gold mine, which is why 13 feature films (and countless documentaries and concert films) have shot scenes inside the Green Mill, making it the most oft-filmed locale in the city aside from the big downtown landmarks.

Thief (1981), an intense study of a professional burglar and the first film for director and former Chicagoan Michael Mann, utilized the Green Mill for several scenes. The bar serves as a sort of headquarters for the main character, played by James Caan. The Green Mill is also the setting for a pivotal moment between Caan and crime boss Robert Prosky.

The end of *Thief* has a determined Caan destroying any place associated with his past, including his home and a car dealership. Caan also firebombs the Green Mill, destroying the front of the building in a massive explosion.

The filmmakers took down the classic Green Mill sign and replaced it with a replica, which they blew up. The original was then returned.

On a less violent note, the Green Mill was a place of leisure for characters in the romantic comedies *Prelude to a Kiss* (1992) and *Kissing a Fool* (1998). Kathleen Turner, in the title role of Disney's wretched butchering of Sara Paretsky's great detective novels, *V. I. Warshawski* (1991), hangs out here, as does the mob family of *Next of Kin*, a 1989 thriller featuring Patrick Swayze as a Chicago cop (and what looks like a 12-year-old Ben Stiller as a mobster's son).

In the wrong-on-many-levels comedy *Folks!* (1992), Don Ameche ends up wandering into the Green Mill, standing in for an all-black South Side blues bar (the few minutes featuring Magic Slim and the Teardrops are the film's only bearable ones). The Green Mill also plays an all–African American South Side bar in *A Family Thing* (1996). In an oddly touching scene, a drunken Robert Duvall, having recently learned he was born to an African American mother, interrupts a private party at the lounge. Awkwardly, Duvall, a white southerner dressed in simple, dirty clothing, tries to ingratiate himself with a group of friends, explaining that he, too, is a member of their race.

Soul Food (1997) used the Green Mill as the debut club for the band Milestone, a group formed by Michael Beach's character. The band features the film's executive producer, Kenneth "Babyface" Edmonds, on guitar and vocals.

The uneven thriller *Excessive Force* (1993) shows a mob thug being murdered in the famed Capone Booth via the unpleasant method of being stabbed in the ear with a pen. The actor, Turk Muller, is actually a good friend of owner Dave Jemilo, and Jemilo found it oddly unsettling to see one of his best friends slain (even fictionally) in his own joint.

The Green Mill doubles as a New Orleans comedy club in the sequel of a remake, *Oceans 12* (2004). In *High Fidelity* (2000), it's there that John Cusack recounts his all-time-worst breakup number five, which he is in the midst of. Keanu Reeves has a serious talk with his brother at the Mill in *The Lake House* (2006); Jemilo recalls getting rather inebriated with Reeves and the actor playing his brother at the end of a long day shooting that scene. Finally, scenes from the mobster film *Chicago Overcoat* (2009) and the buddy comedy *The Dilemma* (2011) were shot inside the Green Mill.

Aside from the many movie scenes shot here, visiting celebrities (like Johnny Depp when he was in town shooting 2009's *Public Enemies*) make a point of stopping at the Green Mill, mostly for the music but also because, in Jemilo's words, "nobody makes a big deal about it."

One of the most enjoyable things about seeing music at the Green Mill is the club's policy toward excessive talkers, whereby folks jabbering away not paying attention to the show will be told in no uncertain terms to either shut up or leave. "If people are payin' 12 bucks to see a show, they oughta be able to listen to the music," explains Jemilo. This provides a welcome respite for serious jazz fans in a world often overrun by dilettantes and poseurs.

Jemilo and his wife, Andrea, plan to continue the way they have since 1986, just doing what they do and paying no mind to fads and fashions. "We just do our thing, and if it's trendy, that's just great. If it's not trendy, that's just fine too."

To find out who's playing at the Green Mill, call (773) 878-5552 or visit http://greenmilljazz.com.

The Uptown Theatre
Broadway at Lawrence Avenue

Located half a block north of the Green Mill, the Uptown Theatre was once the North Side's golden movie palace. Built at a cost of $4 million by Balaban and Katz, the Uptown opened in August 1925.

Eight stories tall, the Uptown combined modern technology with a regal Spanish Renaissance decor. Hanging from the ceiling of the five-story lobby was a magnificent chandelier. The theater itself contained 5,000 seats (still not enough for the estimated opening-night crowd of 12,000!), a custom-made Wurlitzer organ (at the time, the world's most expensive), and a full-sized orchestra pit. Best of all, this movie palace had an elaborate air-conditioning system—no small accomplishment for the 1920s.

The Uptown Theatre offered patrons the latest in Hollywood features, as well as big-name vaudeville acts. A night at the Uptown meant glamour, prestige, and a good time for countless Chicagoans.

Then came the Depression. With declining revenues, theater maintenance was cut back and the Uptown underwent a slow, painful decay. Second- and third-run movies replaced the lavish premieres, and by the late 1970s the Uptown was mainly a venue for rock 'n' roll shows. Ultimately, the theater closed its doors in 1981. It's been slowly rotting away ever since, and various organizations have been ineffective in raising the millions of dollars it would take to restore this gem to its former glory.

Currently the Uptown is owned by
live music entrepreneur Jerry Mick-
elson (Jam Productions) who has
been unable in the present economic
climate to secure the estimated $40
to $70 million it would take to restore
the theater. Meanwhile, this national
treasure continues to rot.

If you want a glimpse of what ex-
ists behind the plywood covering
the Uptown Theatre's doors, check
out *Home Alone 2: Lost in New York*
(1992). The grand lobby of the theater was remade into a Manhattan
toy store for this John Hughes / Chris
Columbus slapstick comedy. The

Ornate facade of the Rapp & Rapp–
designed Balaban and Katz Uptown
Theatre. *(Photo by Kate Corcoran)*

horror suspense flick *Soul Survivors*
(2001) uses the same lobby (with eight more years of neglect behind it)
as a decrepit goth-ish nightclub. The moldering movie palace is also featured in *Backdraft* (1991) and *I Love Trouble* (1994).

For the straight story on the Uptown Theatre, however, check out
the excellent documentary *Uptown: Portrait of a Palace* (2006). It
occasionally airs on WTTW Channel 11, or you can order it at www.
compassrose.org/dvds/uptown-portrait.html (proceeds go to an organization promoting restoration).

People's Church
941 W. Lawrence Avenue

The People's Church was built in 1926 for the congregation of progres-
sive Chicago clergyman Dr. Preston Bradley. Today the building is also
used by theater companies and for public meetings. In the 1930s-period
gangster drama *Hoodlum* (1997), the People's Church is transformed
into New York's Harlem Faith Church.

Loyola University of Chicago
6525 N. Sheridan Road

The camera sweeps across Lake Michigan, zeroing in on a solitary figure
walking along a rocky beach, framed by campus buildings. Against the

brilliance of a rising sun staring him in the face, an isolated young man (Kiefer Sutherland) dramatically declares, "Today is a good day to die." So begins *Flatliners* (1990), a surreal story of medical students who attempt to cheat death. This histrionic opening takes place at Loyola's North Shore Campus; other scenes were shot in Hyde Park and the Museum of Science and Industry.

The Suburbs

Evanston Township High School
1600 Dodge Avenue, Evanston, Illinois
In *Rookie of the Year* (1993), Evanston Township High School is transformed into a junior high where pint-sized pitching sensation Thomas Ian Nicholas is a student. Actors Joan Cusack and Jeremy Piven are two real-life alumni of this north suburban institution.

Northwestern University
North Sheridan Road in Evanston, Illinois
Northwestern Memorial Hospital
Superior Street and Fairbanks Court in Chicago
Founded on June 14, 1851, Northwestern University is one of America's premier schools, with a sprawling campus along the Lake Michigan shoreline in north suburban Evanston. A second campus, in downtown Chicago, comprises Northwestern's law and medical schools.

The Northwestern School of Speech includes divisions in Communication Studies, Radio/Television/Film, Theater, and Performance Studies. The film program is housed in the Barbara and Garry Marshall Studio Wing of Louis Hall, on the north end of the campus. Yes, that's the same Garry Marshall who hit it big in Hollywood as a television writer and film director. A 1955 alum of Northwestern's Medill School of Journalism, he was the driving force behind the 1970s sitcoms *The Odd Couple*, *Happy Days*, and *Mork and Mindy*. Marshall later switched to movies and directed a string of comedy films, including *The Flamingo Kid* (1984), *Pretty Woman* (1990), *Runaway Bride* (1999), *Georgia Rule* (2007), and *Nothing in Common* (1986), which was partially shot at Marshall's alma mater.

Northwestern provides a full range of film production and history classes, sometimes working in tandem with other departments such as

the School of Speech. Guest lecturers have included director Robert Alt-
man, playwrights Alan Ayckbourn and Tony Kushner, producer Robert
Greenhut, and actors Ellen Burstyn, Richard Benjamin (class of 1960),
William Daniels (class of 1950), Gene Hackman, Cloris Leachman (class
of 1948), John Malkovich, Dermot Mulroney (class of 1985), Robert
Redford, David Schwimmer (class of 1988), and Gary Sinise.

In addition to Marshall, Benjamin, Daniels, Leachman, Mulroney,
and Schwimmer, Northwestern has produced a considerable array
of film and television talent. Laura Innes (of *ER* fame, class of 1979),
comic actor Richard Kind (class of 1978), *Seinfeld's* Julia Louis-Dreyfus
(class of 1982) and her husband, writer/producer Brad Hall (class of
1980), screenwriter Dana Olson (class of 1980), Stephen Colbert (class
of 1986), and Kimberly Williams-Paisley (class of 1993) all trod the
boards at Northwestern.

When it comes to Hollywood productions, Northwestern's ivy-covered
buildings and beautiful lakefront locations provide filmmakers with a
wealth of opportunities. *Nothing in Common* features both the Evanston campus and the downtown Northwestern University Hospital.
The film's story revolves around Tom Hanks, a self-centered yuppie
who must come to terms with his dying father, played by Jackie Gleason. Hanks's movie girlfriend, Bess Armstrong, holds the on-screen job
of an acting teacher at Northwestern, with her classes meeting in Annie
May Swift Hall. Meanwhile, Gleason is hospitalized at the downtown
medical center.

Baseball player cum scholar Tom Berenger hangs out at Northwestern's
Deering Library in *Major League* (1989). While on campus he might have
caught a lecture at the Technological Institute, where Dan Aykroyd rules
the classrooms in the dreadful comedy *Doctor Detroit* (1983). When not
being seduced by older women in glass elevators, the prep school boys of
Class (1983) live in Northwestern dormitories.

Other films shot at Northwestern's downtown campus include *The
Babe* (1992), *Richie Rich* (1994), *With Honors* (1994), *Road to Perdition*
(2002), and *Soul Survivors* (2001), which made some good use of the
campus backdrop.

Two other Northwestern-based films are worth noting. In 1942, some
students from the School of Speech took a camera to north suburban
Winnetka and filmed Henrik Ibsen's classic play *Peer Gynt*. Making his
film debut in the title role was none other than Charlton Heston. Seven

years later, many of the same gang scouted out Romanesque buildings in Evanston and Chicago, then used these locations (including the
downtown post office and the Elks Club at Diversey Parkway and Sheridan Road) to shoot a lakeshore version of William Shakespeare's *Julius
Caesar*. Heston had the role of Mark Antony, and David Bradley, who
directed both films, played Brutus.

The Charles G. Dawes House
225 Greenwood Street, Evanston, Illinois
This magnificent mansion, owned by Northwestern University, is home
to the Evanston History Center. Its exterior and gorgeous interiors
were featured in *Road to Perdition* (2002) as the mansion of mob kingpin Paul Newman.

For more information on the Evanston History Center and Charles
Dawes (who was vice president under Calvin Coolidge and a noted
Renaissance man) visit http://evanstonhistorycenter.org.

Niles East High School
Lincoln Avenue at Skokie Boulevard, Skokie, Illinois
When Niles East High School closed its doors in 1980, the north suburbs lost an educational institution but gained a movie facility. Part of
Skokie School District 219, East's demise was instigated by declining
enrollment. Yet the building itself, which was razed a few years ago, was
a moviemaker's dream. Complete with hallways, classrooms, a gym,
lockers, and other scholastic accouterments, Niles East found new life
as a movie set.

In the early-to-mid 1980s, John Hughes almost single-handedly carved
out the north suburbs as a hotbed of adolescent movie locations. With
Sixteen Candles (1984), *The Breakfast Club* (1985), and *Ferris Bueller's
Day Off* (1986), Hughes put together an offbeat trilogy of films that were
solidly rooted in the Skokie / Wilmette / Winnetka / Glencoe / Highland
Park region.

Yet someone beat Hughes to the punch with a film that crystallized the
culture of north suburbia: Paul Brickman in *Risky Business* (1983), a star-
making vehicle for young actor Tom Cruise. Cruise plays Joel Goodson,
a high school senior worried about his future and curious about all matters sexual. Niles East served as both Cruise's school and home. Scenes
inside and outside the school are obvious. The exterior sequences for

his house were filmed at a private residence in the north suburbs. The interior of the home, however, including the famous living room where Cruise dances in his underwear to the music of Bob Seger, were sets built inside the school's old gymnasium.

Not to be outdone, Hughes brought his first group of high schoolers, led by Molly Ringwald and Anthony Michael Hall, to Niles East, where he filmed some scenes of *Sixteen Candles*.

Walker Brothers Original Pancake House
153 Green Bay Road, Wilmette, Illinois
In *Ordinary People* (1980), Robert Redford's Oscar-winning adaptation of Judith Guest's novel, Timothy Hutton and Dinah Manoff meet at this Wilmette restaurant to trade life stories over coffee. They should have stayed for the apple pancakes. Walker Brothers is practically an institution in Wilmette, serving up a delectable array of breakfast creations. The apple pancake is a meal unto itself; eat one and you'll be hooked for life.

Winnetka Congregational Church
725 Pine, Winnetka, Illinois
Remember how Kevin Bacon felt over his nuptials to Elizabeth McGovern in 1988's *She's Having a Baby*? Yeah, me neither. But the happy couple had their ceremony in this quiet Winnetka church.

New Trier West High School
7 Happ Road, Northfield, Illinois
When New Trier West closed down in 1984, John Hughes's movie machine moved in. The former high school's three gymnasiums were converted into movie sets where Hughes filmed parts of *Sixteen Candles* (1984), *Uncle Buck* (1989), and *Curly Sue* (1991). *Uncle Buck* also used the New Trier West exterior as the school where the title character, played by John Candy, drops off his niece and nephews. New Trier West reopened in 1998 as an all-freshman school.

Interestingly, New Trier West's sister school, New Trier (formerly New Trier East) in Winnetka, has been a spawning ground for several film personalities. Ann Margaret, Rock Hudson, Charlton Heston, Adam Baldwin, and *About Last Night . . .* (1986) director Edward Zwick are all alumni of this North Shore institution, which is often described as one of the finest public high schools in the country.

John Milinac: Master of Effects

Born and raised in rural McHenry County in northeastern Illinois, John Milinac was always interested in making home movies and "little story lines" with the neighborhood kids using his parents' 8mm camera. He got a Super 8 sound camera when he graduated from High School in 1978 and "it ratcheted up a little more." All the while, he was trying to figure out an entree to the real film industry.

He and his brother tracked down the production crew of *The Blues Brothers*, which was filming a stunt scene in Wauconda, and visited the set. "We managed to infiltrate the set close enough to start talking to people and figure out how to approach getting into the film industry, and it seemed like a pretty big task at the time."

John Milinac. *(Photo by Michele Wiesler)*

Milinac never gave up on his dream, however, and the itch to make movies just grew too intense. This led to him moving out to Los Angeles in 1985, where he worked as a special effects assistant until his son was born in 1989.

John and his wife decided that L.A. wouldn't be the best place to raise a family, so they moved back to McHenry and bought a home. Illinois was still an infrequent site for moviemaking, however, and John had resigned himself to the fact that his career in film production might be coming to an end.

That all changed when Ron Howard's multimillion-dollar special-effects-laden production *Backdraft* (1991) started filming in several locations around Chicago. Milinac knew the special effects crew and was hired immediately.

Backdraft was the first of a new wave of films to be shot in Chicago, and John soon realized he might be able to return home to his rural roots yet still work in the movie business. "I just had to approach the industry a little bit differently than if we'd stayed in Los Angeles."

The experience that he gained working out west proved invaluable to Milinac, as he was able to work his way into the local film unions and become a mainstay of the Chicago/Midwest crew scene. He's now a top-tier special effects coordinator, having worked in various capacities on over 50 films in the last 25-plus years, including *Next of Kin* (1989), *Dennis the Menace* (1993), *The Relic* (1997), *I Know What You Did Last Summer* (1997), *The Negotiator* (1998), *A Simple Plan* (1998), *Stir of Echoes* (1999), *Road to Perdition* (2002), *8 Mile* (2002), *The Last Samurai* (2003), *The Weather Man* (2005), *The Break-Up* (2006), *The Lake House* (2006), *The Express* (2008), *Wanted* (2008), *The Unborn* (2009), *Contagion* (2011), and *The Dilemma* (2011). He also worked on several television shows, including *Prison Break*, *Boss*, and *The Beast*.

Looking over Milinac's extensive resume, the first question that leaps to mind is: what is the difference between a special effects coordinator, supervisor, foreman, rigger, technician, and assistant? Milinac elaborates on the distinctions. "The special effects coordinator or supervisor is at the top of the food chain; they answer directly to the visual effects coordinator [who is responsible for all visual effects, whether done in front of the camera or added in postproduction]. The next level is the special effects foreman (or gang boss), then technicians, riggers, and finally the assistants."

The next question: looking at certain movies on the list, *The Break-Up*, for example, I don't recall Vince Vaughn's head exploding, or he and Jennifer Aniston having a gunfight down on Michigan Avenue (although about halfway through the movie I was hoping for it)—so was that a pretty easy gig? Milinac sets me straight and explains that the production built a full-scale version of Vaughn and Aniston's apartment down in the South Side Armory to shoot all the interior apartment scenes, which composed much of the movie. Since the special effects coordinator is in charge of all mechanical and physical effects that occur in front of the camera, it was Milinac's responsibility to make sure that it was a completely functional apartment. "The phones had to work, the sinks had to work, the showers had to work, the air-conditioning had to work. Hot water had to be controlled. The scene where she [Aniston] is burning pictures in the fireplace had to be worked out with the fire department and the city."

The special effects department's duties don't end there. "We're also viewed as the on-set mechanics. If something breaks, we fix it. If the camera department needs to do something unique, we help build a rig. If the grips need something manufactured, we're kind of the in-house manufacturing department, working kind of like R&D on-site as we're doing it."

Two views of a Volvo S80 from *The Weather Man* with sections of its side and roof removed. "We needed to accommodate a camera on a dolly as it moves to show Nicholas Cage from behind looking forward, then to a profile as a drink gets thrown in his lap," says Milinac. *(Photos by John Milinac)*

Milinac's job begins long before filming even starts: "A special effects coordinator will take the script and interpret what each scene may request of them. Things like snow, rain, the car blows up or flips over on its side, someone is hanging off a cliff, all the way down to the kitchen sink works and the stove works. So a supervisor will break it all down, probably make an elaborate list, depending on the scope of the picture, and then start consulting with the director or the production designer or many departments and say, 'Are we interpreting this correctly? Are you going to see this? What do you need for that?' This will lead to more meetings with stunt and visual effects [departments] and continues on to what we'll need in the real world, how much labor it will take, how many people it will take. There's a lot of brainstorming among your own people, saying, 'How do you approach this gag? What's the best way to do it?'"

By the way, "gag" is special effects–person slang for any piece of business that happens in a film that requires a mechanical or physical effect (stunt people sometimes use the term as well). Gags don't necessarily have to be funny, although they often are. Regardless of the dramatic or comedic intent, however, all gags have to be "repeatable and controllable," as the scene may have to be done dozens of times to get a usable take.

Sometimes the least noticeable gags are the most time-consuming. In *Wonder Boys* (2000), there's a scene where Michael Douglas takes a pill and tries to wash it down with a shot of whiskey, but he accidentally spits out the pill and it sticks to his jacket. Milinac and crew worked several hours to create a "pill" to be used (a magnet coated with dental material, so it wouldn't be harmful if Douglas accidentally swallowed it), then inserted various pieces of metal under Douglas's jacket lapel so that when he spit the pill out it would adhere to his jacket. "So the viewer isn't paying any attention, because they figure that it's just wet and it stuck, but it has to be repeatable and somewhat controllable," Milinac notes. "It was one of those gags that had absolutely no moving parts, but it was something that needed to be thought about because the director was very specific about what he wanted it to do. It worked well, but it was one of those 'nobody's gonna know what it took to make this little thing work.'"

Often, the effects are unobtrusive but are still very important to the tone of the film. "Sometimes a movie is very slow and drama-driven and very subtle things have to happen. You know, wind on curtains is kind of cliché, but it's the kind of stuff we would do," says Milinac. "That sort of stuff isn't often seen by the ticket-buying public as a special effect because hopefully they're drawn into the story enough that they're not even thinking about it. But these are subtle effects that are seamless and you don't get caught up in them; they're just little things that keep the story moving."

No matter what effect is being attempted, safety is always the primary concern with any production. "Safety discussions go on all the way through a production to ensure that all those things are being addressed well before it gets to the set," Milinac explains. "If there is a safety issue, it can be either changed or shut off or we can just shoot it in a different way. It's something you have to take into consideration. It's an industrial environment; you have to treat it like you're at a factory and you could get hurt at work any day, just like you could anywhere else. And there are a lot of things in place in the industry to make sure that people bring up the safety issues and do the things that are industry standards so that people don't get themselves compromised. It'll be the simplest thing you'll do that somebody gets injured on, because it was taken for granted. On a big day, everyone's focused, everybody's on edge, everyone's paying attention and there's no mishap, then on the smallest day somebody falls."

This is especially difficult on lower-budget pictures: "A lot of times on a small picture, you may have only one or two or three guys working in your department, so you're trying to do stuff on a very frugal basis. On a large-budget picture, you have much greater resources. But on a smaller picture, you're trying to make things happen safely and quickly with almost no expense involved. You don't want to spend much because they didn't budget for it. Because when a film was being greenlit a year earlier and a hypothetical budget was put in, they didn't consider the small little pill that had to be stuck to a guy's shirt."

But these challenges are part of the reason Milinac enjoys his job so much: "Making something out of nothing is part of the day-to-day challenge. I bet if you interviewed a hundred special effects guys, myself included, they'd say their favorite thing about the job is that it's always different. And it can be nerve-wrackingly different, but very rarely will you say, 'I'm really bored from doing the same thing over and over again.'"

The shoot for *The Weather Man* (2005) provided Milinac's greatest challenge. Aside from the gag where Nicholas Cage gets beaned with a Frosty and the spoon sticks to his jacket (reminiscent of the pill gag in *Wonder*

Early morning setup for a funeral scene in *The Weather Man* (2005). Says John Milinac, "We were shooting in a very confined space in Oak Woods Cemetery, so we needed three cranes with 60-foot rain bars to be able to make the scene look right during wider camera shots. There had to be rain as all the limousines pulled up. Each 60-foot rain bar gave us about 80 feet of rain. Three cranes made for a long day; usually it's about two hours for one crane. Here we set up about four hours before the 7 AM call, ran water from across the street into the cemetery for the water trucks, put together the rain bars, did all the positioning and rigging in order to be ready for the 'rain test' by 7:00. After the light was gone and the shooting done, we took it all down again." *(Photos by John Milinac)*

Boys) and lots of shooting of arrows (often done with a special pneumatic cannon), Milinac was responsible for creating winter where there was none. Continue on to the next sidebar, gentle reader. . . .

Putting the Weather in *The Weather Man*

The Weather Man (2005), which stars Nicholas Cage, is undoubtedly one of the finest films ever to be shot in Chicago. Directed by Gore Verbinski (known mostly for the *Pirates of the Caribbean* saga) from a brilliant script courtesy of Steve Conrad, the film is by turns hilarious and heartbreaking. It features an excellent performance by Cage in the lead role, Dave Spritz, a Chicago TV "weather personality" whose personal life is crumbling just as his career may be about to take off. Film legend Michael Caine gives his usual brilliant performance as his stern father, and Hope Davis shines as Dave's estranged wife.

If you're one of the many people who've had the pleasure of seeing this film, you'll be shocked to know that, aside from a handful of second unit shots done months before principal photography was begun, all of the snow, ice, rain, sleet, and fog was completely fabricated by the special effects crew. The shoot was scheduled for the dead of Chicago's winter in the hopes that Mother Nature might assist in dressing the sets, but a freak warm spell hit the city a week before filming began and the real-world snow went away.

This unlucky turn of events provided veteran special effects coordinator John Milinac with the greatest challenge of his career. Over the next month, Milinac and his special effects crew performed a series of labor-intensive tasks, covering a number of locations with ice and snow, including along the lakefront at Belmont Point, numerous downtown areas, a neighborhood up in Evanston, and even an entire golf course in the north suburbs for a pivotal scene. There was a whole week where John's crew swelled to as many as 60 people: 10 to 20 getting a location ready, several more on the shooting crew dressing and modifying the set as filming was going on, and yet another large group cleaning and restoring the locations being struck. Milinac was even forced to call in the big guns, bringing in trusted colleague Dieter Sturm (the world's greatest winter effects specialist) and his crew to assist with the slew of places requiring "weatherization." As location manager James McAllister says, "Basically every form of fake snow that existed was used."

TOP LEFT: On scene for *The Weather Man* (2005) at Belmont Point: special effects technicians first roll out and spike down a special fabric-like ground cover, which is then covered with a variety of materials, from actual chipped ice to foam or cellulose-based artificial snow. "Depending on the intensity of foot traffic and the shooting schedule, we'll regroom the site after several hours. For *The Weather Man*, we had about 56 crew members working round-robin on three locations to set up snow effects and to tear them down," says Milinac. *(Photos by John Milinac)*

BOTTOM LEFT: Special effects technician John Rigden uses a dual component caulk gun that mixes a resin compound to make icicles for the set of *The Weather Man*. *(Photo by John Milinac)*

RIGHT: Icicles dried and ready to use: "Once the resin hardens, we can remove and screw them to any set piece," notes John Milinac. "It's part of a kit we keep on hand to use as needed for random set dressing." *(Photo by John Milinac)*

Interaction with McAllister was a key component of Milinac's coordination tasks. "James and I would talk constantly. He's got a lot of people he's got to keep satisfied as far as street closures and buildings or whatever, and he's coming to me asking, 'OK, now how badly are you going to impact the location when you show up?' For example, putting snow dressing down on Wacker and Wabash; we'd have to be there at 3:30 in the morning and start putting ice down at 4:30 in the morning because the shooting crew is going to be there at 6:30 in the morning. So we've got two good hours of good work done before they show up because they can't be waiting for us to dress the set. And James will say, 'You can't make any noise until after 7.' And I'll say, 'Well, we've gotta do snow dressing.' 'Well, you'll have to do this, we'll get a permit for that.'"

Chicago's capricious winds were a major hurdle to overcome, particularly when they worked downtown. Sturm elaborates: "Chicago is notorious for wind going left, right, up, down, sideways, and summersaults. When creating falling snow, you generally have to be upwind to allow the flakes to fall in a specific direction so it ends up falling through the frame of the camera. But often in Chicago, the wind will go one direction for three or five minutes, then all of the sudden it's going totally in the opposite direction. There are times when we actually have to set up two different types of falling snow systems to anticipate the wind changes in Chicago."

The city's winds became even more of a problem when director Gore Verbinski insisted that several shots have a light atmospheric fog. Milinac brought in two trucks that had navy-sized foggers (normally used for camouflaging entire ships during battle) on the back with big wind machines on them. Because of the swirling winds, they were often forced to just drive around the neighborhood to try to put layers of fog and haze over everything to create the proper ambience.

McAllister was especially frustrated by this, as it was his responsibility to keep the city apprised of the situation and to get the requisite permission for all crew activities. "There was no way we could 'permit' an area for them to be, to say, like, 'Here's where they'll be parked.' So I was kind of responsible to make sure they didn't get too far afield. It was a nightmare because the trucks would always have to move according to the wind, and there were times when they would end up blocks away with fog just pouring out the back. The trucks would be nowhere to be found, except you could see the fog bank rolling across the Loop and I'm screaming 'Where are the fog trucks?' into the radio."

Things weren't any better on Milinac's end. "It would look like we had a whole building on fire because three blocks away we were trying to get a light fog. People from that building who didn't know that we're filming a movie would come out and say, 'What the hell are you doing out here?'

"'We're doing smoke.'

"'Why?'

Special effects technicians roll out fabric on a North Shore golf course prior to application of snow dressing on *The Weather Man*. *(Photos by John Milinac)*

"'Because *waaay* over there there's a camera that needs a light fog in front of it.'"

Milinac is used to working with residents and property owners of the locations he works his effects upon (as are McAllister and Sturm), answering questions and assuaging their concerns as best he can. He finds that Chicagoans are "generally great" about film crews and the inconveniences they cause, "but there's always somebody who's trying to get to work or get to sleep, and we're like, 'Well, we're sorry.'"

The wind fostered further frustration during preparations for the scenes on the "snowy" golf course up in Evanston. One of Milinac's crews worked almost two weeks blanketing several acres with a white fabric that simulates a blanket of snow, but high winds swept through the area just days before the scenes were scheduled. "It looked like Mother Nature had TP'd the golf course," he recalls. Milinac and company scrambled to recover the tattered tarp and managed to have the course ready for its close-up.

The epic amounts of faux snow even presented challenges when striking sets, due to the duration of the shoot and the large amounts of material to collect and clean up. For example, the lawns of the Evanston neighborhood were covered with fabric blankets for such a lengthy period that Milinac was concerned the grass would be harmed, something that movie crews try desperately to avoid. "We're always paranoid we could be damaging someone's property." It was mid-April by the time the crews began removing the fabric.

But instead of having a negative effect, when they pulled up the covering, the lawns were thick and green "as if they been in a hothouse. The grass had been growing so much it looked like upholstery in people's lawns." This caused a flurry of activity in the neighborhood as residents rushed to reacquire the new miracle lawn product: "All the locals were going into the dumpsters pulling out that fabric because they wanted to put it on their lawns next year. They're all like, 'What is that stuff?'"

RIGHT: In this Evanston neighborhood series, special effects technicians dress the neighborhood and yards with foam and crushed ice. "We use crushed ice for those areas that are 'premium to camera,'" notes Milinac, "especially when actors interact with the snow or it needs to twinkle properly in the light. For large areas or backgrounds, we use foam on fabric or the cellulose-based snow. If snow is supposed to be melting or in clumps, we use Dream Cloud, a polyester-cotton mix that clumps well around trees or creates islands of snow." A final step is adding the atmospheric haze in the background. To add this effect, a truck with a wind machine and fogger spews "water-based smoke" to add a look of hazy humidity. "If there's no wind, it'll just sit there," notes Milinac, "which is why we have the wind machine on the truck." *(Photos by John Milinac)*

Dieter Sturm: The Snowmaker

Dieter Sturm and his company (he has a core crew of six and then hires various union pros as needed) can provide the full range of special effects

services. "We handle rain, wind, fog, snow. We do pyrotechnics, mechanicals, electronics, chemicals, and special riggings. Anything that's got to do with live action or special effects. Snow just happens to be our big specialty." That specialty, however, has earned him a worldwide reputation and garnered he and his crew an Academy Award.

Sturm started as a special effects coordinator in his mid-teens, creating pyrotechnics for corporate shows and

special events: "I was always considered the kid inventor." Soon he discovered it was in his blood and began seeking full-time work as a special effects person for film and video. "I started working with Kirk Smith, who was the go-to guy for snow effects in Chicago and vicinity." After Smith retired, Dieter became the main special effects snowmaker for the Midwest.

Compelled by his inventive streak, Sturm immediately set out looking for new ways and means of creating snow—ways that would be faster and more economical, perhaps using different types of materials. His first project was to invent the "Snowmaker Truck," which chips and shaves 400-pound blocks of ice down to the consistency of real snow, then sprays it as far as fifty feet at a rate of 800 pounds per minute.

Over his career, Dieter has done snow effects for dozens of films in Chicago and around North America, including *Planes, Trains & Automobiles* (1987), *Christmas Vacation* (1989), *Dennis the Menace* (1993), *While You Were Sleeping* (1995), *Fargo* (1996), *A Simple Plan* (1998), *The Weather Man* (2005), *The Lake House* (2006), *The Guardian* (2006), *The Vow* (2012), and *Public Enemies* (2009).

Actually, his wife, Yvonne (who is his second-in-command), and his crew completely handled the effects for *Public Enemies* (and notoriously brilliant, intense, and demanding director Michael Mann) while Dieter was recovering from a knee injury, something for which he gives them high praise. "They did a great job on a really difficult picture."

Not that dealing with enormous 11th-hour requests (as he did for friend and colleague John Milinac on *The Weather Man*) or working for exacting directors like Mann or James Cameron bothers Dieter and company: "We're the A-team that's supposed to perform." Nor do tight deadlines: "Our particular crew knows how to deal with these last-minute get-it-done scenarios. Where in other instances it might take a lot of time and people, we work together so well as a unit that we can get things done that other groups can't." That's about as close as he gets to bragging.

Sturm wasn't even fazed when he arrived at the set of what turned out to be his most challenging job ever, *The Horse Whisperer* (1998), directed by Robert Redford. "We drove up to New York State to work on this movie, and at that point it was strictly to manage the real snow that was physically there already, so I only had three crew members with me, thinking that it wasn't going to be that big of a job. But as we kept driving and getting closer, it became apparent that there was no real snow anywhere, and as we pull up to the set, everyone is standing there waiting for us going, 'Uh, there's no snow on this mountain. What are you gonna do?' I said, 'Well give me a day here to analyze it and figure out what needs to get done.'"

Dieter ended up needing to use two separate crews with 30 workers total to satisfy the needs of that production. *The Horse Whisperer* shoot also required a record amount of ice. "Generally on snow movies, we may go through an average of maybe eight to fifteen semi trailers of block ice over the course of five days to a week. In this movie, we went through 56 semi trailers of block ice (at 400 pounds per block) in the course of three weeks."

In addition to snow from the Snowmaker Truck, they may use upwards of 15 to 20 different types of material. "It all depends very specifically on what's taking place in the scene. Some scenes are so quick we may not need to have anything really detailed, just as long as it's white and perhaps a few pieces of detail so that it looks proper. If it's a shot where they hold on the scenery, where you can look at things and analyze it more closely, then we have to upgrade the types of materials we use."

When Dieter first began fabricating snow, some materials were not eco-friendly (plastics and Styrofoam flakes), and although crews were as fastidious as possible about cleaning up after themselves, a very small amount of nonbiodegradable material was getting into the environment. Dieter took it upon himself to solve this problem by creating an artificial snow material that not only was nontoxic but would also biodegrade. He spent years studying various compounds and formulas and invented BioSnow 1, which was nontoxic and water-soluble but could only be used in extremely dry environments. He went back to the drawing board for a few years, then created BioSnow 2, a nontoxic artificial snow that could "retain its integrity as a flake" for up to three months and then dissolve into the environment.

Sturm began using it himself and put it on the market for other effects professionals to sample. Dieter's new eco-friendly crystals became industry standard, replacing the old plastic or Styrofoam flakes. "All of a sudden, we received a notice from Hollywood that we were being considered for an Academy Award for Science and Technical Achievement by the Academy of Motion Picture Arts and Sciences, and we should send all our data and research."

Sturm went to L.A. and underwent the evaluation process for the technical achievement award, which was much like a high-tech science fair. Each nominee displayed his or her innovation and then appeared before the board of governors to explain the methodology. A few weeks later, Sturm was informed he had won the Oscar and was invited to attend the ceremony to accept it (crew category winners are informed in advance to guarantee attendance, because unlike actors, they're usually working on their next production).

In fact, Dieter and his cohorts were in the midst of making snow for the movie *Beautiful Girls* (1996). "We had to actually ask off work that weekend so we could go pick up our Academy Awards." (That has to be the best excuse to take off work ever!) "We worked until 4 AM and got about two hours of sleep, if that. Then we got on a plane in Minneapolis and flew out to L.A. Got out there in the afternoon, got turned around getting our tuxes and dresses together and such, and boom, we're off to the awards." Jamie Lee Curtis handed them their Oscar, and they got back on a plane to Minneapolis. "It's quite a privilege, and it's definitely something that was a surprise," Dieter says.

Normally his work is done by the time movie stars arrive on the set, so his interaction with them is minimal; but he does fondly remember spending an afternoon standing in a snow field while working on *A Simple Plan*, listening to Billy Bob Thornton tell him his life story.

As a spin-off of his snowmaking work, Dieter also is trying to "change the course of winter sports" by teaming with a British engineering firm that has designed and manufactures the world's finest synthetic snow surface system for skiing and snowboarding. He handles North American promotion for facilities that allow skiing and snowboarding 365 days a year without any real snow but rather a high-tech, highly refined synthetic snow. The first one, Liberty Mountain, has opened in Lynchburg, Virginia, and soon synthetic snow slopes will be popping up all over the United States.

Which means that the Winter and Summer X Games can finally be held simultaneously!

Lake Forest Academy

1500 W. Kennedy Road, Lake Forest, Illinois

Is Lake Forest Academy a private prep school or flexible movie location? Actually, it's both. Located on 140 acres of wooded property, Lake Forest Academy has played a considerable role both in education and recent Chicago film history.

Founded in 1857, Lake Forest Academy provides a college preparatory education within a unique setting. Though always located in north suburban Lake Forest, a 35-minute drive north of Chicago, the academy has been headquartered at the former estate of meat-packing magnate J. Ogden Armour since 1948.

Hollywood is no stranger to the unique splendor of this gorgeous campus. Unfortunately, its first foray onto the academy grounds was less than exemplary. *Damien: Omen II* (1978), the second movie adventure of Satan's spawn, turned Lake Forest Academy into a military school. The evil title youngster is enrolled here, using it as a headquarters to commit his crimes against humanity.

Two years later, Robert Redford, Timothy Hutton, Mary Tyler Moore, and Donald Sutherland entered the grounds for *Ordinary People* (1980). The production made extensive use of the wooded campus and school buildings. So did *The Babe* (1992), a retelling of the Babe Ruth legend, when the campus was turned into a spring training facility. For another example of Lake Forest Academy as a movie playground, see the sidebar on *The Package* (1989), below.

The Package: East Berlin, Illinois

Andrew Davis's 1989 film *The Package* was among the last of a dying genre breed: the Cold War thriller. Incorporating historical events with the worst nightmares a conspiracy theorist could conjure up, the film explores a shadow alliance of Soviet and American officials who want to sabotage an impending nuclear peace treaty.

The Package stars Gene Hackman as Johnny Gallagher, an army sergeant who inadvertently stumbles on to a plot to assassinate the Soviet premier during an impending visit to Chicago. The action opens in what was then East Berlin, switches to Washington, DC, and winds up in the Windy City. Yet with the exception of some establishing footage shot in East Germany, the entire film was made in the Chicago area.

"In preparing *The Package*, we visited East Germany, including Berlin," says Davis. "Once you've seen the real location, it's easy to compare and analyze what similarities exist in Chicago. Many Germans immigrated here at the turn of the century and created architecture exactly like they had at home."

The film opens at a peace conference between Soviet and American military officials. The meeting takes place in a chalet outside the Black Forest—or so it would appear. Head north to Lake Forest Academy in suburban Lake Forest and you'll find yourself transported to East Germany, at least as far as *The Package* is concerned.

Another major scene involves a shooting within the Black Forest witnessed by Hackman and his troops. The scene was filmed just outside the city, in a forest preserve on Archer Avenue in south suburban Palos Hills. Add German police cars, American troops, and a few explosions amidst the snow-covered trees, and there's nothing within the sequence to suggest this is anywhere but Germany.

The film's title comes from Gene Hackman's initial mission: to bring insubordinate soldier Tommy Lee Jones—a "package"—from Germany to Washington, DC. Hackman picks up Jones along a bridge between East and West Berlin. Look closely at the scene, though, and you may spot some familiar-looking buildings in the background.

Hackman actually picks up Jones at the Cermak Road bridge at Canal Street. By far, this is one of the most creative movie redecorating jobs Hollywood ever pulled off in Chicago. The bridge was outfitted with barbed wire, guard booths, and ominous warning signs with German lettering. Filmed in the dark of night, the sequence has all the look and feel of a Cold War–era border. When dawn broke, some early-morning commuters were reportedly a bit perplexed over the apparent invasion taking place on Cermak Road.

"We were able to find old hospitals and residential areas, specifically in the Pullman neighborhood, which had the flavor of Berlin," says Davis. With a little set dressing, the Pullman area was turned into the streets of

Berlin, where an American soldier is rousted from his bed by the conspirators and hurled into a complicated web of deceit.

Switching locales to Washington, DC, Davis again was able to shoot in and around Chicago. O'Hare Airport became Washington National Airport. The stately exterior of the Field Museum stood in for a government building where Pam Grier (who also appeared in Davis's Above the Law in 1988) is gunned down. The highways outside the city doubled for roads leading out of Arlington, Virginia.

Harold Ramis: Serious Filmmaker

For someone who has written or directed some of the funniest and most enjoyable comedies ever made, Harold Ramis sure is taken seriously by a lot of very serious people. Take his classic movie *Groundhog Day* (1993), which was named one of the 100 best comedies of the last 100 years by the American Film Institute. Quite understandable, as the saga of an egomaniacal weatherman (Bill Murray) forced to relive the same day over and over again until he learns to mend his self-centered ways, and in the process earns the love of an earnest and loving news producer (Andie MacDowell), is extremely funny. But how about the fact that in 2006, *Groundhog Day* was added to the National Film Registry for being "culturally, historically, or aesthetically significant"?

That honor is also understandable, actually, as there is more insight into the pitfalls of the eternal struggle to become a good person and the Sisyphean nature of human existence in that skewed yet sweet romantic comedy than any number of Sunday sermons or philosophy texts. And, according to Ramis, the recognition from the registry is just the tip of the iceberg.

"The serious conversations have continued in both the religious and psychiatric communities about what

Harold Ramis. *(Photo by Chuck Hodes)*

the movie represents," he says, "and I keep hearing anecdotally about psychiatrists who require their patients to watch *Groundhog Day* as part of their therapy. Danny Rubin, who wrote the original screenplay, is finishing a book about the screenplay itself and how the movie is different from his original conception; someone else has written a book that uses *Groundhog Day* as a basis for motivational teaching, and a few years ago the Museum of Modern Art in New York did a film festival entitled Films of Faith: The Hidden God—and they led the festival with *Groundhog Day*, which was interesting."

His duo of films starring Robert DeNiro and Billy Crystal as a Mob kingpin and his reluctant therapist, *Analyze This* (1999) and *Analyze That* (2002), further endeared him to mental health professionals. "If *Groundhog Day* introduced me to the psychiatric community, then *Analyze This* cemented my place with them," he says. "I've spoken a couple of times to the Institute for Psychoanalysis in Chicago, and I was asked to join the board of the Institute, which I did. I was recruited to do a panel at the national meeting of the American Psychiatric Association at the Waldorf in New York. And then I did a panel on Movies and Mental Illness, and on that panel was Oliver Sacks, the neurologist [who wrote the book that the film *Awakenings* (1990) was based upon], and Akiva Goldsman who wrote [the screenplay for] *A Beautiful Mind* (2001)."

All this is pretty somber stuff for the *Second City Television* (*SCTV*) veteran who wrote the scripts for such rollicking, boisterous comedies as *Animal House* (1978), *Meatballs* (1979), and *Caddyshack* (1980). "Well, the shocking thing now is that I have a son who's a freshman in college, and now *Animal House* is kind of the legacy that I have to live down."

Of course, the reason why people take his films so seriously is simple: because *he* does. "Because I take my films seriously, I do sufficient research and enough thinking about these topics that I feel I can discuss them on a higher level. And I think the psychiatric community in general appreciated the amount of work on those scripts, the way I vetted them with several analysts to make sure that our psychiatric technique that we were describing in the films was good." Ramis's fastidious scholarship on the subject is noteworthy, especially considering how psychiatric professionals are normally portrayed, particularly in comedies: "Either every shrink is Sigmund Freud, like they're a genius, or they're a complete loser."

Despite having penned such a fine script, at first it seemed that circumstances would prevent Ramis from directing his screenplay for *Analyze This*.

"The project was offered to me right when I had moved back to Chicago and I had committed to my family that I wouldn't just pick up and leave as soon as we got here," he remembers. "So when they first offered me the film [to direct], I said I'd do it only if we could shoot the bulk of it in Chicago. Of course, DeNiro and Crystal were heavily invested in filming it in New York and said unfortunately not, so I passed. I turned down the project and they got another director, and after about eight months that relationship fizzled, and they came back to me and said, 'Well, have you been in Chicago long enough to consider leaving now?' A year was up at that point, so I said, 'Yeah, let's do it.' In fact, I took the family to New York when we made the first one."

Nice family vacation. Forget Disney World, kids, let's pack up and go make a movie with Robert DeNiro and Billy Crystal! And if *Groundhog Day* and the *"Analyze* diptych" weren't enough to make Ramis a legend amongst the mental health community, there was *Stuart Saves His Family* (1995), which Ramis directed for his friend Al Franken. "It was really a hit with the recovery movement. The movie is a favorite in 12-step programs everywhere. That was really fun to do and maybe my most underappreciated film."

Ostensibly a feature-length version of the *Saturday Night Live* sketches featuring Franken's 12-step-obsessed character, Stuart Smalley (and his mantra "I'm good enough, I'm smart enough, and doggone it, people like me."). *Stuart Saves His Family* is also a poignant and sincere look into family dysfunction that never shies away from the trauma and pain that brings people into 12-step programs to begin with. Wonderful performances from veteran actors Shirley Knight, Harris Yulin, Lesley Boone, and Vincent D'Onofrio as Smalley's mother, father, sister, and brother, respectively, add to the depth of the film, as does Laura San Giacomo's comic turn as Stuart's dear friend Julia. It is truly a shame that this darkly hilarious film never found a wider audience when it was released. "The fact that it was a *Saturday Night Live* character kind of doomed the movie. It got great reviews from important critics, but as far as reaching the public, one of the critics said, 'It's unfortunate, but people who would see this movie won't like it, and people who would like it won't see it.'"

Another dark yet hilarious Ramis-directed film is *The Ice Harvest* (2005), which stars John Cusack, Billy Bob Thornton, Oliver Platt, and Connie Nielsen. Cusack plays a cynical, burned-out Wichita lawyer who embezzles a large sum of money from his employer, a vicious mob-connected strip club owner. He and his partner in the scheme (Thornton) must escape town before they are found out. Unfortunately, an enormous ice storm complicates the issue, as does a series of plot twists and double-crosses, which take the audience on an adventure through the seedy underbelly of a medium-sized American town.

Although he spends much more time behind the camera these days, Ramis's acting cameos in several more recent comedies, such as *Orange County* (2002), *Knocked Up* (2007), and *Walk Hard: The Dewey Cox Story* (2007), have introduced him to a whole new group of fans who weren't even born when *SCTV* first ran—something that Ramis finds amusing and gratifying: "As I kind of observe my own career, I had been known in Chicago and then got established in Hollywood as a writer and director before I even did any movie acting. Then I did *Stripes* (1981) and became known as a movie actor. So then I was 'the guy from *Stripes*,' and then I was 'the guy from *Ghostbusters*,' and then all that time went by where I didn't do a lot of acting, but *Ghostbusters 2* (1989) kind of cemented the Egon Spengler thing. But after I did *Orange County*, I kind of noticed a generational change with people on the street. The first time it happened I was in New York and someone yelled out, 'Hey, *Orange County* guy!' It was the first time I had not been referred to as 'Hey, Egon!' or 'Hey, Ziske from *Stripes*!' I knew something had changed and that I'd definitely been introduced to a new generation."

Harold's most recent feature, *Year One* (2009), which he cowrote and directed, is further endearing him to that youthful fan base. *Year One* stars Jack Black and Michael Cera as two slacker hunter-gatherers who are banished from their Neolithic tribe and embark on an odyssey across the ancient world. Despite being a much broader comedy than he's done in recent years, it's an ambitious epic with all the requisite research and thoughtfulness for which Ramis is known. "I've never done a period film, particularly a biblical epic," he says. "But I kind of went to school on it; I looked at all the Bible pictures, both Hollywood and European ones. *The Life of Brian* (1979) and of course all the Cecil B. DeMille pictures. It's not a parody of those films, it's not *Blazing Saddles* (1974), it's almost like 'Rosencrantz and Guildenstern walk through the world of Genesis.'"

Harold's comic oeuvre will again come full circle when *Ghostbusters 3* becomes a reality. Columbia Studios has hired the duo who cowrote the screenplay for *Year One*, Gene Stupnitsky and Lee Eisenberg, both veterans of the hit television comedy series *The Office*, to write and produce the long-awaited sequel. "They're in the very early stages of hammering out a story."

Given the "kid appeal" a *Ghostbusters* sequel will have, Ramis's talent will be on display to yet another generation of comedy fans. It's something that he's grown used to: "Most boys are grabbed by comedy, maybe just a little before the time that rock 'n' roll gets a hold of you. It's a tremendous shaping force in someone's adolescence, because as you get socialized, I think the kind of comedy you're exposed to may determine your social orientation—how ironic you're going to be, how sarcastic you're going to be, how much of a rebel you're going to be. How irreverent or impertinent you're going to be."

Which everyone can agree is a very serious thing.

Michael Shamberg: Major Hollywood Player

One of Hollywood's top producers hails from the North Shore suburb of Winnetka. Michael Shamberg's name may be unfamiliar to many of those outside Hollywood, but his films certainly aren't. He's been one of the movers behind the scenes of some of the most popular and critically acclaimed films of the last three decades.

Shamberg gained an early appreciation for movies from his parents, film enthusiasts who had a yearly ritual in which they would take the entire family to see that year's Oscar winner. They also made a point to bring Michael with them to all the major films at the time (age-appropriate, of course). On weekends, he'd ride the train down to Evanston with his friends. "We'd go to one of those big theaters with a double bill with movies like *Godzilla vs. Mothra* (1964), and there'd be 1,200 kids screaming and the ushers trying to calm them down."

In high school, his cinematic education continued when he was fortunate enough to have a great teacher, Mr. McKendall, who would show the class the great Italian Realist, French New Wave, and other European art films.

After graduation, Shamberg left home to attend college at Washington University in Saint Louis. On his first day he met Harold Ramis, and they eventually became lifelong friends.

Michael Shamberg. *(Photo courtesy of Michael Shamberg)*

Shamberg coasted through college as a C student until he had an epiph-
any midway through his senior year when he read Marshall McLuhan's
seminal media studies text *Understanding Media*. "It swept away about
three and a half years of college, because I felt that someone had actually
written a book about the times I lived in and the influences," Shamberg
recalls. "I mean, now media studies is common, but back then nobody
had a clue, or at least it didn't occur to anybody how much effect television was having on the culture and how kids grew up, except for this guy.
It was the first thing I'd ever read that really inspired me and helped me to
understand my world." Fueled by this inspiration, Shamberg became an A
student for the brief remainder of his time in school and began a lifelong
fascination with learning, culture, and the world of ideas.

Shamberg put his new ideas to work, first as a Time/Life correspondent,
then as one of the founders of a video collective called Raindance Corporation, which later became TVTV (Top Value Television). TVTV's mission
was to encourage ordinary citizens to use the (relatively) portable new
video technology of the day to create their own media. This grassroots
movement would subvert the large media outlets that controlled broadcast
television and produce positive social change. He elucidated his theories
and mission in a book titled *Guerilla Television*, in which he exhorts people
to take up a nonviolent struggle against "beast television," as he had nicknamed broadcast television.

His words might sound almost quaint in light of today's YouTube world
of ubiquitous self-produced video content, but *Guerrilla Television* was
incendiary stuff in the three-network world of the early 1970s. In fact, the
do-it-yourself video movement that Shamberg helped found was a direct
forerunner of YouTube, Current TV, and the slew of grassroots media outlets we see today, with one major distinction: "What the YouTube people
did, and I wish I had thought of it, was that they democratized the distribution of the product and removed all the barriers that used to exist."

TVTV opened the door to self-produced video, but it wasn't until the
spread of the Internet that the world could see all that content without the
filter of the media gatekeepers. Not that everything on YouTube and its
hosts of clones is wonderful stuff (far from it, as anyone who's spent time
there will attest), but the paradigm they created has, and will have, far-
reaching effects on world society and culture.

Shamberg 's tenure in the more conventional world of feature film production began in the late 1970s, when he moved to Los Angeles and needed

to earn money to support his young family. Of course, his entree was far from conventional. "Using a credit card, I optioned a little book called *Heart Beat* about the Beat Generation, and a friend of mine knew a guy who gave us $40,000 to get into the film business. Then we hired a screenwriter and we were lucky enough to get the movie made. At the same time, through Harold Ramis, I knew all the *Saturday Night Live* people, and the studios wanted comedies. So with my partner from *Heart Beat* (1980), Alan Greisman, and Doug Kenney, who started the *National Lampoon*, we founded a company and I was just lucky enough to get into the movie business."

The first movie they produced, *Modern Problems* (1981) with Chevy Chase, was a moderate success. The second film, *The Big Chill* (1983), was a huge runaway hit and cemented Shamberg's status as a top-tier Hollywood film producer. He's now produced over 50 films and television shows, including *A Fish Called Wanda* (1988), *Reality Bites* (1994), *Pulp Fiction* (1994), *Get Shorty* (1995), *Gattaca* (1997), *Man on the Moon* (1999), *Erin Brockovich* (2000), *Be Cool* (2005), *Garden State* (2004), *Freedom Writers* (2007), *Reno 911!: Miami* (2007), *Extraordinary Measures* (2010), and *Contagion* (2011).

Many of Shamberg's most successful movie ideas have come about via serendipity or through a confluence of factors. *A Fish Called Wanda* came to him because he had worked with Kevin Kline on *The Big Chill* and a relative had introduced him to John Cleese. When Cleese wanted Kevin Kline to play the role of Otto in *A Fish Called Wanda* and also wanted the movie to be produced by Americans, Shamberg was a logical choice.

In 1990, Shamberg founded a new production company with actor Danny DeVito, Jersey Films. The first employee they hired was Stacey Sher, who proved to be so valuable that she was made a partner in the firm two years later. Sher and Shamberg have worked as a producing tandem ever since, and he credits much of his success to her.

It was Sher's efforts that brought the pair one of their most successful movies to date. She had run across and read writer/director Quentin Tarantino's script for *Reservoir Dogs* (1992), which he was working on at the time, and was completely wowed by it. She suggested they take a meeting with Tarantino and "let's just do whatever he wants to do after *Reservoir Dogs*."

That project turned out to be *Pulp Fiction*, and after reading Tarantino's script, Shamberg told him, "This is the *Lawrence of Arabia* of whatever it is." His words were oddly prophetic, as the film went on to not only break box office records for independent features but also to deeply insinuate itself into the pop-culture landscape (from which Tarantino had assembled the various threads of his story to begin with). "Quentin thought the movie would gross $35 or $40 million and establish his career, but none of us knew it would have such an impact." At last count, the film has grossed over $212 million worldwide. It has also spawned innumerable catch-phrases, fashion trends, parodies, and film imitators (almost all of them unable to capture any of the charm and panache of the original).

In 2003, Shamberg and Sher split with DeVito to form their current production company, Double Feature Films. The title came from Sher's husband, Kerry, who thought of it "because there were two of us."

It was Shamberg's wife, Carla, who was the impetus for the making of *Erin Brockovich*. "She had met the real Erin Brockovich and thought her story would be a great idea for a movie. It's funny, because when she first came to me and told me about her, I said, 'That's a crazy idea for a movie,' and she said, 'You're wrong,' and she talked to Stacey, and they both said, 'You're wrong.'" Later, when Susannah Grant delivered an excellent script, the writing was on the wall. "And of course, I met Erin, and once you meet her, you really get behind it."

Julia Roberts won an Oscar for her portrayal of the feisty paralegal who almost single-handedly brought a utility company to its knees while winning justice for the small town poisoned by its negligence. The film was also nominated for Best Picture, Best Screenplay (Grant), Best Director (Steven Soderbergh), and Best Supporting Actor (Albert Finney). "It's certainly the kind of movie that you're proud of," Shamberg says with characteristic understatement. Carla ended up putting so much work into the making of it that she received executive producer credit and is now vice president of special projects at Double Feature Films.

Michael also credits the vision of the writers, directors, and everyone else involved with the success of his movies. "What we do most often is just to try to support and protect the vision of the filmmakers through the process of creating the film."

Always looking to the future, Double Feature Films has over seven productions in various stages of development. So in the unlikely event you haven't seen one of Shamberg's films in the past, you almost certainly will soon.

4

West

The City

Jane Addams Hull-House Museum

The University of Illinois at Chicago, 800 S. Halsted Street

"In the days before the inspection of films and the present regulations for the five-cent theaters, we established at Hull-House a moving picture show."
—*Jane Addams,* Twenty Years at Hull-House, *1910.*

Social pioneer Jane Addams understood the power of art to germinate ideas. Consequently, painting, music, and theater became a powerful factor in the vitality of Addams's Hull-House. With the development of motion picture technology, Addams decided to make part of Hull-House a nickelodeon for neighborhood children. Though she had to combat objection to the new medium by many of her peers, Addams insisted on holding regular screenings. When her experiment ended, Addams worked closely with local officials to improve the quality of neighborhood motion picture theaters.

The Jane Addams Hull-House Museum is open Tuesday through Friday from 10 AM to 4 PM and Sundays from noon to 4 PM. Admission is free. For more information, including booking group tours, call (312) 413-5353 or visit the Hull-House homepage at www.uic.edu/jaddams/hull/.

The scene of a bank robbery in the opening sequence of *The Dark Knight* (2008), the immense old Chicago Post Office sits vacant above Congress Parkway. *(Photo by Kate Corcoran)*

Cook County Hospital

1835 W. Harrison Street

Cook County Hospital was the largest and busiest medical facility in the city, consisting of 13 common buildings with more than 500 physicians on staff. As a public hospital, it was a true lifeline for many Chicagoans unable to afford medical insurance.

The hospital played a pivotal role in *The Fugitive* (1993). It's here where Harrison Ford, a brilliant surgeon on the run, begins his search for the mysterious one-armed man who killed his wife. Disguised as a janitor, Ford uses the prosthetics lab to research possible suspects but ultimately gives himself away when coming to the aid of a misdiagnosed youngster.

Cook County Hospital was also used for scenes in *Red Heat* (1988) and *Hero* (1992). Independent filmmaker Jim Sikora shot part of *Walls in the City* (1994) outside the hospital, opening the movie's second tale with local artist/actor Tony Fitzpatrick lighting up a cheap stogie to celebrate his release from the medical facility.

When it comes to show business, Cook County Hospital is best known as the inspiration for NBC television's popular show *ER*. This Emmy-winning dramatic series revolved around the people who worked in the "Cook County General Hospital" trauma unit. In early February 2009, *ER* finished filming Chicago exteriors for its 15th and final season, and the two-hour series finale was aired on March 12, 2009, marking the end of a major epoch in network television and Chicago production history. Although no actual filming took place within the real hospital, the show did come to Chicago three or four times a year to shoot exterior scenes around town. Cook County's operations were moved to the new Stroger Hospital in 2002, and the beautiful old main building sits derelict. Preservationists are working furiously to have the structure granted landmark status, but the building remains on their "endangered" list, and the land it sits upon is coveted by several parties.

Mid-City National Bank
800 W. Madison Street
The white supremacists of *Betrayed* (1988) attempt to further their twisted underground movement by staging a holdup at this near-Loop bank (now an MB Financial Bank).

Fulton Street Market
600–800 W. Fulton Street
Head to Fulton Street for a wide variety of fruits, vegetables, bullets, bodies dropping, and cars crashing. A typical day at Chicago's center for restaurant produce? Not really, but then again most produce workers don't look like steely-eyed undercover cop Nico Toscani (Steven Seagal) and his drop-dead gorgeous, tough-as-nails partner Delores Jackson (the irrepressible Pam Grier) in *Above the Law* (1988). The first of the film's many action sequences is set here.

Harpo Studios
1058 W. Washington Boulevard
At first glance, this cluster of buildings doesn't seem that different from anything else in this Near West Side neighborhood. But don't let first impressions fool you. Behind the renovated art deco facade is a billion-dollar empire that can still be summed up in one word: *Oprah*.

When Oprah Winfrey came to Chicago in 1984, her initial role was to serve as host of WLS-TV's morning talk show *A.M. Chicago*. Within a few years, Winfrey had mastered the talk-show form and recreated it in her own image. The program was renamed *The Oprah Winfrey Show*, and it dove headfirst into oddball Americana, with topics ranging from celebrity interviews to dysfunctional families to frank discussions of that old ratings standby, sex.

Legend has it that Quincy Jones saw a broadcast of *The Oprah Winfrey Show* while staying at a Chicago hotel. This led to Winfrey's being cast in Steven Spielberg's *The Color Purple* (1985), an Oscar nomination for Best Supporting Actress, and, ultimately, unbridled success. Shortly after finishing work on *The Color Purple*, Winfrey took her show national. Acquiring the 1058 W. Washington building, she started her own production company, dubbed Harpo. The title was no tribute to Harpo Marx, but rather a backward spelling of Winfrey's first name.

Former home of *The Oprah Winfrey Show*, Harpo Studios (that's "Oprah" spelled backwards) is a state-of-the-art television and film production center. *(Photo by Kate Corcoran)*

The Harpo Studios building has some significant history. Its original purpose was as the Second Regimental Armory. The armory served as temporary morgue for victims of the 1915 Eastland disaster.

The armory's vast spaces made it ideal for film production, and eventually the building was transformed into the Fred Niles Studios. For years these soundstages were a center for commercial and industrial filmmaking, though occasionally feature filmmakers made use of the facility. Herschell Gordon Lewis came to Niles Studios for his first nudie cutie, *The Prime Time* (1960). Arthur Penn and Warren Beatty also utilized the Niles facilities for some of the surreal street scenes of *Mickey One* (1965).

Today, Harpo Studios is a state-of-the-art showcase for film and television production. *Code of Silence* (1985), *Men Don't Leave* (1990), and *Only the Lonely* (1991) are only a small sampling of Chicago-shot Hollywood productions that made use of the Harpo soundstages. Winfrey-produced television films like *The Women of Brewster Place* (1989) and *There Are No Children Here* (1993) have also been based out of Harpo. And even though Oprah ceased her talk show in 2011, the facilities are still an important part of Chicago's production landscape.

The Chicago Academy for the Arts
1010 W. Chicago Avenue

New York has the High School for the Performing Arts, which inspired the 1980 movie and subsequent television series *Fame*. In the Windy City, we have the Chicago Academy for the Arts. This private high school is for students who aspire to careers in visual and performing arts, offering studies in music, theater/musical theater, dance, visual art, and communication arts. Offering fully accredited college preparatory classes in the morning, the school devotes afternoons to the study of a student's chosen discipline.

Famous alumni of the academy include Lara Flynn Boyle, perhaps best known for her work on the cult television series *Twin Peaks* but also featured in such Chicago-based movies as *Wayne's World* (1992), *Baby's Day Out* (1994), and the made-for-TV offering *Since You've Been Gone* (1998); and Adam Rifkin, whose work ranges from directing and writing the little-seen black comedy *The Dark Backward* (1991) to performing under the name "Rif Coogan" in such forgettable junk as *Bikini Squad* (1993) to scripting the big-budget DreamWorks comedy *Mouse Hunt* (1997).

A sort of fictional version of the school, "the Chicago School of Music and Dance," was central to the independent film *Make It Happen* (2008), which involved a small-town dancer with a dream of attending the school. After failing her audition, she finds employment in a burlesque club, where she learns to dance with a greater sensuality and is eventually able to re-audition and fulfill her dream. Oh, and did I mention that she finds love and learns valuable lessons about life and friendship in the process? The script was penned by Duane Adler, who also wrote the Chicago-set Julia Stiles dance movie *Save the Last Dance* (2001)—and who apparently has designs on cornering the "dancer with a dream" movie market.

For more information on the Chicago Academy for the Arts, call (312) 421-0202 or visit its website at www.chicagoacademyforthearts.org.

Christina Varotsis: Making It Happen

Of all the various types of producers that appear at the beginning of a film, the line producer is the most logistically important. What does a line producer do? This definition comes courtesy of Christina Varotsis: "The line producer is one of the first persons to get hired on a film's production team, traditionally during the later stages of development. The line

Christina Varotsis on the set of *Ca$h!* in 2008. *(Photo by Raul Esparza III, courtesy of Three Good Men, LLC)*

producer plays a key role in estimating the cost of making a film. The line producer breaks down the script into a schedule, then based on this schedule, drafts the initial budget, estimating the amount of funding required. As soon as financing is completed and the film is 'greenlit,' the film can go into preproduction. At that point, the line producer supervises the final preparation of the film's budget and the daily planning and running of the production. The line producer is in charge of all the physical aspects of the making of a film and is responsible for overseeing and approving production expenditures; he/she is responsible for hiring and supervising the crew and for the day-to-day operation of the production, from preproduction to principal photography, and through the wrap of the shoot. The line producer is ultimately responsible for ensuring that the production is completed on time and on budget."

While keeping in mind the creative needs of the film, of course. In essence, the line producer is the person who is most responsible on a day-to-day basis for actually getting the film made. It's one of the most complicated and demanding jobs on the planet; part CFO, part office manager, part military procurement officer, and part general. Although he or she works in concert with many others, any number of mistakes by the line producer could doom or severely hamper a production. If the line producer doesn't estimate the budget correctly, the film can run out of funding before principal photography is done. If he or she doesn't hire the right vendors, equipment suppliers, or crew, the budget is broken due to time wasted waiting for late deliveries or rigging to be set up. If the line producer doesn't take the personalities of the people he or she hires into consideration, friction between crew members or between cast and crew might poison the atmosphere on the set. A poorly constructed shooting schedule causes a production to hemorrhage money every day due to unnecessary travel and wasted time.

Varotsis has mastered this Herculean occupation and become one of the best line producers in the business. Her love of Chicago has kept her from moving to Hollywood; and given a choice, she prefers to work on independent features because of the creative freedom and autonomy they offer.

One of Varotsis's first jobs when hired (sometimes years before filming begins or financing has even been found) is to break down the script and figure out a budget and preliminary shooting schedule according to the parameters given her. Once financing has been obtained and preproduction actually begins, she sits down with the assistant director, who finalizes the shooting schedule. Many factors affect this process. "Actors' schedules, specific locations, the action that goes on, basically whatever parameters need to be considered," Varotsis says. No matter what factors come into play, the finished schedule must always be within the set budget and the time allotted for shooting.

This balancing act can be very tricky, especially since certain locations can only be used at certain times. For example, the CTA only allows shooting during certain off-peak hours, and certain actors might only be available for short periods of time, like on the shooting of *The Promotion* (2008), when they had to film all of the scenes with actress Jenna Fischer in just one week.

Other challenges came into play on the shoot for *The Promotion*. Although they were fortunate enough to find a grocery store that had recently closed and were able to fill it with products, mostly through product placement deals and various donations, Varotsis recalls that one of the requirements for filming caused a huge problem: "While you record sound for film, you don't want to have anything on."

This meant that not only did the store's air-conditioning units have to be turned off, but all of the various coolers and freezers also had to be shut down as well. Since the shoot happened during the hot summer months, it wasn't just uncomfortable for cast and crew, but "all of the meat products and everything else we had in the coolers rotted out, so we had to shoot the perishable parts of the supermarket very quickly so we could get rid of some of that stuff. You just can't have things rotting away in the background."

Varotsis managed to work out all the problems, however, something that has earned her a reputation as a top-tier line producer—a fact to which producer Steven A. Jones attests: "She has worked as coproducer with me on several projects. When people want to get the most for their money and still have a great project, she is the person they hire."

One project that took all of Varotsis's considerable skills was the contro-versial yet brilliant 2006 pseudo-documentary *Death of a President*, which required her to not only oversee hundreds of extras in various downtown locations, but also keep the exact nature of the film's plot (a fictional assas-sination of President George W. Bush) confidential from the authorities and the public.

Despite the incendiary nature of the subject matter and the maelstrom of controversy that surrounded its release, *Death of a President* is an extremely balanced and thoughtful film that portrays Bush not as some inhuman monster but as a real human being surrounded by a staff who care deeply about him. His assassination is a traumatic event in the film and is deeply moving even to those who opposed his policies or derided his administration. And the not-so-fictional aftermath of the shooting, involv-ing an extreme reduction in civil liberties under a Dick Cheney presidency and the railroading of an innocent Muslim suspect, is more chilling than a thousand Hollywood thrillers.

The techniques used by the filmmakers, Gabriel Range and Simon Finch, were brilliant as well, using a variety of means to create a hyper-realistic feel to the film. Digital cameras on poles were used to simulate outdoor security cameras, and staged protest scenes were shot with a variety of cameras (even cell phones) from several angles to give the edited sequences a documentary feel. The filmmakers even went Haskell Wexler one better by not only placing their own actors in real antiwar protests on the streets of Chicago, a la *Medium Cool*, but also recruiting actual anarchist protestors to appear in their own staged protests. For the assassination sequence outside a downtown Chicago hotel, Range and Finch spent hours poring over stock footage of an actual "rope line" handshake session that Bush had done a year earlier at that same hotel, casting actors who looked just like the real people in the footage and costuming them so that it is virtually impossible to separate the real from the fictional.

The filmmakers needed to create complete believability and consis-tency in the protest scenes, particularly the one on LaSalle Street, where Varotsis had to coordinate over 400 extras. That scene provided a unique experience for the producer: "You rarely spend so much time focusing on background, but because of the nature of the film, we spent a lot of time focusing on extras and extras being dressed the right way. We're usu-ally more concerned with talent and actors, and it was really interesting to strictly focus on extras and the logistics of them running around and stuff. This time the extras were in the foreground."

The mélange of filmic techniques is also accompanied by documentary-style "talking head" interviews of actors playing White House staffers, Secret Service and law enforcement agents, and various citizens and witnesses. The performances of the actors (especially James Urbaniak as a forensic analyst) are completely believable, and the final result is a faux-documentary that seems as real as an episode of *Frontline*.

Despite the controversy its release engendered, *Death of a President* was widely acclaimed by critics the world over after its premiere at the Toronto International Film Festival. Varotsis attended the premiere and remembers the electric atmosphere surrounding it. "There was a lot of attention on the film as soon as it was revealed that it was premiering there; there were a lot of rumors about what the film was about, lots of excitement, lots of angry people. It was a packed screening; I remember it was the hot ticket of the festival. Going into the screening; room it was a packed house with people fighting for seats."

Ironically enough, the main reaction from a lot of the audience, who were expecting a searing indictment of Bush and were prepared to wallow in his fictional killing, were disappointed at the film's somber, evenhanded tone. Varotsis elaborates: "I think a lot of people were surprised because they were hoping for something much more controversial. I think there was a bit of disappointment in the room because people thought that it was going to be much more exploitative and much more sensationalistic, and it was a serious film. There was a real letdown for those in the crowd who were hoping it would be much more controversial than it ended up being."

Despite the chagrin of those who were expecting a left-wing revenge fantasy, *Death of a President* received the International Federation of Film Critics Award (the FIPRESCI Prize) at the festival.

Although working on intensely creative independent films such as *D.O.A.P.* (as it was called during production to preserve secrecy) is extremely rewarding for Varotsis, there is one large pitfall to working on the cutting edge of indie filmmaking: the fact that the finished product, no matter how good, may never be seen by the general public if the makers are unable to find a distributor. This is something she feels almost comes with the territory: "What you do a lot of times as an independent filmmaker is that you do a film on 'spec.' You raise the money, you get everything together, you shoot it; and then you have to go around and shop it around and get into festivals to get it attention, and even then it doesn't guarantee you'll get it released. It's an uphill battle throughout the whole process of making the film, from raising the funds to shooting the film to attempting to get it released. It is very, very difficult, and a lot of times I'll tell student filmmakers that making the film is sometimes the easiest part! Raising the money and getting distribution are in my mind the two hardest things, because you just have to keep on knocking on doors, keep on begging for mercy!"

But keeping on is something that she is used to, and it's one of the many qualities that make her so popular with those filmmakers who are fortunate enough to have her working on their productions.

Humboldt Park
1400 N. Sacramento Avenue
This picturesque park forms the heart of the Humboldt Park neighborhood, which has been the port of call for immigrants from the US territory of Puerto Rico since the early 1950s. The area has risen and fallen over the decades, but it retains its Puerto Rican flavor and vibrancy. In addition to writer/director (and Columbia College grad) Marisol Torres's big, bold, and often bawdy shoestring indie feature *Boricua* (a.k.a. *Chicago Boricua*, 2004), the neighborhood's bodegas, restaurants, and clubs were featured in the 2008 film *Nothing Like the Holidays*, which was produced by Chicago stalwarts George Tillman Jr. and Bob Teitel.

State Street Pictures' George Tillman Jr. and Bob Teitel: Steadfast Chicago Supporters

On the weekend of September 26–28, 1997, the lives of George Tillman Jr. and Bob Teitel, two Columbia College film school graduates, changed forever. Their film *Soul Food*, which Tillman wrote and directed and Teitel produced, opened in theaters nationwide. Made for $7.5 million, small change by Hollywood standards, *Soul Food* hauled in $11.1 million worth of tickets over that three-day period.

This nationwide take was good enough for second place at the box office. One week later, *Soul Food* was the top box office draw in the country, topping films with budgets several times its own. In a business that's often run by the bottom line, the made-in-Chicago *Soul Food* proved itself

On the set of *Soul Food* (1997) with Bob Teitel (left), George Tillman Jr. (center), and Mekhi Phifer (right). *(Photo courtesy of Bob Teitel)*

a dollar-for-dollar champ. And suddenly Tillman and Teitel were the hottest things in Hollywood.

Tillman, an African American from Milwaukee, and Teitel, a Puerto Rican / Jewish kid from Arlington Heights, Illinois, first met as film students at Columbia College. "I lived in the dormitory at Roosevelt University and so did Bob," says Tillman. "Then we both took the same production class, and that's when we started working together." By the time Tillman and Teitel were seniors, the duo had established a solid working relationship. Teitel handled the business and producing end of the partnership, while Tillman did the writing and directing. Their first film, *Paula* (1990), was Tillman's senior thesis film.

Made for $12,000, which the enterprising duo raised themselves, *Paula* is about a 17-year-old single mother who wants to continue her education beyond high school. Shot in the Uptown area, the film ended up winning six national awards, including the Student Academy Award and recognition from the Black Filmmakers Hall of Fame.

With the success of *Paula*, Tillman sat down to write his next screenplay, a feature-length film called *Scenes for the Soul*. Containing a tapestry of stories, the film intermingled characters and situations with different scenes set on the North, South, and West Sides of Chicago.

"We used *Paula* as a vehicle to raise money for *Scenes for the Soul*," says Teitel. "We raised $150,000 between 44 different people—everyone from plumbers to stockbrokers. We shot in 1993 and it took us a year for postproduction before the film was finally done."

What happened next is the kind of stuff Hollywood legends are made of. With just $400 in their collective pockets and a copy of *Scenes for the Soul* on a videocassette, Tillman and Teitel drove out to Los Angeles in November 1994. "We'd never been to California," says Teitel. "George and I stayed at a friend's house, and we knew one person who knew one person who knew someone at the William Morris Agency. We were fortunate enough to show *Scenes for the Soul* to them and they liked it.

"About a week later we were signed by William Morris, and a month later, on December 23, 1994, we sold the film to Savoy Pictures for $1 million."

But Savoy went bankrupt in 1995 and the film was never seen. Down but not out, Tillman and Teitel remained determined. Tillman wrote a new script, a family drama he called *Soul Food*. "I got the ideas from my family in Milwaukee, the Sunday dinners and family dinners that we had," says Tillman. "The get-togethers at my grandmother's, how important and influential she was on the family, how she kept everybody together. I wanted to make a film about that."

"We were supposed to do George's script with Savoy," says Teitel, "but after that fell apart, we got it out of Savoy and had a deal to make it for a couple million dollars for a small production company. Since we were tied with William Morris, we were always looking for a soundtrack. Some people suggested we show it to Babyface for just a possible soundtrack."

Kenneth "Babyface" Edmonds is one of the music industry's hottest talents, having won numerous Grammy Awards for both his singing and his producing. When he saw Tillman's script, Babyface realized he wanted to do more than the film's soundtrack.

At the time, Babyface and his wife, Tracey E. Edmonds, were starting their own film production company through the auspices of Fox 2000 Pictures (a division of 20th Century Fox). Having just produced the soundtrack album for the movie *Waiting to Exhale* (1995), the Edmondses were looking for the right vehicle to get their company started. Serendipity ensued when the *Soul Food* script crossed their desk. "They felt like this would be a great first project for them to do," says Teitel. "We met in June 1996, and on November 6, we started shooting."

With the Edmondses' connections, it wasn't hard to get Vanessa L. Williams and Vivica A. Fox signed on to the cast. Next was Chicago-based actor Irma P. Hall. "We were huge fans of Billy Bob Thornton's film *A Family Thing* (1996), which starred Irma," says Teitel. "Once we saw that movie, we knew without a doubt that she was *Soul Food*'s Mother Joe."

Still, getting *Soul Food* up and running the way Tillman and Teitel wanted wasn't an easy task. "Originally they didn't want me to direct the film, because my first film didn't come out and they didn't know anything about me," says Tillman. "But we stuck to our guns. I knew I could always raise the money independently if I had to. They gave in, and then they wanted to shoot the film in Los Angeles. I wanted to shoot the film in Chicago. I didn't know anything about Los Angeles neighborhoods. I feel comfortable in Chicago and I held out again."

"Shooting in Chicago is the only way we would make the film," adds Teitel. "They didn't want us to shoot in Chicago, and we said we were going to walk and we did. For a couple of days *Soul Food* was off because of that."

"Finally," says Tillman, "they gave in to shoot in Chicago. I wanted to stick to my guns and do what I believe in, and it worked out to our advantage. We gave them the final script in August and two months later we had started production."

Soul Food was a huge success—and for good reason. The film is an insightful look at family life, honestly portraying the whole gamut of emotions that bubble to the surface when crises strike. The actors are a tight ensemble cast; Williams, Fox, Long, Hall, Beach, Mekhi Phifer, and youngster Brandon Hammond work well together, and their warmth for one another radiates from the screen. Watching *Soul Food*, you really believe these characters are a family.

By January 1998, *Soul Food* had brought in $43.4 million at the box office, making it a certifiable hit. The home video release was also a bestseller, as was the soundtrack album. Tillman and Teitel then adapted the story into a successful television series, which ran for four years on the Showtime cable network.

The pair's next feature found them both living a lifelong dream, working with Oscar winner Robert DeNiro on the powerful period drama *Men of Honor* (2000). Based on a true story, *Men of Honor* depicts the life of Carl Brashear, played by another Oscar winner, Cuba Gooding Jr. Brashear, the son of a sharecropper, joins the navy in 1948 and is inspired by the heroic exploits of Master Chief Petty Officer Billy Sunday (played by DeNiro) to attempt to become a master diver. He is eventually accepted to the elite Diving and Salvage School, where he will train under his idol. Sunday, however, is under orders from the racist commanding officer to make sure that the young Brashear fails the program. Brashear is then put through a brutal hazing regimen that borders on the homicidal. Not only does he endure the agonizing ordeal, but he even saves a fellow cadet in the process, which earns him the grudging respect of Sunday.

The two men meet again several years later. Brashear has become a national hero by recovering a lost atom bomb, an incident in which he lost his leg. Sunday, now a depressed and angry alcoholic, is lifted from his gloom by Brashear, and the two endeavor to fight the US Navy for the chance for Brashear to return to active duty and finally become a master diver.

Men of Honor was a critical and box office hit, and working with such big stars on a serious drama opened up new vistas for Tillman and Teitel. "It was a major turning point just to work with DeNiro and Cuba," says Teitel. "And the film being so well received, it just opened so many doors for us. It's one of those movies that just resonates with people, and we're very fortunate to have that. People still talk to us about it to this day."

Tillman and Teitel returned to comedy with their next project, 2002's *Barbershop*, on which they shared producing duties. Set in one of the most important African American social institutions, the neighborhood barbershop, the film depicts a day in the lives of its customers and employees. Ice Cube and Cedric the Entertainer lead an awesome ensemble cast, and the film's mixture of raucous comedy and poignant drama moves smoothly along without ever ringing a false note. Truly embodying the definition of the little indie comedy with a heart, *Barbershop* was a huge success, grossing over $75 million (its budget was just over $12 million).

Teitel observes, "I think it's interesting, because on the surface it looks like a straight comedy, but I think the thing that made that film resonate so much was that it did have a heart. And at the core was a really good story. And when we all were making the movie, it was something that we always talked about, in that the comedy is going to be there already with that great ensemble and everybody being in a barbershop. It's naturally going to be funny, but for us it's 'Let's get the story right first.'"

The sequel, *Barbershop 2: Back in Business* (2004) was that rarest of creatures, the sequel that not only is successful financially but also meets or exceeds the original from a creative standpoint. The backstory on Cedric the Entertainer's character is provided via a series of hilarious flashback sequences set in the late 1960s, and the greater issue of homes and businesses being displaced by neighborhood gentrification is explored with a balanced treatment not often found in any film, much less an ensemble comedy. All in all, *Barbershop 2* satisfies on several levels, and audiences and critics ate it up with a spoon, pushing the film to gross almost as much as its predecessor.

From left: John Leguizamo, Jay Hernandez, and Bob Teitel enjoy a freezing Chicago winter moment on the set of *Nothing Like the Holidays* (2008). *(Photo courtesy of Bob Teitel)*

Another one of the plot threads of *Barbershop 2* involves a neighboring beauty shop, run by the no-nonsense Gina Norris (played by Queen Latifah). That character and concept are fleshed out and given life in *Beauty Shop* (2005), with Latifah relocating to Atlanta and opening a brand-new beauty shop. The film was a spinoff of sorts, which Tillman and Teitel were only marginally involved with. "George first came up with the idea [of a beauty shop counterpart] the week that *Barbershop* came out. And when Queen Latifah came on for the second *Barbershop*, it seemed she was perfect. And they [Latifah and her writers] took that idea and kind of ran with it. That was one where it was our name and she kind of was the franchise."

A franchise that did the parent proud, grossing over $30 million at the box office. In addition, 2005 saw the release of *Roll Bounce*, another Teitel/Tillman coproduction, which starred hip-hop teen heartthrob Bow Wow. Much of *Roll Bounce,* a roller-skating saga set in the early 1970s, was shot in a pair of roller rinks in the southern suburbs of Summit and Lynwood. The film is a kind of African American version of one of those Disney kids movies from the 1970s (the sort of movie that Disney should have also been making back then), and although it didn't achieve the box office success that the pair had grown accustomed to, it is an extremely popular family rental on DVD.

With the 2008 release of *Nothing Like the Holidays* (which he cowrote), Teitel was able to achieve a long-held dream of creating a filmic portrait that reflected his own Puerto Rican heritage, much like how *Soul Food* provided a positive portrayal of African American family values. "I'm Puerto Rican and my mom's family grew up in Humboldt Park," Teitel says. "My aunts, my uncles, my cousins, and my grandparents were up in Humboldt Park, so I used to spend a lot of time there. And all my cousins have always been like, 'Well, why don't you do a movie on us, you know, with a Latin family?' And I've always thought it was a good idea; it just took a little longer than I would have liked to put it all together. But in the long run it was worth it. I had this idea, it took a while to develop, but when George and I started working on it, we were so fortunate to have this amazing cast."

And an amazing cast it is: Alfred Molina, Elizabeth Peña, John Leguizamo, Debra Messing, Luis Guzmán, Jay Hernandez, Vanessa Ferlito, Melonie Diaz, and Freddy Rodriguez. Rodriguez (most known for his excellent work on HBO's *Six Feet Under*) who originally hails from Humboldt Park, had

TOP: Bob Teitel on the set of *Nothing Like the Holidays* (2008). *(Photo courtesy of Bob Teitel)*

BOTTOM: On the set of *Nothing Like the Holidays* (2008) with Luis Guzmán, Alfred Molina, Bob Teitel, and Freddy Rodríguez. *(Photo courtesy of Bob Teitel)*

been talking for almost 12 years with his good friend Teitel about making a movie that reflected their Latin roots.

Finally the idea came to fruition with this fine ensemble comedy/drama that nicely captures the rhythm and vitality of the area that Teitel and Rodriguez love so much. Shot in Humboldt Park over a frigid winter, the film provides a slice of life of a clan of residents who may be experiencing their last Christmas together as a family due to strife between the mother and father (Peña and Molina) and a sense of general alienation among the siblings. Love and persistence win the day, however, as the various members of the household work through their problems and pull together. The acting is tremendous, the film is beautifully shot (something rarely said about an ensemble comedy), and the film score by club legend Paul Oakenfold crackles with energy.

Tillman and Teitel's next film, *Notorious* (2009), a biopic of slain rapper

Christopher Wallace (a.k.a. the Notorious B.I.G.), marked Tillman's long-awaited return to the director's chair after several years of solely producing films. Tillman continued the directing trend with the action-packed film *Faster* (2010) and the inner-city coming-of-age picture *The Inevitable Defeat of Mister and Pete* (2013).

Their wild ride through the Hollywood system isn't going to let up anytime soon, as the pair currently have several new projects in various stages of development. But no matter where their success takes them, Tillman and Teitel remain committed to their Chicago roots, often poring over the local papers and magazines for stories that can be transformed into films set in the city where their journey together started. As Teitel says, "There's so many stories to be told in Chicago. I don't believe we've even scratched the surface."

Midway Airport
5500–6300 S. Cicero Avenue

The city's first major airport, Midway, was originally known as Chicago Municipal Airport. It opened in 1927 and quickly developed a reputation as the world's busiest airport, a position that now belongs to O'Hare International Airport on the Northwest Side. In 1949, when 3.2 million passengers passed through its gates, Chicago Municipal Airport was renamed in honor of the World War II Battle of Midway.

Midway has been used in just a handful of films. In *Henry: Portrait of a Serial Killer* (1987), dimwitted Otis (Tom Towles) picks up his sister Becky (Tracy Arnold) there. The microbial paranoia suspense thriller *Contagion* (2011) also spends a little time there, as does the indie comedy *Divorced Dudes* (2012).

Midway plays a more pivotal role in Alfred Hitchcock's cross-country thriller *North by Northwest* (1959). Having just been arrested for creating an art gallery disturbance, Roger Thornhill (the rakish Cary Grant) is brought to Midway by two Chicago cops. Shocked that he's being taken to the airport rather than jail, Grant demands some answers. He's quickly handed over to master agent Leo G. Carroll ("FBI ... CIA ... ONI ... We're all in the same alphabet soup," he tells Grant), and the already twisted plot takes another sharp turn.

Look closely during this scene and you'll notice two men in the background. Extras? Hardly. During the shoot, Bill Blaney, an airport worker at the time, and one of his colleagues snuck onto the runway to catch a peek at Cary Grant. Upon seeing the two men on the runway, Blaney recalled, Hitchcock was outraged. The master of suspense berated the duo for ruining his shot and ordered them to leave. Nevertheless, Blaney and his pal remained in the final cut, giving *North by Northwest* a slightly more realistic look, albeit through a volunteer effort.

Joe Mantegna: From Bleacher Bum to Hollywood Star

He's played a romantic interest opposite Mia Farrow in Woody Allen's *Alice* (1990), appeared as Al Pacino's nemesis in *The Godfather: Part III* (1990), and played a delightfully twisted cameo as Dr. Rondog "Doc" Savage in *Witless Protection* (2008). But in many ways, Joe Mantegna's career has been indelibly linked to his hometown and his friend from the 1970s Chicago theater scene, David Mamet.

"The first professional thing I did in Chicago was the play *Hair*," Mantegna recalls. "In fact, my wife and I were both in the same show; that's where we kind of hooked up. We did that at the Shubert Theatre and then we moved to the Blackstone, and after that I did *Godspell* at the Studebaker. So I was kind of on the musical comedy track early on.

"I'm trying to remember the first time I met David Mamet. I think basically he and I just bumped into each other on the stairs of the Goodman Theatre, as I recall. He had seen me in Organic Theater stuff. He introduced himself and said he was a playwright and hoped we could somehow hook up, and I was like, 'Yeah, great.' I think the first full-length play I did for him was *A Life in the Theater* with Mike Nussbaum, and then it was on from there."

While working at the Organic, Mantegna, like many Chicago actors, also acted in industrial films and occasional commercials. But a 20-minute student short led to Mantegna's first feature film, *Towing* (1978). Based on the escapades of the notorious Lincoln Towing Service, immortalized in song by folk singer Steve Goodman as "the Lincoln Park Pirates," *Towing* was a goofy little satire that didn't get much play outside of Chicago. Still, it gave Mantegna an opportunity to further develop his craft: "My first day of shooting, here I was, I hadn't really done much filming at all, all of the sudden they say, 'OK, in this scene you're going to be driving this tow truck, pulling a car behind it.' And I did. I never had driven a tow truck before, let alone hauling a car behind it. From the world of the theater you had weeks to rehearse things like this. In subsequent films I've done in different conditions, it's not so far-fetched. Sometimes you get thrown into stuff. You just do it. You just jump in and do it."

Over the years, Mantegna has developed an accomplished acting resume. He appeared in several Mamet plays and ultimately won both a Joseph Jefferson Award and Tony Award for his searing performance of the amoral salesman Richard Roma in Mamet's *Glengarry Glen Ross*. With his fellow members of the Organic, Mantegna created an improvisational play based on what they observed watching the Cubs play at Wrigley Field. *Bleacher Bums* looked at baseball from the fan's perspective. The piece was a huge success and was performed in both New York and Los Angeles, where Mantegna served as the show's director. A television version, done for PBS at Channel 11, ended up winning an Emmy Award.

In 1986, Mantegna was cast as the conniving lead in *House of Games* (1987), the screen directorial debut of his old pal Mamet. The next year, Mantegna came back to Chicago to appear in Mamet's mobster fairy tale *Things Change* (1988). Mantegna was cast as a low-level mobster assigned to babysit an innocent Italian shoeshine man, played by Don Ameche. "We wrapped *Things Change* on my 40th birthday in Chicago," he recalls, "and Dave's birthday is actually only two weeks later than mine, so we combined the wrap party and made it a double birthday party for the two of us. At the party, somebody in the mayor's office who we kind of knew was able to get this done. They read this proclamation. At the time it was Mayor Washington, and he made it 'Joe Mantegna Day' in Chicago. It was November 13, 1987."

After *Things Change*, Mantegna played a series of gangster and cop roles, including Joey Zaza in Francis Ford Coppola's *The Godfather: Part III* (1990), a Jewish detective torn by his faith in Mamet's *Homicide* (1991), and actor George Raft in Barry Levinson's crime saga *Bugsy* (1991). Then Mantegna returned to Chicago to play the lead kidnapper in the John Hughes–scripted slapstick comedy *Baby's Day Out* (1994). "That was like a dream come true," Mantegna says, "to be able to come into Chicago and spend that much time there. We were there almost four months, and that was great to be able to do that. The other two guys in the movie, Brian Haley and Joe Pantoliano, they'd always get a kick out of it because every day there might be somebody, either a relative or a friend out of my past, that would come up on the set and Brian and Joe were like, 'Hey, do you know everybody in this town?'"

Mantegna again returned to Chicago in 2002 for the film *Uncle Nino* (2003), which also features his daughter Gina. "Chicago is accommodating," he says. "It's indigenous to the kind of people that are in Chicago in the first place. It's what makes Chicagoans and people from the Midwest different from the East Coast and the West Coast, period. The Midwest, there is a different temperament in a way. It's the center of the country and it's a different kind of thing there."

Mantegna has also been a reader for a number of books on tape (including Robert Parker's Spenser series) and narrated the Oscar-nominated documentary films *Crack USA: Country Under Siege* (1989) and *Death on the Job* (1991). Awards include Emmy nominations for *The Last Don* (1997) and for his role as Dean Martin in *The Rat Pack* (1998), a Golden Globe nomination for *The Rat Pack*, and the Savannah (GA) Film and Video Festival Grand Prize as director of Mamet's *Lakeboat* (2000), which he also produced. Mantegna also starred in *The Last Hit Man* (2008), which won Best Feature Film at the Canadian Filmmakers' Festival. Other varied roles have included Spenser in several A&E movies—*Spenser: Small Vices* (1999), *Thin Air* (2000), and *Walking Shadow* (2001)—Justice Joseph Novelli in the series *First Monday* (2002), Will Girardi in the series *Joan of Arcadia* (2003–2005), Lou Manahan in *The Starter Wife* (2007), and most recently David Rossi in CBS's *Criminal Minds* (2005–), joining the cast in 2007. And, of course, Mantegna appears regularly as the voice of Fat Tony on *The Simpsons*. According to his website, www.joemantegna.com, "Nothing interferes with my doing *The Simpsons*!"

R. S. Owens & Company
5535 N. Lynch Avenue

Tucked away in a little pocket of the Northwest Side is one of the most important manufacturing plants in the world, at least as far as the denizens of Hollywood's dream factory are concerned. Movie talents work hard to win a coveted Academy Award statuette, which are produced here at R. S. Owens & Company, a Windy City trophy company that has an exclusive contract to produce Oscars only for the purposes of the Academy of Motion Picture Arts and Sciences.

If you aren't in the movie business, maybe you have a chance to nab one of the other trophies produced by R. S. Owens. They also make the mementos handed out to winners of MTV Video Awards, Emmys, and the advertising industry's CLIO Awards.

Herschell Gordon Lewis: "Godfather of Gore"

He graduated from Senn High School, then earned his bachelor's and master's degrees in journalism from Northwestern. After obtaining a doctorate in psychology, he taught English at Mississippi State University. He has worked in television and advertising and has authored numerous books on direct marketing. He's a connoisseur of the fine arts, penning volumes on such varied topics as plate collecting and Norman Rockwell. So what is Herschell Gordon Lewis's best-known contribution to film history? Gore.

Known among horror fans as the "Godfather of Gore," in the 1960s and early 1970s, Lewis personally annihilated every taboo Hollywood filmmakers had set for themselves. *Blood Feast* (1963) features a maniacal caterer with a taste for human innards; *2000 Maniacs* (1964) is a carnival of torture as Confederate ghosts wreak vengeance on hapless Northerners, and is considered Lewis's best film (and is his personal favorite). Other titles, like *A Taste of Blood* (1967), *The Wizard of Gore* (1970), and Lewis's swan song, *The Gore Gore Girls* (1972), continued to break new ground in on-screen carnage, if not artistic merit.

Blood Feast still holds fond memories for Lewis. He remembers that it "broke open a door that had not only been shut but had been sealed and filled in with lead, and we smashed right through it. The only way to do gore was with a low-budget picture where the entire movie industry wouldn't be on your neck, saying, 'What are you trying to do?'

"We decided to open it in Peoria. We figured, if we die in Peoria, who would know? We not only didn't die in Peoria, we crocked 'em. Of course, we pulled out many stops. We had these vomit bags, and printed on them was 'You may need this when you see *Blood Feast*.' We had an ambulance with a Mars Light running and we put together a 'wowser-bowser' of an ad campaign. Word got out about the movie."

Following the unexpected success of *Blood Feast*, Lewis cranked out gore movies like cinematic sausages. Forsaking expenses other filmmakers face, such as a production crew, Lewis often served as producer, director, cameraman, editor, and composer. In winter he would head to Florida for the hospitable filming weather. Spring and summer brought production back to Chicago, where extensive use was made of area locations. For the most part, Lewis's movies were popular in theaters and drive-ins throughout the southern and western United States but rarely played in Chicago or other northern cities.

In the late 1960s, Lewis returned to his pre-gore roots of sexploitation movies, along with two children's pictures—considered by many to be unwatchable. Often working in multiple capacities on each film, Lewis adopted a variety of pseudonyms, including Lewis H. Gordon, Mark Hansen, George Parades, Armand Pays, Sheldon Seymour, and Sheldon S. Seymour.

Though film work kept him busy throughout the decade, Lewis opened a successful ad agency in the Wrigley Building. He also returned to education on a part-time basis, teaching graduate courses in marketing at Roosevelt University for 20 years and training film students for five years at Columbia College.

Lewis's last Chicago film hurrah was *The Gore Gore Girls*. Notable as the first film ever to be rated X for violent content, *The Gore Gore Girls* was shot in Old Town and other North Side locations. But by that point Lewis was altogether sick of the movie business—and aware that the day of exploitation movies was coming to an end. He now heads Lewis Enterprises in Florida, through which he writes and consults. But despite his retirement from filmmaking, the number of Lewis cultists continues to grow around the world; a few moments of Lewis's delightful gore even appeared in the prize-winning comedy-drama *Juno* (2007).

O'Hare International Airport

Located on the far Northwest Side and surrounded by suburbs, O'Hare International Airport is considered the world's busiest airline terminal. On a typical day, more than 165,000 passengers come and go through O'Hare's gates.

The airport was originally a military airfield and manufacturing facility known as Orchard Place. A remnant of this history can be found on baggage tickets: the "ORD" luggage tags attached to O'Hare-bound luggage is a contraction of the former name. In 1949, Orchard

Place was renamed after navy lieutenant Edward "Butch" O'Hare, a World War II Medal of Honor winner lost in action over the Pacific on November 23, 1943. In 1955, O'Hare began operations as a commercial airport.

Filmmakers love O'Hare, though it's taken a while for the airport to warm up to cameras. An early film to use O'Hare as a backdrop was Philip Kaufman's *Goldstein* (1964), but it took almost another 20 years for the next major production to land at O'Hare. In *Risky Business* (1983), O'Hare is the airport from which Tom Cruise's parents leave town for vacation, and also where they wait endlessly upon their return for a ride home. A few scenes for the Billy Crystal / Gregory Hines buddy-cop flick *Running Scared* (1986) also take place here, as does the "planes" portion of *Planes, Trains & Automobiles* (1987). *The Package* (1989) uses O'Hare as a substitute for a Washington, DC, airline terminal; Gene Hackman takes a nasty hit to the head in an O'Hare bathroom, enabling his "package," Tommy Lee Jones, to disappear.

With *Home Alone* (1990), O'Hare came into its own as a popular movie location. The kiddie comedy (written and produced by John Hughes and directed by Chris Columbus) made significant use of the American Airlines terminal. American had allied itself with the production in exchange for on-screen promotion. This slapstick comedy, while not the most creative film ever made, was an enormous hit, going on to become one of the biggest-grossing comedies in movie history.

In *Home Alone*, O'Hare not only plays the Chicago airport; it also stands in for the Paris airline terminal. Ultimately, that's been a running theme in the *Home Alone* trilogy. *Home Alone 2: Lost in New York* (1992) has O'Hare playing New York's Kennedy Airport, while *Home Alone 3* (1997) pretends Chicago's airline hub is the San Francisco airport.

My Best Friend's Wedding (1997) features another example of the airport switcheroo. In an early scene, Rupert Everett drives Julia Roberts to LaGuardia Airport, located in the Queens borough of New York City. Sharp-eyed Chicagoans will note that the duo drive under the Mannheim Road overpass—quite a detour from the East Coast.

Next thing you know, Roberts is landing at the United Airlines terminal at O'Hare. There she shares an accidental kiss with her old pal Dermot Mulroney, a prelude to the romantic chaos Roberts is about to unleash.

O'Hare has also shown up in such varied films as *Contagion* (2011), *Couples Retreat* (2009), *The Jackal* (1997), *Music Box* (1990), *Rookie of the*

Year (1993), *Sleepless in Seattle* (1993), *U.S. Marshals* (1998), and *Wicker Park* (2004), and television shows *Boss* and *Early Edition*.

The Suburbs

Maine North High School
9511 W. Harrison Street, Des Plaines, Illinois
Once a high school, now a conglomeration of offices for the State of Illinois, the former Maine North had a brief stint as one of John Hughes's mid-1980s movie high schools. Though the title came from a nickname New Trier students in Winnetka gave their Saturday detention group, *The Breakfast Club* (1985) was shot at Maine North.

The Breakfast Club revolves around five archetypal high schoolers: the Athlete (Emilio Estevez), the Princess (Molly Ringwald), the Brain (Anthony Michael Hall), the Criminal (Judd Nelson), and the Basket Case (Ally Sheedy). Assigned Saturday morning detention for various crimes, the quintet proceed to push each other's buttons, whine about life, and come to the mutual conclusion that adults in general and parents in particular are at the root of all adolescent evils.

The film uses the exterior of Maine North, where the kids are dropped off in the morning and picked up at the end of the day. And most of the action takes place in the school library, which was actually a set built in the old Maine North gymnasium.

Perhaps the unrelenting teen angst of *The Breakfast Club* was a little too much for Hughes. The next year he returned to Maine North with something considerably lighter, *Ferris Bueller's Day Off*. The exterior of the school building and classroom interiors were used in the prelude to Ferris (Matthew Broderick) and company's mad trip to downtown Chicago.

Grace Episcopal Church
924 Lake Street, Oak Park, Illinois
A bride, a groom, two wildly disparate families, and a minister barely able to get through a ceremony—you're at *A Wedding* (1978), Robert Altman's over-the-top satire of marriage ceremonies and receptions. The whole shebang gets started in Grace Episcopal Church, a beautiful Oak Park house of worship. Macaulay Culkin also makes a stop here during *Home Alone* (1990).

Robert Altman's *A Wedding*

"I thought it was like going to summer camp."
—Steven B. Poster, Cinematographer

In the summer of 1978, filmmaker Robert Altman brought a crew of 60 technicians and an all-star cast, including Mia Farrow, Lauren Hutton, Paul Dooley, Howard Duff, Dina Merrill, Nina van Pallandt, Carol Burnett, Geraldine Chaplin, Pam Dawber (in a pre–*Mork & Mindy* role), Pat McCormick, Desi Arnaz Jr., a newcomer named Dennis Franz, and the First Lady of American movies, Lillian Gish, to Lake Bluff for a comic extravaganza. Titled *A Wedding*, the film revolves around two unlikely families coming together to celebrate a marriage. The majority of the shoot took place on the estate of Aleka Armour, widow of meatpacking magnate Lester Armour.

This elegant Sheridan Road home, complete with a guest wing and servants' quarters, was ideal for Altman's plans. It occupied 64 acres of a wooded area along Lake Michigan, giving the large cast plenty of physical room to romp through *A Wedding*'s multitude of storylines. In return for using the mansion, Altman agreed to make a considerable donation to Mrs. Armour's favorite charity, the Rehabilitation Institute of Chicago. Altman also promised to hold a fundraising premiere of the film on behalf of the Institute.

So Mrs. Armour moved out and a cast of crazies moved in. Steven Poster, who has photographed such films as *The Boy Who Could Fly* (1986), *The Cemetery Club* (1993), *Rocket Man* (1997), and the made-in-Chicago features *Next of Kin* (1989) and *Opportunity Knocks* (1990), was then a young film technician: "I thought it was like going to summer camp," Poster says, recalling the making of *A Wedding*. "Here we had this huge estate. You had to get into a van and be driven up this long kind of camp road. Every actor in the movie was there every day for that entire summer. Altman worked that way. He wanted to have everyone there."

"There was a real party atmosphere on the set. People hung out together. Everyone went to dailies at night. It seemed more like people on vacation than 120 people making a movie.

"The children working in the movie would love to have Carol Burnett do her Tarzan yell. Every day, somewhere on the Armour estate you would hear way off in the background this wonderful person doing her Tarzan yell.

"One day I was sitting in the front of the main house. There was a big circular driveway and this huge limousine drove up. Maureen O'Sullivan,

Mia Farrow's mother, got out of the car. At that moment, somewhere on the estate, Carol was doing her Tarzan yell, because the kids got her to do it again. For a second, I saw Maureen O'Sullivan's eyes glass over. Of course, she had played Jane opposite Johnny Weissmuller's Tarzan. I think she thought she was back in the Tarzan movies! It was hysterical. Carol found out about it later and was extremely embarrassed. It was one of those golden moments."

O'Sullivan wasn't the only member of Hollywood's glamour age to visit the set of *A Wedding*. Grace Kelly, a.k.a. Princess Grace of Monaco, was another visitor. And of course, cast and crew had the rare privilege of working with one of Hollywood's legendary actors, Lillian Gish. Gish was the star of the silent cinema's first American epic, *The Birth of a Nation* (1915), directed by film pioneer D. W. Griffith. Her performance in the chilling picture *Night of the Hunter* (1955) is a classic example of great screen acting.

"Working with Lillian Gish was like working with a fairy princess," Poster says. Gish plays a family matriarch who dies early in the film and subsequently spends the whole film in her deathbed. "She was in the bedroom the whole movie," Poster recalls. "While preparing a camera set in the shooting room, she would rest in another room and tell stories of the old days to crew members."

Finally, the summer came to an end, the filmmakers packed up, and Mrs. Armour moved back in. The Armour estate was ultimately sold and broken up into a series of smaller lots.

American Movie Palace Museum / Theatre Historical Society of America

York Theatre Building, 2nd Floor, 152 N. York Road, Elmhurst, Illinois

If you long for the days when going to a movie theater meant stepping through the doors of something spectacular, then head to the western suburbs of Chicago. Nestled on the second floor of the York Theatre in Elmhurst, you'll find the remnants of a bygone era. Though the location seems unlikely, the American Movie Palace Museum is a genuine treat. The museum highlights a grand period of moviegoing, from the 1920s through the 1940s. Here you'll find old posters, blueprints, photographs, programs, and other memorabilia from long-gone movie palaces. They even have the conductor's stand saved from the orchestra pit of Chicago's razed Granada Theatre on display. The collection covers a vast sweep of global filmgoing, with information on more than 7,000 theaters, both American and foreign.

As part of the Theatre Historical Society of America, the museum offers considerable research facilities for students, historians, and movie buffs. Staff members will also comb through the archives for an hourly fee.

Admission to the museum is free of charge (although donations are accepted) Tuesday through Friday from 9:00 AM to 4:00 PM. No appointments are necessary. Weekend and evening open houses are also occasionally scheduled. For more information, including research rates, call the Theatre Historical Society of America at (630) 782-1800 or visit www.historictheatres.org.

Aurora, Illinois

Ah, beautiful Aurora, Illinois. One of Chicago's western suburbs, it ranks as the area's best place to relax among fragrant palm trees or beautiful Rocky Mountains while nibbling on pastries from Stan Mikita's Donut Shop.

OK, OK, so there aren't any palms or peaks in Aurora. But in *Wayne's World* (1992) and *Wayne's World 2* (1993), just about anything is possible. So what if California streets substituted for Aurora? It's the spirit of Aurora that really counts! But be prepared for tart disappointment: although both films paid homage to the former Chicago Blackhawk hockey star, you won't find any donut shops topped by a mechanical Stan Mikita amidst Aurora's swaying palm trees.

Grace Is Gone: An Understated Family Drama

In *Grace Is Gone* (2007), John Cusack is an unassuming store manager struggling to raise his two young daughters while his wife is deployed in Iraq. When he receives word that his wife, Grace, has been killed in combat, something snaps inside him emotionally and he finds himself unable to tell the girls the bad news. Instead, he takes them on an impromptu road trip to a theme park in Florida. The small-town landscape rolls by as he struggles with his own grief and guilt, trying all the while to overcome his fear and the emotional barriers between himself and his daughters.

The streets and strip malls of several Chicago suburbs fill in as the towns along the way. Carol Stream, Niles, Westmont, Itasca, and LaGrange all make appearances, and the familiar interchangeability of the scenery makes a poignant statement about the loss of small-town America's uniqueness in the face of monolithic chains and franchises.

John Cusack gives the most understated and accomplished performance of his career, the entire supporting cast is fantastic, and young actress Shé-lan O'Keefe gives a complex and sophisticated performance as the eldest daughter, Heidi, who is old enough to know that something is amiss but caring enough not to confront her father directly. *Grace Is Gone* won the Audience Award and the award for Best Screenplay at the Sundance Film Festival in 2007. Also features a fabulous score by Clint Eastwood (although it gets a little intrusive on occasion).

Groundhog Day in Woodstock, Illinois

Groundhog Day (1993), the ethereal romantic comedy starring Bill Murray and Andie MacDowell, was set against the backdrop of the annual Punxsutawney, Pennsylvania, Groundhog Day Festival. In recreating Punxsutawney, director Harold Ramis needed a location that visually represented small-town America while providing an atmosphere conducive to shooting a major motion picture. Unsuccessful in his initial search of Illinois, Ramis was on the verge of sending location scouts to Pennsylvania. A drive through Woodstock changed everything.

Located about an hour northwest of downtown Chicago, the town was founded in 1837 as Centerville, and changed its name to Woodstock four years later. In its 160 years of existence, Woodstock has grown into a picturesque community and serves as the seat of McHenry County.

Before *Groundhog Day* was ever conceived, Woodstock was home to several movie-related people. Chester Gould, creator of comic strip cop Dick Tracy, lived here. The square-jawed detective inspired a series of low-budget films in the 1940s and a big-budget rendition by Warren Beatty in 1990. Orson Welles, the boy genius behind *Citizen Kane* (1941), also spent his early creative years in Woodstock. Sent to an all-male boarding school located just outside of town, Welles earned his initial acting and directing credits in Woodstock by staging shows at the Woodstock Opera House.

So Ramis settled on Woodstock, chock-full of history and blessed with a unique small-town look, as Punxsutawney's stand-in. The town square offered him a filmmaker's dream: a series of wonderful locations all within walking distance from each other. What's more, Ramis found himself immersed in a friendly community that was glad to cooperate with the often-crazed atmosphere of moviemaking.

"Shooting in a small town like that, in one place, you get to be a citizen of the town," Ramis recalls. "You go from never having seen the place to being the leading citizen of the town. Everyone welcomes the movie people. You kind of become part of the community. And as much as they love you, people on the movie will fall in love with the place itself."

Groundhog Day was shot largely in Woodstock's historic town square, which is anchored by the beautiful Woodstock Opera House (121 Van Buren Street). In the movie, the opera house plays the Pennsylvania Hotel, where Bill Murray leaps from the tower, only to live and see another February 2 roll around.

Across the street from the Opera House, at Van Buren Street and Johnson, is Square Park. The southwest corner of the park stands in for Punxsutawney's famed "Gobbler's Knob," where Phil the Groundhog makes his annual entrance. Incidentally, that is Bill Murray's brother, gravel-voiced writer/comedian Brian Doyle-Murray, playing the mayor of Punxsutawney during the Groundhog Day festivities. A few yards east, near the corner of Van Buren and Benton, is the site where Murray and MacDowell have several snowball fights on their rocky road to love.

Along Johnson Street, between Van Buren and Cass, is Tavern on the Square, the bar where Murray, MacDowell, and Chris Elliott, the cameraman, enjoy a few adult beverages. At 101 Cass Street, you'll find one of the movie's recurring jokes and landmarks—the icy puddle that Murray first steps into but gradually learns to avoid over the course of his endless day. Further east at 109 E. Church is the bowling alley that serves as "Wayne's Lanes." A few blocks further is Woodstock's Moose Lodge, Chapter 1329. Located at 306 Clay Street, this is where Groundhog Day's big dance scene takes place.

Heading along Jefferson Street, go to the northwest corner of Jefferson and Calhoun Street. Drive carefully—this is the spot where Murray and the groundhog take a suicidal plunge after a high-speed chase. Apparently Murray and his rodent costar had their differences offscreen; over the course of shooting, Murray was bitten at least twice by the feisty groundhog.

The Cherry Street Inn, the bed-and-breakfast where Murray supposedly stays, is actually a private residence in Woodstock. Only the exteriors of this stately house were used; interiors were shot at a home in Cary, Illinois.

"The shooting of *Groundhog Day* sort of froze Woodstock in a certain way," says Ramis. "The movie got connected with the identity of the town." Indeed, the film became something of an event for Woodstock. With the belief that any time is a good time for celebrating, Woodstock now holds the annual Groundhog Days festival, a five-day jubilee honoring the town and its movie. Events include a pyrotechnic display known as "the Lighting of the Groundhog," a dinner/dance and auction, a special February 2 breakfast, a free screening of the film at Woodstock's Opera House, and a walking tour of Woodstock's *Groundhog Day* locations. In the past, this jaunt has sometimes been led by Ramis himself, who dedicated a plaque at 101 Cass Street to mark the spot of Bill Murray's puddle nemesis.

For more information about Woodstock's Groundhog Days, visit the website at www.woodstockgroundhog.org.

5

South

The City

Maxwell Street District Police Station
943 W. Maxwell Street
Opened in 1888, in part as a response to the Haymarket Riots, the former Maxwell Street District police station is listed on the National Register of Historic Places. Legend has it Al Capone once spent a night in the station lockup. After more than 100 years of service, the building was closed in 1997 and is now owned by the University of Illinois–Chicago.

Movie fans will probably recognize the Maxwell Street District as the police station Edward Norton is brought to for questioning in 1996's *Primal Fear*. (Interiors were filmed at a now-closed police precinct at 39th and California.) However, the Maxwell Street precinct is better known as the station house shown in the opening credits of the 1980s police drama *Hill Street Blues*. This landmark television series revolved around the cops of an unnamed city and included Chicago actors Betty Thomas and Dennis Franz among its cast.

US Soccer Federation Building / William W. Kimball House
1801 S. Prairie Avenue
OK, you say your movie is about a Catholic bishop who runs the Archdiocese of Chicago, only it turns out that he's also a crazed sex maniac and gets murdered by a sweet-faced young man who appeared in the clergyman's homemade pornographic videos—and you want to film it where?

With a hook like that, it was obvious from the word *go* that the makers of *Primal Fear* (1996) weren't going to be doing a whole lot of creative work in cooperation with the officials of our local Catholic church.

259

The Kimball Mansion in the Prairie Avenue District appeared in the films *Primal Fear* (1996) and *Chain Reaction* (1996). *(Photo by Kate Corcoran)*

Consequently, a substitute rectory had to be created for the murder scene. To accomplish that, *Primal Fear* came to the US Soccer Federation Building on Prairie Avenue.

This gorgeous mansion is one of many to be found along the Prairie Avenue district. Once owned by organ magnate William Kimball, the house now serves as offices of the US Soccer Federation. To turn the home into a cathedral and rectory required a bit of movie magic. Across the street from the property was a warehouse. A false front was built to link the two structures together. This created "Saint Michael's Cathedral," where the bishop is murdered.

The US Soccer Federation Building was also used in the Andrew Davis thriller *Chain Reaction* (1996).

Elbridge G. Keith House
1900 S. Prairie Avenue

Another lovely Prairie Avenue mansion is the Keith House, which is currently owned by GLBT media mogul Tracy Baim. Baim's Windy City Media Group owns several gay and lesbian publications, including *Windy City Times* and *Nightspots*. In 2008 Baim formed Ripe Fruit Films, a limited liability corporation (LLC) with the mission to produce a Chicago-based film about lesbian lives. (For a variety of financial and legal reasons, producers almost always create a separate LLC or other corporation for each film they make.)

The feature film that Ripe Fruit produced, *Hannah Free* (2009), was filmed primarily here in the Keith mansion and coach house, with every room serving either as one of the seven sets, dressing or makeup departments, editing facilities, or production offices for the film. Based on a play by Claudia Allen, *Hannah Free* stars Sharon Gless as Hannah, a woman who recalls her multi-decade love affair and friendship with Rachel. Although both are hospitalized in different wings of the same nursing home, Hannah is unable to visit her partner because Rachel's daughter won't allow it. The film points out the hypocrisy and unfairness of the second-class status forced upon gay life partners, and has been characterized as "the lesbian *Brokeback Mountain*."

After the successful release of *Hannah Free*, Baim started another company, Sam I Am Films, to produce *Scrooge & Marley* (2012), a modern, gay-friendly reworking of *A Christmas Carol*.

For more information on *Hannah Free* and *Scrooge & Marley* visit their websites at www.hannahfree.com and www.scroogeandmarleymovie.com.

The Ripe Fruit Films production *Hannah Free* (2009) used every room of the Keith House and its coach house as either an interior set or a work space. *(Photo by Kate Corcoran)*

All-American News

2901 S. Prairie Avenue

Before television beamed daily news into our living rooms, audiences hungry for pictures of major events soaked in the weekly newsreel. Series such as *March of Time* and *Fox Movietone News* kept film audiences informed and entertained. The only thing they seemed to be missing was the weather report.

Yet like so many Hollywood productions of the 1940s, newsreels all but ignored African American viewers. To serve this important audience, three Chicagoans—Joseph Plunkell, E. M. Gluckman, and J. R. King—formed the All-American News, once located at this site on Prairie Avenue. Intending to bring an improved kind of news and entertainment to African American filmgoers, the All-American News released its first newsreels in October 1942. Aiming to help with the country's war effort, All-American News released some films under the title *March of Freedom*. These newsreels would "record each week the activities of Negro men and women in the service of their country throughout the world," the company stated.

Other newsreels from All-American News examined how the Urban League looked at America's labor struggles, introduced audiences to President Franklin Delano Roosevelt's personal valet, and provided information about the famed Tuskegee Institute. Sports and entertainment figures were also highlighted. The newsreels also included advertisements for Chesterfield tobacco products.

In 1946, All-American News shut down its newsreel production and switched to entertainment films. They made several short pictures with Lollypop Jones, a popular comic in the African American community. Another All-American production, *Killer Diller* (1948), was a musical revue featuring the Nat "King" Cole Trio, comedian Jackie "Moms" Mabley, and *Gone with the Wind*'s Butterfly McQueen.

Eventually, poor production values and financial hardship overtook the company's mission. By the time the 1950s rolled around, All-American News was out of business.

Chicago Film Archives
329 W. 18th Street

One of the newer film-related organizations in the city, the Chicago Film Archives has quickly grown into an important resource for all of the Midwest. Like many worthwhile nonprofit endeavors, the Chicago Film Archives was created for a specific purpose and then expanded its mission in order to fill a larger need. Started at the end of 2003 to save and preserve approximately 5,000 16mm films that the Chicago Public Library was letting go, they originally set up shop in a donated space on LaSalle Street but soon grew out of it. After a long search, they found their current home in a renovated industrial warehouse right on the river at 329 W. 18th Street.

With climate-controlled storage facilities, roomy freight elevators, and plenty of room to grow, the CFA almost immediately began looking to collect and preserve as many other old films as possible. Executive director Nancy Watrous elaborates: "We started talking about the mission of the organization and what we should be doing, aside from just taking care of this collection from the CPL, and it quickly became clear to all of us that this part of the country needed a regional film archive. There simply was no existing place to take in, track, and try to save the films that represent [the heritage of] the Midwest. So slowly but surely we morphed into a regional film archive."

They worked out an expanded mission. "We take in films that either reflect in their content the Midwest, or that are made by Midwest filmmakers," Watrous explains. Other donated films began pouring in, expanding the collection to over 7,000 items. This success has caused its own set of problems, since the CFA also needs to view and catalog each film it receives, and many remain unarchived.

The collection itself is a wondrous hodgepodge of professional and amateur works that includes industrial films, the home "hobby" films of several professionals, documentaries from the 1950s and '60s, travel films from the early 1900s, and countless other varieties of cinematic output. The rarest and/or most important films are selected, and grants are submitted on their behalf to the National Film Preservation Foundation for protection as part of our national cultural heritage. Those films that receive grants are then sent to labs that specialize in restoration and preservation of old films. Preservation is an elaborate and painstaking process that involves creating a new "archival negative" (among many other things).

One of the most fascinating and unexpected aspects of the CFA's mission is the collecting of home movies, which are considered by film archivists and a growing segment of the public to be an important part of our shared cultural heritage. This has led to a fascinating outreach activity known as "Home Movie Day," where CFA technicians and archivists set up inside a location (such as the Chicago Cultural Center) for a daylong celebration of home movies. During the afternoon, interested persons can bring in their old home movies for inspection and evaluation by professionals or donate their films to the archive (they can also arrange to make use of the CFA's transfer and repair services, which are done for a fee). Later that night, the movies that are most interesting or in the best condition are shown to large crowds who gather for a taste of midwestern home (movie) cooking. From the folks who bring in film to the audiences who view it to the CFA staff themselves, Home Movie Day is huge fun for everyone involved.

Never content to remain a static organization, the CFA is constantly evolving and expanding its mission and services, offering new public programs and attempting to create better facilities for researchers and scholars. One of the CFA's more recent initiatives has been to present programs in conjunction with the Chicago Cultural Center and the Siskel Film Center, as it did in January 2009 with its extremely well-received series *Howard Alk: A Life on the Edge*, a retrospective of 10 films by the late director/editor/cinematographer, whose portraits of musicians (*Janis*, 1974) and documentaries of controversial events (*The Murder of Fred Hampton*, 1971) chronicle the tumultuous period of the late 1960s and early '70s. The series, which was held both at the Cultural Center and the Siskel Film Center, also featured a number of filmmakers who paid homage to Alk and discussed his work.

If you have home movies or amateur films that might fit the Chicago Film Archives' mission, want to take advantage of their transfer and/or restoration services, or are interested in discussing a donation, please visit www.chicagofilmarchives.org or call (312) 243-1808.

Stranger Than Fiction: An Unmistakable Everytown

Bertrand Goldberg's River City at 800 S. Wells Street, the location of Harold Crick's friend Dave's apartment in *Stranger Than Fiction* (2006). *(Photo by Michael Corcoran)*

One of the finest movies ever to be shot in Chicago is actually set not here but in an anonymous "every-city" that Chicagoans will still recognize as theirs. Although writer Zach Helm claims that Chicago is his favorite city in the world, the story of Harold Crick (a bland, bureaucratic functionary) required a generic, indistinguishable setting. In an ironic twist, Chicago (one of the most recognizable cities in the world) became director Marc Forster's choice to shoot the movie, mainly because of its large number of buildings designed by Ludwig Mies van der Rohe and other modernist architects—the International Style providing a visual shorthand for monotonous conformity. The IRS office where Harold works is in the CNA Building Annex (the bright red main CNA Center building is seen looming outside the window in many shots), and several other International Style buildings are used, including the Daley Center, Illinois Center, and the Federal Buildings on Dearborn.

In his script for *Stranger Than Fiction* (2006), Helm (a graduate of the Theatre School at DePaul University) was attempting to capture the spirit of the great 1970s Hal Ashby comedies such as *Harold and Maude*. He succeeds wonderfully in this task.

One day, Harold (Will Ferrell) begins to hear the voice of a narrator, describing his life "accurately and with a better vocabulary." He is confused and discombobulated by this odd phenomenon, and when the third-person-omniscient voice portends his own demise ("Little did he know that this simple, seemingly innocuous act would result in his imminent death"), Harold seeks help from English professor Jules Hilbert (Dustin Hoffman). Visiting him in his office in the concrete and glass rabbit warren of Walter Netsch's UIC Campus complex, Harold manages to convince a skeptical Hilbert to help him find a way to prevent the voice's prediction from coming true. In one particularly amusing scene, Hilbert sits down with Harold to determine what type of story he is in, a comedy or tragedy: "Tragedy you die, comedy you get hitched." Unable to determine the origin of Harold's narrator, Professor Hilbert tells him that if he is in a story, then Harold should live the story he's always wanted.

Hilbert's advice inspires Harold to break out of his monotonous rut by fulfilling a lifelong dream of learning to play the guitar. He also begins pursuing a romance with bakery owner Ana Pascal, played by the fabulous Maggie Gyllenhaal in an especially adorable role. The location of Pascal's bakery is at 2500 S. Christiana Avenue in the Little Village neighborhood.

In a parallel story, depressed writer Gwen Eiffel (Emma Thompson) is hopelessly locked in writer's block over how to kill the protagonist of her latest book (her novels always end with the death of the main character), an IRS accountant named Harold Crick. Losing patience, the publishers have sent an assistant/taskmaster to help her finish the long-overdue work, the no-nonsense Penny Escher

The perfect office for *Stranger Than Fiction*'s Emma Thompson was located in the R. R. Donnelley/Lakeside Press Building near 18th Street. *(Photo by Kate Corcoran)*

(Queen Latifah). Eiffel's loft is located in the old R. R. Donnelley & Co. printing plant (now the Lakeside Technology Center) at 350 E. Cermak Road near McCormick Place. In real life, it was one of several lofts that were used to house visiting executives from companies having their catalogues printed at the plant.

The audience is charmed and horrified as these two narrative threads move toward their inevitable meeting. The end result is a film that is heartfelt without being mawkish, and uplifting without being sappy.

Denise Hughes: Behind the Wheel and in Front of the Camera

Denise Hughes. *(Photo by Brian McConkey)*

When *Stranger Than Fiction* (2006) needed someone to play a bus driver in a few pivotal scenes, they decided to go for the real thing and put up notice of an open casting call for female bus operators in all of the seven CTA bus barns around the city.

Driver Denise Hughes, who had acted in plays and pageants as a little girl and up through high school, decided to try her luck and attended the mass audition. She was interviewed by the casting director, who told Denise to come back for an audition with director Marc Forster. After one session with Forster, which involved improvising scenarios at the wheel of an imaginary bus, she was brought back for a second look and then finally chosen to play the driver of the fateful bus who severely impacts the story of Harold Crick (literally).

Hughes worked almost a month shooting her three scenes, an experience she found very rewarding. "I enjoyed it. I had a ball. I can see why actors do what they do. You definitely have to love it, because it's a lot of hard work but the end result is fulfilling." As far as her take on the oft-discussed atmosphere of blissful collegiality on the set of *Stranger Than*

Fiction, "It was like a family. I really loved it. People were telling me, 'This doesn't always happen on every movie.'" Denise even got to walk the red carpet at the film's premiere at the Chicago Theatre. "It was kind of scary, because a lot of people were there."

The experience reawakened her youthful enthusiasm toward acting, and she subsequently found an agent and began auditioning around town. Having managed to land a Com Ed commercial and an appearance on an episode of *Prison Break*, she hopes to eventually be able to work regularly in front of the camera. Until then, if you're ever riding the #66 Chicago Avenue bus (her most regular route these days) and your driver looks familiar, she just might be.

Comiskey Park (now US Cellular Field)
300 W. 35th Street

Home of baseball's Chicago White Sox, the mall-like ballpark on 35th Street is the second incarnation of Comiskey Park. The original, first known as White Sox Park, opened on July 1, 1910; it was located just north of the current park on the other side of 35th Street. Designed by Zachary Taylor Davis, with input from team owner Charles Comiskey and pitcher Ed Walsh, Comiskey Park stood for 80 seasons.

Old Comiskey got into the movie business late in its life. Scenes from *Red Heat* (1988) and the climactic scenes of the obscure *Pastime* (a.k.a. *One Cup of Coffee*, 1990) were shot here. Sadly, the stadium's age-old beauty was never really captured on film until the very end, in the 1991 Chris Columbus romantic comedy *Only the Lonely*.

The film revolves around a shy Chicago cop (John Candy in a nice change of pace from his usual comic styling) and his attempts to woo a mortician's assistant (Ally Sheedy). Candy's character has some pull with the groundskeepers at Comiskey, which enables him to treat Sheedy to a sweet postgame picnic on the field. While the pair dine, they are treated to a special fireworks show, a Comiskey Park trademark that was instituted by former owner Bill Veeck. Though it's an unlikely "only in the movies" moment, the scene has a special kind of charm.

It's also a tad bittersweet, particularly to fans of the old ballpark. Shooting took place on a warm Friday in October, just a few days before demolition was to begin on Old Comiskey. "It was a special night," recalls Jacolyn J. Baker, a location manager on the film. "Everybody knew that this was going to be the last time anybody would be in Comiskey Park, since they were going to start demolition on Monday. Everybody brought their families out. It was an unusually balmy night, about 70 degrees—a perfect Indian summer night. In between takes, people were playing catch on the field. You felt that this history was about to be taken away. It was really special. We all knew it was going to be the end."

The new Comiskey Park opened the following spring on April 18, 1991. The park was bigger, shinier, and had better sight lines, but lacked the warmth of old Comiskey. Still, it looked pretty good in *My Best Friend's Wedding* (1997), the offbeat Julia Roberts comedy in which Cameron Diaz plays the daughter of fictional White Sox owner Philip Bosco.

Jane Alderman: A Casting of Thousands

"We have a great work ethic in Chicago. You've got actors who are willing to work, they're good, they're not seen all the time. They're great faces, they're real people."   *—Jane Alderman*

You may not recognize Jane Alderman's name, but chances are you've seen her listed in the credits for many films and television shows. She's been an important player in Chicago filmmaking, having worked on such produc-

tions as *Four Friends* (1981), *Bad Boys* (1983), *The Color of Money* (1986), *Lucas* (1986), *Child's Play* (1988), *Poltergeist III* (1988), *Music Box* (1990), *Backdraft* (1991), *The Babe* (1992), *Candyman* (1992), *Natural Born Killers* (1994), *A Family Thing* (1996), *Love Jones* (1997), *U.S. Marshals* (1998), *The Straight Story* (1999), *Return to Me* (2000), *Novocaine* (2001), *Normal* (2003), *The Prize Winner of Defiance, Ohio* (2005), and *The Unborn* (2009).

For over three decades her company, Jane Alderman Casting, helped place local actors in supporting roles

Jane Alderman. *(Photo by Brian McConkey)*   for the many feature films that came through town. "We were hired by the production company or the producer to find the actors for the project," she says.

"To do it is truly, I believe, an art. You can't just say, 'I know Bobby, Bobby's a nice guy, he's 30, he can be a cop.' You can't just do that. There has to be a whole look to a picture. If I brought someone in for the part of a cop, the director could say, 'That's really nice, but that's not the way we're going. I want all of our cops to look like they're on *Baywatch*. He looks like he could be from Manhattan or any other city.'

"If the lead is Robert DeNiro and this person has a scene with him, then he's got to be one of the finest actors. Even if the actor says something like, 'Oh, I'm sorry, sir, your bus left' and he's opposite DeNiro, there has to be a presence with that actor. Otherwise he'll evaporate into nothingness because DeNiro's so powerful. To have a very strong actor, even if it's for just one line, up against somebody that brilliant, is smart.

"I loved working on *Backdraft*. That took me into the fire culture, both arsonists and firemen, and learning their code. That really was so exciting. I found a lot of real firemen who could act—and there are firemen actors just like there are cop actors.

"What was very exciting—and I've had this happen before—is where you get actors who don't know about the kind of people they're playing. Getting them together and finally watching everyone learn from each other was great. I had quite a few real firemen in long, big roles. They took the actors under their wings and taught them everything about fighting fires. At the same time the actors, like Billy Baldwin and Kurt Russell, were giving the firemen acting tips.

"For *The Color of Money*, I had to find pool players, real ones that could possibly act. There were some real ones that Scorsese wanted in the movie as themselves. I found myself on this network of pool and pool halls in the city. Word got out really fast within that pool underground. My phone rang off the hook—some of the most fascinating characters I have ever met. I'd go out just about every night into various pool halls in the city; I would arrange for these guys to shoot pool and do their tricks. Scorsese could talk to them, then take them off into a corner and have them read."

Sometimes, a director's desire for "real" actors can be a detriment, as it was during the process of casting the wonderful Robert Duvall/James Earl Jones vehicle *A Family Thing*. For the crucial role of Aunt T (an elderly blind woman whose stern yet loving presence holds both the characters and film together), director Richard Pearce informed Alderman that he wanted her to audition actual elderly African American blind women. "I told him that I could do that, but that I don't have any actors that fill those criteria and I'd have to go into the general population and see if they can act."

Pearce insisted, so she contacted the Lighthouse for the Blind and similar places to try and find a suitable candidate. "And I did manage to get three candidates, and bless their hearts, they all came in and read, but it was absolutely hopeless." The role of Aunt T was just too substantial for someone who'd never acted. An L.A. actor (who wasn't blind) was hired but just didn't work out. "So the director called me in a panic and said, 'Put Irma Hall [whom Alderman had earlier auditioned for a much smaller role] on tape doing this role and being blind.' So Irma came in with very little notice—I mean, she'd read the script. But honestly, she was so fantastic on that tape, you really believe she was blind. So I sent that tape to him and he immediately hired her."

No matter what the film director wants, Alderman feels that it is the casting director's duty to try to fulfill his or her wishes. "You can't be at odds with them. Otherwise, you might as well just pull yourself off the project and let someone else handle it." The job requires a certain empathy and ability to make a connection. "Sometimes the needs are so specific that the casting director really needs to be inside the director's head."

This was definitely the case when Alderman worked with the brilliant and legendarily eccentric director David Lynch on his 1999 film *The Straight Story*. Despite collaborating on all the casting of that award-winning film, Alderman and Lynch never actually met (nor have they to this day). After a few initial telephone conversations, the entire process happened through correspondence and via intermediaries. "My initial chats were very few when he hired me, over the phone. And after that (this was in the days before we were doing e-mail) he would send faxes to me from a motel room where they were on location, and I would come in the morning and there would be a fax with a note or people he wanted, and then if I had any questions I would usually get his assistant on their cell phone and put my questions to him through them."

As if that weren't odd (dare we say, Lynchian?) enough, the entire casting process Alderman used consisted entirely of interviews with the prospective actors, with absolutely no script readings or normal auditions. "All any of them knew was that they were going in for an interview for David Lynch's next film," she explains. "So everyone just came in as themselves, and it was up to me to get inside David Lynch's head and interview them, whether I knew them well or not, as if I were David Lynch, and the concentration was . . . it was quite a test. And I had to listen to them and use my intuition. It was a gorgeous process, but I had to trust him, he had to trust me, the actors had to trust me."

Despite their being physically removed from each other, this unique method caused Alderman to almost meld with Lynch. "I had to become an extension of his perception, and that actually was mind-boggling for me," she recalls. "And it frightened me at first, but then I just dove into it. It was like diving into the deep end but trusting I would know what to do when I got there and I would be able to swim up and out."

In addition to her efforts for veteran directors such as Lynch, Alderman has worked with a number of first-time directors, which can be a challenge. "First-time directors are sometimes more difficult to cast for," she says. "I find that actors who are directing their first films aren't as bad, because they've experienced the process from the other end, but if they were an editor or a writer or a cameraman, then sometimes they need to be educated a little bit."

Alderman feels that her own experience as a professional actor provided her with important insights when she took on the role of casting director, both about the casting process and how to treat actors properly: "I am very, very, very aware of how an actor feels and what they need. And what upsets them and what makes them feel like a million dollars." This empathy occasionally led her to chastise a director for being unkind to an auditioning performer: "I've very rarely had to tell a director, 'God, you can't do that,' but I have. When the actor has left the room, I've said, 'What the hell are you doing!' And sometimes they listen and sometimes there's an argument. But that is so rare."

Alderman actually returned to her acting roots in the late aughts, appearing in small roles in such films as *The Man in the Silo* (2008), *Dustclouds* (2007), and the Vince Vaughn / Jennifer Aniston film *The Break-Up* (2006), something she found very refreshing and liberating. "I love it because it's just me and I don't have to worry about 800 other people on a daily basis."

That feeling of liberation proved to be too powerful to resist, and in late 2009 Alderman officially retired from casting and returned to acting, heading to Broadway for several months to reprise her role in Tracy Letts' play *Superior Donuts* before returning to Chicago to teach acting and continue her own career.

Although it was wonderful for her to spend time in the theater mecca of New York, she had no doubt she would be returning here once the production was completed. She had just grown to love Chicago too much and would be loath to permanently leave, not only because of the city's beauty and charm but for its realism and rawness as well. "There's earth here. There's grit and scars and wrinkles." And like all of us who call Chicago home, she wouldn't have it any other way.

Palace Loan Company
216 E. 47th Street

Looking for a bargain? So were Joliet Jake and Elwood Blues in the 1980 romp *The Blues Brothers*. The Palace Loan Company, complete with a wonderful outdoor mural painted on the building's outdoor wall, was where the singing siblings and their bandmates came to buy instruments from shopkeeper Ray Charles. The loan company has shut down and the mural has been covered over, but the vintage signage currently remains on the exterior.

The Museum of Science and Industry
57th Street and Lake Shore Drive

Nestled off Lake Shore Drive in the Hyde Park neighborhood, the Museum of Science and Industry was originally built in 1893 for the Columbian Exposition. Dubbed the "Palace of Fine Arts," the building was loosely

The Museum of Science and Industry stands on the former grounds of the World's Columbian Exposition of 1893.
(Photo by Kate Corcoran)

modeled on a variety of Greek temples on the Acropolis at Athens. After the fair, it housed a museum that moved in 1920 and become what we know as the Field Museum.

The building remained empty for the next several years. A $5 million donation from philanthropist Julius Rosenwald revitalized the former Palace of Fine Arts for the 1933 Century of Progress Exposition. Now dedicated to highlighting technical achievements, the building has been renamed the Museum of Science and

Industry. It's been a staple for school field trips and a genuine Chicago treasure ever since.

For movie lovers, the Museum of Science and Industry has a lot to offer. Hollywood pictures shot here include *Damien: Omen II* (1978) and *Endless Love* (1981). *Flatliners* (1990) staged its surreal Halloween festival here, making effective use out of the looming Greek columns on the museum's exterior. Take a trip inside to the airplane exhibit and you'll see where Keanu Reeves leaped around on a model 747 fuselage during the chase sequence of *Chain Reaction* (1996). If you want to recreate other moments in Reeves's flight, you'll have to go to the Field Museum (see page 139). Through the magic of movie editing, two of the city's most popular attractions were fused together, much to the amusement of audiences in multiplexes around town.

The museum is also home to a couple of movie-related permanent exhibits. Colleen Moore's Fairy Castle is a sheer delight. Moore was a silent screen star who personified the jazz babies of the flapper era. One of Hollywood's highest-paid talents of the 1920s, she retired from the picture business a few years after talkies arrived. Moore invested her earnings in the stock market and ultimately made a fortune. One of her hobbies was the construction of this Fairy Castle, which houses more than 1,000 miniaturized items.

The Fairy Castle measures nine square feet and actually is made up of 200 separate parts. The majority of the structure is made out of aluminum. It also has its own electrical system and running water.

The museum's second cinematic attraction is the World War II–vintage U-505 German submarine. This U-boat, one of only three left in the world, was captured by American forces during a battle off the coast of Africa. Brought to Chicago in 1954, it remains one of the museum's most popular attractions. Its cinematic significance? When German director Wolfgang Petersen was researching his World War II epic *Das Boot* (1982), a gripping tale of life aboard a German submarine, extensive research was done at the U-505 in order to maintain on-screen accuracy.

Additionally, the Museum of Science and Industry is home to one of the two IMAX theaters in the city. True to the mission of this institution, the films screened here use imagination and a sense of wonder to look at the world's gains in science and industry.

The Museum of Science and Industry is open every day of the year except Christmas Day. Hours are Monday through Saturday 9:30 AM–4:00 PM and 11:00 AM–4:00 PM on Sunday. For admission prices to exhibits call (773) 684-1414 or check out the museum's interactive website at www.msichicago.org.

The University of Chicago
Hyde Park

In 1891, William Rainey Harper founded the University of Chicago in Chicago's South Side Hyde Park neighborhood. In its century of service, the university has become one of America's most prestigious institutions.

The Gothic architecture of the University of Chicago campus is distinctly recognizable. *(Photo by Kate Corcoran)*

Nobel Prizes abound throughout the faculty roster, particularly in the field of economics.

Filmwise, U of C has a great deal of significance. In 1932, a group of students founded the Documentary Film Group, commonly referred to as Doc Films. Devoted to the exhibition and discussion of cinematic arts, Doc Films is the oldest continuously running student film society in the United States.

Looking to engage in a thoughtful deliberation over genre and authorship in postclassical cinema and other arcane topics? Then check out the University of Chicago Film Studies Center. Located in Cobb Hall at 5811 S. Ellis Avenue, the Film Studies Center (FSC) concentrates in three specific areas: film education and research through its Cinema and Media Studies courses, archives and collections with the Gerald Mast Film Archive (named after the university's highly renowned late film historian), and film- and media-related events and activities.

The University of Chicago cinema and media studies program offers undergraduate, graduate, and doctoral degrees in film studies. Classes concentrate on cinematic theory and history. For those who want to make movies as well as study them, the program offers referrals to other area institutions where students can learn production skills.

The Gerald Mast Film Archive contains more than 10,000 film, video, and digital titles, ranging from Hollywood features to noncommercial avant-garde work.

Of course the University of Chicago has also shown up on-screen from time to time. In *When Harry Met Sally* (1989), Billy Crystal and Meg Ryan begin their decades-long friendship at the main quadrangle near University and 58th Avenues.

Looking for a little life after your death? Parts of *Flatliners* (1990), a neo-gothic drama about near-death experiences, were filmed around the university and in the Hyde Park neighborhood.

Andrew Davis brought his last three locally shot productions to the University of Chicago. Before taking it on the lam in *The Fugitive* (1993), Dr. Richard Kimble (Harrison Ford) was based at "Chicago Memorial Hospital." Don't look for their number in the phone book; Chicago Memorial was actually the redressed University of Chicago Hospital at 5812 S. Ellis Avenue.

One of the University of Chicago's most significant historical events ultimately served as a backdrop for Davis's 1989 film *The Package*. On December 2, 1942, in a converted squash court beneath Stagg Field, Italian physicist Enrico Fermi led a group of scientists in the world's first controlled nuclear reaction. Splitting the atom ultimately led to development of nuclear weapons, which brought an end to World War II but a beginning to the Cold War.

After Stagg Field was torn down, the university installed the Henry Moore sculpture *Nuclear Energy* near the site of this flashpoint. In *The Package*, much of the plot revolves around a US-Soviet pact on nuclear weapons. Davis filmed the symbolic signing of this fictional arrangement in front of the Moore sculpture, heightening the dramatic qualities within the moment.

Chain Reaction (1996) was the third Davis film to shoot around this illustrious institution. Keanu Reeves plays a University of Chicago researcher (typecasting this was not!) who assists in an experiment to harness energy from water molecules. When rogue elements within the project blow up a good chunk of the South Side, Reeves finds himself inadvertently tangled in a web of deceit. Most of the Hyde Park scenes take place at the Museum of Science and Industry, though Reeves's

Henry Moore's sculpture *Nuclear Energy* sits near the site of the first self-sustaining nuclear chain reaction. *(Photo by Kate Corcoran)*

movie girlfriend, Rachel Weisz, lives in an apartment building at 4801 S. Ellis Avenue. In another university connection, the role of Keanu's boss (who gets murdered near the beginning) is played by a real U of C professor, Nicholas Rudall.

The University of Chicago played a key role in the movie *Proof* (2005), which was set on the campus. The film's plot revolves around a brilliant yet mentally ill mathematician and professor, played by Anthony Hopkins. When he passes away after a long bout with delusion and dementia, his daughter (played wonderfully by Gwyneth Paltrow), who dropped out of grad school several years earlier to care for him, is left to deal with not only her grief but also her own worries that she may have inherited the same mental instabilities as her father. Her anguish is compounded by the arrival of her overbearing and manipulative older sister (Hope Davis) and by her increasingly complicated relationship with a young math student (Jake Gyllenhaal) who has been studying her father's notebooks. The story is partly revealed through Paltrow's flashbacks of Hopkins's troubled last years and her attempts to assist him and ease his suffering. This powerful and touching film uses several locations on campus, including the offices of the *University of Chicago Chronicle*, the Midway Plaisance, and Rockefeller Chapel (where Hopkins's funeral is set).

For more information on the University of Chicago, check out www .uchicago.edu. Doc Films is also on the web, at http://docfilms.uchicago .edu. The Film Studies Center maintains an excellent website at http:// filmstudiescenter.uchicago.edu.

The *Monkey Hustle* Block Party
6300–6400 S. Ellis Avenue
On a summer day in 1976, this stretch of South Ellis turned into one big movie set. Block parties are nothing new, but throw in some cameras, a

script, and a few hundred well-fed neighborhood extras and you have a movie scene. That's essentially what happened here for a scene in *Monkey Hustle*, a goofy blaxploitation caper comedy starring Yaphet Kotto and Rudy Ray Moore.

By the way, look closely in that crowd of extras and you'll see future film writer-director-actor Robert Townsend. Before going on to such features as *Hollywood Shuffle* (1987), *The Five Heartbeats* (1991), *The Meteor Man* (1993), and the 1990s sitcom *The Parent 'Hood*, Townsend made his movie debut playing a street band member in the *Monkey Hustle* block party.

Irma Hall: Actor and Screen Chameleon

"When I was a kid growing up, one of the things that pushed you to do your best all the time was the fact that you were representing your family, your church, your school, your neighborhood, your race, your country—you had this big bag! I still do that. Whenever I'm doing a project, I'm very conscious that I'm representing not only my family and friends, but also Chicago actors."   *—Irma Hall*

Irma Hall is a screen chameleon. Whether she's playing the family matriarch in *Soul Food* (1997), a mysterious voodoo practitioner in *Midnight in the Garden of Good and Evil* (1997), or a fiercely indestructible churchgoing boardinghouse owner in *The Ladykillers* (2004), Hall completely disappears into her roles. Watch any of her films back-to-back and you'll find it hard to believe that she's the same person, so complete is her character transformation. Offscreen, Hall is a vivacious and deeply spiritual person who brings a lifetime of experience to her work.

The actor recalls, "I was in Dallas, Texas, teaching school and working for a newspaper, the *Dallas Express*. I was the publicity person for my school, so when I heard the oldest black newspaper in Dallas was in trouble because they were short-staffed, I went and volunteered. I figured that would kill two birds with one stone. I'd be doing something to help and I would make sure our school news got in the paper.

"I became the cultural page editor, and they also needed someone to cover school sports and eventually sports. I ended up doing sports, period! I knew this lady named Peggy Taylor who was an agent. She told me that Raymond St. Jacques was coming to Dallas to look at it as a possible location for his film *Book of Numbers* (1973) and that I should interview him. Someone sent him a copy of all the articles I had written. He liked them and asked if I would work as interim publicist for the first five weeks until his regular publicist could come to Dallas. I said great, because I was going to get a chance to learn to do something else.

"I also write poetry and was involved in a group called Advancing Artists and Writers. We had just gotten a grant for workshops for young people in the summer. St. Jacques heard I was reading some poetry and asked me to read for a part in the film. I got the part because they thought I read well, and I said, 'Well, I teach school. I hope I read well!'

"Originally it was just a day's work, but when he saw me in the dailies, St. Jacques said he was going to expand the role and that I had a lot of natural talent. I was what they called 'an instinctive actor' and I should develop it. As God would have it, there was a young man named Reginald Montgomery who was the first black clown with Ringling Brothers. He was in Dallas as a guest director for the Dallas Theater Center. I had met him through some of my ex-students. Montgomery asked me if I would work with him to found a community theater and that I would be the executive director. I found myself plunged headlong into community theater for the next five years.

"That's how I learned the craft. I figured if God gave me the talent then I'm obligated to develop it. But I really felt it was something I was supposed to use in my teaching. I was interested in showing students how they could use theater in school. I did that for the next 12 years, until 1984, when my arthritis got so bad and my parents got so sick that I had to retire.

"I came back to Chicago to take care of my parents in 1987 and have been here ever since. After my father died, it's like he went and started working for me because right away between him dying and being interred, I got a role in the television movie *The Kid Who Loved Christmas* (1990). Then I got a day's work on Oprah Winfrey's television series *The Women of Brewster Place*."

While doing these small television roles, Hall was becoming an established presence on the local theater scene. Her home theater at the time was the now-departed Chicago Theatre Company, a tiny black equity house whose building was at 500 E. 67th Street. Hall ended up winning a Jeff Award, then was cast by Steppenwolf in the play *Stepping Out*. The company won a Jeff Award for Best Ensemble, and Hall's place in Chicago theater was established.

"Mainly I thought I'd be doing stage work and then every once in a while I'd get a day part in a film," she says. "I was in Rochester when I heard about the movie *A Family Thing*. I came back and auditioned for it. I had written a note and put it on my altar table asking God if it was His will to be in the movie. When I got the part of 'Maotis,' I thought, This is the answer to my prayer.

"A few days later, I was extremely tired and took a nap. I didn't hear the phone ring, and when I woke up there were two messages. The first one was telling me that my uncle had died, and the next one was telling me that I needed to come and audition for the part of Aunt T [in *A Family Thing*], a role that all of us who read for it thought was going to someone in Los Angeles. I guess I have these relatives who die and then go and help me! So I went and did the audition. I said, 'All right, if I get it fine, then I still have a part, I'm still going to be in it.' I had to go to Memphis and read, and they all liked it. On my birthday, June 3, I found out I had the part.

"It's just been lucky for me, and that role seemed to be the door-opener. It was very surprising to me, and I was taken aback. At first I didn't understand what they meant when they said I stole all the scenes. I wasn't trying to upstage anybody. I'm so used to ensemble work and this was such a beautiful ensemble piece and I was thinking, Oh gosh! I was worried about that. I said, 'Oh well, I didn't intend to do that.' But I remember Robert Duvall used to say all the time on the set, 'They're going to say that we were good but that Aunt T stole the show!' I thought they were trying to make me feel good."

Hall's next major project was the sleeper hit *Soul Food*. "That was indeed a labor of love. I was in L.A. working on a project when George Tillman Jr. and Bob Teitel came to see me and brought the script to see if I would be interested in doing it."

In Hall's eyes, this project seemed to be fated for her: "When I opened the script, I knew it was something I was supposed to do, because the character's name was 'Mother Joe' and my mother's name was Josephine. So I said, 'My mother sent this, I have to do it.' When I read the script I found more reason to think that, because my paternal grandmother was a diabetic and amputee. She had three daughters and her death was similar [to the Mama Joe character]. I said, 'Oh my, this is too close.' My mother had a brother who lived with her sister, and he had typhoid fever or something when he was a child. It had affected his speech some kind of way, so he rarely talked and he stayed to himself. He always stayed in his room. I knew about him and I said, 'Oh, wow, he's even in [the script].' It was like, whoa—my whole family is in here! So I knew I had to do it.

"The hardest thing for me was lying flat on my back all day. That's hard on you! Everything goes to sleep and you start cramping all over. You're not in bed where you can turn from side to side; you just have to lie there. They would be rehearsing something when I was supposed to be in a coma, especially during the argument, and I would be so tickled and I would want to laugh, but I couldn't."

Hall ended up winning an NAACP Image Award for her work in *Soul Food*. That same year she appeared as Minerva opposite John Cusack and Kevin Spacey in the major studio adaptation of the bestselling book *Midnight in the Garden of Good and Evil*, which was directed by Clint Eastwood. This film exposed her talent to an even larger audience and was a positive experience professionally and personally. "I really enjoyed working with Clint, because I grew a lot because of his directing style," she says. "He hires actors to do the roles that he thinks can do them, then lets them do it. You feel safe, because you know that he always knows exactly where he is going and he will be there for you if you get off-track."

Hall closed out the 1990s with several television roles and an appearance in the Robin Williams comedy *Patch Adams* (1998). The year 1999 saw her in the most intense project of her career, *A Lesson Before Dying*, the heartrending story of an African American man in the 1940s South (Mekhi Phifer) who is falsely accused of murder and sentenced to death. After his white defense attorney compares him to an animal during the trial in a perverse attempt to gain leniency for him, Phifer's mother (Hall) and aunt (Cicely Tyson) convince a local schoolteacher (Don Cheadle) to visit him on death row every day in an attempt to instruct him and to help him regain his lost humanity in the face of a dehumanizing and unjust society. Playing a part in this searing period drama brought back many of Hall's own painful childhood memories of the Jim Crow–era South. "I think I would have to say *A Lesson Before Dying* was most painful, because I remember the period in our history where black people had little chance of justice."

Hall began the new millennium with the project she considers the most fun and enjoyable, the Billy Graham–financed Christian musical *Something to Sing About* (2000). "*Something to Sing About* was the most fun because it verifies that God does have a plan for our lives. At least for me it does." For the next several years she mostly appeared in television roles, most notably in the television-series version of *Soul Food* and as a recurring character on *The Bernie Mac Show*.

The late and much-lamented Mac was a dear friend of Hall's. She recalls, "I first met Bernie Mac at the Cotton Club through Jimmy Spinks (another great Chicago actor whom I met in Dallas when he came as part of the cast of *Guys and Dolls*; it was Jimmy who pushed me into acting in Chicago). I think it was 1989 or 1990. Bernie and I kind of adopted each other after discussions about his being the father of a young daughter, but who had to be on the road a lot—much like my own father, who for the first 10 years of my life was a big band musician on the road. I called Bernie my 'play son.' I always thought he should have his own show. It was while working on his show that my own son, Shed Jr., died of DVT [deep vein thrombosis—a condition that often causes deadly blood clots], and Bernie was a big spiritual shoulder for me to lean on. He started a college fund for my son's son. He was such a good person. A gifted actor, wonderful family man, and beloved friend, I am so glad God brought us together for a while."

In 2004, Hall gained an international audience via her role in the Coen Bothers comedy *The Ladykillers*, which won her the Jury Prize for acting at the Cannes Film Festival. "It was a great boost in my worldwide exposure, but even before that I was receiving fan mail from all over the world."

As fate would have it, that same year saw another life-changing event, when she was involved in a bad auto wreck on a snowy Chicago night, almost losing her life to her terrible injuries. As always, Hall views the accident through the perspective of her deep religious faith: "I feel that the accident was a series of miracles. First, having two broken ribs puncturing my aorta, that they found me in time. Second, that they took me to Christ Hospital, where there was a heart specialist and a bone specialist on call that particular night. Finally, that I was able to recover and go on with my work. I feel I am a living testimony to God's grace."

The accident led to another change in her life: "My daughter felt it would be best if I were closer to her so that she could better care for me. She teaches here in Dallas. Also, I needed knee replacement and back surgery, so in 2006 I moved back to Dallas." Despite the change in geography, Hall hasn't forgotten the city where she lived and worked so many years: "I still call both Chicago and Texas home, and I come to Chicago as often as I have time. I have a street named for me in Chicago [Honorary Irma P. Hall Way on W. 95th Street], so I could never give it up. Both Chicago and Texas have a way of attracting people and claiming parts of their hearts forever. I think it is the spirit. Always growing and welcoming, always changing, always creating, and always honest. I will always love Chicago and I will always love Texas. That's why I call myself a Texigoan."

After all these years of film and television acting, the stage is still Hall's first and greatest love, and where she spent several years acting, singing, and dancing before even thinking about acting for a profession. Because of her live theater roots, Hall encourages a do-it-yourself spirit amongst those young actors she encounters: "I tell young people, if you really want to learn your craft, this is a place where if you get two or three people of like mind together and you don't see a theater of your liking, then you start your own!"

No matter how many kudos and awards she has received, Hall still credits others for helping her develop her craft: "I have been so fortunate to have worked in film with such great directors. Stan Lathan, Dick Pearce, Ron Howard, Joe Sargent, Jonathan Demme, Joel Schumacher, Ernest Dickerson, the Coen Brothers, and Michael Mann, among others, and all have greatly contributed to my growth as an actor and a person. I have great admiration for them all."

Despite having endured a near-fatal car accident and being at an age when most people are looking to rest and take it easy, Irma shows no signs of slowing down. "I am still here and still working. In 2008 I cofounded another theater, the African American Repertory Theater–Desoto, worked on two films that summer, *Hurricane Season* and *I Wanna Dance*, and did *A Raisin in the Sun* here at AART to celebrate the 50th anniversary of the play. I have also done several indies, among which were *Uncross the Stars* (2008), *Wolf* (2012), and *Rain* (2008), which opened the Bahaman Film Fest. So I stay pretty busy."

Her legion of fans and admirers around the world certainly hope it continues that way.

The Community Film Workshop of Chicago
6200 S. Drexel, Room 201

Budding filmmakers will find a friendly home at the Community Film Workshop of Chicago (CFWC), a vibrant institution that's been around since 1971. Originally funded in part by the American Film Institute and the Chicago Office of Economic Opportunity, the CFWC provides hands-on film training at bargain prices.

This is a great place to learn all aspects of the film and video arts, from scripting to postproduction. Aesthetics and film history classes are also available, as are summer programs for high school students. And if you become a member of the CFWC, you'll have access to low-cost equipment rental, sound transfer, and 16mm editing facilities.

The CFWC is committed to putting cameras into the hands of all Chicagoans, regardless of age, education, or background. Over the years, graduates of the program have gone on to success in commercial and independent filmmaking careers.

For more information about the Community Film Workshop, call (773) 752-9335 or visit www.cfwchicago.org.

The "Barbershop"
79th Street and Exchange Avenue

Fans of the two *Barbershop* films (2002 and 2004) will recognize this picturesque intersection as the site where Calvin (actor/musician Ice Cube) had his barbershop. Producer Bob Teitel relates how the location was serendipitously chosen: "When we were looking for locations, there were a couple barbershops we wanted to pattern it after. But on our first day of scouting, we came across this set of three abandoned storefronts at 79th and Exchange. It was literally the first place we looked at; we got right off the plane and drove right to that, saw the place, saw the train tracks right across the street, and it felt like it was just the natural place to shoot it."

"Donaldson's" Grocery Store from *The Promotion*
100 W. 87th Street

The closing of a former Cub Foods store at this location was a godsend to the producers of *The Promotion* (2008), who were able to have complete use of an actual grocery store building with all the various fixtures and equipment intact. This is where Seann William Scott and John C. Reilly engage in their fevered battle for the coveted promotion to store manager, and where their anger with each other boils over in the parking lot, resulting in a hilariously inept tussle between two men with absolutely no idea how to fight.

Philip Kaufman: American Indie Film Pioneer

One of America's most intelligent and literate filmmakers, Philip Kaufman has directed such compelling films as *The White Dawn* (1973), *Invasion of the Body Snatchers* (1977), and an adaptation of Czech writer Milan Kundera's novel *The Unbearable Lightness of Being* (1988). His screen version of *The Right Stuff* (1983), Tom Wolfe's chronicle of the Mercury astronauts, is an American masterpiece, skillfully combining social satire, history, and the human story behind the space program. Kaufman also provided the original story for *Raiders of the Lost Ark* (1981) and wrote the screenplay for Clint Eastwood's *The Outlaw Josey Wales* (1976).

In 1990, working with his wife Rose, Kaufman adapted Anais Nin's memoirs into the lyrical *Henry and June*, a biography of writer Henry Miller, Nin, and Miller's wife June. It was a fitting subject for the director; after meeting at the University of Chicago in 1962, Nin encouraged Kaufman to become a filmmaker.

Kaufman grew up on Chicago's North Side and attended college at the University of Chicago. He then enrolled in Harvard Law School but ended up returning to U of C to work on a master's in history. After living in San Francisco and then Europe, Kaufman returned to Chicago. Exhilarated by the new styles of filmmaking that were sweeping France, Czechoslovakia, and other European countries, Kaufman took Nin's advice and in 1963 began work on his first motion picture.

Teaming up with cowriter/producer/director Benjamin Manaster, Kaufman reworked a Hassidic tale by Martin Buber into a $50,000 satire, *Goldstein* (1964). "It was sort of a fable of a young couple whose relationship is falling apart," says Kaufman. "The young guy encounters a prophet—Elijah, really—who comes out of Lake Michigan and is supposed to be this kind of bum and unrecognizable guy who we leave a seat for at the table.

"He's played by Lou Gilbert. Gilbert had been blacklisted [in the 1950s]; he was a good friend of Studs Terkel and Nelson Algren. Algren also tells a wonderful story in *Goldstein*. There were also a lot of Second City people in the film—Del Close, Severn Darden, Anthony Holland.

"Our offices were on the North Side, around Rush Street. I'd been living in Europe for a couple of years and seen the New Wave [films] and there really wasn't much being done in America. So for us, it was the idea of starting a new wave of filmmaking based on local talent in Chicago."

Goldstein was entered in the 1964 Cannes Film Festival, where French director Jean Renoir hailed it as "the best American film I have seen in 20 years." The film was awarded the Prix de la Nouvelle Critique, the festival's prize for new filmmakers. This honor was shared with another rising filmmaker, Bernardo Bertolucci, and his work *Before the Revolution* (1964). "*Goldstein* showed for a while. It showed in New York and Los Angeles and had a very good run in Paris and then it disappeared! And that's how things happen."

Kaufman's next film was *Fearless Frank* (1967), originally titled *Frank's Great Adventure*, which featured an unknown actor named Jon Voight in his movie debut. "I'd seen him off-Broadway in New York in a play, *A View from the Bridge*," recalls Kaufman. "Dustin Hoffman was the stage manager of that play, and Robert Duvall was in it."

Following *Fearless Frank*, Kaufman headed west and ultimately was signed by a major studio. Moving into the world of bigger-budgeted films, Kaufman rose through the ranks as both writer and director.

The historical drama *Quills* (2000), with Geoffrey Rush, Kate Winslet, and Joaquin Phoenix, brought Kaufman a nomination for best director at the London Critics Circle Film Awards and the film's writer (Doug Wright) and actors a slew of nominations and awards. Kaufman's latest efforts are as director for *Interrupted* (2009), about the final years in the life of filmmaker Nicholas Ray, and *Hemingway and Gellhorn* (2012), a biopic centering on the romance between Ernest Hemingway and WWII correspondent Martha Gellhorn, which premiered at the Cannes Film Festival and aired on HBO.

Kaufman still looks fondly back on his early days in Chicago: "In general, back then, film seemed very fresh and Chicago seemed very fresh. It seemed like you could start a new type of filmmaking. John Cassavetes and Shirley Clarke were just beginning to make an alternative cinema in New York. But there really wasn't that kind of thing in Chicago, and it was tough. It was hard to get recognition, hard to break through with some of the New York critics. There was a certain kind of competitiveness as to which way the independent movement should go."

Pullman State Historic Site

11111 S. Forrestville Avenue

Dismayed by the violence resulting from the bitter 1877 rail strike, George M. Pullman resolved to not only build the new factory for his luxury sleeping cars far from what he saw as the corrupting influence of Chicago's workingman's neighborhoods, but also to construct an entirely self-sufficient town around the factory, so as to create a positive environment for his workers.

He commissioned architect Solon Beman to create a planned community, which would include a hospital, stores, schools, housing, parks, a

Workers passing in front of the Pullman factory site open *Road to Perdition* (2002),
but look closely and you'll see the image is reversed: the Pullman administration
building appears to the right rather than left. *(Photo by Kate Corcoran)*

theater, and all the amenities found in any town or village (except a saloon,
as he wanted his workers to remain pure). Beman designed all the various
brick structures in the Queen Anne Style, and anchored the community
around the administration building with its imposing clock tower, and the
Hotel Florence, which Pullman named in honor of his daughter.

The town Beman built was a marvel of its day, and its clean streets and
beautifully uniform dwellings were a major side destination for those
attending the Columbian Exposition of 1893. There was an undercurrent
of paternalism in the seemingly bucolic hamlet, however, and Pullman
himself was definitely no humanitarian. This became abundantly clear
during the deep economic depression of 1894, when Pullman sliced
the wages of his workers but refused to lower the rent on the dwellings,
which he also refused to let them own. Tensions grew, and the Pullman
workers began a strike that spread to include the country's entire rail
system. Pullman refused to back down and was vilified in the national
press for his penurious ways.

When Pullman died in 1897, his coffin was buried under tons of concrete, so as to prevent desecration by enraged unionists. In 1898, the
Illinois Supreme Court ordered the Pullman Company to divest itself of
all real estate holdings in the town.

The factory continued manufacturing railcars until 1981, when the
last Pullman car was built in the neighborhood and the company
closed the plant and moved on to other endeavors. The administration

building sat vacant for many years, becoming a dwelling for homeless squatters, one of whom set the complex afire in 1998; much of the structure was gutted.

Ironically, this tragedy had a silver lining, as it became the impetus for then-governor James Thompson to allocate funding to create the Pullman State Historic Site, which included the charred administration/factory complex and the Hotel Florence, which had fallen on hard times and had also been badly neglected.

Today, through the hard work of the site's employees and a legion of volunteers, the Pullman State Historic Site has rebounded. The administration building has been rebuilt, and the restored clock tower now rises over the neighborhood again. Restoration work continues on the Hotel Florence.

Hollywood has loved the neat brick cottages and unique structures of the Pullman neighborhood for years. *The Untouchables* (1987) used a neighborhood bistro for the restaurant scene in which Kevin Costner allows a photographer to snap a picture of himself and his crime-fighting compadres; a Pullman building plays an East German hospital in *The Package* (1989); and Dr. Richard Kimble discovers the dwelling of the one-armed man who killed his wife in one of Pullman's row-house apartments in *The Fugitive* (1993). The distinctive clock tower was the inspiration for the tower from which Santa emerges in the animated hit *The Polar Express* (2004); the film's director, Robert Zemeckis, grew up

The Pullman State Historic Site's Hotel Florence, designed by architect Solon S. Beman, is dressed with artificial snow and alternative signage for *Road to Perdition* filming. *(Photos by Ed Beyer, courtesy of Pullman State Historic Site)*

The dining room of the Hotel Florence, shown here with furniture from the original hotel, was transformed into part of the home of John Rooney (Paul Newman) in *Road to Perdition*. *(Photo by Kate Corcoran)*

in nearby Roseland. The administration building was also the location of the opening scene of the pilot episode of the television series *Boss*, where Kelsey Grammer's character, Mayor Tom Kane, learns of his irreversible and fatal brain condition during a clandestine meeting with a neurologist.

The riveting period drama *Road to Perdition* (2002) made the most extensive use of Pullman, spending several months shooting scenes in the Hotel Florence, the hotel's annex building, and around the administration/factory complex. *Road to Perdition* was directed by Sam Mendes of *American Beauty* fame and stars Tom Hanks as a hitman for the organized crime boss (Paul Newman) of an unnamed downstate Illinois city in the 1920s. When one of Hank's young sons inadvertently witnesses Newman's son (played by the current James Bond, Daniel Craig) commit a murder, a chain of events is set in motion that results in Hanks and the boy on the run from the entire Chicago mob. Jude Law oozes with demented menace as the hitman hired to hunt down the pair.

Another fine period drama, *The Express* (2008), which stars Dennis Quaid and *Finding Forrester's* Rob Brown, uses Pullman's picturesque Greenstone Church as the site of a 1950s NAACP meeting.

TOP LEFT: A false wall and doorway were constructed to cover the lobby entrance to the hallway; alternate lighting fixtures were installed. *(Photo by Mike Wagenbach, courtesy of Pullman State Historic Site)*

TOP RIGHT: Main-floor hallway of the Hotel Florence being transformed into interiors for the home of John Moody (Paul Newman) for *Road to Perdition*. *(Photo by Mike Wagenbach, courtesy of Pullman State Historic Site)*

MIDDLE: A variety of period vehicles parked at the Pullman factory site for use during filming on *Road to Perdition*. Although originally scheduled for three months, the production remained on the site for nine months. *(Photo by Mike Wagenbach, courtesy of Pullman State Historic Site)*

BOTTOM: Resin icicles ready for use on *Road to Perdition* at the Pullman State Historic Site. *(Photo by Ed Beyer, courtesy of Pullman State Historic Site)*

The Suburbs

Stateville Correctional Center
16300 Illinois 53, Crest Hill, Illinois
Joliet Correctional Center
1127–1299 Collins St., Joliet, Illinois

South of Chicago in Will County is Joliet, Illinois. A unique city in and of itself, it is also the site of two Illinois Department of Corrections prisons: the Stateville Correctional Center and the Joliet Correctional Center.

Despite Stateville technically being located in nearby Crest Hill, the two penitentiaries are sometimes collectively referred to as "Joliet," which leads to some confusion if you're not familiar with the different sites. The original Joliet Correctional Center opened in 1860 as a prison for Confederate soldiers. Following the Civil War, the site was converted to part of the Illinois prison system. Stateville opened in 1925 and over the years became the main facility for prisoners in Joliet.

Prison films have been popular since the birth of the movies. Shooting a big-budget movie inside a prison, however, poses a unique set of obstacles to any film crew. For one thing, access is restricted within the prison walls. Every item brought onto the set must be cataloged and accounted for at the day's end. The sort of fraternization and horseplay inherent to movie sets must be strictly curtailed.

With that said, it's still not impossible to bring camera crews inside a prison, and Stateville has been cooperative with Hollywood over the years. Director Robert Florey brought Preston Foster, Harry Morgan (then using the name Henry Morgan), and Anthony Quinn to Stateville for the 1944 crime flick *Roger Touhy, Gangster*, a primarily fictional account of the notorious Chicago crime figure.

In *Call Northside 777* (1948), James Stewart comes to Stateville to research the truth of prisoner Richard Conte's story. Filming took place in Cellhouse F, which is designed in the "panopticon," or circular, fashion. Filmed in stark black-and-white, this rounded cellblock and an imposing central guard tower provide an eerie backdrop as Stewart walks along the balcony to meet Conte.

The cinematic possibilities of Stateville were stretched to the limit by Oliver Stone's over-the-top satire *Natural Born Killers* (1994). This wasn't just a straight shoot like *Roger Touhy* or *Call Northside 777*; Stone's vision was a hyperkinetic, surreal nightmare, culminating in a frenzied prison riot. Shooting under the strict controls of prison regulations was a daunting challenge, to say the least. Yet Stone pulled it off, creating a compelling sequence that sucks viewers right into the heart of the action.

The entire production team was extremely cautious, because if anything went wrong, no movies would ever be allowed to shoot in Stateville ever again. Interestingly, real convicts were given an opportunity to be film extras for the riot scenes. To be eligible, the prisoners were carefully screened for the least troublesome candidates.

Ultimately, the prison riot went off without a problem. Mingling convicts with stuntmen and real guards with their movie counterparts, Stone's hallucination was pulled off without a hitch.

More recently, the Joliet Correctional Center was used extensively in the first season of the television show *Prison Break* and for the ingeniously goofy Bob Odenkirk–directed comedy *Let's Go to Prison* (2006), which starred Will Arnett and Dax Shepard.

Of course, no discussion of movies and the Illinois Department of Corrections would be complete without mentioning *The Blues Brothers* (1980). In the film's opening, Elwood Blues (Dan Aykroyd) picks up his newly paroled brother Jake Blues (John Belushi), a.k.a. "Joliet Jake," in front of the Joliet Correctional Center gates. What goes around comes around; by the film's end, both Aykroyd and Belushi, along with their reunited Blues Brothers Band, are back in the slammer, providing an invigorating version of "Jailhouse Rock" for an inmate audience.

Acknowledgments

Michael Corcoran

First off, I must give a huge thanks to Cynthia Sherry and Chicago Review Press for rescuing this update project from several years of limbo. In addition, I could never have completed this project without the assistance and expertise of the following people (in no particular order). Any errors and/or omissions in this volume are entirely mine.

Sharon Woodhouse and everyone at Lake Claremont Press; Bob Teitel; Harold Ramis; Pam Kasper at Ocean Pictures; Irma Hall; Harrisse Davis; Michael Shamberg; Richard Salamone; Jennifer Girard; Bob Janz and Patricia Mglej; Bart Wurtzebach (a.k.a. "CTA Bart"), Bill Reilly; CTA Media Relations; Steven A. Jones; Steve Conrad; John Milinac; Dieter Sturm; James McAllister; Nathan Crowley; Christina Varotsis; Tim Kazurinsky; Jane Alderman; Jeff Garlin; Denise Hughes; Rich Moskal and Kathy Byrne at the Chicago Film Office; the Illinois Film Office; Nancy Watrous at Chicago Film Archives; Marty Rubin and Barbara Scharres at the Siskel Center; Dave and Andrea Jemilo and Michael Polino at the Green Mill; Andrea Tichy at the Theatre School at DePaul University; Luis Lopez and Jesus Lopez at St. Augustine College; Mike Wagenbach at the Pullman State Historic Site; Tony Dzik; Eileen Fitzsimons; Ruth Ratny at ReelChicago; Robin Hammond and Andrew Alexander at Second City; David Rosenberg, Martha Lavey, Molly Kobelt, and Ed Sobel from Steppenwolf; Ora Jones; Paula Muzik; Natalia Derevyanny from the Illinois Institute of Art; Jeff Kemp; Ted Okuda; Donna Primas; Al Walavich; Holly Jensen; Ariana Swan and Julie Heath at Warner Bros.; Vanessa Valliere at Northwestern University; Sarah Marcus at the Chicago History Museum; Gillian Smith; Lars Ullberg at the Illinois Production Alliance; Wayne Kubacki at Essanay Studio and Lighting; Maria Norman; Pat Kingsley; Lisa Schmidt; Izzy Arias; Dan Bodansky; Scott Melrose; Christian Meier; Ashley Hunt; Bonnie Hunt; Justine Nagan, Gordon Quinn, Jerry Blumenthal, Steve James, Peter Gilbert, David Simpson, and Frederick Marx at Kartemquin Films; and everyone at the Tuesday Night Domino Game (sorry I've missed so many sessions). Apologies to anyone I may have missed.

Finally, a special thanks to Kate Corcoran, with whom I've shared an incredible journey over the last 30 (very) odd years. Her wonderful photographic talent is evident in this volume, and without her hours of assistance, this update would have never been possible.

Arnie Bernstein

Special thanks to Dave Drazin and Carol Seymour for help, wisdom, and good thoughts. Sharon and everyone at Lake Claremont Press. Cheryl, as always. And for being good sports, Gene and Sheila Bernstein, and Chuck and Nancy Diddia.

Appendix

Films Shot in Chicago and the Surrounding Area

The 1,250+ films below were shot either all or in part in Chicago and/or the suburbs. This list is by no means complete. Many of the silent titles of Selig Polyscope, Essanay, and others have been lost to history. Other films of more recent times can be difficult to catalog due to the sometimes slippery nature of independent film distribution.

The list also does not include TV series, such as *Crime Story*, *Lady Blue*, *Early Edition*, and others. Made-for-TV movies are also omitted. Also keep in mind that many of the films may only feature exterior shots of Chicago and/or merely had a few tangential scenes filmed here.

4 and a Half Terrorists (2008)
5 Girls (2001)
5 Star Day (2010)
7 soles (2009)
8 of Diamonds (2006)
9 to 5 (2008)
10 MPH (2007)
13 Genders (2004)
16th Street (2008)
21 Up America (2006)
'77 (2007)
400 Miles to Freedom (2009)

500 Years Later (2005)
813 Lake Street (2008)
Aah, Beer (2007)
About Last Night . . . (1986)
Above the Law (1988)
Access Nation (2004)
Act Naturally (2011)
Acting Class, The (2000)
Adam's Rib (1923)
Adrift in the Heartland (2002)
Adventures in Babysitting (1987)
Adventures of Kathlyn, The (1914)

Business Rivalry (1903)
Busted Romance, A (1918)
Busy Body, The (1967)
Butch Camp (1997)
Butterfly (2008)
Butterfly on a Wheel (2007)
Ca$h! (2010)
Cab Ride, The (2009)
Cabbie (2007)
Cabin, The (1998)
Cakewalk (2002)
Caligari's Cure (1983)
Call Northside 777 (1948)
Calling All Stations (2005)
Campaign (1968)
Candyman (1992)
Captain Ron (1992)
Carl Panzram: The Spirit of Hatred and Vengeance (2011)
Carving Out Our Name (2001)
Caseys, The (2003)
Cast in Gray (2005)
Casting About (2004)
Catching Hell (2011)
Caught (2006)
Chain Reaction (1996)
Chains (1912)
Challenge of Chance, The (1919)
Chamber, The (1996)
Chances of the World Changing, The (2006)
ChangingMan (2000)
Chasing October (2007)
Chasing Robert (2007)
Cheat You Fair: The Story of Maxwell Street (2006)
Check Please (2007)
Chemistry of Dating, The (2007)

Chi Girl (1999)
Chicago (2002)
Chicago 10 (2007)
Chicago After Midnight (1928)
Chicago Blues (2009)
Chicago Cab (1998)
Chicago Calling (1951)
Chicago Deadline (1949)
Chicago Filmmakers on the Chicago River (1998)
Chicago Fire Run (1903)
Chicago Fireboats on Parade (1903)
Chicago Heights (2009)
Chicago Maternity Center Story, The (1976)
Chicago Overcoat (2009)
Chicago Police Parade (1901)
Chicago Politics: A Theatre of Power (1985–87)
Chicago Street, A (1898)
Chicago Syndicate (1955)
Chicago360 (2006)
C-H-I-C-K-E-N Spells Chicken (1910)
Children of the Revolution: Tune Back In (2005)
Children on Their Birthdays (2002)
Child's Play (1988)
Child's Play 2 (1991)
Christians, The (2008)
Christmas Vacation (a.k.a. *National Lampoon's Christmas Vacation*, 1989)
Christmas with the Kranks (2004)
Citizen Saint (1947)
City Lights (2006)
City of Purple Dreams, The (1918)
City That Never Sleeps (1953)
City Wasp (2008)
Class (1983)

Clearance (2004)

Cliffhanger, The (2003)

Club Paradise (1986)

Coasting (2009)

Cocked (2005)

Code of Silence (1985)

Cold Justice (a.k.a. *Father Jim*, 1989)

College, The (1964)

Color Me Obsessed: A Film About the Replacements (2011)

Color of Money, The (1986)

Columbiana (2011)

Comeback of Barnacle Bill (1918)

Coming of Columbus, The (1912)

Common Senses (2005)

Company, The (2003)

Compensation (1999)

Confession, The (1908)

Connie and Carla (2004)

Contagion (2011)

Continental Divide (1981)

Contract Killers (2003)

Cookie Bandit (2002)

Cooley High (1975)

Coop's Night In (2006)

Cop Show (2007)

Copasetic (2008)

Copywrite (2001)

Corner Madison and State Streets, Chicago (1897)

Corner of, The (2006)

Count of Monte Cristo, The (1908)

Countess, The (1914)

Counting Backwards (2007)

Country Western Hoedown (1967)

Couples Retreat (2009)

Cousin Jim (1916)

Cracked Ice (1917)

Crave (2012)

Crazy Like They Are (2004)

Crime Fiction (2007)

Crime Spree (2003)

Crimson Wing, The (1915)

Crisis, The (1918)

Cup of My Blood (2005)

Curly Sue (1991)

Currency (2011)

Cushion (2005)

Damien: Omen II (1978)

Dancing Nig, The (1907)

Dancing on Water (2008)

Dandy Kids Documentary (2008)

Dark (2003)

Dark Avengers (2009)

Dark Knight, The (2008)

Dark Knight Project, The (2008)

Darling (2007)

Date Me Save $40 (2008)

Days of Fall (2007)

Dead End (2013)

Dead On: The Life and Cinema of George A. Romero (2008)

Dead to Rights (2003)

Death and Taxis (2007)

Death in Progress, A (2008)

Death of a President (2006)

Debt (2003)

Decaf (2005)

Decker (2007)

Decomposed (2009)

Deep End of the Ocean, The (1999)

Demon Possessed (1993)

Dennis the Menace (1993)

Derailed (2005)

Desertion (2008)

Detention Teacher, The (2006)

Eight Men Out (1988)

Einstein's God Model (2012)

Ekho: Fall of an Empire (2004)

Elder Brother, The (1914)

Elephant in the Living Room, The (2010)

Elly Glass Project, The (2009)

Empathy (2004)

Empty Boxes (2006)

End of the Line (1987)

End of the Road, The (1915)

Endless Love (1981)

Ends Runway (2008)

Envying Alice (2004)

Epitaph: Bread and Salt (2011)

Estes Avenue (2005)

Eugene (2003)

Eugene and the Worm (2007)

Euro-Central (2009)

Even Trade (2004)

Every Inch a King (1914)

Every Other Day (2004)

Everybody Sins (2005)

Examined Life (2008)

Excessive Force (1993)

Exile, The (1931)

Expelled: No Intelligence Allowed (2008)

Express, The (a.k.a. Express: The Ernie Davis Story, The, 2008)

Eye of Cruelty (2004)

Eye That Never Sleeps (1912)

Eyelids (2008)

Eyes of an Angel (1991)

Fable of Hazel's Two Husbands and What Became of Them (1915)

Fable of the Bush League Lover Who Failed to Qualify, The (1914)

Fahrenheit 9/11 (2004)

Fairies (2003)

Fairylogue (1910)

Faith of Millions (1927)

Fall of Montezuma, The (1912)

Fallen Souls (2010)

Family Thing, A (1996)

Fancypants (2011)

Farewell Darkness (2007)

Farmer's Daughter, The (1913)

Fast as You Can (2008)

Fat Head (2009)

Fate Twisted Simply (2006)

Fate's Funny Frolic (1911)

Fatty Drives the Bus (1999)

Faustian Tale, A (2007)

Fearless Frank (a.k.a Frank's Great Adventure, 1967)

Fence, The (1994)

Ferris Bueller's Day Off (1986)

Few Years Older, A (2003)

Fifth Horseman, The (2002)

Finding Preet (2006)

Fingerprints (1914)

Finney (1969)

Fireproof Gloves (2008)

First Bass (2008)

First Breath of Tengan Rei, The (2009)

Fish Out of Water (2009)

Fixing the Faker (1918)

Flags of Our Fathers (2006)

Flatliners (1990)

Flipping the Whale (2001)

Fly (2005)

Flying (2002)

Flying Aarons, The (2004)

Folks! (1992)

Fonder Heart, A (2009)

For Love Alone (2010)

For the Honor of the Eighth Illinois Regiment (1914)

Foreign English (2008)

Forgetting Betty (2006)

Forgiving Dr. Mengele (2006)

Formosa Betrayed (2009)

Four Friends (1981)

Frankenstein: Day of the Beast (2011)

Freaky Circus Guy (2005)

Fred Claus (2007)

French Fries and Curry (2004)

From the Submerged (1912)

Frozen Warning, The (1917)

Fugitive, The (1993)

Fundamentals of the Stoma (2003)

Funkytown (1998)

Fury, The (1978)

Futbolanthropology (2009)

Gaily, Gaily (1969)

Gameshow and Tell (2008)

Gangster with a Heart of Gold: The Noonie G. Story (2006)

Gans-McGovern Fight (1901)

Gathering, The (2003)

Gentle Julia (1923)

Get A Job (2010)

Get Pony Boy (2007)

Get2Gether, A (2005)

Ghosts (1917)

Girl in Blue, The (1903)

Girls Just Want to Have Fun (1985)

Girls Room (2007)

Gladiator (1992)

Gnaw (2008)

Go Fish (1994)

Go for It! (2009)

Go Mom (2006)

God's Smile or The Odessa Story (2008)

Golden Days (2007)

Golden Glove Story, The (1950)

Goldstein (1964)

Golem (2008)

Golf Champion "Chick" Evans Links with Sweedie (1914)

Golub (1988)

Gomer and Ed Turn Gay (a.k.a. *Gomer and Ed in West Hollywood*, 2001)

Good Band Is Easy to Kill, A (2005)

Good Catch, A (1912)

Good Luck in Old Clothes (1918)

Gordian Knot, The (1911)

Gore Gore Girls, The (1972)

Gotch-Hackenschmidt Wrestling Match (1908)

Gotch-Zbyszko World's Championship Wrestling Match (1910)

Gotham, IL (2004)

Grace Is Gone (2007)

Grace Quigley (a.k.a. *Ultimate Solution of Grace Quigley, The*, 1985)

Grafter, The (1907)

Gran tabu, El (2007)

Grand Piano (2013)

Graustark (1915)

Great Heights (2009)

Green Story, A (2012)

Greg's Leg (2008)

Ground Chuck (2001)

Groundhog Day (1993)

Group, The (2008)

Grudge 2, The (2006)

Gypsy Blood (2001)

H. H. Holmes: America's First Serial Killer (2004)

Lost (2002)

Lost Along the Way (2008)

Lost Girls (2005)

Lost Years (1911)

Love. Blood. Kryptonite. (2008)

Love It, Leave It (1970)

Love Jones (1997)

Love Shorts (2004)

Love: The Movie (2004)

Love Your Mama (1993)

Lover for My Husband, A (2003)

Lovers (2006)

Lucas (1986)

Luci D (2004)

Lucky Ones, The (2008)

Lucky Strike (2001)

Mad at the World (1955)

Mad Dog and Glory (1993)

Madison (2001)

Madman, The (1911)

Magic Act, The (2000)

Magic Melody, The (1909)

Magic Wand, The (1912)

Mahogany (1975)

Maid in Manhattan (2002)

Mail Order Bride, The (1912)

Major League (1989)

Major League II (1994)

Make It Happen (2008)

Making the Man (2007)

Mama Black Widow (2008)

Mama Medea (1998)

Man in the Silo, The (2008)

Man Who Shot Dogs, The (2009)

Manhunter (1986)

Map of the World, A (1999)

Marching Banned (2013)

Marked for Death (1990)

Marquette Park I (1976)

Marquette Park II (1978)

Masked Wrestler, The (1914)

Mass Romantic (2008)

Maxwell Street Blues (1981)

Meat Tricks, The (2005)

Medium Cool (1969)

Meet the Browns (a.k.a. *Tyler Perry's Meet the Browns*, 2008)

Meet the Fockers (2004)

Meet the Parents (1992)

Meet the Parents (2000)

Melody and the Old Sock (2012)

Melody of Love, The (1912)

Memoirs of Don Walker, The (2005)

Memorial Stadium: True Illini Spirit (2008)

Men Don't Leave (1990)

Menmaniacs: The Legacy of Leather (1995)

Merci (2006)

Mercury Rising (1998)

Mercy, the Mummy Mumbled (1918)

Merry Gentleman, The (2008)

Message in a Bottle (1999)

Michael (1996)

Mickey One (1965)

Microfísica (2008)

Midnight Run (1988)

Migrating Forms (2000)

Milk Fed Hero, A (1918)

Mindy (2004)

Minx, The (2007)

Miracle, The (2007)

Miracle on 34th Street (1994)

Misanthrope: The Movie (2001)

(Mis)Leading Man (2008)

Miss Ohio (2009)

Mix Tape (2003)
Mo' Money (1992)
Modulations (1998)
Mole Man of Belmont Avenue, The
  (2010)
Money Talks in Darktown (1916)
Monitors, The (1969)
Monkey Hustle (1977)
Monster a-Go Go (1965)
Moon's Ray, The (1914)
More Than Gravity (2004)
Mortal Kombat (2013)
Motel 666 (2012)
Motivational Growth (2012)
Motorcycles & Mayhem (2004)
Mourning After Mirabelle (2008)
Movie Boy (2005)
Movie Marionettes (1918)
Mr. 3000 (2004)
Mr. Id (2003)
Mr. Sophistication (2012)
Muhammad and Jane (2003)
Mulligan (2011)
Murder of Fred Hampton, The (1971)
Music Box (1990)
Music Box (2008)
Musician (2007)
My Best Friend's Wedding (1997)
My Big Fat Greek Wedding (2002)
My Blood Doesn't Clot Right (2004)
My Bodyguard (1980)
My Brother's Light (2002)
My Buddy Rick: The Making of a One-
  Man Show (2009)
My First Tooth (2009)
My Friends Told Me About You
  (2008)
My Life (1993)

My Nappy Roots: A Journey Through
  Black Hair-itage (2005)
My Porn Star (2004)
My War, My Story (2007)
Myra (2008)
Naked Ape (1972)
Naked Face, The (1984)
Nashville Rebel (1966)
Nate & Margaret (2012)
National Vampire (2006)
Native Son (1951)
Native Son (1986)
Natural Born Killers (1994)
Natural Born Shooter, A (1917)
Navy Way, The (1944)
Nebata the Greek Singer (1912)
Negotiator, The (1998)
Neptune's Daughter (1912)
Nerdcore for Life (2008)
Nest, The (2003)
Never Been Kissed (1999)
New Manager, The (1911)
New Port South (2001)
Next of Kin (1989)
Nice Bombs (2006)
Nice Threads (2006)
Night Fangs (2005)
Night Hawks, The (1914)
Night in the Life of Jimmy Reardon, A
  (a.k.a. Jimmy Reardon, 1988)
Nightingale in a Music Box (2002)
Nightlight (2008)
Nightlights (2012)
Nightmare on Elm Street, A (2010)
No Applause: Joe Frank (2009)
No Mercy (1986)
Normal Life (1996)
North by Northwest (1959)

Not Another B Movie (2010)

Note of Triumph: The Golden Age of Norman Corwin, A (2005)

Nothing in Common (1986)

Nothing Like the Holidays (2008)

Novice, The (2005)

Novocaine (2001)

Now We Live on Clifton (1974)

Oak Tree, The (2009)

Ocean's Eleven (2001)

Ocean's Twelve (2004)

Of Bass and Men (2001)

Of Boys and Men (2008)

Oh My Soul (2008)

Oh Shit (2005)

Oh You Teacher! (1911)

Old Maid (2005)

On the Desert's Edge (1911)

On the Downlow (2004)

On the Line (2001)

On the Right Track (1981)

Once Upon a Time in the Hood (2004)

One in a Million (2009)

One Ordinary Woman, One Extraordinary Journey (2004)

One Small Hitch (2012)

One Way (2007)

One Week (2000)

One Week (2008)

One Wonderful Night (1914)

One^3 (2005)

Only the Lonely (1991)

Open Door, An (2006)

Opera Lover, The (1999)

Opportunity Knocks (1990)

Opposite of Life, The (2008)

Orange Cactus (2004)

Ordinary People (1980)

Original Gangstas (1996)

Orphans of Apollo (2008)

Osso Bucco (2007)

Other Girl, The (1914)

Other Man, The (1914)

Other People's Mirrors (2004)

Other Tongue (2006)

Our Story Our Voice (2007)

Out of Faith (2006)

Out of the Depths (1912)

Out of the Loop (2009)

Out of the Shadow (2004)

Outing Riley (2004)

Outlaw and the Child, The (1911)

Overcome (2011)

Owner, The (2012)

Package, The (1989)

Painters, The (1918)

Palooka (2006)

Paper Plane (1999)

Parents (1968)

Partyline (2007)

Passing Shadow, The (1912)

Passover (2007)

Pastime (a.k.a. *One Cup of Coffee*, 1990)

Pastime, The (2009)

Pat Gets a Cat (2005)

Patriarchs, The (2009)

Patriot Acts (2004)

Payback (1999)

Pea vs. Carrot (2008)

Pearl Diver (2004)

Peeling It Off (2008)

Peer Gynt (1941)

Penitent, The (1912)

Pennies from Heaven (1981)

Penny Philanthropist, The (1917)

People vs. Paul Crump, The (1962)

Pep Talk (2006)

Perfect Model, The (a.k.a. *Sweet Perfection*, 1990)

Permute (2008)

Personal Foul (1987)

Petty Cash (2010)

Philip Greeley Goes Hollywood (2004)

Phunny Business: A Black Comedy (2010)

Piaf: Her Story, Her Songs (2003)

Pickman's Muse (2010)

Pictures on the Wall (2004)

Piece of the Action, A (1977)

Pimps Up, Ho's Down (1999)

Pinball Passion (2008)

Pioneer Days (1917)

Pirates and Pills (2007)

Pit, The (1914)

Plain and Simple (2008)

Planes, Trains & Automobiles (1987)

Please Wait to Be Seated (2004)

Plum Tree, The (1914)

Poker House, The (2008)

Polish Bar (2010)

Poltergeist III (1988)

Pop Machine (2006)

Porters, The (1918)

Possessed, The (2008)

Post Mortem, America 2021 (2009)

Power (1916)

Power of Conscience, The (1913)

Prelude to a Kiss (1992)

Present Perfect (2001)

Preserve Me a Seat (2006)

Press Start (2007)

Pretty in Pink (1986)

Primal Fear (1996)

Prime Time, The (1960)

Primer for Dental Extraction, A (1999)

Prince Test (2009)

Professional Interview, The (2008)

Prologue (1970)

Promise Keeper, The (2006)

Promises in the Dark (1979)

Promises Kept (2008)

Promotion, The (2008)

Proof (2005)

Providence (2009)

Public Enemies (2009)

Public Eye, The (1992)

Public Housing (1997)

Puncher's New Love, The (1911)

Purple Gang, The (2008)

Put the Needle on the Record (2004)

Pyrite (2008)

Qwerty (2012)

Race for Mayor, The (1983)

Radio Free Albemuth (2009)

Railed (2008)

Railroad Porter, The (a.k.a. *Pullman Porter, The*, 1912)

Rain Today (2004)

Raisin in the Sun, A (1961)

Rape of the Soul (2006)

Rapid Fire (1992)

Raw Deal (1986)

Ray (2004)

Reach the Rock (1997)

Réactivision de Marilyn, La (2004)

Reborn (2009)

Reckless Rover, A (1918)

Red Heat (1988)

Red, White & Blue: A Tale of Two Americas (2009)

Relic, The (1997)

Stolen Summer (2002)

Stonecutter, The (2011)

Stony Island (a.k.a. *My Main Man from Stony Island*, 1978)

Straight Talk (1992)

Strange as Angels (2003)

Strange as Angels (2005)

Stranger Than Fiction (2006)

Stray Dogs (2002)

Street Thief (2006)

Streets of Fire (1984)

Strip, The (2009)

Stuart Saves His Family (1995)

Subtle Seduction (2008)

Subway (2005)

Sugar (2008)

Summer Silenced (2006)

Super Size Me (2004)

Superman: Man of Steel (2013)

Superpower (2008)

Surviving Christmas (2004)

Swap Meet (2006)

Sweedie and Her Dog (1915)

Sweedie at the Fair (1914)

Sweedie Goes to College (1915)

Sweedie in Vaudeville (1915)

Sweedie Learns to Swim (1914)

Sweedie the Swatter (1914)

Sweedie's Hopeless Love (1915)

Sweedie's Suicide (1915)

Sweet Adeline (1926)

Switching Channels (1988)

T.R. Baskin (1971)

Take Down (2006)

Tale of a Suicidal Narcoleptic, The (2008)

Talent Given Us, The (2004)

Tales of Terror and Love (2001)

Tapioca (2009)

Taylor Chain I (1980)

Taylor Chain II (1984)

Team Picture (2007)

Temple Builder, The (2006)

Ten Nights in a Barroom (1909)

Terra Incognita: The Perils and Promise of Stem Cell Research (a.k.a. *Mapping Stem Cell Research: Terra Incognita*, 2007)

That Asian Thing (2008)

That One Moment (2006)

That Royle Girl (1925)

Theft by Deception (2010)

They Call Me Bruce (1982)

Thief (1981)

Things Are Tough All Over (1982)

Things Change (1988)

Third Rail, The (2001)

Thirteenth Man, The (1913)

This Old Cub (2004)

This Promise I Made (2013)

Three Days (1997)

Three Girls Lost (1931)

Three Pals (1916)

Three the Hard Way (1974)

Three to Tango (1999)

Thriller Theater! (2011)

Through the Storm (1914)

Through Walls (2004)

Thumbs Down (1968)

Thunder in Guyana (2003)

Time Traveler's Wife, The (2009)

Timebox Twins, The (2007)

Toll of the Marshes, The (1913)

Tomboy and the Champ (1961)

Tony the Fidler (1913)

Touch and Go (1986)

Wizard of Oz, The (1910)
Women & Manue (2007)
Wonton (2005)
Working Class Rock Star (2008)
Working Title (2008)
World of Weird (2004)
World's Championship Series (1910)
World's Smartest Man, The (2007)
Worst Date (2002)

Wrestled (2003)
Wrong All Around (1917)
You Don't Say! (2013)
You May Not Kiss the Bride (2011)
You'll Never Amount to Anything
   (2009)
Young Runaways, The (1968)
Your Astronauts (1969)
Zombie(zero) (2001)

Selected Bibliography

Addams, Jane. *Twenty Years at Hull-House*. New York: New American Library, 1981.

Arce, Hector. *Groucho*. New York: Perigee, 1980.

Bach, Ira J. *Chicago on Foot: Walking Tours of Chicago's Architecture*. Chicago: J. Philip O'Hara, 1973.

Balaban and Katz Historical Foundation. www.balabanandkatzfoundation.com.

Balaban, David. *The Chicago Movie Palaces of Balaban and Katz*. Charleston, SC: Arcadia Publishing, 2006.

Bergreen, Laurence. *Capone: The Man and the Era*. New York: Touchtone, 1996.

Cawelti, John G., ed. *Focus on Bonnie and Clyde*. Englewood Cliffs, NJ: Prentice-Hall, 1973.

Chaplin, Charles. *My Autobiography*. New York: Pocket Book, 1966.

Cinema Treasures. http://cinematreasures.org.

Cripps, Thomas. *Slow Fade to Black: The Negro in American Film, 1900–1942*. London: Oxford University Press, 1977.

Dardis, Tom. *Harold Lloyd: The Man on the Clock*. New York: Penguin Books, 1984.

Friedman, David F., with Don DeNevi. *A Youth in Babylon: Confessions of a Trash-Film King*. Buffalo, NY: Prometheus Books, 1990.

Gabler, Neal. *An Empire of Their Own: How the Jews Invented Hollywood*. New York: Anchor Books, 1989.

Geduld, Harry M., ed. *Focus on D. W. Griffith*. Englewood Cliffs, NJ: Prentice-Hall, 1971.

Gelmis, Joseph. *The Film Director as Superstar*. New York: Doubleday, 1970.

Graf, John, and Steve Skorpad. *Chicago's Monuments, Markers, and Memorials*. Chicago: Arcadia Publishing, 2002.

Greene, Bob. "It Wasn't 777: New Twist to Old Number." *Chicago Sun-Times*, November 12, 1975.

Grossman, James R., Ann Durkin Keating, and Janice L. Reiff., eds. *The Encyclopedia of Chicago*. Chicago: University of Chicago Press, 2004.

Hansberry, Lorraine. *A Raisin in the Sun: The Unfilmed Original Screenplay*. New York: Signet, 1994.

Hayner, Don, and Tom McNamee. *Chicago Sun-Times Metro Chicago Almanac*. Chicago: Bonus Books, 1991.

Heise, Kenan, and Mark Frazel. *Hands on Chicago: Getting Hold of the City*. Chicago: Bonus Books, 1987.

Holli, Melvin G., and Peter d'A. Jones. *Ethnic Chicago: A Multicultural Portrait.* Grand Rapids, MI: Wm. B. Eerdmans Publishing Company, 1995.

Houston, Gary. "A Real-Life Chicago Murder Mystery: Few Stories Compare with 'Northside 777.'" *Chicago Tribune,* January 9, 1995.

Hucke, Matt, and Ursula Bielski. *Graveyards of Chicago.* Chicago: Lake Claremont Press, 1999.

Katz, Ephraim. *The Film Encyclopedia.* New York: Harper-Perennial, 1994.

Kenney, William. "Chicago's 'Black-and-Tans,'" *Chicago History,* Fall 1997.

Lake Claremont Press. *A Native's Guide to Chicago.* 4th ed. Chicago: Lake Claremont Press, 2004.

Lahue, Kalton C., ed. *Motion Picture Pioneer: The Selig Polyscope Company.* Cranbury, NJ: A. S. Barnes and Company, 1973.

Leab, Daniel J. *From Sambo to Superspade: The Black Experience in Motion Pictures.* Boston: Houghton Mifflin Company, 1975.

Leaming, Barbara. *Orson Welles: A Biography.* New York: Viking, 1985.

Lehman, Ernest. *North by Northwest.* New York: Viking, 1972.

Library of Congress, Prints and Photographs Division. "Historic American Buildings Survey." HABS ILL, 16-CHIG, 60-. http://hdl.loc.gov/loc.pnp/hhh.il0034.

Lowe, David. *Lost Chicago.* New York: American Legacy Press, 1985.

Marill, Alvin H. *Movies Made for Television: The Telefeature and the Mini-Series 1964–1986.* New York: New York Zoetrope, 1987.

Marx, Arthur. *Son of Groucho.* New York: David McKay Company, 1972.

Marx, Groucho. *The Groucho Phile: An Illustrated Life.* Indianapolis: Bobbs-Merrill, 1976.

Mast, Gerald. *A Short History of the Movies.* 3rd. ed. Indianapolis: Bobbs-Merrill, 1981.

McBrien, Judith Paine. *Pocket Guide to Chicago Architecture.* 2nd ed. New York: W. W. Norton, 2004.

Monaco, James. *American Film Now: The People, the Power, the Money, the Movies.* New York: Plume, 1979.

Morton, Jim, ed. *RE/Search No. 10: Incredibly Strange Films; A Guide to Deviant Films.* San Francisco: RE/Search Publications, 1986.

Mosley, Leonard. *Disney's World.* New York: Stein and Day, 1985.

Pierson, John. *Spike, Mike, Slackers & Dykes: A Guided Tour Across a Decade of American Independent Cinema.* New York: Miramax Books, 1995.

Ramsaye, Terry. *A Million and One Nights: A History of the Motion Picture Through 1925.* New York: Touchstone, 1986.

Robinson, David. *Chaplin: His Life and Art.* New York: McGraw-Hill, 1985.

Royko, Mike. *Like I Was Sayin'*. New York: Jove Books, 1985.

Sampson, Henry T. *Blacks in Black and White: A Source Book on Black Films*. Metuchen, NJ: Scarecrow Press, 1995.

Sawyers, June. "The True Story that Led to 'Call Northside 777.'" *Chicago Tribune Sunday Magazine*, March 19, 1989.

Sawyers, June Skinner. *Chicago Portraits: Biographies of 250 Famous Chicagoans*. Chicago: Loyola University Press, 1991.

Sawyers, June Skinner, and Sue Telingator. *The Chicago Arts Guide*. Chicago: Chicago Review Press, 1993.

Schickel, Richard. *D. W. Griffith: An American Life*. New York: Simon and Schuster, 1984.

Schulze, Franz, and Kevin Harrington. *Chicago's Famous Buildings*. 5th ed. Chicago: University of Chicago Press, 2003.

Sheetz, George H. *The Chicago Film Industry: Beginnings to 1918*. Unpublished senior thesis. University of Illinois at Champaign-Urbana, Department of English, Spring 1974.

Siegel, Arthur, ed. *Chicago's Famous Buildings: The City's Architectural Landmarks and Other Notable Buildings*. Chicago: University of Chicago Press, 1967.

Sinkevitch, Alice, ed. *AIA Guide to Chicago*. 2nd ed. Orlando: Harcourt, 2004.

Swanson, Gloria. *Swanson on Swanson*. New York: Random House, 1980.

Sweet, Jeffrey. *Something Wonderful Right Away*. New York: Discus, 1978.

Wolfe, Gerard R. *Chicago in and Around the Loop: Walking Tours of Architecture and History*. New York: McGraw-Hill, 1996.

Index